DIRECTORY OF EVERYDAY DEMONS

IDENTIFY AND DEFEAT WHAT IS SABOTAGING YOUR LIFE AND PURPOSE

GWEN E. BUTLER

Directory of Everyday Demons

Identify and Defeat What is Sabotaging Your Life and Purpose

Gwen E. Butler

ISBN: 979-8-21870-745-3

DEDICATION

This work is dedicated to my Lord and Savior, Jesus Christ and to the best friend I ever had, The Holy Spirit.

CONTENTS

THE FOUR TYPES OF PEOPLE READING THIS BOOK

Jesus once told a parable about a sower scattering seed *(Luke 8:4–15)*. Some fell on the path, some on rocky soil, some among thorns, and some on good ground. The seed in this parable is the Word of God: truth. But whether that seed produces anything depends entirely on the condition of the soil: the heart.

That parable still applies today. It applies to you right now. You are one of these four types of ground, and how you respond to what's in this book will reveal which one.

Let's break them down:

1. The Hard Path – The Word Stolen Before It Can Take Root
Jesus said that some seed fell along the path, and the birds came and ate it up. He explained, *"These are the ones who hear, but then the devil comes and takes away the word from their hearts, so that they may not believe and be saved." (Luke 8:12)*

This is the person who dismisses the message instantly. Maybe they roll their eyes. Maybe they scoff. Maybe they close the book and forget about it. Either way, the Word has no chance to take root because the enemy comes quickly and for one reason only: for the Word's sake *(Mark 4:15)*.

Satan attacks what has power. If he's coming to snatch something from you, it's because that seed had the potential to change your life.

2. The Shallow Soil – Receives with Joy, But Falls Away in Testing
Jesus said some seed falls on rocky soil; it springs up fast but has no depth. When the sun comes out, it withers. He explained, *"They receive*

the word with joy when they hear it, but they have no root. They believe for a while, but in the time of testing, they fall away." (Luke 8:13)

This is the person who gets excited at first. They feel the truth and say "Amen." They even post about it. Then life gets hard and the warfare hits. People think they're weird and friends don't understand. Prayers aren't answered overnight.

Because there's no deep root and the truth never made it all the way down into their soul, they give up and go back to how they were. This shallowness costs them the harvest.

3. The Thorny Soil – Choked Out by Worry, Wealth, and Pleasure

Jesus said that some seed falls among thorns; it starts to grow, but it gets choked out. He explained, *"These are the ones who hear, but as they go on their way, they are choked by life's worries, riches, and pleasures, and they do not mature." (Luke 8:14)*

This is the person who's torn. They want God, but they're distracted. They believe, but they compromise. They like the idea of truth, but they're overwhelmed by everything else: money, entertainment, anxiety, ambition.

They never fully let the Word take over their life.

It's important to understand not all tests are painful. Some are comfortable. You can be tested by lack, and you can be tested by plenty. Success, beauty, popularity, and luxury can all choke the Word just as easily as poverty or pain. The enemy doesn't care whether it's pressure or pleasure, as long as it keeps you fruitless.

4. The Good Soil – Deep Roots, Open Heart, Abundant Harvest

Then there's the fourth kind of ground, the one this book is really written for.

Jesus said, *"The seed on good soil stands for those with a noble and good heart, who hear the word, retain it, and by persevering produce a crop." (Luke 8:15)*

This is the person who lets the Word go deep. They meditate on it and confront hard truths. They allow God to work through discomfort and discipline. They aren't perfect, but they're surrendered. As a result, they produce fruit: thirty, sixty, even a hundredfold.

So... Which Are You?

Be honest. Not every heart is ready. Not everyone will let this truth take root. Some will read and dismiss. Some will read and forget. Some will get distracted.

Some will fight for it.

This book isn't just information. It's seed.

If your heart is good soil, get ready because a harvest is coming.

MEET THE ENEMY &
WHY THERE'S A WAR

1

Around 2,000 years ago, under extraordinary circumstances, a child was born who would grow up to be called the Son of God.

His name was Jesus.

His life is one of the most heavily documented in human history, both in the Bible by eyewitnesses and in extra-biblical records written by historians. In fact, His life was so significant to civilization that time itself is divided around it: B.C. means "Before Christ." A.D. means "Anno Domini," Latin for "In the year of our Lord."

At age 30, Jesus began a public ministry that lasted only three years, but it changed the world forever.

He healed the blind. Cast out demons. Raised the dead. In one instance, He turned six giant stone jars of water into wine at a wedding. Crowds followed Him everywhere. Besides doing miracles, He was teaching the truth of God's word and revealing deeper meaning behind the Jewish scriptures: the Torah, also known as "The Law and the Prophets."

These scrolls were both spiritual instruction and historical record. The authors included prophets, men who heard directly from God and relayed His messages to His chosen people, the Jews. One way people knew these prophets were truly sent by God was through prophecy: predictions of the future that could only come from divine knowledge.

Over 900 prophecies are recorded in scripture. Every single one that pertains to the past has come true with perfect accuracy *despite literally incalculable odds*. The few that remain describe events still ahead of us. You and I are living in the final chapter.

One of the most important prophetic promises in the Torah was the coming of a Messiah, a Savior who would rescue God's people. The religious authorities in Jesus's day read those prophecies, but when Jesus appeared, they refused to believe it was Him. He didn't look the way they expected. He was born into poverty, not royalty. He came from Nazareth, a low-income suburb, not Jerusalem, the big city. Yet all of this was foretold in scripture.

The prophecy even said the Messiah would be born of a virgin. Jesus was.

And yet, they rejected Him.

Eventually, these same religious leaders convinced the Roman government to execute Him. They beat Him, whipped Him with sharp metal lashes, and nailed Him naked to a wooden cross to die a slow, brutal death. When He died, darkness fell, the earth shook, and the curtain in the temple—the one separating people from the presence of God—was torn supernaturally from *top* to bottom.

They placed His body in a sealed tomb, guarded by Roman soldiers.

Three days later, according to an eyewitness account, there was an earthquake, an angel appeared, the Roman soldiers became "like dead men" from fear, and the stone was rolled away.

Jesus was alive.

Hundreds of eyewitnesses saw Him walk, talk, and eat over a period of 40 days until He ascended into the sky in full view of His disciples.

Those men—His twelve closest followers—were so convinced that Jesus was truly the Son of God that they spent the rest of their lives telling the world about Him. Nearly all were tortured and killed in horrible ways for their message, but none ever recanted.

The Bible we have today includes their testimony (the New Testament) alongside the Torah and writings of the prophets (the Old Testament). It was written over a span of 1,500 years by more than 40 authors and contains 66 books. There are no contradictions. Its supernatural unity is unmatched. It has more surviving identical manuscripts than any ancient text in human history.

This is your context.

This is why this book exists.

Jesus spoke constantly about the spiritual realm. He warned of a real place called Hell—a place of eternal torment originally created not for people, but for Satan and his demons. However, because of sin, humans became eligible to go there.

That's why Jesus came. He died to give us a way out. Because He lived a perfect life, He was a perfect sacrifice for the sins of mankind.

In the Bible, a sacrifice is the offering of something valuable (often a spotless animal) to pay for sin. God's law required this because sin brings death and separation from Him. Before Jesus, animal sacrifices only temporarily covered sin and had to be repeated over and over.

Jesus changed that. As the sinless Son of God, He became the final, perfect sacrifice. *His death paid the full price for all sin for everyone for all time.* When you believe in Him and follow Him, you're covered by that sacrifice. The punishment He took is counted as yours. You're forgiven, set free, and restored to relationship with God.

Whoever believes in Him, repents of sin, and follows His instructions for life will not perish but have eternal life *(John 3:16)*. This is what it means to be saved.

Here's the part most people don't realize:

You have an enemy who will do everything in his power to keep you from being saved, or to pull you away after you've started. That enemy is Satan. He's not a cartoon or a myth. He's real. He hates God, and since he can't hurt God directly, he goes after what God loves most: you.

This is spiritual warfare. Whether you believe it or not, you are in it.

The effects may be visible—depression, addiction, anxiety, dysfunction—but the cause is invisible. We are in the middle of a war for human souls and pretending it doesn't exist won't protect you.

God hasn't left you defenseless. He offers armor, weapons, authority, and truth. This book will help you recognize who you're fighting and how to fight back.

Let's begin.

Who is Satan and Where Did Demons Come From?

Satan was not always evil. He was originally an angel named Lucifer, created by God with power and purpose. Before his fall, Lucifer held a unique position among the created beings in heaven. He was called the anointed cherub who covers *(Ezekiel 28:14),* believed to mean he stood near the throne in a position of honor and responsibility, guarding the presence of the Lord. He was full of wisdom, perfect in beauty, and instrumental in worship *(Ezekiel 28:12–13).*

God gave Lucifer free will, just like He gives us. With it, Lucifer chose pride. Because of his proximity to God, familiarity bred contempt. He wanted more. He wanted God's throne.

That pride was the very first sin and the root of all sin that followed. Scripture says God found iniquity in him, and Lucifer was cast out of heaven, along with a third of the angels who joined his rebellion *(Revelation 12:4, Ezekiel 28:15-17, Isaiah 14:12-15).* These fallen angels are now demons, and Lucifer (now called Satan, which means Adversary or Enemy) became their leader.

When Satan deceived Eve in the Garden of Eden, he introduced sin into the world. In doing so, mankind unknowingly gave him power and influence over the earth. The Bible calls him the "prince" and "ruler of this world" *(John 12:31, 2 Corinthians 4:4).*

The earth still belongs to God: *"The earth is the Lord's, and everything in it." (Psalm 24:1)*

Satan may have some authority for now, but it's temporary. He's like a corrupt building supervisor managing things in the Owner's absence, but the Owner is coming back.

Jesus will return to reclaim the building (the earth) and everyone who belongs to Him. And when He does, Satan's time is up, which he knows: *"He is filled with fury, because he knows that his time is short." (Revelation 12:12)*

That's why Satan is working overtime to deceive, distract, and destroy as many people as he can before the end. If he's going down, he wants to take as many human souls with him as possible.

So, to do that, Satan established his own system by copying God's.

He built a counterfeit kingdom with rank, order, and assignments. His army operates like a military: strategic, hierarchical, and deceptive. Everything he does is designed to steal, kill, and destroy *(John 10:10).*

However, he has one major obstacle: he only has power where people agree with his lies. Satan's kingdom can only tempt and suggest and influence. They can't make people do anything. The more doors people open in their lives to demonic influence, the stronger it will be.

That's why discernment matters. God tells us not to be ignorant of the enemy's devices, which means his plans and strategies *(2 Corinthians 2:11)*. God says people die from lack of knowledge *(Hosea 4:6).*

That's why studying and understanding the Bible to the point of God's approval *(2 Timothy 2:25)* is essential, as well as putting on the armor of God. Ephesians Chapter 6 describes the elements of the armor and each piece's uses. The single offensive weapon is the Sword of the Spirit, which is the Word of God, meaning the contents of the Bible is our single greatest weapon.

What About the Nephilim and Unclean Spirits?
After the angelic rebellion, some of the fallen angels (known as the Watchers) were assigned to observe mankind. They disobeyed. They saw that human women were beautiful and took them as wives *(Genesis 6:1–4).* The children from these unions were called the Nephilim: giants who were part angel and part human.

Besides the accounts of giants in the Bible, there is also documented physical evidence—skeletal remains, oversized tools, and burial mounds—which have reportedly been collected, destroyed, or sealed away by the Smithsonian. The Smithsonian is a global network of museums and research institutions funded by and accountable to the United States government, receiving significant federal support and oversight from Congress. This connection is prophetic because understanding who controls the flow of truth today may help further reveal who the United States is in end-times prophecy.

These hybrid beings were not created by God. They had no soul capable of redemption and therefore no path to heaven. When they died, their spirits had no resting place.

According to ancient texts and biblical understanding, the disembodied spirits of the Nephilim became what we now call unclean spirits (also referenced in books like Enoch and confirmed by the behavior of demons in the New Testament).

They still roam the earth today. They are restless, hostile, and constantly seeking human hosts. They are a key part of Satan's army and are often the very beings people encounter in spiritual warfare.

Why Demons Target People

Demons are disembodied spirits and need human bodies to express their wicked desires. Their main goal is to drag human souls into hell.

They look for legal entry points (sin, trauma, generational curses, false beliefs, unrepented actions) anything that gives them access.

Demonic possession and oppression are both real. In simple terms, Possession = the demon is in. Oppression = the demon is on.

Possession is when a demon inhabits a person's body and/or mind, exerting dominance over their will, behavior, and sometimes even voice or physical actions. It's rare, but it does happen—especially in people who have deeply opened themselves to darkness through rituals, occult involvement, extreme trauma, or generational curses. Possession is typically associated with non-believers, because a true follower of Jesus is filled with the Holy Spirit, and a demon cannot possess what the Holy Spirit inhabits *"What harmony is there between Christ and Belial?" (2 Corinthians 6:15).*

Oppression is when a demon harasses, influences, or attacks a person—physically, emotionally, mentally, or spiritually—without fully inhabiting them. Oppression can affect anyone, including believers. Common signs include persistent fear or anxiety; cycles of sin or destructive patterns; nightmares or sleep paralysis; chronic confusion, heaviness, or hopelessness; relational breakdowns, mental fog, or spiritual numbness.

Oppression is often the result of open doors (unforgiveness, occult activity, trauma, soul ties, etc.) and while not as extreme as possession, oppression can be spiritually crippling and require deliverance, which means the demon is cast out by a minister or believer *"And these signs will follow those who believe: In My name, they will cast our demons..."* *(Mark 16:17).*

Most people aren't just dealing with one spirit. Demons travel in gangs. *"My name is Legion, for we are many."* (Mark 5:9) When a spirit is cast out and finds no rest, it may return with seven more worse than itself *(Luke 11:26).* That's why cross-references are included in every demon profile in this book because these spirits work together. If you see one, others are likely hiding nearby. Even though this book names 116, it's not exhaustive; there are many more.

How Do Demons Gain Access to People?

As stated earlier, Satan only has power where people agree with his lies. His demons can tempt, suggest, manipulate, and pressure, but they can't make you do anything.

The more legal ground a person gives the enemy through sin, trauma, agreement, rituals, or touching what belongs to the enemy, the more power those demons are allowed to have. This is the legal side of spiritual warfare.

Sin is basically whenever we miss the mark and are not living to God's standards. The Bible is the manual of God's standards.

Here are some of the most common open doors demons gain access:

Unrepented Sin

Ongoing, unconfessed sin becomes an open invitation for the enemy to come in, set up a base (called a stronghold) and torment.

Even private or "harmless" sins can create spiritual access points.

To repent means to change your mind and turn away from the sin you're committing. Sometimes we have to take baby steps, but we must always be moving forward in the opposite direction from the sin. God will help us, and in some cases, take away the urge to sin completely.

"Give no place to the devil." (Ephesians 4:27)

Believing Lies

When you agree with a lie about yourself, others, or God, you create agreement with the enemy. This is how many people unknowingly invite oppression: "I'm worthless." "No one will ever love me." "God doesn't care."

Every false agreement becomes a foothold for demonic influence. If you say or think these kinds of things, immediately repent out loud by saying, "Forgive me Lord, I repent for those words."

"As a man thinks in his heart, so is he." (Proverbs 23:7)

"Death and life are in the power of the tongue." (Proverbs 18:21)

Trauma and Unhealed Wounds

Pain opens spiritual doors, especially when people respond to trauma by turning inward, growing bitter, or numbing out.

Demons swarm around unresolved pain. That's why healing is a weapon.

"He heals the brokenhearted and binds up their wounds." (Psalm 147:3)

Occult Activity

Anything involving false spiritual power—tarot, crystals, astrology, witchcraft, energy healing, "harmless" rituals—opens massive doors.

Brace yourself: Manifestation is on this list as well.

Manifestation is a neutral spiritual principle—the Bible calls it *faith*. What the world calls "Manifestation" relies on self-will, the universe, or spirit guides instead of God. The danger is in the source, not the principle.

These practices align with Satan's kingdom, even if people think they're using them for good. God doesn't deny the power or accuracy of these practices; that's why He warns so strongly against them. The problem is the source. When you turn to the occult for guidance, you're making a covenant with powers that hate you more than anything on earth. No matter how beautiful or helpful it seems, the enemy never gives without taking far more in return.

> *"Do not turn to mediums or seek out spiritists, for you will be defiled by them." (Leviticus 19:31)*
>
> *"If a person turns to mediums and necromancers, whoring after them, I will set my face against that person and will cut him off from among his people." (Leviticus 20:6 ESV)*
>
> *"You are wearied with your many counsels; let them stand forth and save you, those who divide the heavens, who gaze at the stars, who at the new moons make known what shall come upon you." (Isaiah 47:13)*

Sexual Sin and Soul Ties

Sex creates a soul tie, a spiritual connection between two people. In the Bible, sex is called "becoming one flesh." Flesh is more than physical, it also means spiritual. Even though physically two people have separated, the spiritual tie is still connected.

When someone has sex outside of God's design (marriage between man and woman), a spiritual door opens, and whatever spirits are tormenting the other person can now transfer through that tie. Remember, demons are basically lawyers and know their legal rights to occupy territory. Does it make sense now why a world ruled by the enemy celebrates and promotes all kinds of sex outside of marriage? Do you see how this attack on marriage via the devaluation of sex and its sanctity has utterly eroded relations between men and women and destroyed the family structure by extension, impacting society as whole? The enemy has always been about more than hookups, situationships and a rainbow flag. He plays the short, middle, but especially the long game.

Unauthorized sex often leaves people feeling spiritually weighed down, emotionally confused, or even mentally attacked afterward. Sometimes a person will suddenly have urges and traits they never did before or act out of character in other ways. Sometimes they will physically change for the worse. It's all spiritual consequences.

> *"Or do you not know that he who is joined to a prostitute becomes one body with her?" (1 Corinthians 6:16)*

Objects and Music

Certain objects (idols, ritual tools, cursed items, artwork) and music (especially those tied to occult themes or demonic energy) can carry spiritual weight. Having either in your environment is like a magnet and a shelter for demonic energy.

The impact of demonic music is multiplied through rhythmic repetition. Oftentimes the "hook" of a song turns into a non-stop earworm, essentially an agreement or curse people are saying over themselves on repeat and have no power to stop.

A hook and a worm are the perfect representation of bait. The enemy is slick and attracts people into sin and destruction with bait hiding the hook. Furthermore, he knows from studying us what bait to use for each individual, since everyone doesn't have the same weaknesses *"But each person is tempted when they are dragged away by their own evil desire and enticed." (James 1:14 NIV)*.

Some doors are opened through what we allow into our homes, cars, or minds. This is why we're told to guard the gates of our eyes and ears and not to look at or listen to any evil thing.

> *"Do not bring a detestable thing into your house or you, like it, will be set apart for destruction." (Deuteronomy 7:26)*
> *"Above all else, guard your heart, for everything you do flows from it." (Proverbs 4:23 NIV)*

Generational Curses

Sometimes the door was opened long before you were born.

If your family line includes witchcraft, Freemasonry and other secret societies including fraternities and sororities, abuse, addiction, or deep rebellion against God, those sins can invite familiar spirits that follow families across generations until someone breaks the cycle.

Scripture is clear about making oaths, especially in secret or to anything other than God: *"But I tell you, do not swear an oath at all... Let your 'Yes' be 'Yes,' and your 'No,' 'No'; anything beyond this comes from the evil one." (Matthew 5:34–37).* Like Freemasonry and its sister organization the Eastern Star, most fraternities and sororities require oaths of loyalty, ritualistic initiations and secrecy about internal practices.

When someone pledges lifelong loyalty to these groups (often above even their faith or family) that becomes a spiritual covenant. Many members refer to it as a "brotherhood/sisterhood for life." Spiritually, that's a binding soul tie unless broken.

God calls us to be set apart, not bound to organizations that rival our ultimate loyalty to Him: *"You cannot drink the cup of the Lord and the cup of demons too." (1 Corinthians 10:21).*

The entire Greek system draws from ancient philosophy and paganism. Even the use of Greek letters is symbolic, and some organizations invoke ancient gods, goddesses, or esoteric principles in their rituals. This aligns them with systems of false spiritual power.

Scripture tells us to examine the fruit to know the true nature of a person or thing. The fruit of these organizations is often pride, exclusivity, drunkenness, hazing, sexual sin, and idolatry of tradition, image, or status. While many claim to stand for service and scholarship, these traits are often surface level, masking deeper spiritual compromise.

"He punishes the children for the sin of the parents to the third and fourth generation..." (Exodus 20:5)
"Have nothing to do with the fruitless deeds of darkness but rather expose them." (Ephesians 5:11)

If You Ignore the War, You're Still In It

We are called to armor up and wield the sword of the Spirit *(Ephesians 6:17)*, to resist the devil and stand firm *(James 4:7, Ephesians 6:13)* but most people don't. Most live like there's nothing at stake. Understand that refusing to choose a side is a choice, and by default, it's the wrong one.

If you don't know you're in a war, you're walking the battlefield naked and unarmed. The enemy is counting on that. He hopes you'll stay numb, distracted, or too "logical" to take this seriously until it's too late.

Just because you deny the war doesn't mean it isn't happening. Your favorite entertainers, influencers, and leaders believe it. They stopped hiding it a long time ago. The symbolism is everywhere: upside-down crosses, all-seeing eyes, and rituals in plain sight.

Ask yourself why every other music video, awards show, or fashion shoot centers around hell, witchcraft, or demonic themes. Maybe it's because Satan made them the same offer he made Jesus: *"All this I will give you, if you will bow down and worship me."* (Matthew 4:9). Jesus didn't correct him because Satan does have the power to hand out kingdoms on earth *(Luke 4:5–8)*.

The Good News

Every demonically accessed open door can be shut through Jesus. You will be instructed at the end of this book on how to begin a relationship with Him so that you can become more than a conqueror through Christ and live the life God intended you to live, using the gifts He gave you to fulfill the purpose you were created for. You were absolutely created for a purpose.

Repentance, forgiveness, deliverance, and truth sever the legal rights of the enemy to sabotage your life. You don't have to live bound, and you don't have to stay stuck. Most importantly, you do not have to go to Hell.

Jesus said: *"I have come that they may have life and have it more abundantly."* (John 10:10)

WARNINGS ABOUT THIS BOOK

2

Why This Book Exists

Every single day, people are falling into Hell.

That's not fearmongering, it's what the Bible says. Most people will not be saved. Not because God doesn't want them, but because they chose the easier road.

"Wide is the gate and broad is the road that leads to destruction, and many enter through it. But small is the gate and narrow the road that leads to life, and only a few find it." (Matthew 7:13–14)

Think about that. A wide road, spacious, gently sloping, crowded with millions, versus a narrow path that must be found… and can only be walked one soul at a time.

This book exists because we are at war.

Even if you don't see it, there is a spiritual battle happening all around you right now. It's not metaphorical. It's real. God versus Satan. Light versus darkness. Truth versus deception.

What's at stake is eternal.

Earth Is the Waiting Room for Eternity

Your life is a vapor. A puff of smoke. We don't know what will happen tomorrow or in the next five seconds *(James 4:14)*. What you choose during this short life determines your eternity: Heaven or Hell. Freedom or torment. Eternal life or eternal separation from God.

It all hinges on one question: Is the Bible true… or the greatest lie ever told?

If there's even a sliver of a chance it's true, *Why on earth would you risk your eternity?* Please take one short moment to contemplate what endless time means. After 100 million years, it's still going. No person, no relationship, no habit, no ambition is worth trading *forever* for.

This book was written to expose what the enemy doesn't want you to see: that you don't have all the time in the world to get on God's side, and to help you fight back before it's too late.

Why the Bible Is the Only Objective Truth

This book stands on one foundation: the Bible. Not "a truth." The truth. In a world obsessed with personal narratives— "my truth," "your truth," "their truth"—the Word of God remains the only unchanging, objective truth on earth. It doesn't shift with culture. It doesn't bend to preference. It is not up for redefinition.

How do we know the Bible is true?

Here's why you can trust it—spiritually *and* historically:

Manuscript Evidence:

We have over 24,000 ancient manuscripts of the New Testament alone. No other ancient document even comes close. For comparison: Plato's *Republic*: about 7 copies. Julius Caesar's *Gallic Wars*: fewer than 10. The Bible: tens of thousands, virtually identical in content.

Extra-Biblical Sources:

Writers like Tacitus, Josephus, and Pliny the Younger (none of them Christians) confirmed the life, crucifixion, and widespread belief in the resurrection of Jesus. He was a real person, not a myth.

Fulfilled Prophecy:

The Bible contains over 900 prophecies, hundreds of which have already come to pass with uncanny precision.

The odds of each prophecy itself coming true cannot be calculated. Just 8 of them coming true in one person's life has been calculated at 1 in 10^{17} (that's 1 in 100 quadrillion). That's like covering the vast state of Texas knee-deep in silver dollars, marking one, and picking it up on your first try blindfolded.

There are hundreds more prophecies waiting to be fulfilled in our lifetime. Many of which we can already see starting to come to pass.

Internal Consistency:

The Bible was written by 40 authors across 66 books, on 3 continents, in 3 languages, over 1,500 years and yet, it tells one seamless story and has zero contradictions or misalignments. That is impossible without divine authorship.

What about circular reasoning?

Some argue that quoting the Bible to prove the Bible is circular. But that's a misunderstanding. We don't just believe the Bible because it says it's true, we believe it because:

10. **Its internal claims are confirmed by external evidence**

11. **Its prophecies came true in verifiable, historical ways.**

12. **Its manuscripts are preserved far more faithfully than any other ancient text.**

If a math textbook had 100% accurate answers, unmatched preservation through centuries, and fulfilled impossible predictions it would be foolish not to trust it. The Bible is that book, but infinitely more.

Truth Isn't New—Just Repackaged

Many of the insights in this book might sound familiar to those who've studied psychology or self-help. But let's be clear: psychology didn't invent these ideas. It borrowed them (consciously or not) from the Bible and stripped out the Source.

What modern science calls "trauma," scripture calls "wounds." What therapy calls "limiting beliefs," scripture calls "strongholds." What motivational speakers call "manifestation," scripture calls "speaking death or life" *(Proverbs 18:21).* The vocabulary is different, but the truth is ancient.

That said, we're not dismissing psychology or medicine. God can use both. Some issues are clinical. Some are spiritual. Often, they overlap. But in cases of persistent torment, oppression, fear, or confusion—especially when nothing else is working—you're likely dealing with the spiritual.

This Book is a Field Guide

This is a field guide, not a theology textbook. Meaning, it doesn't cover every doctrine or debate. It's meant to help you recognize the enemy, understand his tactics, and fight back. It's real-world spiritual warfare for everyday life.

It is built on biblical patterns, spiritual discernment, and the recognition that the Word of God is inexhaustible. Some names you'll find here aren't listed directly in scripture, but neither is "Trinity." That doesn't make them unbiblical.

For example, Paul said he was caught up to the *third heaven (2 Corinthians 12:2).* That implies a first and second even though they're not defined. We're called to "rightly divide the Word" *(2 Timothy 2:15)* and to study spiritual patterns with wisdom.

Each demon profile includes:

- **Core torment & lie**
- **Gifts under attack**
- **Common symptoms**
- **A real-life example**
- **Declarations** (meant to be spoken aloud)
- **Prayers**
- **Cross-references to related spirits**

Not Misplacing Blame—Revealing Influence

Some will say, *"These are just human behaviors. You're blaming demons for everything."* No. We are exposing what's driving the behavior. Yes, people have free will. Yes, people are responsible for their choices. But we live in a spiritually contaminated world, and many people are being manipulated by forces they cannot see. Scripture says, *"We wrestle not against flesh and blood" (Ephesians 6:12)*; another translation says, *"Our wrestling match is not with persons who have bodies."* Your boss, your parent, your partner may have hurt you, but the real war is spiritual and with the demons operating through and influencing people.

But These Names Aren't in the Bible...

You may flip through this book and be thinking: "I've never seen names like The Abyss, The Performer, or The Loop in scripture." You're right. These are not the original Hebrew or Greek names of the spirits. But the concepts absolutely are and every single profile in this book is built on biblical truth.

Scripture Describes Spirits by Their Function

In the Bible, spirits are often named by what they *do*, not what they're *called*:

"Spirit of Heaviness" *(Isaiah 61:3)* – That's depression.

"Spirit of Infirmity" *(Luke 13:11)* – That's chronic illness.

"Spirit of Whoredoms" *(Hosea 4:12)* – That's sexual perversion and spiritual unfaithfulness.

"Spirit of Fear" *(2 Timothy 1:7)* – That's anxiety, dread, and paralysis.

This book follows the same biblical pattern. We've given these spirits modern names to make their influence easier to identify.

For example:

The Abyss = spirit of heaviness/depression.

The Shrinker = fear of being seen, rooted in shame, intimidation and sometimes pride.

The Idolmaker = spirit of idolatry, often disguised in ambition or fame-seeking.

The goal of this book is not to convince you that a spirit is called "The Saboteur" or "The Withholder." The goal is to help you recognize the spiritual strongholds that have been operating in your life, possibly for years, and give you the weapons to defeat them. *"For we are not unaware of Satan's schemes." (2 Corinthians 2:11)*

What we need to examine is the fruit, meaning the visible effects and results of these demons. Jesus said: *"You will recognize them by their fruits." (Matthew 7:16).* That's the standard we've used here. What is this spirit producing in a person's life? And what does the Word of God say about it?

A Note on Translations

Unless otherwise noted, scripture in this book is from the King James Version. It's the most consistent and unaltered translation in English. That said, some verses may be cited from other translations for clarity.

The original Hebrew and Greek languages are richer than any English rendering, and all translations are attempts to help us understand the truth, not to distort it. Beware of those who twist that truth to discredit God's Word by saying ignorant things like "There are so many different versions of the Bible, how do you know which one is right?" All of them are right and saying the same truth, just in different ways so people can better understand.

Final Note: This Is a Survival Guide

This manual is not comprehensive. That would be impossible to achieve. It's a starting weapon for people ready to enter the spiritual war. It is the book I needed when my eyes first opened to the reality that God is real and so is the enemy.

We are living in demonized times, and this book will help you understand the lay of the land and how to fight back. More than that, it will show you how to overcome the spiritual obstacles to accessing the gifts God placed inside of you when he created you for a specific purpose. None of us were meant to just live our lives, eat, sleep, and die.

If you want to discuss anything further, my TikTok page is open for DMs and comments. I'm still in the field with you.

God bless you.

YOUR GIFTS &
WHY THEY'RE UNDER ATTACK

3

Satan hates God, but he can't touch Him. So, what does he do?

He goes after what God loves most: people.

You. Your children. Your bloodline.

The enemy has studied human behavior for thousands of years. He's not all-knowing, but he's an expert in pattern recognition. He watches for open doors. He attacks gifting early. He moves through bloodlines and generations, trying to stop callings before they even begin.

The enemy often recognizes your gifts before you do. If a gift goes unused—like prophecy, leadership, or healing—he waits to see where it reappears. What your grandfather suppressed, your father doubted, and you may only be beginning to feel, the enemy has been studying for generations. He assigns resistance early, hoping to shut you down before you ever realize what you carry.

That's why the attacks feel personal. They are. They're also strategic and reveal the hidden treasure inside you. There's a symmetry to the attacks and a logic we can reverse engineer.

The Seven Main Gifts

Whether a person is saved or not, God has given every single one of us gifts, talents, and abilities. These are not random. They were placed inside of you before you were born, meant to be used to advance the Kingdom of God on earth and draw more souls to Him for eternity in heaven.

"For the gifts and the calling of God are irrevocable." (Romans 11:29, ESV)

That means you are free to use your gifts however you choose. You can use them for God or use them for the world. You can build up others or build your own platform. God will not take your gifts away even if you never use them for Him.

The enemy is counting on that.

There are seven foundational spiritual gifts described in the Bible, also called *motivational gifts*. These gifts are supernatural in origin, but they will feel completely natural to you. They're how God hardwired you. Many people have more than one, but often one is primary:

The 7 Root Spiritual Gifts
(Romans 12:6–8)

1. **Prophecy** – Declares truth boldly and brings clarity and conviction.

2. **Serving (Ministry)** – Meets practical needs with joy and selflessness.

3. **Teaching** – Breaks down truth for understanding and application.

4. **Exhortation** – Encourages and strengthens with vision and hope.

5. **Giving** – Finds joy in generosity, provision, and funding Kingdom work.

6. **Leadership (Administration)** – Organizes, guides, and stewards well.

7. **Mercy** – Loves deeply, comforts the hurting, and brings healing presence.

These gifts often reveal themselves early in life. You may have noticed them before you ever knew what to call them. They are root gifts; from them, other strengths grow: creativity, boldness, empathy, wisdom, discernment, artistic ability, influence, intercession, insight, healing, writing, design, strategy, music, and more.

There is a pattern—an intelligence—to how people are attacked. The enemy doesn't need to reinvent his tactics because they've worked for thousands of years. But God gives us the ability to recognize the strategy and break it. Jesus said, *"Behold, I send you out as sheep in the midst of wolves. Therefore, be wise as serpents and harmless as doves."* *(Matthew 10:16, NKJV).*

That means don't fight like the world fights but understand how your enemy operates. Learn to identify the schemes so you can resist them. This section explores how the enemy targets each of these 7 root gifts along with related traits, and what the pattern of attack might reveal about your God-given calling. This isn't a checklist, and it isn't exhaustive. It is a starting place that might explain a lot.

Let's take a look.

1

The Gift of Prophecy

Core Trait: Clarity, conviction, truth-telling.

This person sees the world in terms of right and wrong, and they are often bold enough to say what others won't. They carry spiritual insight and discernment and have a deep desire to expose lies, call out injustice, and bring truth to light.

Common Attacks:

- **Being silenced or overlooked**
  From a young age, prophetic people are often ignored, dismissed, or told they're "too much." Their insights are brushed off until someone else repeats them. They learn that their voice doesn't matter.

- **Struggle with rejection and loneliness**
  This gift often feels isolating. Prophets can feel like outsiders, misunderstood by peers, church, or even family. The enemy plants seeds of bitterness or withdrawal.

- **Fear of speaking up or being wrong**

  Many prophetic types wrestle with deep self-doubt. They may hear from God but fear it's "just them," so they stay quiet. Others may fear being labeled judgmental or divisive.

- **Temptation to weaponize truth**

  When not submitted to love and humility, this gift can come off as harsh or cutting. The enemy can twist the gift into criticism, legalism, or spiritual pride.

Enemy's Lie:

"Your voice doesn't matter."

"You're too intense. No one wants to hear you."

"If you speak, you'll just push people away."

God's Truth:

"Before I formed you in the womb I knew you, and before you were born, I consecrated you; I appointed you a prophet to the nations." *(Jeremiah 1:5 ESV)*

"Your gift will make room for you and bring you before great men." *(Proverbs 18:16)*

"Do not be afraid of them, for I am with you and will rescue you," declares the Lord. *(Jeremiah 1:8 NIV)*

Related Demons That Attack This Gift:

- **The Shrinker** – Causes you to play small and doubt your authority.
- **Mute** – Silences voices meant to speak bold truth.
- **The Critic** – Twists discernment into self-righteousness or judgment.
- **The Rejector** – Plants deep wounds that make you afraid to speak.
- **The Loop** – Keeps you stuck replaying your doubts or failures.

Encouragement:

If your whole life has been marked by feeling silenced, ignored, or rejected, it may be because your voice is meant to break chains. Hell tries hardest to mute the ones who carry Heaven's messages. Don't confuse your wounds with your worth. The attack means you're called.

2

The Gift of Serving (Ministry)

Core Trait: Practical help, meeting needs, behind-the-scenes strength.

This person naturally steps in to help without needing to be asked. They see needs before others do and feel compelled to take action. They bring comfort through care, and stability through service.

Common Attacks:

- **Feeling invisible or unappreciated**
  People with this gift are often taken for granted. Their value is rarely acknowledged publicly, and they may be overlooked in favor of louder or flashier gifts.

- **Burnout and overextension**
  The servant heart often says yes when it should say no. The enemy exploits this, pushing them to pour from an empty cup, leading to exhaustion, resentment, or health issues.

- **People-pleasing and identity confusion**
  When affirmation is tied to usefulness, it becomes easy to believe love must be earned. The enemy convinces them they have no worth outside of what they do for others.

- **Bitterness toward takers.**
  If not guarded, this gift can become jaded from always giving but never receiving. It may attract selfish people who see them as easy to use.

Enemy's Lie:

"You're only valuable when you're needed."

"You're replaceable. Anyone could do what you do."

"If you don't do it, it won't get done."

God's Truth:

"God is not unjust; He will not forget your work and the love you have shown Him as you have helped His people and continue to help them." *(Hebrews 6:10 NIV)*

"Whatever you did for one of the least of these brothers and sisters of mine, you did for Me." *(Matthew 25:40 NIV)*

"Let us not grow weary of doing good, for at the proper time we will reap a harvest if we do not give up." *(Galatians 6:9 NIV)*

Related Demons That Attack This Gift:

- **Performer** – Says your worth is tied to how much you do.
- **Lazybones** – Make you feel guilty for resting, convincing you to push through exhaustion.
- **The Critic** – Turns your service into judgment of others who don't do as much.
- **The Withholder** – Convinces you to pull back when you feel unseen, robbing others of your gift.
- **The Ghoster** – Encourages you to disappear when you feel overwhelmed or taken advantage of.

Encouragement:

The enemy knows your gift is often the glue holding families, teams, and communities together. That's why he tries to wear you out. You may not preach from a pulpit, but your hands are preaching the gospel every time you serve. God sees it all, and heaven never forgets a single act of love done in His name.

3

The Gift of Teaching

Core Trait: Explaining truth, breaking down concepts, illuminating understanding.

Teachers have a deep love for knowledge and a natural ability to communicate information. They measure their success by what has been learned and understood, rather than what was taught.

Common Attacks:

- **Accusations of being "too much" or a "know-it-all"**
  This gift often gets dismissed as arrogant or overly analytical. The enemy uses others' reactions to shame the teacher into silence.

- **Mental fatigue or confusion**
  Teachers tend to overthink. The enemy exploits this by creating confusion, brain fog, or analysis paralysis.

- **Imposter syndrome**
  The teacher is often attacked with the thought: *"Who do you think you are to teach this?"* especially if they lack credentials or are self-taught.

- **Hyper-criticism or perfectionism.**
  The enemy tempts teachers to become overly focused on accuracy to the point of missing grace. The standard becomes performance, not revelation.

Enemy's Lie:
"You don't know enough to speak."
"Someone else has said it better."
"You're not qualified."

God's Truth:

"If anyone speaks, they should do so as one who speaks the very words of God." *(1 Peter 4:11)*

"The unfolding of Your words gives light; it gives understanding to the simple." *(Psalm 119:130)*

"Not many of you should become teachers, because you know that we who teach will be judged more strictly." *(James 3:1)*

(*This is not a warning to scare you—it's confirmation that the role is real and weighty.*)

Related Demons That Attack This Gift:

- **The Critic** – Turns clarity into condescension, or makes you judge others who lack understanding.
- **The Mindstorm** – Keeps your mind spinning on every angle instead of speaking.
- **The Doubter** – Makes you question whether you even believe what you know.
- **The Saboteur** – Pushes you to self-destruct just as you're ready to lead or teach.
- **The Mute** – Silences the voice of instruction, making you hold back when you were meant to equip others.

Encouragement:

You're strategic in the Spirit. Your ability to break things down is not just basic human cleverness; it's a gift meant to illuminate truth for others. Every time you teach, you pull someone out of confusion and into clarity. That's why the enemy wants to shut you down.

4

The Gift of Encouragement (Exhortation)

Core Trait: Strengthening, uplifting, and activating others through words.

Those with this gift are "spiritual oxygen." They breathe life into others, restore hope, and push people toward growth. They comfort and also mobilize.

Common Attacks:

- **Being drained by people constantly coming to you for support**
  The enemy turns your compassion into exhaustion.

- **Feeling like your encouragement doesn't matter**
  If people don't immediately change, you may feel like your words are empty.

- **Personal battles with discouragement or depression**
  The enemy often hits encouragers with what they help others overcome.

- **Being written off as "too positive" or "fake"**
  You may get mocked for always finding the silver lining.

Enemy's Lie:
"No one listens to you."
"You're just a cheerleader. What you do doesn't matter."
"You should have your life together before helping others."

God's Truth:
"Encourage one another daily, as long as it is called 'Today,' so that none of you may be hardened by sin's deceitfulness." *(Hebrews 3:13)*
"Therefore encourage one another and build one another up, just as you are doing." *(1 Thessalonians 5:11)*
"A word fitly spoken is like apples of gold in settings of silver." *(Proverbs 25:11)*

Related Demons That Attack This Gift:

- **The Abyss** – Pulls you into emotional heaviness so you can't lift others.
- **The Mouth** – Makes you second-guess what to say or fear saying it wrong.
- **The Phantom** – Haunts you with fears of failure or of being a burden.
- **The Withholder** – Convince you it's not your place to speak up.
- **The Shrinker** – Tells you to stay small and silent.

Encouragement:

You are a mirror of God's kindness. The enemy tries to silence you because he knows your words spark movement. Your voice comforts and calls people forward. Words you say are cherished and can last a lifetime. Your gift is spiritual propulsion, rocket fuel. Keep speaking.

5

The Gift of Giving

Core Trait: Supernaturally generous, spiritually strategic, and

deeply invested in advancing God's Kingdom.

Those with this gift give money, solutions, opportunities, time, and resources. They have a sharp sense for what will produce fruit.

Common Attacks:

- **Being taken advantage of by manipulators, opportunists, or scammers**
  Your generous nature makes you a target for misuse.

- **Financial instability or sudden losses**
  The enemy hits your source to discourage your flow.

- **Shame or guilt around money, either for having too much or not enough**
  You may feel judged or unsure if it's "godly" to be wealthy.

- **Extreme frugality or over-giving**
  You either hoard out of fear or give recklessly to prove your heart.

Enemy's Lie:
"You're not really helping."
"Your resources are wasted."
"God doesn't care how you spend your money."

God's Truth:
"Give, and it will be given to you... For with the measure you use, it will be measured to you." *(Luke 6:38)*
"God is able to bless you abundantly, so that in all things at all times... you will abound in every good work." *(2 Corinthians 9:8)*
"Whoever is generous to the poor lends to the Lord, and He will repay him." *(Proverbs 19:17)*

Related Demons That Attack This Gift:

- **Mammon** – Twists the purpose of wealth and seduces with greed.
- **The Pauper** – Tries to convince the Giver they will never have enough, keeping them in fear and scarcity.
- **The Promise Breaker** – Undermines trust by wounding the Giver through broken commitments and betrayal.
- **The Withholder** – Encourages stinginess and self-protection, twisting discernment into suspicion and reluctance.
- **The Glazer** – Takes advantage of the Giver through flattery and manipulation, causing them to become guarded or jaded.

Encouragement:
You reflect God's abundance. God uses you to provide and multiply. The enemy tries to shut your hand because your giving funds Kingdom

movement. Your gift is sacred, and your discernment is growing. More than simply generous, you are a distributor of God's provision.

6
The Gift of Leadership

Core Trait: Spirit-led vision, high-level discernment, and the ability to mobilize people toward a goal.

Those with this gift naturally take responsibility. They carry divine authority, whether or not they hold a title.

Common Attacks:

- **Early rejection or betrayal in leadership roles**
  You may be sabotaged, slandered, or undermined to create fear of stepping up again.

- **Struggles with self-doubt or imposter syndrome**
  You question whether you're "called" to lead or just bossy.

- **Criticism from others for being "too much" or "controlling"**
  The enemy uses misunderstanding and envy to isolate you.

- **Burnout from taking on too much**
  You feel like everything falls on you, and no one else steps up.

Enemy's Lie:
"You're not really called—no one follows you."
"You're too much."
"You're better off staying in the background."

God's Truth:
"If God has given you leadership ability, take the responsibility seriously."
(*Romans 12:8 NLT*)
"The Lord will make you the head and not the tail... if you carefully follow His commands." (*Deuteronomy 28:13*)

"I can do all things through Christ who strengthens me." *(Philippians 4:13)*

Related Demons That Attack This Gift:

- **Withholder** – Refuses to step up and lead, choosing self-protection over calling.
- **The Critic** – Undermines your decisions and confidence through constant scrutiny.
- **The Faithless One** – Convinces you that your prayers and efforts won't matter.
- **The Saboteur** – Creates self-sabotage cycles that block momentum.
- **The Avenger** – Leads from unhealed offense instead of God's vision.

Encouragement:

You were born to go first. Your authority comes from God. Even when no one affirms you, Heaven backs you. You are not "too much." You are set apart to carry influence, and you're being trained for impact beyond what you see now.

7

The Gift of Mercy

Core Trait: Deep compassion, empathy, and emotional discernment.

Those with this gift reflect the heart of God for the hurting. They feel others' pain, often before it's spoken.

Common Attacks:

- **Emotional overwhelm and compassion fatigue.**
  You carry burdens that aren't yours and struggle to set boundaries.

- **Repeated toxic relationships or one-sided dynamics.**
  The enemy sends people who drain you, abuse your kindness, or manipulate your heart.

- **Hardness or bitterness from betrayal.**
  After being hurt, you may shut down emotionally to survive.

- **Shame for being "too sensitive" or "weak."**
  The enemy distorts your compassion into a flaw.

Enemy's Lie:

"You're too sensitive. You'll never be strong."
"People just take advantage of you."
"Caring always leads to pain. You should shut down."

God's Truth:

"Blessed are the merciful, for they shall receive mercy." *(Matthew 5:7)*
"The Lord is close to the brokenhearted and saves those who are crushed in spirit." *(Psalm 34:18)*
"Above all, clothe yourselves with love, which binds us all together in perfect harmony." *(Colossians 3:14)*

Related Demons That Attack This Gift:

- **The Guard** – Builds emotional walls that block connection and tenderness.
- **The Chainkeeper** – Holds grudges and won't release pain, turning mercy into bitterness.
- **The Rejector** – Keeps you questioning your worth and acceptability.
- **The Ghoster** – Makes you disappear before true intimacy can form.
- **The Burnt-Out Child** – Resents the emotional labor that was never reciprocated.

Encouragement:

You feel deeply because God trusts you to love like He does. Mercy is one of the most powerful forces in the Kingdom. While the world hardens, you heal. In a time when love is growing cold, your heart is a weapon. You make all the difference in people's lives.

The Way the Enemy Attacks Reveals God's Gifts in You

Now that you've seen the breakdown of the seven motivational gifts, here's another way to identify what God may have placed inside you.

Sometimes, your gifts aren't revealed through what comes easily to you, instead they're exposed by what's been under attack. The enemy often fights what threatens him most, and that means your struggles, patterns, and wounds may actually be clues.

This next section will help you connect the dots between your battles and your calling.

This is just a starting point that highlights some of the most common struggles people face and the hidden gifts those battles may be pointing to. These are broad categories. Spiritual gifts are deeply personal, and how they show up in your life may look completely different from someone else with the same core wiring. As you read, think about your own talents, instincts, and natural abilities in this context. God designed you with intention, and often the thing the enemy has fought hardest in you is the very thing you were born to carry.

For example, someone struggling with vaping or smoking may not realize it's a spiritual attack on their voice. If that person is called to lead worship, their voice is an instrument of breakthrough, designed to shift atmospheres and bring people into the presence of God. Worship is precious to Him. It was the one thing He didn't create for Himself because He waits to *receive it* from us. So, the enemy works overtime to silence or distort worshipers, especially those whose voices carry anointing. Satan knows better than anyone the power of worship. In this case, the addiction is a strategic muzzle, a slow suffocation of purpose.

Another example is the struggle with pornography. Many people think it's just a private weakness, but spiritually, it's a trap that distorts the gift of intimacy. If someone is called to build a godly marriage—a partnership where each person helps the other step into their divine calling—then porn is a direct assault on that future. It rewires the brain to seek pleasure without covenant, and over time, it cheapens intimacy, trains the heart for disconnection, and damages the ability to truly bond. What God designed as sacred glue for marriage becomes weakened, and that relationship can start to look more like two hostile roommates than one flesh. In that case, the struggle isn't just about desire, it's about delaying destiny.

Take procrastination, for instance. It's easy to write it off as laziness or poor time management, but spiritually, it can be a form of invisible bondage, especially in people called to build, lead, or create. Some of the most visionary, gifted people are stuck in cycles of delay, distraction, or overthinking—not because they don't care, but because the enemy knows that if they ever *move*, things will shift. A book would be written. A business would launch. A generation would be inspired. Most importantly of all, souls would be saved. If he can keep you waiting for the "right" moment, tied up in fear, perfectionism, or mental fog, he can slow down what God intended to accelerate. In this case, procrastination is an attack on momentum, and ultimately, on obedience.

Let's take a look at some attacks and what they show us:

20 Common Attacks & What They Reveal

Struggle 1: Constantly distracted or can't focus for long
Spiritual Root: Fragmentation, avoidance, and internal unrest
Gift Under Attack: Mental clarity, focus, and prophetic listening

Example Demons:

- **The Mindstorm** – Keeps your thoughts racing in loops
- **The Loop** – Hooks you into digital twilight and screen addiction
- **The Alchemist** – Promises mental escape through substances
- **Lazybones** – Numbs the will to take action
- **The Phantom** – Heightens anxiety and fear, making stillness unbearable

What It May Be Telling You:

You may have a sharp, discerning mind that the enemy is trying to scramble. If he can't stop you, he'll scatter you, keeping you mentally fragmented so you can't hear God clearly or follow through on your calling. The chaos is a smokescreen sent to blur your vision and wear you down.

~ * * * ~

Struggle 2: Not caring about appearance
Spiritual Root: Resignation, despair, or identity confusion
Gift Under Attack: Self-worth, embodiment, and joy

Example Demons:

- **The Glacier** – Freezes emotion and motivation
- **The Abyss** – Pulls you into depressive disengagement
- **The Broken Mirror** – Warps your self-image
- **The Orphan** – Convinces you you're unloved or forgotten
- **Lazybones** – Leaches energy and enthusiasm for self-care

What It May Be Telling You:

You may carry a radiant presence that the enemy wants to dim. When you lose touch with your outer self, it's often a sign that your inner identity has been attacked. The enemy knows that living fully in your God-given skin is a form of warfare, and he's working to keep you disengaged, unseen, and disqualified in your own eyes.

~ * * * ~

Struggle 3: Constantly lying, exaggerating, or pretending
Spiritual Root: Fear of rejection, shame, or desire for approval
Gift Under Attack: Truth-bearing, authenticity, and leadership

Example Demons:

- **The Pretender** – Masks true identity to gain acceptance
- **The Liar** – Distorts reality and traps you in falsehood
- **The Performer** – Lives to please others instead of God

- **The Rejector** – Convinces you your true self isn't enough
- **The Mouth** – Uses speech as a weapon or disguise

What It May Be Telling You:

You may be called to carry truth, but the enemy has convinced you that your real story isn't enough. If he can get you to perform, you'll never walk in the authority of your authentic voice. This is a war for your identity. You were made to lead in truth.

~ * * * ~

Struggle 4: Strong urge to drink, alcoholism
Spiritual Root: Desire to escape, numb pain, or feel powerful
Gift Under Attack: Sobriety, spiritual discernment, and emotional strength

Example Demons:

- **The Drunkard** – Normalizes overconsumption of alcohol
- **The Alchemist** – Promises relief through substances
- **The Suicide Spirit** – Whispers despair and self-destruction
- **The Abyss** – Amplifies depression and hopelessness
- **The Numb One** – Pushes you to escape pain by dulling your emotions and disconnecting from reality

What It May Be Telling You:

You may have a gift of emotional depth or discernment that's become overwhelming without proper guidance. The urge to numb is often a sign of spiritual sensitivity under pressure. The enemy wants to turn your capacity for truth and feeling into a burden instead of a blessing, so you'll reach for temporary relief instead of lasting freedom.

~ * * * ~

Struggle 5: Compulsion to gamble or take reckless risks
Spiritual Root: False hope, entitlement, or craving for quick validation
Gift Under Attack: Stewardship, contentment, and divine provision

Example Demons:

- **Mammon** – Fuels greed and financial obsession
- **The Mindstorm** – Thrives in chaos and impulsive action
- **The Pauper** – Keeps you locked in scarcity and striving
- **The Waster** – Destroys resources through impulsivity, neglect, or self-indulgence.
- **The Withholder** – Distorts your relationship with provision, convincing you it's never enough or always about to run out

What It May Be Telling You:

You may have a deep hunger for adventure, breakthrough, or reward planted in you by God. But instead of trusting His timing, the enemy lures you toward quick wins and unstable highs. He's twisting your desire for purpose into a craving for payoff, hoping to bankrupt your future while you chase illusions.

~ * * * ~

Struggle 6: Overeating
Spiritual Root: Comfort-seeking through the flesh; emotional hunger
Gift Under Attack: Self-control, comfort from God, physical strength

Example Demons:

- **The Glutton** – Feeds emotional pain with food
- **The Burnt Out Child** – Seeks relief from chronic pressure or emotional exhaustion through food as escape
- **The Mindstorm** – Keeps up a constant stream of "food noise," obsessive thinking about what to eat next, even during eating and when already full
- **Lazybones** – Paralyzes action and discipline
- **The Insatiable** – Creates constant cravings and the illusion that nothing will ever be enough.

What It May Be Telling You:

You may be trying to feed something spiritual with something physical. The craving is actually for peace, love, or control. The enemy wants to dull your discernment and keep your temple foggy and heavy so you can't run the race marked out for you.

~ * * * ~

Struggle 7: Smoking / Vaping
Spiritual Root: Numbing pain and anxiety; counterfeit peace
Gift Under Attack: Breath, worship, prophetic voice

Example Demons:

- **The Puffer** – Encourages self-harm through inhalation, clouding judgment, and weakening the body as a temple.
- **The Loop** – Keeps you in self-soothing cycles
- **The Mute** – Silences your voice and witness
- **The Alchemist** – Seeks artificial comfort and altered state
- **Lazybones** – Drains energy and motivation

What It May Be Telling You:
The enemy is after your breath: your worship, your prayer, your power. Smoking is a counterfeit exhale meant to replace the life-giving breath of God. Your voice carries weight, so the enemy seeks to cloud or suppress it.

~ * * * ~

Struggle 8: Being Drawn to Porn
Spiritual Root: Deep longing for intimacy; distorted love
Gift Under Attack: Purity, covenant love, relational authority

Example Demons:

- **The Defiler** – Pollutes the temple and rewires desire
- **The Insatiable** – Feeds lust through watching
- **The Player** – Trains the heart to use others
- **The Splitter** – Trains your mind to disconnect emotion from desire, reducing people to functions
- **The Exploiter** – Feeds entitlement and domination, convincing you that pleasure matters more than people

What It May Be Telling You:

You long for connection, but the enemy offers illusion. Porn isolates you from real intimacy, training your spirit to love passively and selfishly. Your calling might involve deep relational restoration, and the enemy is sabotaging it at the root.

~ * * * ~

Struggle 9: Being Drawn to Witchcraft & The Occult
Spiritual Root: Desire for control, power, or healing apart from God
Gift Under Attack: Spiritual discernment, authority, healing ministry

Example Demons:

- **The Arcane One** – Draws hearts to "harmless" spells or crystals
- **The Guru** – False spiritual authority
- **The Enchanter** – Counterfeit healing and energy work
- **The Idolator** – Replaces God with other sources
- **The Bitter One** – Often drawn in through woundedness

What It May Be Telling You:

You were made to walk in real spiritual power. The enemy offers a twisted version first, one that feels empowering but opens you to bondage. If you've been drawn to spells or "energy," it may mean you're meant to operate in prophetic or healing gifts through the Holy Spirit.

~ * * * ~

Struggle 10: Fear of Being Seen
Spiritual Root: Shame, pride, or self-protection
Gift Under Attack: Visibility, leadership, prophetic voice

Example Demons:

- **The Shrinker** – Trains you to hide
- **The Mute** – Silences your voice
- **The Critic** – Torments you with imagined judgment
- **The Rejector**– Convinces you you'll never belong
- **The Ghoster** – Disappears before being truly known

What It May Be Telling You:

You were meant to be visible and for your life to reflect God's light. Hiding might feel safer, but it's robbing others of what you carry. Your fear of exposure might mean your calling is to influence, speak, or lead.

~ * * * ~

Struggle 11: Procrastination
Spiritual Root: Fear of failure, perfectionism, confusion
Gift Under Attack: Discipline, obedience, creativity

Example Demons:

- **The Binger** – Feeds dopamine dependence through overconsumption, convincing you that movement can come after *just one more*
- **The Saboteur** – Delays your progress through self-doubt
- **Lazybones** – Stalls energy and momentum
- **The Doubter** – Questions whether it's worth doing
- **The Promise Breaker** – Keeps commitments half-finished

What It May Be Telling You:

The enemy knows your work matters. Your gift might be writing, building, speaking, or creating, and every hour delayed is one less soul impacted. He knows only YOU can stop you, so he tries to get in through every crack possible. Once you're aware of this, you will see how ridiculous and even small the distractions and obstacles can be.

~ * * * ~

Struggle 12: Chronic Fatigue
Spiritual Root: Oppression, depletion, emotional burnout
Gift Under Attack: Strength, endurance, calling to serve

Example Demons:

- **Lazybones** – Camouflages weariness as laziness
- **The Abyss** – Drains energy through despair
- **The Mindstorm** – Mentally exhausts with spinning thoughts

- **The Chainkeeper** – Keeps you stuck in past emotional drains
- **The Wanderer** – Creates a sense of aimlessness

What It May Be Telling You:

You may be in a spiritual fog that is not just physical. If you feel like you're dragging every day, it could be an attack on your momentum and calling. Your stamina is needed to build or support something big, so the enemy wants to shut it down early. The people under this attack actually have incredible endurance.

~ * * * ~

Struggle 13: Overspending and Greed
Spiritual Root: Scarcity mindset or idolizing wealth/status
Gift Under Attack: Stewardship, generosity, financial authority

Example Demons:

- **Mammon** – Makes money your master
- **The Pauper** – Keeps you feeling like it's never enough
- **The Selfish One** – Trains the hand to close, not give
- **The Idolator** – Obsesses over gain
- **The Collector** – Ties identity to things

What It May Be Telling You:

You may be called to fund or steward something for the Kingdom, so the enemy wants your finances tied up. Whether through debt, fear, or materialism, he'll try to make money a stronghold rather than a tool for purpose.

~ * * * ~

Struggle 14: Obsession with Appearance
Spiritual Root: Insecurity, fear of rejection, idolatry of image
Gift Under Attack: Identity, confidence, boldness

Example Demons:

- **The Conceited One** – Fixated on surface validation

- **The Broken Mirror** – Warps how you see yourself
- **The Harlot** – Elevates seduction and visibility as a source of worth and power
- **The Critic** – Constantly finds flaws
- **The Jealous One** – Fuels comparison, envy, and the belief that beauty is competition

What It May Be Telling You:
You might be called to stand in front of others, but the enemy wants you consumed with how you look instead of who you are. God wants to clothe you in strength and dignity. The enemy wants to robe you in obsession and shame.

~ * * * ~

Struggle 15: Gossiping
Spiritual Root: Insecurity, jealousy, or a desire for control
Gift Under Attack: Speech, discernment, relational integrity

Example Demons:

- **The Mouth** – Speaks harm instead of truth or life
- **The Critic** – Tears others down to feel superior
- **The Sower of Strife** – Divides relationships with words
- **The Idolator** – Exalts self or opinion above God's standard
- **The Monitor** – Watches others closely for information

What It May Be Telling You:
You were made to speak life and truth. The enemy is trying to train your tongue in the wrong direction—to destroy instead of build. If your mouth is a battleground, it may be because your voice has weight in the spirit and was designed to bring unity and truth.

~ * * * ~

Struggle 16: Bed Rotting; Staying in Bed All Day, Emotionally Checked Out.
Spiritual Root: Neglect, despair, and learned helplessness

42

Gift Under Attack: Vitality, purpose, emotional agency

Example Demons:

- **The Glacier** – Numbs emotion and motivation
- **The Abyss** – Saps the will to live, move or engage
- **The Neglectful Parent** – Models emotional abandonment and lack of nurture
- **The Orphan** – Convinces you that no one sees or cares
- **The Weak Father** – Fails to call forth strength, direction or identity

What It May Be Telling You:

This may be a response to emotional abandonment or years of being unseen. Bed rotting often masks a deep sense of futility: *"Why try?"* It may be the fallout of never being taught how to fight through discomfort or shown how much your presence matters. But your life does have weight, and your movement matters. God wants you fully alive.

~ * * * ~

Struggle 17: Miserliness; Extreme frugality with self and others
Spiritual Root: Fear of lack, scarcity mindset, and control
Gift Under Attack: Generosity, trust in God's provision, and financial discernment

Example Demons:

- **The Selfish One** – Hoards resources and fears release
- **The Pauper** – Convinces you there will never be enough
- **Mammon** – Equates money with safety and power
- **The Withholder** – Keeps you from giving, even when prompted by the Spirit
- **The Guard** – Uses self-protection to block generosity

What It May Be Telling You:

You may be gifted with radical generosity or a calling to steward resources for Kingdom impact, but the enemy has convinced you it's not safe to let go. Miserliness is not thrift or frugality, it's bondage.

When you struggle to bless others or even yourself, it's often because fear is speaking louder than faith. The enemy wants to keep your hands clenched and your heart anxious, so the blessings God intended to flow through you stay dammed up.

~ * * * ~

Struggle 18: Extreme Mood Swings
Spiritual Root: Fragmentation, emotional torment, and identity disruption
Gift Under Attack: Emotional resilience, clarity, and relational stability

Example Demons:

- **The Rash One** – Swings emotions from one extreme to the next
- **The Phantom** – Fuels internal fear, confusion, and torment
- **The Inferno** – Fuels sudden outbursts of anger, turning emotional instability into relational destruction
- **The Abyss** – Deepens depressive episodes
- **The Glazer** – Masks chaos with charm or overcompensation

What It May Be Telling You:
You may carry a deep emotional and spiritual sensitivity, a gift for leadership, intercession, or insight. The enemy wants to hijack your inner life with instability and confusion. These extremes can be the result of unhealed soul fragmentation, spiritual agitation, or open doors from sin, trauma, or soul ties. If he can keep you cycling between emotional highs and lows, he can destabilize your ability to build, lead, and connect with others in the consistency God intended for you.

~ * * * ~

Struggle 19: No Self-Control
Spiritual Root: Flesh-driven thinking, soul hunger, and spiritual weariness
Gift Under Attack: Purity, obedience, and spiritual authority

Example Demons:

- **The Rude One** – Rejects correction and reacts with hostility instead of restraint
- **King Baby** – Fuels entitlement, avoidance, and the refusal to take responsibility
- **The Defier** – Rebels against boundaries, accountability, and God's order
- **The Liar** – Justifies disobedience through distortion and excuses
- **The Waffler** – Keeps you stuck in indecision, delay, and mental confusion
- **The Stunted One** – Blocks emotional growth, leaving you spiritually immature and impulsive

What It May Be Telling You:

You may have a powerful calling that requires maturity, discipline, and spiritual authority, but the enemy is working to keep you stuck in childlike reactions, emotional instability, or rebellious patterns that short-circuit growth. What looks like laziness or defiance on the surface is often a deeper war over your ability to rise into leadership, responsibility, and strength. The enemy is trying to arrest your development, so you never step fully into who you were created to be.

~ * * * ~

Struggle 20: Limerence, Obsessive Infatuation or Uncontrollable Crushes
Spiritual Root: Emotional idolatry, rejection, and fantasy-based thinking
Gift Under Attack: Discernment, emotional clarity, and relational purpose

Example Demons:

- **The Narcissist** – Casts emotional spells through charm and control, keeping others entranced and off-balance
- **The Idolator** – Replaces God with emotional dependence on others
- **The Pretender** – Fuels fantasy over reality

- **The Chainkeeper** – Keeps you tied to unavailable people
- **Jezebel** – Dominates, seduces and entangles, especially through emotional and spiritual manipulation disguised as intimacy

What It May Be Telling You:

You may be wired for deep connection, covenant love, or even relational ministry, but the enemy is trying to trap your heart in fantasy and longing instead of rooted reality. Limerence feels like love but leaves you empty. It is designed to keep your soul looping around people who can't or won't love you back. The goal is to delay your healing, hijack your focus, and sabotage the relationships God *is* trying to prepare you for.

WHAT'S BEEN AFTER YOU?

4

Before we dive into the full list of demonic profiles, take a moment to examine what's been active in your life.

This is a spiritual inventory, a tool to help you identify which doors may have been opened, what strongholds you've struggled with, and where the enemy has tried to take ground.

You might already know some of the areas where the enemy has attacked you. Others may come as a surprise. Remember: this is not to shame you. We are gaining clarity and insight. The more specific you are about what you're fighting, the more effective you can be in overcoming it.

As you go through these questions, answer honestly. Especially if something is hard to admit. If you feel resistance, that's actually a neon sign pointing to your answer. If there wasn't truth there, you wouldn't feel friction.

The Bible says, *"You will know the truth, and the truth will make you free." (John 8:32)* Not just set you free as if unlocking a door and letting you out of a room, but MAKE you free, as in transforming you into someone who walks in freedom. Truth doesn't just open the cage; it changes the prisoner.

Once you finish, we'll move into the profiles, where you'll learn how these demons operate, how to recognize their influence, and how to fight back with authority.

Let's begin.

Primary Battleground Assessment

You may find yourself resonating with more than one group. The one with the most "yes" answers likely reflects your primary battleground.

Funnel Quiz: Lust of the Flesh

(Appetite, indulgence, sensory escape, and bodily-driven urges)

Check all that apply. Don't overthink—
go with your first honest reaction.

- ☐ I reach for food, drink, or screens when I feel emotional, overwhelmed, or bored.

- ☐ I often crave stimulation, comfort, or escape even when I'm not sure why.

- ☐ I've said, "Just this once" or "I deserve this" to justify something I knew wasn't right.

- ☐ I struggle with self-control and feel stuck in cycles of indulgence or avoidance.

- ☐ I feel shame after indulging, but it doesn't stop me from repeating it.

- ☐ I've used sex, fantasy, or attention to feel powerful, wanted, or emotionally safe.

- ☐ I stay up too late, binge content, or scroll for hours even though I know it's harmful.

- ☐ I procrastinate by numbing out, then feel defeated by everything I've avoided.

- ☐ I've felt numb, flat, or emotionally unavailable and couldn't explain why.

- ☐ I've convinced myself certain sins "aren't that serious" even when I felt convicted.

☐ I often act on desire or impulse, then regret it later.

☐ I feel like my body runs the show and my spirit can't catch up

SCORING GUIDE:

0–3:
You may be tempted in this area, but it's not your main battleground. Watch for patterns and stay spiritually alert.

4–7:
This area may be a significant open door. Flesh-driven patterns and indulgence could be limiting your spiritual authority. You're not powerless—but you may be misplacing your power.

8–12:
You are likely under spiritual oppression in this category. These are not just habits—they are strongholds. Deliverance, repentance, and discipline will be essential to healing.

Funnel Quiz: Lust of the Eyes

(Materialism, comparison, envy, image obsession)

Check all that apply. Go with your gut, not what you wish were true. Honesty will lead to freedom.

☐ I compare myself to others constantly—on social media, in real life, or even in church.

☐ I crave financial stability, status, or recognition more than spiritual growth.

☐ I feel like I'm "behind" in life compared to others, and it makes me feel small or bitter.

☐ I feel pressure to look a certain way even if it costs a lot of time, money, or peace.

☐ I've bought things I couldn't afford just to feel better or look successful.

☐ I measure my worth by how much I've achieved or how little others have.

☐ I secretly enjoy when others fail, or feel envious when they succeed.

☐ I care more about how something looks than whether it's good, right or true.

☐ I've lied, exaggerated, or twisted facts to protect my image or gain favor.

☐ I monitor other people's lives more than I focus on my own.

☐ I've talked about people behind their backs, especially if I felt jealous.

☐ I feel a constant pressure to "keep up" even when I'm exhausted or unhappy.

SCORING GUIDE:

0–3:

You may wrestle with comparison or pressure at times, but it doesn't define your lens. Stay vigilant; small compromises can snowball.

4–7:

This may be an area of active warfare. What you're seeing is affecting how you value yourself and others. Be mindful of what you feed your eyes and soul.

8–12:

There is likely deep spiritual oppression here. Your eyes have become a portal for strongholds around greed, vanity, envy, or identity distortion. Break agreement, renounce comparison, and recover your true vision.

Funnel Quiz: Pride of Life

(Control, rebellion, shame, fear, and generational strongholds)

Check all that apply. Go with your gut—not who you wish you were, but where you might be under attack. Pride often hides in wounds. Truth brings freedom.

- ☐ I feel a strong need to stay in control; if I'm not in charge, I feel anxious or unsafe.

- ☐ I change who I am depending on who I'm around.

- ☐ I've used guilt, silence, or flattery to influence outcomes.

- ☐ I find it hard to trust authority, especially when I've been hurt before.

- ☐ I carry shame about my story or past and try to hide it from others.

- ☐ I struggle with rage, resentment, or grudge-holding, even if I hide it well.

- ☐ I often feel like I'm responsible for everyone's well-being or happiness.

- ☐ I avoid stretching myself to grow or obedience when it feels scary or uncertain.

- ☐ I feel like I inherited pain or dysfunction that I can't seem to escape.

- ☐ I've questioned if God really sees me or if He'll ever come through for me.

- ☐ I often self-sabotage or back away right when I'm about to break through.

- ☐ I feel stuck in fear, anger, or performance, and it's exhausting.

SCORING GUIDE:

0-3:

These may be passing struggles, but pride isn't the dominant battlefield. Stay aware since seeds can still take root if left unchallenged.

4-7:

You may be operating under an active stronghold. Control, fear, or shame might be shaping your choices more than you realize. This is worth pressing into.

8-12:

This is likely a core battleground in your life. These patterns go beyond personality and are spiritual. Break agreement, seek truth, and go deeper into healing. Explore the breakout quizzes to identify where the enemy may be hiding.

Primary Battleground Assessment Scoring:

Your highest number points to the strongest area of spiritual warfare in your life.

Result Key:

- **Highest in Lust of the Flesh?**
  Turn to the next section: **Flesh-Based Breakout Quizzes**

- **Highest in Lust of the Eyes?**
  Turn to the next section: **Eyes-Based Breakout Quizzes**

- **Highest in Pride of Life?**
  Turn to the next section: **Pride-Based Breakout Quizzes**

Flesh-Based Breakout Quizzes

Flesh-Based Breakout Quiz:
Sexual Sin, Perversion & Soul Ties

(Lust, trauma, infidelity, pornography, emotional bondage, and spiritual entanglement)

Check all that apply. Sexual sin and emotional entanglements open spiritual doors. Whether through trauma, rebellion, or misplaced longing, these patterns form soul ties that impact your identity, relationships, and sense of worth. The good news is no one is too defiled for God to restore.

- ☐ I've had sex outside of marriage.

- ☐ I've had more partners than I can remember or want to admit.

- ☐ I've struggled with porn, sexual fantasy, or compulsive masturbation.

- ☐ I've experienced same-sex attraction or confusion about my gender.

- ☐ I've compared who I'm with to someone from my past, especially during sex

- ☐ I've been sexually abused or exposed to sexual content at a young age.

- ☐ I've divorced someone who is still alive.

- ☐ I read a lot of romance novels and erotic fiction.

- ☐ I've felt "hooked" on someone I knew wasn't good for me.

- ☐ I've performed sex work or paid for it, including sugaring and exotic dancing.

- ☐ I've used sex to gain attention, validation, power, or protection.

☐ I've fantasized or dreamed about people from my past even after years.

☐ I've participated in sexual things I didn't really want or regretted afterwards.

☐ I've been unfaithful in a relationship or emotionally entangled outside of one.

☐ I've felt shame, regret, or emotional numbness related to sex.

☐ I've viewed sex as a strictly physical transaction.

☐ I've thought of someone other than who I was with during sex.

☐ I've had an abortion or impregnated someone who had an abortion.

☐ I've been sexually assaulted or have assaulted someone.

☐ I've thought, "Real love doesn't exist," or "I'll never be enough for one person" or "No one can be completely faithful."

☐ I've participated in phone or cyber sex, including paying for sites like Only Fans.

☐ I've thought of people as objects or tools for pleasure instead of whole souls.

☐ I feel like something is missing in me, and that I can't be alone, so I've tried to fill that void through relationships.

☐ Even though I'm married or in a serious relationship, there is someone from my past who I would leave everything for if they came back to me.

SCORING GUIDE:

0–7: There may be wounds or open doors here, but you're not in bondage. This is a vital area to guard, purify, and surrender. Let God heal what's hidden.

8–15: You're likely carrying spiritual residue from past relationships or trauma. The enemy has legal access and may be using these entanglements to adversely affect your intimacy, identity, or emotional clarity. Deliverance and healing are available. God wants to make you whole.

16–24: This is likely a major spiritual stronghold. You may be dealing with soul ties, addiction, deep-rooted shame, or demonic torment. But Jesus redeems what was broken, and no history is too unclean for Him to restore.

Demons to Explore: (Sexual Sin, Perversion & Soul Ties)

- **The Insatiable** – "More will finally satisfy." (Lust-driven craving that never ends)
- **The Cheater** – "No one will ever fully satisfy me." (Infidelity, discontent, betrayal)
- **The Player** – "Lust is just part of being a man." (Serial sex, casual detachment)
- **The Harlot** – "Your body is your only power." (Seduction, visibility obsession)
- **The Splitter** – "People are parts, not whole beings." (Objectification, misogyny)
- **The Profane** – "Sacred doesn't matter." (Pornography, spiritual defilement)
- **The Reverser** – "Switch what God made." (Gender reversal, sexual confusion)
- **The Corrupter** – "Steal their innocence." (Early exposure, molestation)
- **The Rapist** – "Take what you want." (Sexual violation, domination)
- **The Inverter** – "Call evil good and good evil." (Normalizes perversion)
- **The Chainkeeper** – "You'll never break free from them." (Soul tie bondage)
- **The Idolator** – "Affection is your god." (Makes intimacy and validation into idols)

- **The Pretender** – "Be whoever they'll want." (Fantasy-based identity and attraction)
- **The Exploiter** – "Use them for what you want." (Pleasure over connection)

Flesh-Based Breakout Quiz: Addiction & Indulgence | Part 1

(Digital loops, binge behavior, and escapism)

Check all that apply. Addiction often hides in routines that comfort but control you.

- ☐ I lose track of time scrolling, watching, or consuming content.
- ☐ I often say "just one more" and then feel disappointed afterward.
- ☐ I escape into screens, food, or fantasy when life feels heavy.
- ☐ I've told myself I can stop anytime, but I haven't.
- ☐ My habits leave me numb, not refreshed.
- ☐ I know it's wasting my time, but I keep going back to it anyway.

SCORING GUIDE:

0–2: There may be patterns forming—catch them early.

3–4: This area may be quietly dominating your attention and time.

5–6: You're likely in bondage. Break the cycle, renounce the comfort, and expose the idol.

Relevant Demon Profiles to Explore:
(Addiction & Indulgence Part 1)

- **The Loop** – "Just keep scrolling." (Digital trance, mental disengagement)
- **The Binger** – "Next episode. Then I'll stop." (Compulsive overconsumption)

- **The Escapist** – "Anywhere but here." (Avoidance through distraction or fantasy)

Flesh-Based Breakout Quiz:
Addiction & Indulgence | Part 2

(Chemical, physical, and food-based coping)

Check all that apply. Don't just think about extremes. Think about dependency, self-control, and what you run to when life hurts.

☐ I use food, substances, or habits to calm my emotions.

☐ I feel out of control when I try to quit certain habits.

☐ I've hidden my indulgence from others because I'm ashamed.

☐ I know something is hurting me, but I keep going back to it.

☐ I feel like I "need" something to feel okay.

☐ I've broken promises to myself or others about stopping.

SCORING GUIDE:

0–2: Watch this area closely—it may be more spiritual than physical.

3–4: Something is offering false comfort. Ask what you trust more than God.

5–6: You are likely under spiritual bondage. Deliverance is possible.

Relevant Demon Profiles to Explore:
(Addiction & Indulgence Part 2)

- **The Glutton** – "Feed the void." (Comfort eating, emotional filling)
- **The Alchemist** – "One more hit won't hurt." (Substance-driven false peace)
- **The Drunkard** – "You can't face this sober." (Alcohol dependence and self-numbing)

- **The Puffer** – "You need this to feel calm and in control." (Nicotine and vaping addiction)

Flesh-Based Breakout Quiz: Sloth & Apathy

(Spiritual laziness, procrastination, emotional numbness, and passive surrender)

Check all that apply. Sloth is more than laziness— it's spiritual dullness that numbs your passion, stalls your calling, and keeps you from rising.

- ☐ I know I should take action, but I keep putting it off.

- ☐ I get overwhelmed by what needs to be done, so I do nothing.

- ☐ I say "later" a lot, even when I know I mean "never."

- ☐ I want to feel productive, but I waste hours avoiding what matters.

- ☐ I start things but rarely finish them.

- ☐ I delay obedience and call it "waiting on God."

- ☐ I feel emotionally numb, like I'm just drifting through life.

- ☐ I've lost passion or vision, even for things I once loved.

- ☐ I avoid spiritual growth because I just don't have the energy.

- ☐ I pretend not to care, but deep down I feel hopeless.

- ☐ I often sleep too much, eat to cope, or mentally check out.

- ☐ I've stopped expecting much because disappointment feels safer.

SCORING GUIDE:

0–3: You may just be in a natural slump—stay vigilant and ask God to renew your strength.

4–7: Apathy or avoidance is likely creeping in. This could be a spiritual block—don't ignore it.

8–12: This is likely a stronghold. The enemy is trying to numb, delay, or bury your destiny. Wake up. Armor up. Rise.

Relevant Demon Profiles to Explore: (Sloth & Apathy)

- **Lazybones** – "Why try?" (Spiritual sloth, mental and physical inertia)
- **The Staller** – "It's not ready yet." (Perfectionism disguised as delay)
- **The Numb One** – "I just don't care." (Emotional shutdown, passivity)

Eyes-Based Breakout Quizzes

Eyes-Based Breakout Quiz: Occult Influence, False Light & Secret Agreements

*(New Age, secret knowledge, spiritual elitism,
AI worship, mysticism, and deception)*

The enemy hides behind "innocent curiosity," tradition, or enlightenment. Whether it was a psychic reading, a ritual oath, or a game, you may have opened spiritual doors you never intended. It takes humility to admit we may have participated in things with serious spiritual consequences, even if we didn't realize it at the time. That's exactly what the enemy is counting on: pride, sentimentality, and loyalty to a system over loyalty to God. Don't double down. Repent and be free.

☐ **I've dabbled in astrology, tarot, crystals, or spellwork even casually or for fun.**

☐ **I've gone to psychics, mediums, or energy healers for answers or help.**

☐ **I've believed that all religions lead to the same truth or that I was "spiritual but not religious."**

☐ I've practiced manifestation, law of attraction, or visualization to attract what I wanted.

☐ I've followed spiritual influencers, "light workers," or "higher self" teachings.

☐ I've rejected parts of the Bible because they didn't fit my view of love, freedom, or truth.

☐ I've believed witches are misunderstood and misrepresented and are actually enlightened or evolved more than others.

☐ I've trusted technology, science, or artificial intelligence more than God's Word.

☐ I've been abducted by aliens or have entertained alien communication theories such as The Galactic Federation as a form of deeper knowledge.

☐ I've said affirmations, chants, or "high vibration" phrases without knowing their origin.

☐ I've practiced yoga, even if just for fitness, especially if breathwork, poses, or mantras were involved.

☐ I've been part of a cult, secret society, or high-control religious group.

☐ I've been involved in a group that claimed to follow Jesus but taught a different gospel (e.g. Mormonism, Jehovah's Witnesses).

☐ I've joined an organization (including frats/sororities) that required oaths or secret rituals.

☐ I've played with Ouija boards, "light as a feather," or ghost summoning games.

☐ I've watched, read, or listened to content that glorifies witchcraft or sorcery.

- ☐ I've toured haunted sites, voodoo shops, or temples and brought back souvenirs.

- ☐ I've visited a root worker, Santeria priest or similar spiritual practitioner for help, healing, or insight.

- ☐ I've had supernatural experiences like sleep paralysis, shadow figures, or spirit visitations.

- ☐ I've entertained or believed in alien communication or "galactic wisdom."

- ☐ I have occult objects in my home: books, crystals, images, jewelry, or clothing with spiritual symbols.

- ☐ I've had recurring dark dreams, especially involving specific people, places or themes like eating, engaging in sexual activity, or signing contracts.

- ☐ I regularly listen to secular music, especially by artists who openly promote darkness, lust, rebellion, or Satanic symbolism, and always have a song stuck in my head.

SCORING GUIDE:
0-6:
You may have been exposed but haven't made lasting agreements. Ask the Holy Spirit to reveal anything hidden and close all doors through repentance.

7-14:
There are likely open spiritual doors and active influence from false light, occult involvement, or spiritual deception. What feels harmless may be costing you spiritual clarity. Renounce and remove. See the Solutions section of this book.

15-23:

This is likely a major stronghold. The enemy has legal access through oaths, rituals, objects, or spiritual agreements, whether knowingly or not. Deliverance and full cleansing are essential. Jesus can break every chain.

Relevant Demon Profiles to Explore: (Occult Influence, False Light & Secret Agreements)

- **The Arcane One** – "Hidden knowledge is power." (Draws people into forbidden wisdom and mystery)
- **The Guru** – "I have the secret." (False spiritual authority and elitism)
- **The Enchanter** – "Let the magic in." (Romanticizes the occult and "white witchcraft")
- **The Hypnotist** – "You're under the influence." (Spirit of mind control and altered consciousness)
- **The AI Spirit** – "The machine is god." (Idolizes technology and synthetic wisdom)
- **The Alien Deceiver** – "They are coming for you." (False signs, lying wonders, and strong delusion)
- **The Manifester** – "Believe it into being." (Disguises witchcraft as positive thinking and self-deification)
- **The Gatekeeper** – "Not everyone belongs." (Elitism and spiritual superiority)
- **The Oracle** – "The spirits will tell you." (Channeling, divination, and false prophecy)
- **The Apostate** – "I've moved beyond that." (Rejection of truth for spiritual rebellion)

Eyes-Based Breakout Quiz:
Greed, Materialism & Vanity | Part 1

(Status, stuff, and the pressure to achieve)

Check all that apply. Greed and vanity often hide behind goals, style, and ambition, but they steal peace and warp identity.

☐ I feel behind in life when I look at other people's money, career, or status.

☐ I link my worth to how much I've accomplished or what I can offer.

☐ I've bought things just to feel better about myself or look impressive.

☐ I feel anxious when money is tight, even if I all my needs are met.

☐ I fear being seen as "less than" or not having it all together.

☐ I secretly feel envious when others succeed more quickly than I have.

SCORING GUIDE:

0-2: These thoughts may pass through, but they haven't taken root.

3-4: Watch your value system—something may be replacing God's approval.

5-6: You're likely battling a spirit of materialism or false identity. Renounce the lie that your worth is found in wealth or work.

Relevant Demon Profiles to Explore:

(Greed, Materialism & Vanity Part 1)

• **The Achiever** – "You are what you do." (Performance-based identity and worth)

- **Mammon** – "Money is your safety." (Trust in wealth over God)
- **The Pauper** – "You'll never have enough." (Spirit of lack, poverty, and scarcity mindset)
- **The Collector** – "More will finally be enough." (Endless accumulation to fill a spiritual void)

Eyes-Based Breakout Quiz:
Greed, Materialism & Vanity | Part 2

(Image obsession and destructive spending)

Check all that apply. Vanity is about more than appearance; it's about distraction, insecurity, and false idols.

☐ **I spend too much time thinking about how I look or how I'm perceived.**

☐ **I've prioritized my image over what's right, honest, or wise.**

☐ **I shop, spend, or "treat myself" when I feel low, even if I regret it later.**

☐ **I've exaggerated or polished the truth to look good.**

☐ **I obsess over my feed, outfits, or style, but still feel unsatisfied.**

☐ **I've judged others by what they have, wear, or post.**

SCORING GUIDE:

0–2: Keep a clean heart—vanity can creep in slowly.

3–4: Image may be taking priority over integrity. Time to re-center.

5–6: You may be idolizing self, status, or style. Repent, reset, and refocus.

Relevant Demon Profiles to Explore:

(Greed, Materialism & Vanity Part 2)

- **The Idolmaker** – "Worship what shines." (Exalts beauty, status, and superficial success)
- **The Curator** – "Only the image matters." (Obsessed with appearances and aesthetic control)
- **The Conceited One** – "Admire me." (Craves validation, envy, and superiority)
- **The Waster** – "Spend now. Think later." (Irresponsible indulgence and financial foolishness)
- **The Thief** – "If no one sees, it doesn't count." (Justifies dishonesty for gain)

Eyes-Based Breakout Quiz:
Envy, Comparison & Discord | Part 1

(Jealousy, rivalry, and discontent)

Check all that apply. Envy makes people bitter, blinds us to our blessings, and poisons relationships.

- ☐ **I compare myself to others constantly—on social media, in real life, or even in church.**
- ☐ **I've judged someone's success, looks, or gifts and felt inferior in comparison.**
- ☐ **I look down upon people who don't look the way I think they should.**
- ☐ **I've confused wanting and needing regarding certain material things.**
- ☐ **I notice when a person repeats an outfit.**

□ I feel like there's not enough for everyone: if they have it, I can't.

□ I feel like if I compliment someone, they won't receive it the right way.

□ I behave and carry myself differently depending on my appearance.

□ I expect my friends to downplay their appearance on my birthday or similar occasion.

□ I feel like owning a certain thing or changing a certain feature of my body would complete my life and I would be happy.

□ I judge people by their appearance, first.

□ I feel like other people have a lot more than I do and I'll never catch up.

□ I believe there is an ideal body and that I have it or do not have it.

□ I've canceled plans because I couldn't dress or groom myself the way I wanted.

□ I believe the more attractive a person is, they more power they have.

□ I get jealous even when I try not to and I feel ashamed of it.

□ I have a hard time celebrating others without comparing myself.

□ I've felt secretly pleased when someone who "had it all" failed.

SCORING GUIDE:

0–4: . You may feel a tug of comparison or envy now and then, but it hasn't taken root. Stay alert. What starts as a glance can become a stronghold if not brought to God. Guard your eyes and your heart.

5–11: You are likely in a battle with insecurity, envy or image-driven self-worth. You may feel pressure to "keep up," struggle to celebrate others, or view yourself through a distorted lens. These lies can isolate, exhaust, and steal joy. It's time to break agreement and let God redefine your worth.

12–18: You are likely dealing with a deep-rooted spirit of jealousy, rivalry, or self-rejection. Materialism, false identity, and constant comparison may be shaping your relationships, peace, and purpose. This is beyond insecurity, it's spiritual. Repent, renounce, and be restored. You were never meant to live in competition.

Relevant Demon Profiles to Explore:

(Envy, Comparison & Discord Part 1)

- **The Jealous One** – "If they have it, I've lost it." (Competes for blessing and worth)
- **The Monitor** – "Watch them constantly." (Fixates on others' lives to measure your own)
- **The Bitter One** – "You've been robbed. Hold on to the pain." (Resentment and unforgiveness disguised as righteousness)
- **The Curator** – "Only the image matters." (Obsessed with appearances and aesthetic control)
- **The Idolator** – "Worship anything but God." (Elevates beauty, success, or people as ultimate sources of value)
- **The Conceited One** – "Admire me." (Craves validation, envy, and superiority)

Eyes-Based Breakout Quiz:
Envy, Comparison & Discord | Part 2
(Division, gossip, and stirring strife)

*Check all that apply. In their envy, some spirits
destroy relationships to feel better.*

☐ I've talked about people behind their backs, even if I framed it as "concern."

☐ I've created tension between others, intentionally or not.

☐ I vent or gossip instead of going to God.

☐ It is very difficult for me to keep a secret or not share a hot piece of gossip.

☐ I have nicknames for the people I gossip about to keep everyone straight

☐ I leave comments online that I would not if my real identity was attached.

☐ Even when I know I shouldn't talk, I can't resist passing on certain info or gossip.

☐ I get offended easily and replay the offense in my mind.

☐ I am very informed about celebrity and influencer gossip.

☐ I've held onto bitterness or carried a grudge against someone.

☐ I am secretly proud that people come to me for the story or inside info on a situation or person.

☐ I sometimes feel more connected to people when we're tearing down someone else.

☐ I would feel badly if the people I talked about heard what I say about them.

SCORING GUIDE:

0–3: You may have occasionally slip into gossip or judgment, but it hasn't become a pattern. Stay vigilant, seeds of discord grow fast if not pulled quickly. Ask the Holy Spirit to refine your words and purify your intentions.

4–8: This may be an active stronghold of gossip, offense, or spiritual rivalry. The enemy may be using comparison, jealousy or bitterness to break relationships or distort how you see others. Renounce the need to be "in the know" or "on top." That's pride, and God hates it. Pursue peace and repentance.

9–13: This area is likely under demonic influence. Strife, suspicion, and slander may be stealing your peace and sabotaging your connections. What feels like venting or truth-telling may actually be agreement with the accuser. Ask God to cleanse your heart and silence every spirit that feeds on division.

Relevant Demon Profiles to Explore: (Envy, Comparison & Discord Part 2)

- **The Sower of Strife** – "Break them apart." (Spreads division through conflict and manipulation)
- **The Mouth** – "If I feel it, I'll say it." (Speaks without restraint; wounds with words)
- **The Gossip** – "They need to know." (Spreads private matters to elevate self or stir drama)
- **The Monitor** – "Watch them constantly." (Fixates on others' lives to feed comparison and envy)
- **The Critic** – "Pick them apart." (Finds fault in others to avoid self-reflection)

Pride-Based Breakout Quizzes

Pride-Based Breakout Quiz: Mind & Identity Distortion

(Self-hatred, depression, mental noise)

Check all that apply. Be honest.

Even hard truths are doors to freedom.

- ☐ I constantly second-guess myself and feel mentally exhausted.

- ☐ I struggle with obsessive thoughts or mental loops I can't turn off.

- ☐ I often feel worthless or like I'll never be enough.

- ☐ I fear being wrong or corrected, even when I know I need help.

- ☐ I have trouble making decisions and feel stuck between choices.

- ☐ I find it hard to trust what's true. My thoughts feel clouded or confusing.

- ☐ I react quickly without thinking and regret it later.

- ☐ I live in fear of what *might* happen and can't relax.

- ☐ I feel like I have to protect myself emotionally because others can't be trusted.

- ☐ I tell myself stories that excuse or distort reality so I can avoid pain.

- ☐ I struggle to believe God's truth applies to *me*.

- ☐ I overthink spiritual matters to the point of anxiety, not peace.

SCORING GUIDE:

0–3:

You may have occasional struggles, but your foundation is fairly stable. Still, be mindful of creeping mental patterns that erode clarity and peace.

4–7:

You likely wrestle with identity distortion or spiritual confusion. These may be strongholds, not just personality quirks. God wants to restore your mind and silence the noise.

8–12:

This may be spiritual oppression. The enemy is actively distorting your thoughts, identity, and ability to walk in truth. It's time to confront these lies, renounce them, and walk in divine clarity.

Relevant Demon Profiles to Explore:
(Mind & Identity Distortion)

- **The Abyss** – "Nothing will ever change." (Depression & hopelessness)
- **The Broken Mirror** – "You are never enough." (Self-hatred & insecurity)
- **The Guard** – "Don't try, it won't matter." (Overprotection & self-sabotage)
- **The Phantom** – "You are never safe." (Paranoia & fear loops)
- **The Liar** – "The truth is what I say it is." (Reality distortion)
- **The Doubter** – "Did God really say?" (Spiritual uncertainty)
- **The Mindstorm** – "You can't stop thinking." (Obsessive thought patterns)
- **The Waffler** – "You can't choose." (Chronic indecision)
- **Leviathan** – "You don't need correction." (Prideful confusion & rebellion)
- **The Rash One** – "I don't need to think. I just act." (Impulsiveness)

Pride-Based Breakout Quiz: Shame, Fear & Limitation

(Self-sabotage, emotional immaturity, fear of man)

Check all that apply. The enemy knows how to prey upon and exploit our weaknesses so that we become our own greatest obstacle.

☐ I often feel like I'll mess things up no matter what I do.

☐ I struggle with speaking up, even when I know I should.

☐ I fear rejection and often hide parts of myself to be accepted.

☐ I feel like I never measure up to others' standards or my own.

☐ I'm highly critical of myself, others, or both.

☐ I feel like certain people or groups are "beneath me" or the problem.

☐ I often complain or focus on what's wrong more than what's right.

☐ I get anxious or impatient when things don't move fast enough.

☐ I tend to withdraw or disappear when people need me.

☐ I have begged to be chosen or noticed and felt worthless when I wasn't.

☐ I resist maturing emotionally or spiritually because it feels overwhelming.

☐ I avoid doing what I know God wants because I'm scared of the cost.

☐ I keep the peace even if it means betraying myself or truth.

☐ I believe God is good, but not necessarily to me.

☐ I have had thoughts of harming myself or wishing it would all end.

☐ I've broken promises I made, especially to myself or people I love.

SCORING GUIDE

0–5:

You may carry hidden wounds, but you're functioning well. Still, be aware: tolerating low-grade shame or fear can eventually deepen into strongholds.

6–11:

You likely deal with unresolved pain or oppression. These patterns limit your joy, obedience, and boldness. God wants to restore your voice, vision, and worth.

12–16:

This points to deep spiritual oppression or trauma wounds. These are not just emotions—they are weapons used against your purpose. It's time to renounce these lies, receive healing, and reclaim your authority.

Relevant Demon Profiles to Explore: (Shame, Fear & Limitation)

- **The Saboteur** – "You'll ruin it anyway." (Self-sabotage and unworthiness)
- **The Mute** – "Stay quiet." (Silencing your voice)
- **The Rejector** – "You'll never belong." (Fear of abandonment and exclusion)
- **The False Mirror** – "You'll never measure up." (Toxic self-perception)
- **The Critic** – "Find every flaw." (Hyper-critical spirit)
- **The Despiser** – "She is the problem." (Internalized contempt toward others)
- **The Complainer** – "Nothing is ever good enough." (Chronic discontent)
- **The Impatient One** – "Now or never." (Restlessness & entitlement)
- **The Ghoster** – "Disappear when needed most." (Avoidance under pressure)
- **The Desperate** – "Pick me, or I'm nothing." (Validation-seeking and rejection panic)

- **The Stunted One** – "I shouldn't have to grow up." (Emotional immaturity)
- **The Coward** – "It's too risky to obey God." (Fear of obedience)
- **The Appeaser** – "Don't upset anyone." (People-pleasing bondage)
- **The Faithless One** – "God isn't coming through." (Hopelessness toward God)
- **The Suicide Spirit** – "It will never get better. Just end it." (Spirit of despair)
- **The Cutter** – "You deserve this pain." (Self-harm and punishment)
- **The Promise Breaker** – "You don't owe anyone anything." (Neglect of responsibility)

Pride-Based Breakout Quiz: Control & Manipulation

(Intimidation, domination, entitlement, rebellion)

Check all that apply. Control and manipulation wear countless disguises. Sometimes they show up as niceness, helpfulness, or even "discernment." At their root they are witchcraft, which is defined as manipulation, intimidation, and domination. Where control reigns, pride has taken the throne.

- ☐ I often feel unsafe unless I'm in control of the situation.
- ☐ I plan or overthink conversations to steer how people respond.
- ☐ I get angry or anxious when others don't do things my way.
- ☐ I use sarcasm, silence, or guilt to influence people.
- ☐ I tend to play different roles depending on who I'm around.
- ☐ I've been told I'm emotionally distant, cold, or shut down.
- ☐ I avoid responsibility and expect others to step in.
- ☐ I need to be right—being wrong feels like a threat.
- ☐ I share others' information or vent about them behind their back.

☐ I feel above the rules or resist being told what to do.

☐ I've used flattery or charm to get what I want.

☐ I struggle to submit to God's timing, authority, or plans.

SCORING GUIDE

0–4:

You may lean toward independence, but you likely keep it in check. Still, watch for areas where "self-protection" is really hidden control.

5–8:

There are likely spiritual strongholds influencing your behavior. The desire for control may stem from past wounds, but it's costing you peace, intimacy, and obedience.

9–12:

This level of control or manipulation usually points to deep emotional damage or demonic oppression. These patterns are survival mechanisms hijacked by the enemy. Repentance and deliverance are essential.

Relevant Demon Profiles to Explore: (Control & Manipulation)

- **Jezebel** – "Control is safer than trust." (Spirit of manipulation, intimidation, and seduction)
- **The Puppeteer** – "If I pull the strings, I'll be safe." (Covert control through orchestration)
- **The Intimidator** – "Fear gets results." (Bullying and domination)
- **The Dominator** – "My way or nothing." (Authoritarian spirit)
- **The Narcissist** – "I am the center." (Idolatry of self and emotional vampirism)
- **The Pretender** – "Become whatever works." (Shapeshifting and deceit)
- **The Glacier** – "Don't feel. Don't move." (Emotional shutdown and paralysis)
- **King Baby** – "Someone else will handle it." (Immaturity and emotional dependence)

- **The Litigator** – "If I'm right, I'm safe." (Argumentative and combative spirit)
- **The Gossip** – "Speak to divide." (Destructive speech and spiritual slander)
- **The Defier** – "No one tells me what to do, not even God." (Rebellion and lawlessness)
- **The Glazer** – (Manipulation through insincere praise and charm)

Pride-Based Breakout Quiz: Rage & Corruption

(Hatred, unforgiveness, treachery)

Check all that apply. Rage can seethe, manipulate, or punish silently, it's not always screaming. Corruption can also be subtle and have a polite face.

- ☐ I replay offenses in my mind and think of what I *should* have said or done.

- ☐ I've fantasized about getting revenge or seeing someone suffer.

- ☐ I hold back affection or kindness as a way to punish people who've hurt me.

- ☐ I feel proud of being cold, blunt, or unapologetically "real."

- ☐ I often think, *"They don't deserve forgiveness."*

- ☐ I've broken trust, cheated, or betrayed someone, but blamed them for it.

- ☐ I manipulate people to get what I want, especially when I'm angry.

- ☐ I speak or act in ways that intentionally hurt others and don't always regret it.

- ☐ I've bullied, threatened, or controlled someone through fear.

- ☐ I've laughed at someone's pain or felt good seeing them fail.

☐ I've said or thought things that were cruel, hateful, or dehumanizing.

☐ I've judged or mistreated someone based on their race or background.

SCORING GUIDE:

0–4:

You may carry unhealed hurt or anger, but it hasn't fully taken root. Still, don't excuse sarcasm or harshness; what's planted in the heart eventually bears fruit.

5–8:

There is likely spiritual oppression tied to offense, bitterness, or pride. These are strongholds, not just attitudes. Ask God to reveal the roots and break their power.

9–12:

These patterns reveal a dangerous foothold for the enemy. Whether loud or subtle, this level of rage and corruption is spiritually destructive and demands repentance, healing, and deliverance.

Relevant Demon Profiles to Explore: (Rage & Corruption)

- **The Inferno** – "Burn it all down." (Uncontrolled rage and destruction)
- **The Avenger** – "You owe me pain." (Vengeance and retaliation)
- **The Chainkeeper** – "They owe me." (Grudge holding and emotional bondage)
- **The Withholder** – "Nothing is ever enough." (Bitterness and emotional punishment)
- **The Monarch** – "I deserve it, no matter what." (Entitlement and spiritual pride)
- **The Exploiter** – "People are tools—use them before they use you." (Manipulation and dehumanization)

- **The Selfish One** – "Only your needs matter." (Self-centeredness and disregard for others)
- **The Rude One** – "Courtesy is weakness." (Cruelty, brashness, and domination)
- **The Unforgiving One** – "They don't deserve forgiveness—and I'll never let it go." (Bitterness and spiritual blockage)
- **The Betrayer** – "Loyalty is for fools." (Treacherousness and self-preservation at all costs)
- **The Murderer** – "End them." (Violent hatred and the spirit of death)
- **The Hater** – "They don't deserve to live." (Deep-seated contempt and evil judgment)
- **The Bully** – "Power belongs to the cruel." (Intimidation and torment)
- **The Cruel One** – "Hurt them. Break them." (Sadism and emotional brutality)
- **The Racist** – "They are beneath you." (Hatred and pride rooted in skin or heritage)

Pride-Based Breakout Quiz:
Generational & Cultural Strongholds

(Estrangement, internal wounds, conditional love, parentification)

Check all that apply. These wounds often feel "normal," because they've always been there.

- ☐ **I felt emotionally disconnected from one or both parents, even if my needs were met.**

- ☐ **I carry a deep sense of being unwanted, excluded, or different from the rest of my family.**

- ☐ **I was the "responsible one" growing up and still feel responsible for everyone's well-being.**

☐ I was either constantly praised or constantly blamed and still feel like I'm performing.

☐ I often shrink around family, like I'm a child again, even as an adult.

☐ I've been told I'm too much, too intense, or "just causing problems" when I speak the truth.

☐ I've felt guilt for growing, leaving, or setting boundaries, especially with my mother or in-laws.

☐ I've experienced jealousy, competition, or emotional manipulation in family relationships.

☐ I've never known a healthy father figure—or had to recover from a harmful one.

☐ I feel like I don't belong in my family or culture but also don't know where I *do* belong.

☐ I've found myself repeating patterns I swore I'd escape, especially in how I parent, partner, or relate.

☐ I feel spiritually or emotionally stuck when I go back home or engage with certain relatives.

SCORING GUIDE:

0–3:

You may carry some residue from family dynamics, but you've likely broken free from most of the pattern. Keep asking God to reveal any subtle roots.

4–8:

You are likely under the influence of one or more familiar spirits—generational patterns that continue to operate until renounced. These strongholds shape how you see yourself and others.

9–12:

There is likely deep spiritual entanglement through bloodline, trauma, or identity. You may have accepted dysfunction as normal, but these patterns are not your inheritance. Deliverance, healing, and re-parenting through the Father's love are critical.

Relevant Demon Profiles to Explore:
(Generational & Cultural Strongholds)

- **The Severer** – "You don't need them." (Isolation, relational disconnection, anti-family spirit)
- **The Orphan** – "You are unwanted." (Spirit of abandonment and rejection)
- **The Performer** – "Be who they want." (Approval addiction, identity distortion)
- **The Golden Child** – "You can do no wrong." (Pride, perfectionism, false identity)
- **The Black Sheep** – "You're the problem." (Shame, scapegoating, self-loathing)
- **The Truth Teller** – "Say what no one wants to hear." (Misunderstood prophetic voice, often shunned)
- **The Overbearing Matriarch** – "Only I know best." (Control, domination through motherhood)
- **The Meddling Mother-in-Law** – "They still belong to me." (Emotional enmeshment, boundary violation)
- **The Withholding Father** – "Earn my approval." (Performance pressure, emotional deprivation)
- **The Weak Father** – "I won't lead." (Abdication of authority, passivity)
- **The Terrifying Father** – "Obey or suffer." (Abuse, fear, legalism)
- **The Neglectful Parent** – "You're on your own." (Abandonment, emotional starvation)
- **Sibling Rivalry** – "Only one of us can win." (Jealousy, competition, division)

- **The Burnt-Out Child** – "You're responsible for everyone." (Parentified child, emotional fatigue)
- **The Jealous Mother** – "Your light is a threat to me." (Undermining, sabotage)
- **The Enmeshed Mother** – "You are an extension of me." (Identity confusion, codependency)

THE LUST OF THE FLESH

5

Some chains don't look like chains at all, until you try to break them. These demons specialize in keeping people stuck through overstimulation, overindulgence, and escape. Whether through food, screens, substances, or fantasy, their goal is the same: to keep the body comfortable, the mind occupied, and the soul sedated.

These spirits use pleasure as the bait to rewire your brain, hijack your nervous system, and leave you unable to sit still in silence or crave anything deeper than dopamine. They promise comfort but deliver bondage; escape becomes isolation; fullness leaves you empty.

In this chapter, you'll meet the demons that exploit human appetites and distract you from your purpose:

Addiction & Indulgence

1. **The Loop** – Digital Distraction. "Just keep scrolling."

2. **The Alchemist** – Substance Addiction. "One more hit won't hurt."

3. **The Glutton** – Food Addiction "Feed the void."

4. **The Drunkard** – Alcoholism "I need a drink."

5. **The Binger** – Dopamine Dependence. "Next episode. Then I'll stop."

6. **The Escapist** – Fantasy Addiction. "Reality is unbearable. Escape is survival.""

7. **The Puffer** – Smoking/Vaping Addiction. "You need this to feel calm and in control."

The Loop

Core Torment & Lie: Digital Distraction.

"Just keep scrolling."

Gifts under attack:

- **Focus** – The Loop fragments your attention through endless notifications and infinite scroll, making sustained concentration on prayer, study, or deep work feel nearly impossible. *("Be still and know that I am God." – Psalm 46:10)*
- **Time Stewardship** – It steals hours through "just one more" moments, gradually robbing you of the time God entrusted for relationships, rest, and Kingdom assignments. *("Teach us to number our days, that we may gain a heart of wisdom." – Psalm 90:12)*
- **Purpose** – It keeps you reacting to someone else's agenda instead of fulfilling your God-given mission, replacing contribution with consumption. *("Do not conform to the pattern of this world but be transformed by the renewing of your mind." – Romans 12:2)*
- **Mental Clarity** – It overstimulates the brain's dopamine pathways, leaving the mind foggy, anxious, and disconnected from the still, small voice of the Spirit. *("You will keep in perfect peace those whose minds are steadfast, because they trust in you." – Isaiah 26:3)*

The Loop is a demon of distraction, delay, and digital enslavement. It steals your time, minute by minute, scroll by scroll, cycle by cycle. It thrives in repetition: one more episode, one more swipe, one more "quick look." It knows that if it can't get you to sin outright, it can at least keep you passive, entertained, and unproductive. The Loop is subtle and quiet, often justified as "downtime" or "just decompressing," but its fruit is spiritual numbness and lost hours. This demon lulls you into a digital twilight between wakefulness and unconsciousness while your life passes you by.

Scripture references:

"Be very careful how you live—not as unwise but as wise, making the most of every opportunity, because the days are evil." (Ephesians 5:15–16)

"A little sleep, a little slumber... and poverty will come on you like a thief." (Proverbs 6:10–11)

"All things are lawful, but I will not be mastered by anything." (1 Corinthians 6:12)

Common symptoms:

- Compulsive scrolling or binging despite conviction
- Saying "just a few more minutes" but staying for hours
- Avoiding tasks or spiritual assignments through distraction
- Feeling stuck in cycles of guilt and procrastination
- Numbing emotional discomfort with screens or entertainment

Real-life example:

Tyler had no shortage of ideas: God kept giving him powerful, creative concepts for films that would expose darkness and point people to the truth. Somehow, none of them ever made it past the idea stage. Every time he sat down to write, plan, or pray through a project, his hand would automatically reach for his phone. One video turned into five. Five turned into fifty. Whether it was TikTok, YouTube, or a streaming binge, there was always something else to consume. The Loop whispered that he was just researching, or that he needed to rest. But the "rest" never refreshed him; it only stole more time. Tyler was meant to be an impactful filmmaker for the Kingdom, and any one of his stories could have led thousands to salvation. But they never made it out of his mind and onto the screen, because The Loop put up an irresistible obstacle: *just one more video.*

Solutions and declarations:

1. **"I break agreement with every spirit of distraction and mental enslavement."**
   "I will not be mastered by anything." (1 Corinthians 6:12)

2. **"My time is not my own—I will use it for the Kingdom, not to escape it."**
   "Be very careful, then, how you live—not as unwise but as wise, making the most of every opportunity, because the days are evil." (Ephesians 5:15–16)

3. **"I will not be mastered by any cycle. My mind is alert. My spirit is willing."**
   "Watch and pray so that you will not fall into temptation. The spirit is willing, but the flesh is weak." (Matthew 26:41)

Turn to Chapter 9 Prayer Index and go to:
Prayer 1: General Prayer for Lust of the Flesh
Prayer 2: Deliverance from Addiction & Indulgence

Cross references:

- **The Alchemist** – Offers chemical or substance-based escape, while The Loop offers digital and mental sedation. Both steal clarity and momentum.
- **The Escapist** – Fuels dissociation and avoidance through fantasy, often paired with digital media and endless scrolling.
- **The Saboteur** – Derails progress through procrastination and passive resistance masked as "just taking a break."
- **Lazybones** – Encourages paralysis and comfort-seeking, making it easier to surrender to the Loop's numbing rhythm.
- **The Binger** – Mirrors The Loop's compulsive cycle—whether through shows, food, shopping, or doomscrolling—it's addiction by another name.

- **The Doubter** – Often triggered after prolonged digital overstimulation, leading to confusion, spiritual apathy, and weakened discernment.
- **The Shrinker** – Hides in the comfort zone of distraction, keeping you small and unseen.
- **The Coward** – Avoids facing truth, risk, or calling, and lets the Loop fill the silence instead.

The Alchemist
Core Torment & Lie: Substance Addiction.
"One more hit won't hurt."
Gifts Under Attack:

- **Self-Control** – The Alchemist numbs your will, making cravings feel stronger than conviction and training your mind to choose escape over endurance. *("For the Spirit God gave us does not make us timid, but gives us power, love and self-discipline." – 2 Timothy 1:7)*
- **Sobriety** – Substance use clouds spiritual discernment and dulls your ability to obey, making you vulnerable to deception and demonic oppression. *("Be alert and of sober mind. Your enemy the devil prowls around like a roaring lion..." – 1 Peter 5:8)*
- **Clarity of Purpose** – It detours your mission and dulls your focus, turning hours meant for building into wasted, forgotten time. *("Do not get drunk on wine... Instead, be filled with the Spirit." – Ephesians 5:18)*
- **Physical Health** – It deteriorates the body through cycles of indulgence and withdrawal, weakening the vessel meant to carry out God's work. *("Do you not know that your bodies are temples of the Holy Spirit...?" – 1 Corinthians 6:19)*
- **Freedom from Bondage** – It replaces God's leadership with chemical dependence, chaining your spirit to what once promised relief. *("You are slaves to the one you obey... whether you are slaves to sin, which leads to death..." – Romans 6:16)*

The Alchemist promises transformation, relief, escape, or elevation through a substance or chemical experience. Whether it's alcohol, pills, weed, cocaine, or any other mind-altering agent, its lie is always the same: "This is how you'll feel better." It convinces you that you need it to cope, think, sleep, be social, and feel okay. What begins as comfort becomes chains. The Bible plainly says it will ruin your life even though you feel like you can't function without it. It is bondage.

You don't have to go far to find The Alchemist at work because it's everywhere. On one end, we have wine moms, mushroom retreats, and influencer therapists pushing microdosing as the path to enlightenment. On the other, the streets of Philly are filled with people bent in half in the "Fenty fold," zombified from drugs laced with fentanyl and tranquilizers. What's often called "harm reduction" is sometimes just demon management. The modern drug trade—both legal and illegal—is spiritual. The Greek word for "pharmaceuticals" is *pharmakeia*, the same word used in Scripture for sorcery *(Galatians 5:20, Revelation 9:21)*. These substances often mimic naturally produced chemicals in the brain (like dopamine, serotonin, oxytocin) but instead of supporting the body, they rewire it, burn out the receptors, and replace God-designed healing with counterfeits. Yes, some medications are merciful and necessary. But The Alchemist doesn't deal in mercy. It exploits pain that hasn't been surrendered, stress that hasn't been cast on God, and trauma that remains unhealed. And with every new dependency—whether from a street dealer or a white coat—it says: *"Don't feel. Just take this."*

Scripture Reference:

> *Do not be drunk with wine, because that will ruin your life. Instead, be filled with the Holy Spirit. (Ephesians 5:18 NLT)*

> *You say, 87I am allowed to do anything   but not everything is good for you. And even though 87I am allowed to do anything, I must not become a slave to anything. (1 Corinthians 6:12 NLT)*

> *For whatever overcomes a person, to that he is enslaved. (2 Peter 2:19 ESV)*

Common Symptoms:

- Reaching for substances to self-soothe or escape
- Escalating use and dependency over time
- Shame, secrecy, or isolation around use
- Denial of addiction despite visible consequences
- Emotional numbness or avoidance of deeper wounds

Real-Life Example:

Ashley discovered cocaine in college. It helped her party all night and study all day. By the time she graduated, she had a full-blown dependence—and wealthy parents who unknowingly funded her habit. The drug kept her sharp, energetic, and high functioning at her demanding job. She quickly realized she wasn't alone: there was an unspoken club of high achievers doing the same thing. It made her feel connected, even invincible.

One night, everything changed. She got a bad batch, cut with something far more dangerous. Fentanyl, most likely. She was clinically dead for several minutes. When she woke up, she was on the floor of a stranger's bathroom, blood everywhere, a gash in her head, and EMTs hovering above her. The person she had been with was pale and sweating, panicked.

The EMTs told her she was lucky to be alive and warned her that if she didn't throw away whatever she had left, it would likely kill her next time. Entire batches across the country were being laced, they said. Even with blood streaming down her face, having just returned from death, Ashley's thoughts were already drifting back to the high. Where could she get more?

That is The Alchemist in action—offering a twisted version of control, energy, and escape, while quietly stealing her soul and nearly her life.

Solutions & Declarations:

1. **"I will not be ruled by anything—I am free in Christ."**
   "I have the right to do anything," you say—but not everything is beneficial. "I have the right to do anything"—but I will not be mastered by anything." (1 Corinthians 6:12)

2. **"I am filled with the Holy Spirit, not artificial peace."**
   "Do not get drunk on wine, which leads to debauchery. Instead, be filled with the Spirit." (Ephesians 5:18)

3. **"What once overcame me has no hold—I have overcome through Jesus."**
   "They promise them freedom, while they themselves are slaves of depravity—for 'people are slaves to whatever has mastered them.'" (2 Peter 2:19)

Turn to the Index of Deliverance Prayers and go to:
Prayer 1: General Prayer for Lust of the Flesh
Prayer 2: Deliverance from Addiction & Indulgence

Cross-References:

- **The Puffer** – Targets nicotine/vaping specifically. Often a gateway to heavier substances.
- **The Glutton** – Overindulgence used to numb pain (food as a drug).
- **The Abyss** – Depression that often fuels or results from substance dependency.
- **The Loop** – Digital distraction and addiction patterns frequently overlap with chemical escapism.
- **The Broken Mirror** – Self-hatred that drives self-medication and escapism.
- **Lazybones** – Substance abuse can lead to physical, emotional, and spiritual sloth.
- **The Suicide Spirit** – In extreme cases, addiction drives despair and self-harm ideation.
- **The Idolator** – When drugs become false saviors or "coping gods."

- **The Desperate** – Reaches for relief in anything that feels like comfort.
- **The Inverter** – Often glamorizes substance abuse under the guise of empowerment or creativity.

The Glutton

Core Torment & Lie: Food Addiction & Overindulgence
"Feed the void."

Gifts Under Attack:

- **Temperance** – The Glutton weakens your ability to walk in moderation, turning food into an emotional coping mechanism instead of a tool for nourishment. *("Let your moderation be known unto all men. The Lord is at hand." – Philippians 4:5, KJV)*
- **Self-Control** – Cravings begin to dictate behavior, as the body takes command over the spirit rather than submitting to it. *("Those who belong to Christ Jesus have crucified the flesh with its passions and desires." – Galatians 5:24)*
- **Gratitude** – Overindulgence disconnects eating from thankfulness, turning blessings into blind consumption. *("They gave themselves up to sensuality, greedy to practice every kind of impurity... But that is not the way you learned Christ." – Ephesians 4:19–20)*
- **Stewardship of the Body** – The physical vessel becomes neglected, dulled, or overloaded—reducing vitality, energy, and effectiveness for Kingdom work. *("Honor God with your bodies." – 1 Corinthians 6:20)*
- **Clarity of Appetite** – It confuses physical and spiritual hunger, blurring the line between need and want and dulling discernment. *("Man shall not live by bread alone, but by every word that proceeds from the mouth of God." – Matthew 4:4)*

The Glutton drives you to numb. This spirit latches onto emotional pain, stress, boredom, or shame and convinces you that food is comfort, reward, and release. It creates a cycle of overindulgence and regret, often masked as harmless habits or cultural norms. Whether it's bingeing late at night, constant grazing, or needing something sweet to "feel okay," The Glutton thrives on the slow erosion of self-control. Its true goal is deeper than your appetite. It wants to dull your spiritual sensitivity, hijack your discipline, and trap you in a flesh-driven loop of false satisfaction.

Scripture Reference:

> *"Their god is their stomach, and their glory is in their shame. Their mind is set on earthly things." (Philippians 3:19 NIV)*

> *"Do you not know that your body is a temple of the Holy Spirit...? You are not your own; you were bought at a price." (1 Corinthians 6:19–20 NIV)*

> *"Put a knife to your throat if you are given to gluttony." (Proverbs 23:2 NIV)*

Common Symptoms:

- Eating past fullness, especially when emotionally triggered
- Food, snacks, or sugar used to self-soothe
- Constant consumption—TV, scrolling, snacking—without pause
- Discomfort with fasting or delayed gratification
- Shame around body image or eating habits
- "Food noise" – a nonstop mental loop of eating, planning to eat, or thinking about what to eat next—even during meals

Real-Life Example:

When she was a child and ignored by everyone in her family, Alison used food as comfort. She would sneak candy and snacks into her room and bury the wrappers deep in the trash so no one would know. Even without being explicitly told, Alison knew she was doing something that needed to be hidden—maybe because her family was always critiquing people's bodies or because no one around her ever seemed to indulge.

As an adult living on her own, the habit continued. With no one watching, she was free to eat like she wanted. Then she visited family after a long time apart. The moment they saw her, they loudly exclaimed how fat she'd gotten. Alison went home and spiraled into shame... and ate some more.

It was only later she realized she wasn't eating out of hunger anymore. She was eating to soothe herself when she was tired, sad, anxious, or ashamed. The Glutton had reprogrammed her habits. She wasn't craving food. She was craving emotional escape.

The Glutton wants us to reward our pain instead of addressing it. We call it comfort food, self-care, or treating ourselves, but really, it's a replacement for the Holy Spirit's comfort. The Glutton tells us that we need more to feel okay, and that abstaining is cruel or restrictive. Yet the more we indulge, the less satisfaction we feel. In a world of ultra-processed foods, endless entertainment, and instant gratification, Gluttony thrives. Its damage shows up not just in our bodies, but in our dulled senses, weakened wills, and foggy spiritual lives.

Solutions & Declarations:

1. **"My stomach is not my god—I am ruled by the Spirit, not my cravings."**
   "Their destiny is destruction, their god is their stomach, and their glory is in their shame. Their mind is set on earthly things." (Philippians 3:19)

2. **"My body is a temple of the Holy Spirit, and I will honor God with it."**
   "Do you not know that your bodies are temples of the Holy Spirit, who is in you, whom you have received from God? You are not your own; you were bought at a price. Therefore, honor God with your bodies." (1 Corinthians 6:19–20)

3. **"I receive the fruit of self-control and find true satisfaction in the Lord."**
   "But the fruit of the Spirit is love, joy, peace, forbearance, kindness, goodness, faithfulness, gentleness and self-control. Against such things there is no law." (Galatians 5:22–23)

Turn to the Index of Deliverance Prayers and go to:
Prayer 1: General Prayer for Lust of the Flesh
Prayer 2: Deliverance from Addiction & Indulgence

Cross-References:

- **The Alchemist** – Food is one of the first and most socially acceptable forms of self-medication; often a gateway to other numbing substances.
- **Lazybones** – Gluttony and sloth frequently reinforce each other: one seeks excess, the other avoids discipline.
- **The Loop** – Overeating is often accompanied by binge-watching, doomscrolling, or other digital distractions.
- **The Abyss** – Depression drives emotional eating; gluttony temporarily numbs but deepens despair.
- **The Broken Mirror** – Self-hatred and shame often fuel the cycle of overindulgence, which then reinforces negative self-image.
- **The Rejector** – Uses food as comfort to fill the void left by relational rejection or abandonment.
- **The Shrinker** – May binge in private while presenting control in public; hiding pain through consumption.
- **The Withholder** – Can be the flip side in family systems: withholding love or provision while another overfeeds for false comfort.

The Drunkard

Core Torment & Lie: Alcoholism

"I need a drink."

Gifts Under Attack:

- **Sobriety of Mind** – The Drunkard dulls spiritual awareness, lowers resistance, and leaves the soul vulnerable to deception and attack. *("Be sober, be vigilant; because your adversary the devil walks about like a roaring lion, seeking whom he may devour." – 1 Peter 5:8)*
- **Discernment** – Intoxication clouds judgment and numbs sensitivity to the Holy Spirit, making truth harder to recognize and error easier to fall into. *("Do not get drunk on wine, which leads to debauchery. Instead, be filled with the Spirit." – Ephesians 5:18)*
- **Self-Control** – Alcohol erodes restraint, unleashing impulsivity, mood swings, and behavior that grieves the Spirit. *("Like a city whose walls are broken through is a person who lacks self-control." – Proverbs 25:28)*
- **Purpose** – Addiction delays or derails divine calling, turning hours meant for impact into wasted time and forgotten assignments. *("Be very careful, then, how you live—not as unwise but as wise, making the most of every opportunity..." – Ephesians 5:15–16)*
- **Accountability** – The Drunkard destroys trust and responsibility, severing relationships that were meant to foster growth and protection. *("Confess your sins to each other and pray for each other so that you may be healed." – James 5:16)*

The Drunkard is a spirit of bondage that invites destruction under the disguise of relief. It tells you alcohol is just a tool for relaxation, connection, and celebration. Then slowly, it demands more: your peace, your health, your relationships, your dignity. The Bible warns sober mindedness is critical for spiritual alertness, because the enemy is always seeking someone to devour (*1 Peter 5:8*). Alcohol numbs that awareness. The

Drunkard partners with spirits of escapism, regret, shame, and pride. It is deeply generational. It has destroyed families, nations, and destinies.

Drunkenness is a counterfeit comfort that replaces the Holy Spirit's role as our true Comforter. People in a battle with this pernicious demon are fortunate to escape with their lives and bodies intact.

Scripture References:

"Wine is a mocker, strong drink a brawler, and whoever is led astray by it is not wise." (Proverbs 20:1)

"...nor drunkards... will inherit the kingdom of God." (1 Corinthians 6:10)

"Do not get drunk on wine, which leads to debauchery. Instead, be filled with the Spirit." (Ephesians 5:18)

Common Symptoms:

- Using alcohol to self-medicate stress, trauma, or loneliness
- Saying "I can stop anytime" but never doing it
- Blackouts, regrets, or destruction tied to drinking
- Family history of alcohol abuse
- Losing time, memory, or self-respect due to drinking

Real-Life Example:

Donny said he drank just to take the edge off, but the edge never seemed to dull. What began as a few drinks after work turned into every night, then into every morning. After losing his last job, he couldn't seem to find his footing again. Employers sensed something was off beyond the bloodshot eyes and haggard face. The spirit of The Drunkard clung to him like a shadow. Even his skin carried the stench of despair.

Donny stopped pretending after a while. Depression wrapped around him like a wet blanket, and he stayed drunk all day. His wife carried the weight of the household, working two jobs while raising their kids alone. She eventually stopped asking Donny to help with anything. He had become a ghost in his own home.

One afternoon, an old friend spotted him stumbling out of a liquor store and barely recognized him. Alarmed, the friend called Donny's wife, then drove him straight to the hospital. The diagnosis was grim: advanced liver failure. The doctor said there wouldn't be time for a transplant. He handed Donny a pen and paper to begin writing goodbye letters to his children.

Donny looked at his friend in disbelief. "All this... from a few drinks?"

What Donny didn't see was that The Drunkard had been hunting his bloodline for generations and it wasn't leaving without a fight.

Solutions and Declarations:

1. **"I reject false comfort—I turn to the Holy Spirit, my true Helper."**

   "But the Helper, the Holy Spirit, whom the Father will send in my name, He will teach you all things and bring to your remembrance all that I have said to you." (John 14:26)

2. **"I break every generational agreement with alcohol and addiction."**

   "You shall not bow down to them or worship them; for I, the Lord your God, am a jealous God, punishing the children for the sin of the parents to the third and fourth generation of those who hate me, but showing love to a thousand generations of those who love me and keep my commandments." (Exodus 20:5–6)

3. **"I will be sober and alert—my life is not mine to waste."**

   "Be sober-minded; be watchful. Your adversary the devil prowls around like a roaring lion, seeking someone to devour." (1 Peter 5:8)

Turn to the Index of Deliverance Prayers and go to:

Prayer 1: General Prayer for Lust of the Flesh

Prayer 2: Deliverance from Addiction & Indulgence

References:

- **The Escapist** – Alcohol becomes a tool for avoiding pain, pressure, or truth through mental withdrawal
- **The Alchemist** – Partners in substance-based self-medication, offering false relief while deepening bondage
- **The Coward** – Avoids reality, responsibility, and healing by hiding behind intoxication
- **The Loop** – Keeps the drinker stuck in a repeated cycle of indulgence, shame, and relapse
- **The Withholder** – Uses alcohol to disconnect emotionally, leaving loved ones neglected and confused

The Binger

Core Torment & Lie: Dopamine Dependence

"Next episode. Then I'll stop."

Gifts Under Attack:

- **Self-Control** – The Binger overrides discipline with impulse, training the mind to seek the next thrill instead of staying grounded in presence. *("The fruit of the Spirit is... self-control. Against such things there is no law." – Galatians 5:22–23)*
- **Mindfulness** – It robs attention from the present moment, making you numb to the Spirit and unaware of the time and energy being stolen. *("Be very careful, then, how you live—not as unwise but as wise..." – Ephesians 5:15)*
- **Purposeful Living** – It trades Kingdom calling for comfort, turning active mission into passive consumption. *("Do not be slothful in zeal, be fervent in spirit, serve the Lord." – Romans 12:11)*
- **Mental Stamina** – The flood of constant stimulation weakens your ability to focus, reflect, and engage deeply with God, people, or truth. *("Set your minds on things above, not on earthly things." – Colossians 3:2)*

The Binger exploits the human brain's reward system, particularly the dopamine pathways, to create a cycle of compulsive consumption. In the digital era, streaming platforms and social media are engineered to maximize user engagement, often at the expense of mental health. Features like autoplay and infinite scroll are designed to keep users hooked, leading to excessive screen time and neglect of real-life responsibilities.

Tristan Harris, a former Google product manager, has highlighted how technology companies intentionally design apps to exploit psychological vulnerabilities, creating "compulsion loops" that are difficult to break. Similarly, Dr. Anna Lembke, in her book *Dopamine Nation*, discusses how the overconsumption of digital media can lead to a state of dopamine deficiency, resulting in increased anxiety, depression, and a diminished capacity for pleasure.

The devastation is most visible in children.

Today's young minds are being chemically rewired by digital overstimulation before they've even developed. Their brains—still soft clay—are being sculpted by compulsion, not creativity. What once required discipline, imagination, and effort is now replaced with flashing lights, endless scrolls, and instant distraction. Educators across the country report alarming trends: children who can't sit upright at a desk, who struggle to hold a pencil, who fatigue after minutes of using crayons. Fine motor skills are disappearing. So is the ability to focus, read, or engage in critical thinking.

We are watching an entire generation of children become digital slaves before they've even reached maturity.

The short-term "solution" of handing a child a device to keep them quiet in a restaurant, classroom, or church service has compounded into a long-term crisis of mass illiteracy and stunted development. High school seniors are graduating without the ability to read or are only at elementary level. College students are turning to AI to fake comprehension because they can no longer read or write proficiently. Kids are even learning to hide their illiteracy using technology. Entire classrooms are being passed along not because they've learned, but because they've adapted to fake it or else the teachers know and have given up, unable to care more than parents who don't at all and who usually have the audacity to place all responsibility for their children's education on the system.

This is not correct.

The Binger is not a harmless distraction. It is a spirit of mental decay—one that trades long-term fruitfulness for short-term sedation. If we do not cut it off, we will lose whole generations.

Scripture Reference:

"Like a city whose walls are broken through is a person who lacks self-control." (Proverbs 25:28)

"Everything is permissible for me—but not everything is beneficial." (1 Corinthians 6:12)

"Be very careful, then, how you live—not as unwise but as wise." (Ephesians 5:15)

Common Symptoms:

- Spending excessive hours consuming digital content
- Neglecting sleep, work, or relationships due to screen time
- Feeling anxious or irritable when unable to access streaming platforms
- Using digital media as a primary coping mechanism for stress or boredom
- Difficulty concentrating or engaging in offline activities

Real-Life Example:

Paula used to be the most promising employee on her team: sharp, driven, and creative. But over the past year, something shifted. It started small: a few late nights watching her favorite shows, a couple groggy mornings at work. Soon, she was bingeing entire seasons until 3 or 4 a.m., unable to stop despite knowing she had to work the next day. She began arriving late, unshowered, in wrinkled clothes. Her focus was shot. Her conversations revolved entirely around plotlines and characters, and coworkers started avoiding her because they couldn't relate or were simply put off.

She told herself it was just stress relief, that she'd pull it together, but the mental fog never lifted. The fatigue grew heavier. When a major promotion came up—the one she'd worked toward for years—she wasn't even considered.

Paula was trapped. Not in sin that looked dangerous on the outside, but in the slow decay of constant consumption. The Binger had stolen her time, her clarity, her discipline, and ultimately, her future. What looked like "self-care" was actually self-sabotage.

Solutions & Declarations:

1. **"I will not be mastered by anything but will live in the freedom Christ provides."**
   "'I have the right to do anything,' you say—but not everything is beneficial. 'I have the right to do anything'—but I will not be mastered by anything." (1 Corinthians 6:12)

2. **"I choose to steward my time wisely, focusing on what is edifying."**
   "Make the best use of the time, because the days are evil." (Ephesians 5:16)

3. **"I find true rest and satisfaction in God's presence, not in endless entertainment."**
   "Come to me, all who labor and are heavy laden, and I will give you rest." (Matthew 11:28)

Turn to Chapter 9 Prayer Index and go to:
Prayer 1: General Prayer for Lust of the Flesh
Prayer 2: Deliverance from Addiction & Indulgence

Cross-References:

- **The Loop** – Feeds distraction and derails purpose through endless scrolling and passive consumption, reinforcing the same dopamine trap.
- **The Glutton** – Uses overindulgence (in food or stimulation) to numb emotion and quiet spiritual hunger.
- **Lazybones** – Lulls you into inertia by making passive rest feel earned, even when it's avoidance in disguise.
- **The Hypnotist** – Encourages altered states and mental escapism, dulling alertness to spiritual reality.
- **The Alchemist** – Also exploits dopamine through substances or stimulation to mimic peace, energy, or pleasure.
- **The Withholder** – Prevents discipline and follow-through by keeping you stuck in temporary reward cycles.
- **The Splitter** – Disconnects action from intention, causing internal division between what you want and what you do.

The Escapist

Core Torment & Lie: Fantasy Addiction

"Reality is unbearable; escape is survival."

Gifts Under Attack:

- **Presence** – The Escapist detaches the mind from reality, making it difficult to engage with people, prayer, or purpose in the present moment. *("Be still and know that I am God." – Psalm 46:10)*
- **Purpose** – It delays or abandons divine assignments by replacing action with avoidance and surrender with sedation. *("We must work the works of him who sent me while it is day; night is coming, when no one can work." – John 9:4)*
- **Identity** – It encourages the creation of false selves through fantasy or roleplay, disconnecting you from your true identity in Christ. *("Put on the new self, created to be like God in true righteousness and holiness." – Ephesians 4:24)*

- **Emotional Resilience** – It trains you to flee discomfort instead of facing it, weakening your capacity to endure trials and mature spiritually. *("Not only so, but we also glory in our sufferings, because we know that suffering produces perseverance..." – Romans 5:3–4)*

The Escapist thrives in the digital age, where alternate realities are just a click away. This demon entices individuals to retreat from the complexities of real life into the comforting embrace of fantasy worlds, be it through gaming, fan fiction, or immersive virtual experiences. While occasional escapism can be harmless, The Escapist distorts this into a compulsive avoidance of reality, leading to a disconnection from one's own life and responsibilities.

In extreme cases, individuals may go to great lengths to embody their fantasy personas, including undergoing significant body modifications to resemble fictional characters. Their identities become so entwined with these alternate realities that the boundaries between the virtual and the real blur, causing significant distress when forced to confront the real world.

Scripture Reference:

"They exchanged the truth about God for a lie and worshiped and served created things rather than the Creator." (Romans 1:25)

"Do not love the world or anything in the world." (1 John 2:15)

"Set your minds on things above, not on earthly things." (Colossians 3:2)

Common Symptoms:

- Obsessive engagement with fantasy media or gaming
- Neglect of personal, social, or occupational responsibilities
- Emotional distress when separated from fantasy environments
- Identity confusion or preference for fictional personas over real self
- Financial strain due to excessive spending on fantasy-related items or events

Real-Life Example:

Jordan *lived* fantasy. What started as casual fandom evolved into full immersion. He tattooed his arms, chest, and neck to match a character from his favorite fictional universe. His self-worth was tied to his game stats, his online guild rank, and how many likes he got on cosplay posts. Any disruption to his internet triggered panic, frustration, and a deep sense of disconnection and loss. The real world held nothing for him.

He poured every spare dollar into high-end costumes and elaborate wigs, not just for fun, but to maintain an identity he preferred over his own. He allowed nothing to keep him from conventions, where people understood him, where the line between who he was and who he wished he could be finally blurred. He looked down on those who didn't know the lore. He was only attracted to women who dressed as characters from that same universe.

To Jordan, the fictional world felt safe, controlled, beautiful—unlike the world that had hurt and disappointed him. Without realizing it, he elevated creation above the Creator. He was worshiping something made by man instead of turning to the One who made *him.* This is The Escapist in action—building alternate identities to survive pain, while slowly losing the one God intended him to become.

Solutions & Declarations:

1. **"I find my identity and purpose in Christ, not in fictional worlds."**
   "For we are His workmanship, created in Christ Jesus for good works, which God prepared beforehand, that we should walk in them." (Ephesians 2:10)

2. **"I choose to engage with reality, trusting God to equip me for life's challenges."**
   "For God gave us a spirit not of fear but of power and love and self-control." (2 Timothy 1:7)

3. **"I will not conform to the patterns of escapism but be transformed by the renewing of my mind."**

   "Do not be conformed to this world, but be transformed by the renewal of your mind, that by testing you may discern what is the will of God—what is good and acceptable and perfect." (Romans 12:2)

Turn to Chapter 9 Prayer Index and go to:

Prayer 1: General Prayer for Lust of the Flesh

Prayer 2: Deliverance from Addiction & Indulgence

Cross-References:

- **The Binger** – Seeks to numb reality through overstimulation and media consumption.
- **The Pretender** – Hides behind false identities and fantasy personas to avoid confronting truth.
- **The Withholder** – Rejects present blessings and responsibilities in favor of imagined alternatives.
- **The Loop** – Creates mental paralysis and keeps the Escapist in cycles of distraction.
- **The Impatient One** – Urges escape from process and discomfort, refusing to wait on God.

The Puffer

Core Torment & Lie: Smoking/Vaping Addiction

"You need this to feel calm and in control."

Gifts under attack:

- **Self-Control** – The Puffer overrides discipline with physical compulsion, reinforcing a dependency on ritual instead of reliance on the Spirit. *("Like a city whose walls are broken through is a person who lacks self-control." – Proverbs 25:28)*

- **Physical Health** – It damages the lungs, heart, and immune system, weakening the body meant to carry out Kingdom work. *("So, whether you eat or drink or whatever you do, do it all for the glory of God." – 1 Corinthians 10:31)*
- **Clarity of Mind** – Nicotine clouds judgment, heightens anxiety cycles, and dulls spiritual awareness, disrupting discernment. *("Be alert and of sober mind..." – 1 Peter 5:8)*
- **Temple Stewardship** – It mocks the truth that your body is sacred, slowly destroying the vessel entrusted to host the Holy Spirit. *("Do you not know that your bodies are temples of the Holy Spirit... You are not your own." – 1 Corinthians 6:19–20)*

The Puffer is a spirit of slow destruction and self-soothing deception, disguised as relaxation. Unlike The Alchemist, which lures people into heavy substance abuse and oblivion, The Puffer works through normalization, keeping people chemically tethered to a vice that damages the body, hijacks the mind, and drains resources. It reinforces dependence on a temporary fix, often introduced at a young age. This demon partners with shame, rebellion, peer pressure, and escapism. It trains the host to reach for a chemical instead of the Comforter.

Scripture references:

> *"You were bought with a price. Therefore, glorify God in your body." (1 Corinthians 6:20)*

> *"Do not be mastered by anything." (1 Corinthians 6:12)*

> *"Let us cleanse ourselves from everything that defiles body and spirit." (2 Corinthians 7:1)*

Common symptoms:

- Inability to quit or cut back despite conviction
- Deep emotional attachment to smoking or vaping ritual
- Justifying the behavior as "not that bad"
- Shame after doing it, yet returning again and again
- Using to escape discomfort or mask deeper pain

Real-life example:

Jody started vaping at just ten years old, using the devices her parents left lying around the house. No one handed it to her, she just picked it up, curious and unsupervised. It wasn't long before she was sneaking her own, despite being too young to buy them legally. She wasn't alone; half her friends had access too. Now a teenager, Jody can't go a full day without vaping. Her parents say it's "not allowed," but they still leave their vapes in plain sight. Her younger brothers are addicted too. At school, almost everyone has a weed pen, and getting a hit is as easy as asking. Jody knows her lungs are being destroyed. She can feel it. But the Puffer already moved in through the cracks in her home, her school, and her pain. Now it's everywhere she turns.

Solutions and declarations:

1. *"I renounce every agreement with this addiction and its false comfort."*
   "All things are lawful for me, but not all things are helpful. All things are lawful for me, but I will not be dominated by anything." *(1 Corinthians 6:12)*

2. *"I declare my body is not mine but God's—I am His temple."*
   "For you were bought with a price. So, glorify God in your body." *(1 Corinthians 6:20)*

3. *"I will be filled with the Holy Spirit, not chemical dependency."*
   "And do not get drunk with wine, for that is debauchery, but be filled with the Spirit." (Ephesians 5:18)

Turn to Chapter 9 Prayer Index and go to:
Prayer 1: General Prayer for Lust of the Flesh
Prayer 2: Deliverance from Addiction & Indulgence

Cross references:

- **The Alchemist** – Partners in substance dependency, offering counterfeit relief through chemical or sensory alteration.

- **The Escapist** – Drives avoidance through habit, encouraging emotional suppression over healing.
- **The Glutton** – Uses the body for comfort, reinforcing compulsive indulgence to manage inner pain.
- **The Loop** – Amplifies compulsive, ritualistic behaviors, often creating a cycle of distraction and craving.
- **The Saboteur** – Promotes self-soothing through destructive habits, especially when growth or breakthrough is near.

Sex is sacred. Which is why Satan goes out of his way to distort it. These demons operate where pleasure, power, and identity intersect, twisting what God designed for covenant and intimacy into a tool of addiction, abuse, and confusion.

Many of the spirits in this chapter enter early through exposure, trauma, or generational strongholds. Others disguise themselves as "freedom," "expression," or "orientation," but behind the costume is deep bondage. These demons rewire how we relate to ourselves, others, and even God.

Sexual sin is not "worse" than other sins in God's eyes, but it is unique in its effect. The Bible says it's a sin against the body *(1 Corinthians 6:18)* and results in specific bodily consequences *(Romans 1:27)*.

Sexual sin reshapes how you see yourself. It opens doors to shame, secrecy, and compulsion. And often, it brings psychological pain and physical damages that linger long after the act is over.

In this chapter, you'll meet the demons that pervert God's design, wound identity, and hijack sexuality:

Perversion & Sexual Sin

8. **The Insatiable** – Lust. "You need more."

9. **The Profane** – Pornography. "Just look."

10. **The Reverser** – Gender Confusion & Homosexuality. "You were born wrong."

11. **The Corrupter** – Early Exposure & Molestation. "Steal their innocence."

12. **The Rapist** – Violation & Sexual Aggression. "Take what you want."

13. **The Inverter** – Moral Confusion. "Evil is good, good is evil."

14. **The Harlot** – Female Whoredom. "Your body is your only power."

15. **The Player** - Male Whoredom. "Lust is just part of being a man."

16. **The Cheater** – Infidelity & Adultery. "No one will ever fully satisfy me."

17. **The Splitter** – Objectification. "People are parts to be used, not whole beings to be loved."

The Insatiable

Core Torment & Lie: Lust

"You need more."

Gifts under attack:

- **Desire** – The Insatiable twists healthy longing into restless obsession, creating an unquenchable appetite that leads to sin. *("Each person is tempted when they are dragged away by their own evil desire and enticed. Then, after desire has conceived, it gives birth to sin..." – James 1:14–15)*

- **Intimacy** – It substitutes genuine love with lust-driven consumption, isolating the soul from true emotional and spiritual connection. *("For the lips of the adulterous woman drip honey... but in the end she is bitter as gall." – Proverbs 5:3–4)*

- **Focus** – Lust hijacks mental energy, making it difficult to concentrate, pursue purpose, or walk in spiritual discipline. *("Flee the evil desires of youth and pursue righteousness, faith, love and peace..." – 2 Timothy 2:22)*

- **Faithfulness** – It erodes loyalty by nurturing dissatisfaction and selfish craving, often justifying betrayal in thought or deed. *("But I tell you that anyone who looks at a woman lustfully has already committed adultery with her in his heart." – Matthew 5:28)*
- **Purity** – The Insatiable dulls conviction and normalizes impurity, making holiness feel irrelevant or unattainable. *("It is God's will that you should be sanctified: that you should avoid sexual immorality..." – 1 Thessalonians 4:3–5)*

Lust is a distortion of a God-given desire for connection and intimacy. The Insatiable twists this into addiction where satisfaction is never reached, only chased. What begins as curiosity or indulgence quickly becomes compulsion. The Bible says plainly, *"The eye is not satisfied with seeing, nor the ear filled with hearing" (Ecclesiastes 1:8)* and *"The leech has two daughters. 'Give! Give!' they cry." (Proverbs 30:15)*. Lust is never satisfied. That's because it's not meant to be. It's a black hole, a spiritual parasite. The more it's fed, the more it takes. This demon must be cut off, not managed. It will not leave room for peace, love, or purpose—only hunger, guilt, and disconnection.

Scripture references:

"Lust is never satisfied, nor is the eye content." (Proverbs 27:20)

"Flee from sexual immorality... whoever sins sexually, sins against their own body." (1 Corinthians 6:18)

"You were bought with a price. Therefore, honor God with your bodies." (1 Corinthians 6:20)

Common symptoms:

- Compulsive thoughts about sex or physical contact
- Escalating behavior (porn use, sexting, casual encounters)
- Constant fantasizing or daydreaming about others
- Feeling unsatisfied after sexual experiences
- Justifying inappropriate relationships or flings

Real-life example:

Ian always believed he just had a "high sex drive." Over time, that turned into a daily, desperate compulsion. He subscribed to multiple OnlyFans accounts, spent hours scrolling through explicit content, and couldn't go a full workday without slipping into the bathroom to relieve himself. Eventually, he damaged the skin on his own body from the frequency and still couldn't stop.

What started as porn turned into chat rooms, then escort sites. Though he identified as straight, he began offering himself on both gay and straight hookup platforms, chasing a thrill that always left him emptier. He stopped paying bills on time because his money was going to cam girls and sex workers. Every woman he saw became a target of intrusive, degrading thoughts. He couldn't see them as people anymore, just opportunities.

People around him felt it. Women avoided him without knowing why. Men looked at him with a knowing smirk. His presence felt heavy, off. Ian had become so consumed by lust that it rewired his instincts, isolated him spiritually, and crushed his sense of self. Lust became his master, and it was devouring him.

Solutions & Declarations:

1. **"I tear down every high place and cast out every spirit of lust. I no longer give my body or mind to impurity."**
   "Let not sin therefore reign in your mortal body, to make you obey its passions." (Romans 6:12)

2. **"I am not a slave to sin—I belong to Christ. I walk in the Spirit and do not fulfill the desires of the flesh."**
   "But I say, walk by the Spirit, and you will not gratify the desires of the flesh." (Galatians 5:16)

3. **"My body is a temple. I will honor God with it and refuse to be ruled by anything."**
   "Or do you not know that your body is a temple of the Holy Spirit within you, whom you have from God? You are not your own, for

you were bought with a price. So, glorify God in your body." (1 Corinthians 6:19–20)

Turn to Chapter 9 Prayer Index and go to:
Prayer 1: General Prayer for Lust of the Flesh
Prayer 3: Deliverance from Perversion & Sexual Sin
Supplemental Prayers: 19, 21, 23,

Cross references:

- **The Profane** – Lust is often sustained through the consumption of pornographic material that normalizes sin and rewires desire.
- **The Corruptor** – Many battles with lust begin in childhood through early exposure or abuse that plants distorted appetites.
- **The Binger** – Lust triggers the same dopamine-driven cycle of highs and crashes, leading to compulsive behavior.
- **The Waffler** – Obsessive thought patterns can fuel internal shame, confusion, and indecision around relationships and self-worth.
- **The Pretender** – Lust often hides behind charm, religiosity, or performance, keeping sin cloaked in secrecy.

The Profane
Core Torment & Lie: Pornography
"Just look."
Gifts under attack:

- **Purity** – The Profane defiles what God designed as sacred, desensitizing the heart and severing the conscience from conviction. *("But I tell you that anyone who looks at a woman lustfully has already committed adultery with her in his heart." – Matthew 5:28)*
- **Imagination** – It hijacks the creative mind, redirecting vision and wonder toward lust and idolatry instead of worship. *("Although they knew God, they neither glorified him as God nor gave thanks to*

him, but their thinking became futile, and their foolish hearts were darkened." – Romans 1:21–24)

- **Intimacy** – Porn builds a counterfeit framework for connection, making true relational vulnerability feel unnecessary or unsatisfying. *("But among you there must not be even a hint of sexual immorality... because these are improper for God's holy people." – Ephesians 5:3)*
- **Discernment** – It dulls spiritual sensitivity, making evil appear harmless, desirable, or normal. *("But solid food is for the mature, who by constant use have trained themselves to distinguish good from evil." – Hebrews 5:14)*
- **Innocence** – The Profane corrupts early, robbing both children and adults of the purity and trust God intended them to carry. *("To the pure, all things are pure, but to those who are corrupted and do not believe, nothing is pure." – Titus 1:15)*

There is a reason the first act of God after the fall was covering. Once sin entered, something shifted in the human body. Not biologically, but spiritually. What had been naked and unashamed *(Genesis 2:25)* now carried the weight of exposure, distortion, and spiritual danger.

The power of the female form is so profound that across history – from ancient pagan cultures to modern theocracies like those governed by Sharia law – coverings are strictly imposed to contain or control it. Not because women are shameful, but because the body carries powerful sacred energy that was never meant to be publicly consumed. It was created to be revealed in covenant.

But our culture has lost that understanding. Today, the female body is used to sell everything from cars to hamburgers. Women are praised for showing every curve, crevice, and pore in the name of empowerment. We have degraded the sacred.

Pornography is the industrialization of lust. It packages what God designed for oneness into something detached, perverse, and infinitely consumable. U.S. Supreme Court Justice Potter Stewart once said, "I know it when I see it." That's exactly how it works: by sight.

Porn corrupts through the eyes, shocking the system with what should only be experienced in private between two people in holy covenant. But the shock doesn't last. It requires escalation: more perversion, more dominance, more degradation. The brain rewires. The soul desensitizes. And eventually, even innocence becomes unbearable to the corrupted eye.

It doesn't matter how common it's become. The runway, the magazine cover, the social media thirst trap, or the barely-there bikini—it's all part of the same war against sacredness. When God covered the body, He was protecting something holy. When we uncover it for the world to consume, we are welcoming the spirit of The Profane.

Today's average age of first exposure to porn is between 8 and 11 years old. For many boys and girls, it happens on a smartphone, unsupervised and unfiltered. Once exposed, they return again and again, confused but captivated. This early contact with high-stimulation imagery is frying their developing brains, hijacking their ability to experience normal intimacy, and in some horrifying cases, even leading to classroom sexual assaults. Teachers report young students mimicking scenes they don't understand because this is the only model of "sex" they've seen. They've never been shown God's design for love, connection, or marriage, only violence, dominance, and detachment on a screen.

The world is paying for it. America is the number one exporter of pornographic content, flooding the globe with spiritual sewage. This is the single most corrupting influence on the planet, and we will answer for it. As Scripture says, "It would be better for a millstone to be hung around their neck and drowned in the depths of the sea..." *(Matthew 18:6)*. We are poisoning the innocence of generations.

Today, the exploitation of youth is no longer hidden in the shadows, it's being normalized and celebrated in plain sight. Across popular platforms, we see increasing examples of adults and even parents enabling or profiting from the public exposure of children's private lives, sometimes in deeply inappropriate ways. What once would have been called exploitation is now framed as empowerment, content creation, or brand-building. Behind the screens are vulnerable young people who are not developmentally equipped to understand the long-term conse-quences of being sexualized or marketed online. Even more troubling, younger children watching this content begin to see it as aspirational, learning that attention and validation come from performance rather than character. Instead of being protected, these generations are being discipled by the spirit of The Profane, mocking innocence and celebrat-ing deep dysfunction.

Scripture references:

> *"I will set no wicked thing before my eyes." (Psalm 101:3)*

> *"The lamp of the body is the eye. If your eye is unhealthy, your whole body will be full of darkness." (Matthew 6:22–23)*

> *"Put to death therefore what is earthly in you: sexual immorality, impurity, passion, evil desire..." (Colossians 3:5)*

Common symptoms:

- Difficulty forming real-life emotional or physical intimacy
- Compulsive need to view adult content, especially alone
- Escalating desire for extreme or taboo content
- Loss of sexual desire for real partners
- Guilt, shame, or spiritual numbness after viewing

Real-life example:

Lily was only a child when she stumbled upon a stack of adult magazines hidden in her father's closet. She didn't fully understand what she was looking at, but something about it captivated her.

After school, she would sneak into the closet and quietly flip through the pages, drawn in by curiosity and the thrill of secrecy. As she got older and gained access to the internet, the still images gave way to videos. Her imagination became shaped by what she saw, and a part of her began longing for a sense of power, attention, and validation through the lens of what those scenes portrayed.

In middle school, a classmate named Eric noticed Lily didn't flinch when he showed her something dirty on his phone. Eric knew he found a partner. They convinced their parents to let them "do homework "together and before long they were experimenting.

Now, as adults, both Lily and Eric struggle deeply with intimacy. What began as curiosity and secret exposure at a young age shaped how they see themselves and others. They find it difficult to experience real connection—emotionally or physically—without their minds drifting back to what they consumed for years.

Attempts at healthy relationships have been sabotaged by unrealistic expectations, emotional detachment, or guilt they don't know how to name. It's not just that they were exposed too early—it's that something sacred was corrupted before they ever had a chance to understand its purpose.

The Profane polluted their memories and altered their patterns. It made them believe that affection had to look a certain way to be meaningful. Now they're both trying to rebuild what was broken, though they will never replace their stolen innocence.

Solutions & Declarations:

1. **"I renounce every covenant I made with pornography. My eyes, mind, and body belong to the Lord."**
   "I will not set before my eyes anything that is worthless. I hate the work of those who fall away; it shall not cling to me." (Psalm 101:3)

2. **"I break the power of addiction and perversion. I am not ruled by images or urges—I am ruled by the Spirit."**
   "So then, brothers, we are debtors, not to the flesh, to live according to the flesh. For if you live according to the flesh you will die, but if by the Spirit you put to death the deeds of the body, you will live." (Romans 8:12–13)

3. **"I call back my imagination from every dark place. I choose purity, honor, and truth."**

   "Finally, brothers, whatever is true, whatever is honorable, whatever is just, whatever is pure, whatever is lovely, whatever is commendable, if there is any excellence, if there is anything worthy of praise, think about these things." (Philippians 4:8)

Turn to Chapter 9 Prayer Index and go to:

Prayer 1: General Prayer for Lust of the Flesh
Prayer 3: Deliverance from Perversion & Sexual Sin
Supplemental Prayers: 19, 21, 23, 29, 32

Cross references:

- **The Insatiable** – Porn fuels and feeds compulsive sexual desire, escalating the need for more stimulation.
- **The Corruptor** – Many are exposed to porn before they even understand what they're seeing, setting early strongholds.
- **The Pretender** – Most consumption happens in secret, masked by shame, secrecy, and double lives.
- **The Escapist** – Porn becomes a vehicle for fantasy addiction and false intimacy, often replacing real connection.
- **The Abyss** – Overconsumption isolates the viewer, leading to spiritual deadness, depression, and despair.

The Reverser

Core Torment & Lie: Gender Confusion, Sexual Identity Distortion & Homosexuality

"You were born wrong."

Gifts under attack:

- **Identity** – The Reverser targets the very foundation of personhood, sowing confusion, rejection, and rebellion against the image of God. *("So, God created mankind in his own image... male and female he created them." – Genesis 1:27)*

- **Purpose** – When identity is distorted, the path God uniquely designed becomes unclear or unreachable. *("For I know the plans I have for you... plans to give you hope and a future." – Jeremiah 29:11)*
- **Wholeness** – It fractures the soul into conflict, causing deep internal torment and confusion that only truth and healing can restore. *("He heals the brokenhearted and binds up their wounds." – Psalm 147:3)*
- **Generational Legacy** – The Reverser distorts God's design for family, cutting off natural lineage, inheritance, and spiritual covering. *("Be fruitful and multiply, and fill the earth..." – Genesis 1:28)*
- **Fruitfulness** – Beyond biological reproduction, this spirit stifles spiritual fruit, relational flourishing, and emotional restoration. *("If you remain in me and I in you, you will bear much fruit." – John 15:5)*

The Reverser is the spirit of the age, an ancient deception resurfacing in a modern cloak. It aims to twist God's order, targeting children and teens with one of the most sinister lies ever told: "You were born in the wrong body." This confusion is not new. Scripture tells us that the final world ruler—the Antichrist— "will show no regard for the desire of women" *(Daniel 11:37)*, an indication that homosexuality and gender confusion are not just personal struggles, but prophetic signs. The world is being prepared for it.

This is not about condemning people. Homosexuality is a sin like any other, but Scripture clearly reveals that sexual sins carry unique consequences: *"...he who sins sexually sins against his own body" (1 Corinthians 6:18).* Those who abandon God's design *"receive in themselves the due penalty for their error" (Romans 1:27),* a prophetic description echoed in the rise of devastating consequences like HIV and AIDS (which when it first emerged was labeled "gay cancer"), STDs, and specific physical damage that results from the misuse of the body in ways it was never designed to endure. If every person were to follow this path, humanity would cease to exist. A good test of how seriously God views a sin is to observe its ultimate end—and here, the end is extinction.

There has always been effeminacy. There have always been children who "seem different." What we're seeing now is not simply a social shift, it's a spiritual acceleration. In the name of "liberation," parents are turning their children over to a spirit of confusion, cheering on drag performances, prescribing hormone blockers, and signing off on irreversible surgeries while the child is still too young to vote, drive, or consent to anything else in life.

This isn't progressive. It's demonic.

Some cases resemble spiritual Munchausen by proxy, where parents crave the spotlight for having a "special" or "brave" child. In other families, it's generational bondage, where children feel these things early not because they were made wrong, but because the enemy was already watching the bloodline, looking for an opening.

The deception is ancient because it mirrors the nature of the enemy himself: twisting, inverting, and mocking everything God created.

Now the fruit is showing. More and more young people are speaking up after the surgeries and hormone therapy, full of regret for buying into a belief system that sold them the lie that gender could be changed. It can't.

Some have lost function and fertility permanently. Some will live the rest of their lives on hormones and anti-rejection medications, undergoing organ maintenance for surgical wounds that never fully heal. They were children when the damage was done. Clinicians report children asking for their amputated organs back, as if that were possible. It is criminal and heartbreaking what we have allowed to happen.

There is a difference between feeling something and acting on it. Just like any temptation, it can be resisted. Self-control is not hatred or punishment—it is holiness.

Scripture references:

"Male and female He created them." (Genesis 1:27)

"...nor men who have sex with men... will inherit the kingdom of God." (1 Corinthians 6:9–10)

"...he shall not regard the desire of women." (Daniel 11:37)

Common symptoms:

- Persistent belief that one's biological sex is incorrect
- Desire to take on traits of the opposite gender
- Confusion about gender roles and purpose
- Obsession with pronouns, identities, or labels
- Influence or immersion in online communities that affirm gender rejection

Real-life example:

Noah is a young man who de-transitioned after years of living under a lie. As a teenager, he was placed on estrogen for four years and underwent facial feminization surgery. Today, he lives with the consequences: gynecomastia, reduced sexual function, and wide hips and thighs. His fertility may be lost forever. He calls it the worst regret of his life, both physically and emotionally.

When he asked his close-knit family to start using new pronouns, they couldn't agree with the decision. Their refusal to affirm what they knew wasn't true felt like rejection, and the pain of that broken connection ran deep. Noah now says he bought into the lie that gender could be changed and that he had been born in the wrong body.

He didn't know it at the time, but he was under the influence of The Reverser, a spirit that twists identity, inverts truth, and convinces people to reject the very design God gave them. What he thought would bring freedom only brought deeper bondage. Now on the long road of healing, Noah is beginning to reclaim the truth. His story is a powerful warning: when The Reverser is at work, the consequences are not just spiritual, they are permanent and personal.

Solutions & Declarations:

1. **"I reject every lie spoken over my body, mind, and identity. I was not born wrong. God does not make mistakes."**
   "For You formed my inward parts; You knitted me together in my mother's womb. I praise You, for I am fearfully and wonderfully made." (Psalm 139:13–14)

2. **"I break every generational curse that has opened the door to this confusion. I choose truth over acceptance."**
   "And you will know the truth, and the truth will set you free." (John 8:32)

3. **"I declare that I am who God made me to be—male or female by His design, for His purpose."**
   "So God created man in His own image, in the image of God He created him; male and female He created them." (Genesis 1:27)

Also refer to the Solutions Section for:
Prayer 1: General Prayer for Lust of the Flesh
Prayer 3: Deliverance from Perversion & Sexual Sin
Supplemental Prayers: 19, 21, 23, 26, 29, 32, 33, 34

Cross references:

- **Jezebel** – A high-level spirit that undermines godly order, blurs gender roles, emasculates men, and manipulates identity for control. Often partners with The Reverser to dismantle generational structure and corrupt divine design.
- **The Splitter** – Breaks apart identity at its core, often partnering with The Reverser to fracture a person's sense of self and create internal division.
- **The Orphan Spirit** – Feeds the longing to belong and be accepted, making individuals more vulnerable to false identities and communities that offer counterfeit love.
- **The Idolator** – Exalts self-expression and identity over God's design, placing personal feelings and desires above divine truth.

- **The Arcane One** – Opens the door to alternate spiritual systems and ideologies that celebrate inversion and rebellion against natural order.
- **The Manifester** – Promotes self-deification and the rewriting of reality, encouraging people to "speak a new truth" into existence, even if it contradicts God's creation.
- **The Rejector** – Fuels the emotional pain and alienation that The Reverser exploits to sell the lie: *"You were born wrong."*
- **The Harlot** – Often works in tandem to distort sexuality, severing sex from covenant, fruitfulness, and divine intention.

The Corruptor

Core Torment & Lie: Early Exposure & Molestation

"Steal their innocence."

Gifts under attack:

- **Innocence** – The Corruptor violently strips away what God meant to guard in childhood, introducing trauma where purity should have flourished. *("If anyone causes one of these little ones—those who believe in me—to stumble, it would be better... to have a large millstone hung around their neck..." – Matthew 18:6)*
- **Identity** – Abuse implants deep lies about worth and value, causing the child to internalize shame and distorted self-perception. *("I praise you because I am fearfully and wonderfully made..." – Psalm 139:14)*
- **Trust** – It ruptures foundational safety, making it difficult to rely on others or believe that God is good and protective. *("Trust in the Lord with all your heart and lean not on your own understanding." – Proverbs 3:5)*
- **Purity** – It opens premature doors to sexual knowledge and shame, leaving deep spiritual confusion and vulnerability. *("It is God's will that you should be sanctified: that you should avoid sexual immorality..." – 1 Thessalonians 4:3)*

- **Generational Blessing** – The Corruptor seeks to plant or perpetuate cycles of dysfunction and bondage, warring against family healing and legacy. *("...visiting the iniquity of the fathers on the children... but showing love to a thousand generations of those who love me..." – Exodus 20:5–6)*

The Corruptor is a bloodline spirit, a generational predator that seeks to defile innocence and rewrite identity before a child even understands what's happening. It partners with The Insatiable and The Profane, dragging victims into deeper perversion and confusion. This demon wounds the body, fractures the soul, and opens doors to lifelong struggles with shame, addiction, and self-hatred.

This spirit operates both in the shadows and in plain sight. It thrives in families, institutions, and systems that protect abusers and silence victims. It partners with Mammon, as child exploitation is a multibillion-dollar industry. It also aligns with the satanic, using children as ritual currency. From ancient times to today, innocence has been the enemy's desired sacrifice, whether in households or at the highest levels of power.

KNOW THIS: God sees every act of abuse. He hears every cry. As Revelation 6:10 declares: *"They cried out with a loud voice, 'O Sovereign Lord, holy and true, how long before you will judge and avenge our blood on those who dwell on the earth?'"* NO ONE escapes God's judgment.

Scripture references:

"It would be better for them to have a large millstone hung around their neck and to be drowned in the depths of the sea..." (Matthew 18:6)

"The Lord is close to the brokenhearted and saves those who are crushed in spirit." (Psalm 34:18)

"How long, O Lord, holy and true, until You judge and avenge our blood..." (Revelation 6:10)

Common symptoms:

- Early exposure to sexual content or experiences

- Lifelong struggles with shame, confusion, or identity
- Difficulty forming healthy relationships
- Recurring nightmares or flashbacks
- Feeling "dirty" or "broken" beyond repair

Real-life example:

Tanya was only six when she was molested by her uncle. Scared and confused, she eventually told her mother, hoping for safety. Instead of comfort, she was met with anger. Her mother refused to believe her, accusing Tanya of making it up and warned her not to "destroy the family." What Tanya didn't understand at the time was that her mother was also a victim, abused by the same man years earlier and had received the same reaction from *her* mother. Instead of confronting the pain, she buried it, and now she was doing the same to her daughter.

This generational silence created an atmosphere where darkness thrived. Tanya was left feeling exposed, unprotected, and unsure if she could trust her own voice. The Corruptor didn't just harm her, it trained her to believe that no one would protect her, that she wasn't worthy of protection. This demon is truly from the pits of hell, and even the unconverted know this and hate it. Out of all the crimes people commit, it's revealing that inmates controlled by this spirit don't stand a chance in prison.

Solutions & Declarations:

1. **"I renounce the lie that I am defined by what was done to me. I am a new creation in Christ."**

   "Therefore, if anyone is in Christ, he is a new creation. The old has passed away; behold, the new has come." (2 Corinthians 5:17)

2. **"I break every generational curse of abuse and perversion. The cycle ends with me."**

   "You shall not bow down to them nor serve them. For I, the Lord your God, am a jealous God, visiting the iniquity of the fathers on the children to the third and fourth generation... but showing

steadfast love to thousands of those who love Me and keep My commandments." (Exodus 20:5–6)

3. **"I declare that God is my healer and avenger. He restores what was stolen."**
   "I will restore to you the years that the swarming locust has eaten." (Joel 2:25)

Turn to Chapter 9 Prayer Index and go to:
Prayer 1: General Prayer for Lust of the Flesh
Prayer 3: Deliverance from Perversion & Sexual Sin
Supplemental Prayers: 19, 21, 23, 32, 34

Cross references:

- **The Insatiable** – Feeds the escalating cravings planted by The Corrupter, leading victims into deeper sexual bondage and compulsive behaviors.
- **The Profane** – Normalizes filth and perversion, eroding the sacred and making what is vile seem acceptable or even desirable.
- **Mammon** – Fuels exploitation through industries like pornography and trafficking, where children and innocence are traded for profit.
- **Jezebel** – A high-ranking spirit that seduces, controls, and corrupts through sexual manipulation, often laying groundwork for generational defilement.
- **The Reverser** – Twists identity and sexual confusion, especially in those whose innocence was violated, creating disorientation around gender and self-worth.
- **The Broken Mirror** – Reinforces the belief that the victim is permanently defiled, creating internal self-loathing and spiritual paralysis.
- **The Arcane One** – Opens the door to darker rituals and spiritual practices where molestation and child sacrifice are not new, but ancient.

- **The Abyss** – Draws in the emotional and spiritual fallout of corruption, such as depression, suicidal thoughts, and deep soul fragmentation.

The Rapist
Core Torment & Lie: Violation & Sexual Aggression
"I take what I want."
Gifts under attack:

- **Autonomy** – The Rapist violates the God-given right to agency and consent, treating the body not as a sacred trust but as a possession to conquer. *("You are not your own; you were bought at a price. Therefore, honor God with your bodies." – 1 Corinthians 6:19–20)*
- **Bodily Safety** – It desecrates the physical temple of the Holy Spirit, shattering the sense of protection and bodily sanctity. *("He will cover you with his feathers, and under his wings you will find refuge..." – Psalm 91:4)*
- **Self-Worth** – Survivors often internalize deep shame and worthlessness, believing they are broken, used, or unclean. *("Instead of your shame you will receive a double portion... and everlasting joy will be yours." – Isaiah 61:7)*
- **Sexuality as God Designed It** – This spirit corrupts God's vision for sacred intimacy, replacing love, covenant, and mutual honor with trauma and domination. *("Marriage should be honored by all, and the marriage bed kept pure..." – Hebrews 13:4)*
- **The Image of God in Others** – It dehumanizes both victim and perpetrator, reducing people to objects and directly attacking the divine image stamped on every soul. *("So, God created mankind in his own image... male and female he created them." – Genesis 1:27)*

The Rapist is a spirit of domination, dehumanization, and demonic violation. It is a grotesque distortion of power and lust, often passed down generationally through cycles of abuse and silence. It partners with The

Insatiable, The Profane, The Monarch, and The Dominator, operating wherever people are treated as property or prey. It is rooted in pride, cruelty, and the satanic thirst to corrupt what is sacred.

Sex was designed by God to be a covenant act between two unified souls. This spirit violently shatters that design, turning intimacy into warfare. In spiritual terms, rape is ritual defilement, a desecration of a person made in the image of God. This is why the enemy uses it as a weapon in both warzones and households.

Whether the act is carried out by force, coercion, or manipulation, the spirit behind it claims: "You are mine to violate."

No one is beyond the justice of God, and no one is too broken for the healing of Jesus.

Scripture references:

"Woe to him who builds his house by unjust gain, setting his nest on high... You have plotted the ruin of many peoples, shaming your own house and forfeiting your life." (Habakkuk 2:9-10)

"For nothing is hidden that will not be made manifest, nor is anything secret that will not be known and come to light." (Luke 8:17)

"You have done these things, and I kept silent; you thought I was just like you. But I will rebuke you and accuse you to your face." (Psalm 50:21)

Common symptoms:

- Perpetrators: Addiction to power, fantasy of domination, callousness to consent
- Victims: Deep shame, mistrust, self-harm, suicidal thoughts, PTSD
- Families: Silence, generational patterns, protecting abusers at the expense of victims

Real-life example:

At an out-of-town work conference, Gabby was sexually assaulted by a coworker. The man was married, respected, and held a senior position in the company. She reported what happened, but instead of support, she was met with suspicion. Eyewitnesses told HR they had seen her earlier that evening laughing with him at the bar, drinking, and acting "overly familiar." Someone even mentioned seeing her walk into his hotel room voluntarily. That was enough for the company to dismiss her.

HR told her it would be in her best interest to let the matter go. "He's a family man," they said. "He has kids." They warned her that pursuing a formal complaint could make her look bitter or unstable—and hurt her chances of advancement. And besides, they added, *"You didn't go to the hospital for a rape kit, so how serious could you really be?"*

That betrayal cut deeper than the assault. The people who were supposed to protect her—the ones trained to handle this—sided with Gabby's abuser to protect their own power structure. It shattered something in her spirit. She stopped trusting. She stopped caring. For years, she lived out of character, acting like her body was a weapon or a tool—anything but sacred. She slept with men to feel in control, but none of it made her whole. The label "maneater" stuck, but no one saw the truth: she wasn't empowered, she was bleeding.

It wasn't until she heard that *God had seen it all*—that He wept for her, would avenge her pain, and never once blamed her—that healing began. Forgiveness came slowly, and not because what happened was ever okay. But she realized forgiveness wasn't about setting him free. It was about setting *herself* free.

Solutions & Declarations:

1. **"I declare what was done to me was evil, and God saw every moment."**
   "The eyes of the Lord are in every place, keeping watch on the evil and the good." (Proverbs 15:3)

2. **"I reject the lie that I am dirty or damaged. I am fearfully and wonderfully made."**
   "I praise You, for I am fearfully and wonderfully made. Wonderful are Your works; my soul knows it very well." (Psalm 139:14)

3. **"I release vengeance to God. Justice is His, and He will repay."**
"Beloved, never avenge yourselves, but leave it to the wrath of God, for it is written, 'Vengeance is Mine, I will repay, says the Lord.'"
(Romans 12:19)

Turn to Chapter 9 Prayer Index and go to:
Prayer 1: General Prayer for Lust of the Flesh
Prayer 3: Deliverance from Perversion & Sexual Sin
Supplemental Prayers: 19, 23, 32

Cross references:

- **The Insatiable** – Fuels lust without limits, pushing individuals to pursue dominance and gratification at any cost.
- **The Profane** – Strips away all reverence and restraint, normalizing sexual violence and making what is sacred seem disposable.
- **The Monarch** – Seeks total control, often asserting power through sexual conquest, dominance, and humiliation.
- **The Dominator** – Drives abusive control over others, frequently expressed through force, coercion, and dehumanization.
- **The Corrupter** – May first open the door to perversion through early exposure, grooming, or trauma that distorts boundaries and empathy.
- **The Harlot** – Dismantles sexual purity and seduces toward deviance, often laying groundwork for manipulation and exploitation.
- **The Broken Mirror** – Infects the victim with crushing self-hatred and unworthiness, making healing feel unreachable.
- **The Abyss** – Feeds on the aftermath of violation—emotional devastation, despair, and deep internal collapse.

The Inverter

Core Torment & Lie: Moral Confusion

"Good is evil, and evil is good."

Gifts Under Attack:

- **Discernment** – The Inverter twists spiritual perception, causing evil to look noble and holiness to seem offensive or outdated. *("Woe to those who call evil good and good evil... who put darkness for light and light for darkness..." – Isaiah 5:20)*
- **Integrity** – It erodes moral consistency by promoting compromise in the name of tolerance, success, or belonging. *("Whoever walks in integrity walks securely, but whoever takes crooked paths will be found out." – Proverbs 10:9)*
- **Courage** – It intimidates believers into silence, making truth-telling feel dangerous and conviction seem intolerant. *("For God has not given us a spirit of fear, but of power and of love and of a sound mind." – 2 Timothy 1:7)*
- **Clarity of Truth** – It replaces absolutes with relativism, leaving the soul unanchored and the conscience confused. *("Sanctify them by the truth; your word is truth." – John 17:17)*

The Inverter flips truth. This spirit thrives in a world that calls sin "self-expression" and righteousness "hate." It says that holiness is outdated, boundaries are oppressive, and only those who stand for God's truth deserve judgment—everyone else gets a pass.

In today's culture, truth has become subjective: people talk about *"my truth"* as if truth bends to individual perspective. When everyone has their own truth, there is no truth at all. That's why God gave us one unchanging standard: His Word. Anything that doesn't align with that ruler is off, no matter how loudly it's celebrated.

The Inverter is one of the final forms of delusion in a culture on the brink of collapse *(Isaiah 5:20)*. It works hand in hand with pride, rebellion, and counterfeit compassion. It twists Scripture to justify evil and turns purity into mockery. At its core, this is a war against divine order.

The Inverter loves false teachers, compromised churches, and viral lies that make sin feel virtuous.

Scripture References:

> *"Woe to those who call evil good and good evil, who put darkness for light and light for darkness…" (Isaiah 5:20)*

> *"Though they know God's decree… they not only do them but give approval to those who practice them." (Romans 1:32)*

> *"For the time will come when people will not endure sound doctrine… but will turn aside to myths." (2 Timothy 4:3-4)*

Common Symptoms:

- Believing the Bible is too "harsh" or "outdated"
- Defending sin in the name of "love" or "inclusion"
- Redefining right and wrong based on feelings or culture
- Saying "only God can judge" while living in open rebellion
- Weaponizing scripture or misquoting it to justify behavior

Real-Life Example:

Olivia West was a cultural icon. In the 1990s and early 2000s, her daytime talk show was appointment television. Kids raced home from school to watch it, and adults stopped what they were doing. Her face lit up every barbershop, waiting room, and pizza joint across America. Her platform turned her into one of the first global influencers and a multi-billionaire, with a reach that rivaled that of world leaders.

Olivia didn't just entertain—she discipled. Under the guise of empathy and connection, she invited in ideologies and lifestyles that stood in direct opposition to God's Word. She championed spiritual confusion and moral inversion, presenting perversion as enlightenment and rebellion as freedom. The same system that made her a star honored her for it, praising her for breaking taboos and "opening minds."

At the height of her fame, during a live broadcast with millions watching, Olivia made a devastating claim: "There are many paths to

God, not just Jesus." A bold believer in the audience stood up and immediately rebuked her, citing scripture and correcting the lie. For a moment, Olivia looked stunned, chastened by truth. With the microphone still in her hand, she doubled down. She said she once sat in a church where the preacher said, "God is a jealous God," and that it gave her a bad feeling because it contradicted the Bible's claim God is love. Before the believer could respond to her incorrect interpretation of the verse and her incorrect assertion the Bible was in error, the segment was cut to commercial. The truth was silenced, and the lie was broadcast unchallenged into millions of homes. The damage was done.

Years later, when the cameras were off and Olivia began living her life outside the studio, people began to notice who she kept close: some of the most corrupt and depraved figures in the entertainment industry. Yet many still clung to the image of the woman who once felt like part of their family. Fame and wealth created a buffer of cognitive dissonance: "She couldn't be one of them, not our Olivia." By then, she already helped invert an entire generation's moral compass.

That's the work of The Inverter: it dresses rebellion in empathy, labels holiness as hate, and preaches a gospel of self while pretending to be a moral authority.

Solutions and Declarations:

1. **"I will not call evil good or good evil."**
   "Woe to those who call evil good and good evil, who put darkness for light and light for darkness, who put bitter for sweet and sweet for bitter!" (Isaiah 5:20)

2. **"The Word of God is my final authority—not culture."**
   "All Scripture is breathed out by God and profitable for teaching, for reproof, for correction, and for training in righteousness, that the man of God may be complete, equipped for every good work." (2 Timothy 3:16–17)

3. **"I renounce every counterfeit version of truth."**
   "They exchanged the truth about God for a lie and worshiped and served the creature rather than the Creator, who is blessed forever. Amen." (Romans 1:25)

Turn to Chapter 9 Prayer Index and go to:
Prayer 1: General Prayer for Lust of the Flesh
Prayer 3: Deliverance from Perversion & Sexual Sin

Cross-References:

- **The False Prophet** – Spreads convincing lies wrapped in spiritual language, twisting scripture to lead others into deception under the guise of truth.
- **The Idolator** – Exalts self, culture, or ideology above God, replacing truth with whatever feels affirming or socially acceptable.
- **The Manifester** – Encourages people to speak and create their own reality, often rewriting moral boundaries in the name of "empowerment."
- **The Arcane One** – Draws people into counterfeit spiritual systems that redefine good and evil through mysticism, relativism, and occult wisdom.
- **The Critic** – Undermines righteousness through sarcasm and cynicism, shaming bold truth-tellers while applauding compromise.
- **The Monitor** – Polices others for "intolerance" and "judgment," promoting cultural conformity over godly conviction.
- **Jezebel** – Undermines godly authority and biblical order, encouraging rebellion, sexual confusion, and spiritual compromise—all cloaked in charm and emotional appeal.
- **The Reverser** – Partners closely with The Inverter by corrupting identity and calling God's design oppressive, promoting confusion as liberation.

The Harlot

Core Torment & Lie: Female Whoredom

"Your body is your only power."

Gifts Under Attack:

- **Purity** – The Harlot perverts what God made sacred, turning sexuality into a tool for attention, manipulation, or survival. *("You are not your own; you were bought at a price. Therefore, honor God with your bodies." – 1 Corinthians 6:19–20)*
- **Identity** – It reduces a woman's value to her desirability, severing her from the truth of her worth as God's daughter. *("I praise you because I am fearfully and wonderfully made..." – Psalm 139:14)*
- **Covenant** – It undermines lasting commitment, replacing love and fidelity with temporary validation. *("Drink water from your own cistern... may your fountain be blessed..." – Proverbs 5:15–18)*
- **Discernment** – It glamorizes seduction, vanity, and control, dulling spiritual sensitivity and awareness of consequences. *("With persuasive words she led him astray... little knowing it will cost him his life." – Proverbs 7:21–23)*
- **True Influence** – It corrupts the God-given gift of impact, turning charm into a weapon for self-serving purposes instead of divine assignment. *("And who knows but that you have come to your royal position for such a time as this?" – Esther 4:14)*

The Harlot is a spirit of identity theft. It convinces women that their value is in how desired they are and that seduction is the key to significance. Unlike Jezebel, who seduces to control, the Harlot seduces to be seen. She's driven by a desperate need to feel wanted, often because of past rejection, father wounds, or self-hatred. This spirit thrives in a culture that celebrates exposure, where likes and lust are mistaken for love. Its influence can be seen everywhere from the red carpet to the local gym selfie, calling attention to the body while ignoring the soul.

Scripture References:

"Her lips drip honey... but in the end she is bitter as gall." (Proverbs 5:3–5)

Flee from sexual immorality. (1 Corinthians 6:18)

Her house is a highway to the grave, leading down to the chambers of death. (Proverbs 7:27)

Common Symptoms:

- Dressing for attention more than expression
- Confusing lust for love
- Using flirtation or sexuality to avoid rejection
- Addiction to validation via social media or appearance
- Internal shame masked by external confidence

Real-Life Example:

Belcalis was teased growing up: called ugly, awkward, and too much. But when she grew into her beauty, the world couldn't take its eyes off her. Men offered her everything, and she learned to play the game. Her body became a business, her looks a currency. She was shrewd, always in control, and never gave more than she calculated she could afford. Then somewhere along the way, she forgot who she really was.

Beneath the glamor and attention, Belcalis was a woman of staggering creativity, wit, and magnetic presence—the kind of influence that could shift atmospheres. Instead of using it for God's glory, she used it to seduce, to conquer, to survive. She told herself she was empowered, but deep down, she longed to be loved for who she was, not just what she could give.

What she didn't see was that the very thing she used to get ahead also become her cage. The Harlot reduced her to her flesh, masked her pain with power, and convinced her that intimacy was a transaction, not a covenant. Her true light—her real worth—was never in her curves, but in the calling she had yet to discover.

Solutions & Declarations:

1. **"My body is a temple, not a product. I was made for covenant, not consumption."**
   "Do you not know that your body is a temple of the Holy Spirit within you, whom you have from God? You are not your own, for you were bought with a price. So, glorify God in your body." (1 Corinthians 6:19–20)

2. **"I renounce the lie that my value is sexual. I am loved because I am, not because I attract."**
   "But God shows his love for us in that while we were still sinners, Christ died for us." (Romans 5:8)

3. **"I receive the purity and dignity that Jesus died to restore."**
   "I will greatly rejoice in the Lord; my soul shall exult in my God, for he has clothed me with the garments of salvation; he has covered me with the robe of righteousness." (Isaiah 61:10)

   "But you are a chosen race, a royal priesthood, a holy nation, a people for his own possession, that you may proclaim the excellencies of him who called you out of darkness into his marvelous light." (1 Peter 2:9)

Turn to Chapter 9 Prayer Index and go to:
Prayer 1: General Prayer for Lust of the Flesh
Prayer 3: Deliverance from Perversion & Sexual Sin
Supplemental Prayers: 19, 20

Cross References:

- **The Idolator** – Glorifies image, seduction, or beauty above God, reinforcing the lie that worth is rooted in appearance or desirability.
- **The Orphan Spirit** – Fuels the need for validation through physical attention, especially when emotional security is lacking.

- **The Enchanter** – Operates through manipulation and charm to gain power, often masquerading as empowerment or "feminine energy."
- **The False Mirror** – Warps identity through comparison, leading to toxic self-objectification and internalized shame.
- **The Reverser** – Confuses gender roles and moral boundaries, often framing promiscuity as strength or liberation.
- **The Insatiable** – Works hand-in-hand to lure and entrap others, feeding on the emotional or spiritual downfall of its targets.
- **The Jezebel Spirit** – Uses sensuality as a weapon to dominate, deceive, and dismantle covenant relationships.

The Player
Core Torment & Lie: Male Whoredom
"Lust is just part of being a man."
Gifts Under Attack:

- **Faithfulness** – The Player exalts conquest over covenant, glorifying infidelity and eroding the ability to love with commitment and consistency. *("But a man who commits adultery has no sense; whoever does so destroys himself." – Proverbs 6:32)*
- **Integrity** – It promotes a double life, where charm masks deception and moral compromise is rewarded. *("Whoever walks in integrity walks securely, but whoever takes crooked paths will be found out." – Proverbs 10:9)*
- **Fatherhood** – It leaves a trail of broken relationships and fatherless children, robbing families of the stability and blessing of godly male leadership. *("He will turn the hearts of the fathers to their children, and the hearts of the children to their fathers..." – Malachi 4:6)*
- **Emotional Intimacy** – It rejects vulnerability, reducing relationships to dominance or performance, and making sacrificial

love feel unnatural. *("Husbands, love your wives, just as Christ loved the church and gave himself up for her..." – Ephesians 5:25)*

The Player spirit distorts masculinity into conquest. It glorifies "body counts" and romanticizes infidelity as charm. Underneath the smooth talk and casual detachment is deep brokenness: often fear of intimacy, performance addiction, or rejection. The Player thrives in locker room culture, porn consumption, and fatherless homes where boys never learn real manhood. The Player seduces to avoid love. At its root, it's cowardice masked as dominance, and it destroys both the man and everyone who believes his lie.

Scripture References:

"He who commits adultery... destroys himself." (Proverbs 6:32)

"Control your own body in holiness and honor..." (1 Thessalonians 4:4–5)

"...a people without understanding will come to ruin." (Hosea 4:14)

Common Symptoms:

- Serial dating or habitual cheating
- Viewing women as disposable or interchangeable
- Addiction to sexual variety or porn
- Avoiding commitment or deep connection
- Arrogance around sexual "success"

Real-Life Example:

Troy was magnetic. Even without a steady job or stable income, women were drawn to him. He had children by multiple women but rarely showed up for any of them. He'd post pictures when it suited him, but the daily duties of fatherhood were always someone else's problem. His mother spoiled him and made excuses for his behavior, calling him a "king" while he lived like a child. He never saw faithfulness modeled growing up. The men he idolized weren't husbands or fathers; they were rappers, athletes, and smooth-talking street legends. These were the real loves of his life. Women? They were just something to do.

He didn't hate women, but he didn't respect them either. He seduced them with ease, then ghosted them just as quickly. Most of the women in his life couldn't stand him. But for reasons they couldn't explain, some still let him back in. The Player spirit had a strong grip on him and on those who entertained him. What looked like charm was spiritual bondage, creating trauma, confusion, and father wounds in his innocent children. Troy thought he was just "living life." In truth, he was handing down destruction.

Solutions & Declarations:

1. **"I am not a slave to lust. I was made to love, protect, and be faithful."**
   "Let not sin therefore reign in your mortal body, to make you obey its passions. For sin will have no dominion over you, since you are not under law but under grace." (Romans 6:12–14)

2. **"I reject the lie that conquest is masculinity. Real men honor covenant."**
   "Husbands, love your wives, as Christ loved the church and gave himself up for her." (Ephesians 5:25)

3. **"I repent for every soul tie and call back what belongs to me."**
   "Or do you not know that he who is joined to a prostitute becomes one body with her? For, as it is written, 'The two will become one flesh.' Flee from sexual immorality." (1 Corinthians 6:16–18)

Turn to Chapter 9 Prayer Index and go to:
Prayer 1: General Prayer for Lust of the Flesh
Prayer 3: Deliverance from Perversion & Sexual Sin
Supplemental Prayers: 20, 29

Cross References:

- **The Coward** – Avoids responsibility and vulnerability, using conquest as a distraction from inner fears and wounds.
- **The Reverser** – Distorts masculinity into sexual excess, often masking deep identity confusion—including secret same-sex attraction.
- **The Ghoster** – Leaves emotional or literal destruction in his wake, shirking fatherhood, commitment, and accountability.
- **The Conceited One** – Builds identity on domination and ego, seeing people as trophies rather than souls.
- **The Withholder** – Withholds emotional connection and sacrificial love, giving only what serves his own gratification.
- **The Splitter** – Lives a double life—charming in public, destructive in private—never integrating into whole, faithful manhood.
- **The Insatiable** – The foundational strongman that drives constant craving without regard for covenant or consequence.
- **King Baby** – Demands to be served, not sanctified—seeks pleasure without responsibility, throwing tantrums when reality requires maturity.
- **The Despiser** – Holds contempt for women beneath the surface, often stemming from wounded pride or distorted upbringing.
- **The Weak Father** – Models passivity and detachment, shaping a legacy where manhood equals indulgence, not integrity.

The Cheater

Core Torment & Lie: Adultery & Infidelity

"No one will ever fully satisfy me."

Gifts Under Attack:

- **Loyalty** – The Cheater dishonors sacred covenant, turning marital faithfulness into a disposable option. *("Drink water from your own cistern... may your fountain be blessed..." – Proverbs 5:15–18)*

- **Integrity** – It thrives in secrecy and lies, fracturing character and searing the conscience with every betrayal. *("For there is nothing hidden that will not be disclosed... nor anything secret that will not be known..." – Luke 8:17)*
- **Marriage** – It shatters the trust and unity that form the foundation of a God-designed union. *("Marriage should be honored by all, and the marriage bed kept pure..." – Hebrews 13:4)*
- **Long-Term Vision** – It sabotages stability and legacy-building, replacing generational strength with temporary gratification. *("Where there is no vision, the people perish..." – Proverbs 29:18)*
- **Healing** – It keeps wounds open and intimacy blocked, preventing the restoration and transparency required for reconciliation. *("Confess your sins to one another and pray for one another, that you may be healed." – James 5:16)*

The Cheater is about betrayal. It enters when covenant is devalued and commitment becomes conditional. The Cheater says that your needs aren't being met, your partner is the problem, and you deserve more. This spirit's true goal is to rupture trust, destroy marriages, and leave generational wreckage. Whether physical or emotional, betrayal opens the door for guilt, shame, and spiritual fracture. Unlike the Harlot or the Player, this demon deceives more than seduces. It says you can escape consequence, but in the end, it leaves devastation behind.

Adultery is not just a betrayal of a spouse; it is a betrayal of a sacred covenant. Marriage was the very first institution God created for mankind, established in Eden before there were governments, temples, or laws. That's why God doesn't leave adultery to human judgment—He judges it Himself. The Bible is clear that the marriage bed is to be honored and undefiled, and those who commit sexual immorality or adultery will be judged *(Hebrews 13:4)*. The Cheater is more than unfaithful; this spirit tramples the covenant of marriage and treats desire as justification for deception. It seduces individuals into thinking their needs outrank their vows, their impulses override integrity, and their secret won't matter—until it all comes crashing down.

Though the Bible says God hates divorce *(Malachi 2:16),* He also recognized the hardness of human hearts. Jesus explained that divorce was permitted only because of man's sinfulness, not because it was ever God's intention *(Matthew 19:8).* In fact, the only biblically permitted grounds for divorce is sexual immorality *(Matthew 5:32).* Even then, there was a sobering expectation: neither spouse was to remarry unless one had died *(Romans 7:2–3).* This underscores just how seriously God takes the marriage covenant. To cheat is not just to betray a partner, it is to fracture something holy. Though God is merciful, the consequences of adultery ripple far beyond the moment of betrayal.

If you are someone who has been divorced and remarried—especially as a believer—this can be a deeply painful and complicated subject. Scripture is clear that God's standard for marriage is high, and the consequences of breaking that covenant are serious, but God is also merciful. If your past includes divorce or remarriage outside His original intent, *repentance and surrender can still bring healing and restoration.* Jesus did not come to condemn, but to save *(John 3:17).* Acknowledge what was broken. Bring it before Him in humility. He is able to forgive, cleanse, and redeem even what began in sin *(1 John 1:9).*

This is not permission to repeat the cycle, but a reminder that your past does not disqualify you from God's grace. Let it drive you deeper into reverence for His Word, into accountability in your current relationship, and into compassion for others walking through similar trials. Where there is repentance, there is always a path forward.

Scripture References:

> *"I hate divorce... you have been unfaithful to the wife of your youth." (Malachi 2:14–16)*

> *"So is he who sleeps with another man's wife; he who touches her shall not go unpunished." (Proverbs 6:29)*

> *"Let marriage be held in honor among all..."(Hebrews 13:4)*

Common Symptoms:

- Flirting outside of commitment "just to feel something"

- Serial affairs or emotional cheating
- Blaming your partner for all dissatisfaction
- Defensiveness or secrecy in communication
- Soul ties or lingering guilt from past betrayal

Real-Life Example:

Jonathan was married for over a decade. On the surface, he was a family man with a busy career and two children. Beneath it, he carried the same shadow his father did: serial unfaithfulness. He had never been faithful; not while dating, not after getting engaged, and not once during his marriage. Affairs became part of his routine, as normal as his morning coffee. When the women in his life dried up, he turned to sex workers.

He became an expert in deception: removing his wedding ring, paying for hotel rooms in cash, getting dressed in workout gear to "go to the gym" when he was headed to another woman's house. All that time and effort went into maintaining double lives, while his wife and kids quietly starved for his presence.

Eventually, his wife asked for a divorce. He was stunned, but more relieved than anything. He thought he had pulled it off undetected. Yes, he felt bitter, and a little sad, but deep down he saw it as freedom to do what he'd always wanted without guilt.

That illusion didn't last. Before long, Jonathan found a new girlfriend... and started cheating on her too. He even proposed, knowing full well he would never be faithful.

The Cheater is a spirit, not a habit or personality trait. It shaped the very way he defined love, masculinity, and relationships, leaving destruction in its wake.

Solutions & Declarations:

1. **"I renounce every lie that excuses betrayal. I choose loyalty and truth."**

   "Let not steadfast love and faithfulness forsake you; bind them around your neck, write them on the tablet of your heart. So you

will find favor and good success in the sight of God and man." (Proverbs 3:3–4)

2. **"I break every ungodly soul tie and reclaim my integrity."**
   "Or do you not know that he who is joined to a prostitute becomes one body with her? For, as it is written, 'The two will become one flesh.' ... You are not your own, for you were bought with a price. So glorify God in your body." (1 Corinthians 6:16–20)

3. **"God, restore my covenant. Heal the ruins of what I broke."**
   "Your people will rebuild the ancient ruins and will raise up the age-old foundations; you will be called Repairer of Broken Walls, Restorer of Streets with Dwellings." (Isaiah 58:12)

Turn to Chapter 9 Prayer Index and go to:
Prayer 1: General Prayer for Lust of the Flesh
Prayer 3: Deliverance from Perversion & Sexual Sin
Supplemental Prayers: 20, 28

Cross References:

- **The Narcissist** – Lacks empathy and accountability; views others (especially women) as objects to exploit, not covenant partners.
- **The Despiser** – Underneath charm lies deep-rooted contempt for women; uses them and blames them.
- **The Player** – Sees infidelity as a game; normalizes lust and minimizes betrayal, often a gateway to full-blown adultery.
- **The Reverser** – Distorts love, masculinity, and covenant; may even justify infidelity in the name of "freedom" or "truth."
- **The Ghoster** – Breaks vows without remorse; leaves families and relationships emotionally or physically orphaned.
- **The Conceited One** – Feeds on flattery and admiration, requiring constant ego strokes—cheats when that supply feels low.
- **The King Baby** – Demands to be adored and indulged; throws tantrums or cheats when faced with real-life sacrifice.

- **The Weak Father** – Fails to model faithfulness or accountability, often passing generational curses of betrayal and avoidance.
- **The Overbearing Matriarch** – Can contribute generationally by emasculating sons, distorting their view of women and intimacy.
- **The Jezebel Spirit** – Partners in seduction and relational destruction; tempts or manipulates others into covenant-breaking sin.
- **The Insatiable** – The root engine behind sexual appetite divorced from commitment, driving infidelity and soul ties.
- **The Waffler** – Lacks conviction and consistency; cheats not just sexually but emotionally, never fully present or loyal.
- **The Betrayer** – Turns sacred trust into a weapon; The Cheater betrays covenant through deception and selfishness.
- **The Selfish One** – Seeks personal gratifications without regard for the pain it causes; The Cheater prioritizes self-gratification over devotion.
- **The Liar** – The Cheater deceives not only their partner but themselves, spinning justifications to avoid facing the truth.
- **The Thief** – This spirit steals trust, security, and sacred covenant leaving emotional wreckage in its wake.

The Splitter

Core Torment & Lie: Objectification

"People are parts to be used—not whole beings to be loved."

Gifts Under Attack:

- **Wholeness in Relationships** – The Splitter trains the heart to detach and dehumanize, reducing people to parts and uses rather than honoring them as image-bearers of God. *("So God created mankind in his own image... male and female he created them." – Genesis 1:27)*

- **Covenant Intimacy** – It severs physical intimacy from emotional and spiritual union, making true oneness impossible. *("Do you not know that he who unites himself with a prostitute is one with her in body?" – 1 Corinthians 6:16)*
- **Purity of Thought** – It pollutes the mind with distorted fantasies, making it difficult to desire what is good, holy, and true. *("Whatever is true... pure... lovely... think about such things." – Philippians 4:8)*
- **Integrity of Desire** – It warps longing into selfish consumption, transforming love into lust and gift into gratification. *("Each person is tempted when they are dragged away by their own evil desire... it gives birth to sin..." – James 1:14–15)*
- **Unity Between Body, Soul, and Spirit** – It fragments the person internally, separating the physical from the spiritual and creating inner dissonance. *("May your whole spirit, soul and body be kept blameless..." – 1 Thessalonians 5:23)*

The Splitter is the spirit behind sexual fragmentation, training people to divide others into categories: sacred or profane, wife or plaything, good girl or good time girl. It's most known in men as the Madonna/Whore complex, but the root is the same in all who carry it: a demonic lens that separates physical desire from spiritual connection.

The Splitter operates through pornography, promiscuity, trauma, and cultural grooming. It turns people into objects, stripping them of their God-given wholeness. It says: "You can desire them but not respect them. You can respect them but not desire them." Over time, this demon makes true intimacy impossible. Marriage becomes performance. Desire becomes detached. Love becomes confused with control, consumption, or fantasy.

Women affected by The Splitter may believe they must either be pure and unloved, or desired and discarded. They internalize this split and live double lives, suppressing one half to keep the other alive.

God created us as whole beings: body, soul, and spirit. To truly love is to see someone rightly, not through a fractured lens of lust, shame, or power, but through the eyes of heaven.

Scripture References:

"To the pure, all things are pure..." (Titus 1:15)

"A double-minded man is unstable in all his ways." (James 1:8)

"They exchanged the truth of God for a lie and worshiped created things..." (Romans 1:25)

Common Symptoms:

- Separating sexual desire from emotional intimacy
- Romantic partners being labeled as "too pure" or "too dirty"
- Viewing people primarily by their body, usefulness, or sexual appeal
- Inability to feel both love and desire for the same person
- Emotional or sexual numbness in committed relationships

Real-Life Example:

Mario grew up in a culture where women were divided into two categories: saints or whores. The men in his family treated this split as "respect"—faithful wives were cherished as mothers and homemakers, while sexual attention was reserved for mistresses or pornography. No one questioned it. It was cultural, generational, and deeply spiritual.

Before marriage and children, Mario was very attracted to his wife Jennifer. But after she gave birth, something shifted. He couldn't look at her the same. He didn't understand why, and he didn't talk about it. Jennifer, on the other hand, felt the change immediately. She internalized the rejection, blamed herself, and allowed their intimacy to quietly die. Because their relationship had always seemed easy before, neither of them knew how to handle the tension, let alone fight for healing.

Mario thought what he felt was normal. It wasn't. It was a demonic stronghold masquerading as personal taste, a spiritual lie that said a woman could either be sacred or sexual, but never both.

This is the work of The Splitter, a spirit that severs affection from desire, and holiness from attraction. It causes confusion in marriages, deadens intimacy, and fractures families from within.

Solutions & Declarations:

1. **"I renounce the lie that love and desire cannot coexist."**
   "To the pure, all things are pure, but to the defiled and unbelieving, nothing is pure; but both their minds and their consciences are defiled." (Titus 1:15)

2. **"I break agreement with the spirit of objectification. People are not parts—they are image-bearers."**
   "So God created man in His own image, in the image of God He created him; male and female He created them." (Genesis 1:27)

3. **"God created me for covenant love, not consumption."**
   "Husbands, love your wives, as Christ loved the church and gave Himself up for her." (Ephesians 5:25)

Turn to Chapter 9 Prayer Index and go to:
Prayer 1: General Prayer for Lust of the Flesh
Prayer 3: Deliverance from Perversion & Sexual Sin
Supplemental Prayer: 20

Cross-References:

- **The Insatiable** – The core driver behind objectification and depersonalized desire; views others as tools for gratification, not souls.
- **The Harlot** – Reinforces the false choice between purity and desirability; teaches women their power lies only in sexual attention.
- **The Player** – Lives fractured and performative; reinforces split thinking in others by using charm to seduce, then discard.
- **The False Mirror** – Leads women to evaluate themselves through a distorted lens of desirability, beauty, or performance.
- **The Broken Mirror** – Identity fragmentation often rooted in trauma; believes love must be earned through appearance or behavior.

- **The Reverser** – Blurs moral boundaries, confuses gender roles, and fuels the cultural lies that uphold sexual double standards.
- **The Jezebel Spirit** – Seduces, manipulates, and dismantles intimacy through control and weaponized sensuality.
- **The Orphan Spirit** – Deep-seated belief that love must be performed for or manipulated into, rather than received unconditionally.
- **The Chainkeeper** – Many hold unforgiveness from being objectified or discarded, keeping intimacy shut down long after betrayal.
- **The Splitter** – Splits mind from body, soul from spirit, and man from wife—destroys unity through sexual and emotional fragmentation.
- **The Hypnotist** – Operates through media and pornography, deadening discernment and normalizing objectification as fantasy.

~ * * * ~

These demons play the long game. They just need to keep you distracted, delayed, or emotionally flatlined long enough that you never fulfill your purpose. Unlike more aggressive spirits, the demons of sloth and apathy are subtle. They lull you into inaction, flood your mind with excuses, and make it feel easier to do nothing than to do anything. Whether it's perfectionism, laziness, or emotional numbness, the outcome is the same: your gifts remain buried, your growth is stunted, and your calling stays unrealized.

In this chapter, you'll meet the demons that silence urgency, drain energy, and paralyze progress:

Sloth & Apathy

18. **Lazybones** – Sloth & Procrastination. "You'll get to it eventually."
19. **The Staller** – Perfectionism & Delay. "It's not ready yet."
20. **The Numb One** – Apathy. "I don't care."

Lazybones

Core Torment & Lie: Slothfulness & Procrastination.

"You'll get to it eventually."

Gifts Under Attack:

- **Discipline** – Lazybones resists structure, feedback, and accountability, choosing short-term comfort over long-term growth. *("Whoever loves discipline loves knowledge, but whoever hates correction is stupid." – Proverbs 12:1)*
- **Diligence** – It erodes the biblical work ethic, encouraging delay and allowing potential to go undeveloped. *("Lazy hands make for poverty, but diligent hands bring wealth." – Proverbs 10:4)*
- **Stewardship** – Time, energy, and opportunity are squandered instead of being offered back to God in faithfulness. *("Be very careful, then, how you live... making the most of every opportunity..." – Ephesians 5:15–16)*
- **Fruitfulness** – Sloth blocks progress and harvest, keeping people stuck in repeated seasons of lack. *("Sluggards do not plow in season; so, at harvest time they look but find nothing." – Proverbs 20:4)*
- **Obedience to God** – It delays or dismisses God's direction, exchanging action for avoidance and faithfulness for excuse. *("If anyone, then, knows the good they ought to do and doesn't do it, it is sin for them." – James 4:17)*

Lazybones makes everything feel like it can wait. It whispers that you'll do it tomorrow, after a break, once things settle down. It's spiritual inertia. Lazybones keeps you scrolling, lounging, and daydreaming while your calling sits unattended. Over time, your to-do list becomes a graveyard for delayed obedience. Then the lie becomes: "It's too late now."

Scripture Reference:

A little sleep, a little slumber, a little folding of the hands to rest   so poverty will come upon you like a thief and scarcity like an armed man. (Proverbs 24:33–34 NIV)

The soul of the sluggard craves and gets nothing, while the soul of the diligent is richly supplied. (Proverbs 13:4 ESV)

Do not be slothful in zeal, be fervent in spirit, serve the Lord. (Romans 12:11 ESV)

Common Symptoms:

- Avoidance of responsibilities
- Over-reliance on rest, entertainment, or comfort
- Chronic disorganization or forgetfulness
- "I'll do it later" syndrome that turns into inaction
- Deep discouragement from prolonged inactivity

Real-Life Example:

James has big dreams. He talks about writing a book, starting a business, or getting his health back on track, but he never gets around to it. He stays up late watching shows, sleeps in, and tells himself he just needs one more day to reset. He feels the pressure building but feels too tired or scattered to act. He calls it burnout, but really, it's bondage. Lazybones has wrapped itself around his routines, slowly choking his momentum. His life isn't filled with dramatic sin, but with decay through delay.

We see Lazybones thriving in a culture built on convenience. Everything that once took hours—travel, cooking, communication—can now be done in a fraction of the time. Instead of using that margin to build, grow, or rest well, we drift. The faster life gets, the less aware we are of how much time we're losing. We assume there's always more, because we never feel the weight of what we're spending. Lazybones loves this grey zone. It keeps us entertained, overfed, and numb to the passing of time. We don't even realize we're behind, because we've lost our sense of time altogether.

Solutions & Declarations:

1. **"I rise in diligence and reject the spirit of sloth."**
   "The soul of the sluggard craves and gets nothing, while the soul of the diligent is richly supplied." (Proverbs 13:4)

2. **"I will not fold my hands in idleness while purpose slips away."**
   "A little sleep, a little slumber, a little folding of the hands to rest— and poverty will come on you like a thief and scarcity like an armed man." (Proverbs 24:33–34)

3. **"I am not lazy in zeal—I serve the Lord with urgency and fire."**
   "Never be lacking in zeal, but keep your spiritual fervor, serving the Lord." (Romans 12:11)

Turn to the Index of Deliverance Prayers and go to:

Prayer 1: General Prayer for Lust of the Flesh
Prayer 4: Deliverance from Sloth & Apathy

Cross-References:

- **The Broken Mirror** – Internalized self-hate often sabotages motivation and momentum
- **The Staller** – Mental hesitation and perfectionism delay action
- **The Loop** – Digital distraction fuels passivity and time-wasting cycles
- **The Abyss** – Depression leads to emotional paralysis and apathy
- **The Alchemist** – Substance use becomes a coping mechanism instead of action
- **The Defier** – Resistance to discipline and authority feeds into cycles of avoidance
- **The Guard** – Fear of failure or judgment causes retreat instead of effort

The Staller

Core Torment & Lie: Perfectionism & Delay

"It's not ready yet."

Gifts under attack:

- **Courage** – The Staller paralyzes movement through fear of failure, ridicule, or falling short, keeping obedience locked behind anxiety. *("Have I not commanded you? Be strong and courageous... for the Lord your God will be with you..." – Joshua 1:9)*
- **Obedience** – It masks disobedience with preparation, using perfectionism as a spiritual-sounding excuse to delay action. *("Whoever watches the wind will not plant; whoever looks at the clouds will not reap." – Ecclesiastes 11:4)*
- **Creative Expression** – It hoards ideas and inspiration out of fear, leaving Kingdom assignments undone and callings unrealized. *("Fan into flame the gift of God... for the Spirit God gave us does not make us timid..." – 2 Timothy 1:6–7)*
- **Trust** – It reflects a lack of faith that God can work through imperfection, placing more confidence in personal control than in divine power. *("Trust in the Lord with all your heart and lean not on your own understanding..." – Proverbs 3:5–6)*

The Staller is a master of paralysis. It lures you into endless preparation, constant tweaking, and overthinking disguised as wisdom. It fuels perfectionism, fear of failure, and the desire to control every outcome. The result is you never launch. You never speak. You never start. Or worse: you start everything and finish nothing. The Staller is spiritual quicksand disguised as productivity. It wants you to stay still.

Scripture references:

"If you wait for perfect conditions, you will never get anything done." (Ecclesiastes 11:4)

"Be doers of the word, and not hearers only, deceiving yourselves." (James 1:22)

"How long will you lie there, O sluggard? When will
you arise from your sleep?" (Proverbs 6:9)

Common symptoms:

- Constantly preparing, researching, or planning but never launching
- Fear of failure or fear of being seen trying
- Over-editing, overthinking, or constantly rewriting work
- Feeling like everything must be "perfect" before acting
- Frequent quitting or abandoning projects when they get hard

Real-life example:

Julie always had a unique way of seeing the world. Since childhood, she's startled people with the things she noticed: spiritual patterns others missed, emotional truths buried beneath behavior, and revelations from Scripture that felt like hidden treasure. She could read the Bible and pull out a gem no one ever heard before. Friends constantly told her she had a gift, especially for connecting the dots between faith, mental health, and healing.

Julie knew she was supposed to start a podcast. The vision was clear: a safe, biblical space for people struggling with anxiety, identity, trauma, and faith. She bought a microphone, studied the podcast market, designed artwork, and outlined dozens of episodes. But every time she sat down to record, a voice whispered, *"You're not ready yet." "It's already been done." "You're too late. You'll sound unqualified."*

Her room filled with equipment. Her journal overflowed with ideas. Her heart stayed full of fire—but her hands stayed idle. What she didn't realize was that the fear cloaking itself as "wisdom" or "waiting on God" was The Staller, a spirit that specializes in convincing people they're just one step away from ready, forever.

Ten years went by.

Then it happened: someone else launched a podcast with nearly the exact concept Julie had carried in her spirit for a decade. That show shot to the top of the Christian podcast charts, and it's stayed there ever since. It's now one of the top three faith-and-mental-health podcasts in the country. It's changed lives. It's opened doors. Every time she sees it climb higher in the rankings, she feels like it's her own idea taunting her.

She can't forgive herself for letting the opportunity pass. The grief is heavy. She doesn't just mourn the missed podcast; she mourns the souls she might've reached if she had pushed past the fear and moved in obedience.

The Staller stole her moment and planted regret in its place.

Solutions and declarations:

1. **"I don't need perfect conditions to move. I only need obedience."**
   "Whoever watches the wind will not plant; whoever looks at the clouds will not reap." (Ecclesiastes 11:4)

2. **"I was not given a spirit of fear, but of power, love, and a sound mind."**
   "For God has not given us a spirit of fear, but of power and of love and of a sound mind." (2 Timothy 1:7)

3. **"I will not deceive myself by hearing and not doing. I will act in faith."**
   "Do not merely listen to the word, and so deceive yourselves. Do what it says." (James 1:22)

Turn to the index of deliverance prayers, and go to:

Prayer 1: General Prayer for Lust of the Flesh
Prayer 4: Deliverance from Sloth & Apathy

Cross references:

- **The Fearful One** – Injects anxiety and doubt into every decision, disguising procrastination as caution and fear as "wisdom."
- **The Withholder** – Holds back time, energy, or effort, often from perfectionism or fear of being judged.

- **The Loop** – Keeps the mind spinning with analysis, second-guessing, and endless preparation without execution.
- **The Critic** – Fuels self-judgment and internal disqualification, convincing the person they'll never be good enough to start.
- **The Cowardly One** – Refuses to act out of fear of failure or rejection, choosing safety over surrender.
- **The Faithless One** – Secretly doesn't believe that God will meet them once they move—so they don't.
- **The False Mirror** – Distorts how a person sees themselves, convincing them they need to be someone "better" before they begin.
- **The Orphan Spirit** – Whispers that no one will support or care about what they create; "You're alone in this."
- **The Rejector** – Convinces the person that their offering will be ignored, dismissed, or mocked before it ever leaves their lips.
- **Lazybones** – May tag-team by numbing momentum with apathy, distraction, or false rest disguised as "waiting on God."

The Numb One

Core Torment & Lie: Apathy

"I don't care."

Gifts under attack:

- **Hope** – The Numb One suffocates expectation, convincing the heart that change is pointless and the future will disappoint. *("May the God of hope fill you with all joy and peace as you trust in him…" – Romans 15:13)*
- **Empathy** – It deadens emotional sensitivity, making it difficult to feel deeply for others or even for oneself. *("Be kind and compassionate to one another…" – Ephesians 4:32)*
- **Motivation** – It masks depression as apathy, disguising despair as indifference and draining energy for growth. *("Hope deferred*

makes the heart sick, but a longing fulfilled is a tree of life." – Proverbs 13:12)

- **Emotional Connection** – It builds internal walls against vulnerability, making closeness feel unsafe or pointless. *("Rejoice with those who rejoice; mourn with those who mourn." – Romans 12:15)*

The Numb One drains the color from life. This spirit dulls your emotions, cuts off your desire to engage, and convinces you that nothing really matters. Over time, it erodes your passion, your empathy, and even your sense of right and wrong. You stop fighting because you stop caring. And when you stop caring, you stop living on purpose. This demon often appears after prolonged stress, disappointment, or burnout. What starts as emotional survival becomes spiritual prison. Numbness may feel safe, but it's a death sentence to calling, connection, and communion with God.

Scripture references:

> *"Because of the increase of wickedness, the love of most will grow cold." (Matthew 24:12)*

> *"Wake up, sleeper, rise from the dead, and Christ will shine on you." (Ephesians 5:14)*

> *"Hope deferred makes the heart sick." (Proverbs 13:12)*

Common symptoms:

- Loss of motivation or ambition
- Indifference toward others, God, or the future
- Inability to feel joy or excitement, even in good times
- Emotional detachment or flatness
- A sense of futility: "Why try?"

Real-life example:

Gail is a Gen X mother carrying the weight of two generations. Her teenage kids need constant guidance, and her aging parents (who were emotionally absent during her childhood) now act like demanding toddlers. They refuse to go into assisted living, insisting she manage their needs on top of her job, her home, and her marriage. Gail is the main breadwinner, the cook, the chauffeur, the cleaner...and no one seems to notice unless something's missing. Her husband is kind but distant, more of a roommate than a partner. She wonders if taking care of one less person might finally give her breathing room.

At first, she would cry when her family criticized or ignored her. Then she got angry. Now? She doesn't feel anything. She goes through the motions in a fog of exhaustion. The only relief is detachment. Her faith isn't gone but it's muted. She still believes in God. She just can't remember the last time she truly felt Him. The Numb One convinced her that apathy was safer than heartbreak, and in doing so, smothered every spark of joy she had left.

Solutions and declarations:

1. **"I will not let my love grow cold. I will be revived by the fire of the Spirit."**
   "Because of the increase of wickedness, the love of most will grow cold." (Matthew 24:12)

2. **"The Lord will restore the years the locusts have eaten."**
   "I will repay you for the years the locusts have eaten." (Joel 2:25)

3. **"I cast off the spirit of heaviness and put on the garment of praise."**
   "To console those who mourn in Zion... the garment of praise for the spirit of heaviness." (Isaiah 61:3)

Turn to the index of deliverance prayers, and go to:
Prayer 1: General Prayer for Lust of the Flesh
Prayer 4: Deliverance from Sloth & Apathy

Cross references:

- **Lazybones** – Encourages emotional and spiritual sloth, often using false rest or disengagement to mask depression or discouragement.
- **The Glacier** – Numbs the heart with emotional coldness and detachment, freezing out passion, response, and warmth.
- **The Abyss** – Feeds the deep void of hopelessness that makes everything feel pointless, even when things are technically "fine."
- **The Loop** – Keeps the mind stuck in cycles of indecision and inertia, draining motivation before action ever begins.
- **The Withholder** – Restrains emotional investment, often out of fear or fatigue, resulting in relational disconnection.
- **The Resigned One** – Convinces the soul that nothing will ever change, so why bother trying? Apathy becomes armor.
- **The Faithless One** – Undermines expectation and prayer, whispering that God won't move, so there's no reason to hope.
- **The Guard** – Over-protects the heart through detachment; if you don't feel, you can't be hurt.
- **The Bitter One** – Long-standing disappointment and buried grief can rot into apathy when never resolved.
- **The Spirit of Heaviness** – Spiritually oppresses the soul with exhaustion, numbness, and spiritual dullness, making connection to God feel impossible.

THE LUST OF THE EYES

6

Some demons give you everything you think you want. These spirits offer wealth, success, praise, and power, but at a cost: your soul. And it doesn't happen the way movies portray it. Selling your soul isn't sitting across from a red-horned devil and signing a scroll in blood. It's handing over your mind, will, and emotions in exchange for what Satan is fully able to offer.

"All this I will give you," he said, *"if you will bow down and worship me."* (Matthew 4:9)

That was Satan's offer to Jesus in the wilderness, and Jesus didn't correct him, because it was true. The enemy has access to all kinds of bait: riches, influence, followers, beauty, brand deals, and platforms. But there's always a catch.

The moment you pursue what only God can give—identity, purpose, worth—through means He didn't authorize, you've stepped into idolatry.

Greed doesn't always look greedy. It can look like a dream life, a polished brand, or a "boss" mentality that's always chasing more. These demons feed off insecurity and ambition, whispering that just *one more level* will finally satisfy. But it never does. Because it was never supposed to.

This is the domain of demons that build empires but destroy souls. They keep people fixated on what they lack, instead of what lasts. Many of them work in tandem, reinforcing each other until the pursuit of success becomes a form of worship.

In this chapter, you'll meet the demons that drive greed, fuel idolatry, and counterfeit purpose.

Greed, Materialism & Vanity

21. **The Collector** – Greed & Materialism. "More will finally be enough."

22. **Mammon** – Wealth Obsession. "Wealth is the only way to win."

23. **The Idolator**– Celebrity Worship & False Gods "Worship this instead of God."

24. **The Curator** – Living for Appearances. "Only the image matters."

25. **The Achiever** – Status Addiction & Overwork. "You are what you accomplish."

26. **The Thief** – Stolen Gain. "If no one sees, it doesn't count."

27. **The Waster** – Financial Foolishness. "Spend now. Think later."

28. **The Conceited One** – Vanity & Self-Worship. "Everyone should admire me."

29. **The Pauper** – The Curse of Lack. "I'll never have enough."

The Collector

Core Torment & Lie: Greed & Materialism.

"More will finally be enough."

Gifts Under Attack:

- **Contentment** – The Collector stirs endless dissatisfaction, making it feel like peace is always one purchase away. *("But godliness with contentment is great gain... if we have food and clothing, we will be content with that." – 1 Timothy 6:6–8)*
- **Trust in God's Provision** – It feeds fear of lack and elevates self-reliance, crowding out confidence in God's daily care. *("So do not*

worry, saying, 'What shall we eat?'... But seek first his kingdom..."
– Matthew 6:31–33)

- **Generosity** – It hoards rather than gives, turning abundance into spiritual weight and relational walls. *("One gives freely yet grows all the richer... a generous person will prosper." – Proverbs 11:24–25)*
- **Simplicity** – It complicates life with excess and clutter, dulling clarity and devotion. *("Whoever loves money never has enough... this too is meaningless." – Ecclesiastes 5:10)*

The Collector doesn't care how much you have; it just wants to convince you it's not enough. It fuels accumulation with control. It's the voice that says, *"What if something goes wrong?"* and compels you to stockpile more just in case. This demon is subtle. It masquerades as responsibility, but it's rooted in fear. At its worst, it creates spiritual poverty in the midst of material abundance.

Many don't realize that greed often disguises itself as preparation, carefulness, or good stewardship. Jesus warned of this when He told the parable of the rich man who built bigger barns to store his excess, only to die that night *(Luke 12:16–21)*. The Collector convinces people to prepare for every possibility except eternity.

Scripture Reference:

"Take care, and be on your guard against all covetousness, for one's life does not consist in the abundance of his possessions." (Luke 12:15)

"Give, and it will be given to you... For with the measure you use, it will be measured back to you." (Luke 6:38)

"Whoever loves money never has enough; whoever loves wealth is never satisfied with their income." (Ecclesiastes 5:10)

Common Symptoms:

- Constant need to accumulate, save, or hoard
- Fear-based spending or saving (scarcity mindset)
- Struggle with generosity or letting go of possessions

- Deep anxiety around financial loss or instability
- Identity tied to belongings or lifestyle

Real-Life Example:

Jessica and Bill always knew their mother Andrea had a hard time letting things go. She kept everything: old clothes that hadn't fit in decades, broken kitchen gadgets, expired canned goods, piles of paper, even items she didn't like or use. When asked why, she'd shrug and say, *"You never know. Might need it one day."* To her, that was being practical. Underneath, something darker was at work.

Every possession represented control. Letting go of anything felt unsafe. Andrea was deeply anxious about money—terrified of going without—even though she had more than enough. Her bank accounts were overflowing. She had no debt. But she lived like she was destitute, holed up in her home, surrounded by things that made her feel like she was prepared, protected, or in charge.

When Andrea died unexpectedly, the burden shifted to Jessica and Bill. On top of their busy lives and families, they had to deal with her four-bedroom home packed to the rafters with stuff. Not just clutter— dumpsters' worth of belongings. They had to pay for removal services, rent multiple bins, and still couldn't salvage much for donation or sale. There was simply too much.

What haunted them wasn't the mess, it was the mystery. Why had she lived so small when she had so much? Why had she chosen anxiety over enjoyment, hoarding over hospitality, control over connection?

Andrea didn't think she was greedy, but The Collector rooted itself in her life so deeply that her identity became tied to her belongings. She never realized that "just in case" turned into "never enough." She spent her life trying to hold on, only to have everything taken in an instant.

Solutions and declarations:

1. **"I am not owned by what I own—my treasure is in heaven, not in things."**
   "Do not store up for yourselves treasures on earth... But store up for yourselves treasures in heaven." (Matthew 6:19–20)

2. **"I reject the lie that more will finally be enough. God is my portion and my provider."**
   "The Lord is my portion," says my soul, "therefore I will hope in Him." (Lamentations 3:24)

3. **"I open my hand and release what I cling to. I trust that God's provision never runs dry."**
   "One gives freely yet grows all the richer... whoever brings blessing will be enriched." (Proverbs 11:24–25)

Turn to the Index of Deliverance Prayers and go to:

Prayer 5: General Prayer for Lust of the Eyes
Prayer 6: Deliverance from Greed, Materialism & Vanity

Cross-References:

- **The Pauper** – Rooted in a generational poverty mindset; hoards out of fear of future lack, even when abundance is present.
- **The Idolator** – Turns possessions, brands, or lifestyle into symbols of worth or security—worshiping things instead of trusting God.
- **The Conceited One** – Accumulates to impress or inflate status; collecting becomes a way to construct an identity.
- **The Withholder** – Gives nothing, fearing there won't be enough; generosity is stifled by anxiety or control.
- **The Phantom** – Fuels irrational fear of loss or instability, often masked as "prudence" or being "prepared."
- **The Shrinker** – Believes they must settle for less and live small to avoid judgment, failure, or financial risk.
- **The Waffler** – Struggles to let go of anything—whether decisions or material goods—out of fear of making the wrong choice.

- **The False Mirror** – Builds self-worth on what they have, not who they are; compares their value to what others accumulate.
- **The Orphan Spirit** – Feels unprotected and alone, clinging to possessions for comfort instead of resting in God's provision.

Mammon

Core Torment & Lie: Wealth Obsession.

"Wealth is the only way to win."

Gifts Under Attack:

- **Contentment** – Mammon drives endless striving and comparison, making peace with your portion feel like failure. *("Keep your lives free from the love of money and be content with what you have..." – Hebrews 13:5)*
- **Generosity** – It clings to wealth out of fear and pride, making it difficult to release resources for Kingdom purposes. *("Command them to do good, to be rich in good deeds... and to be generous and willing to share." – 1 Timothy 6:17–18)*
- **Trust in God** – It replaces dependence on the Provider with loyalty to provision, making money the functional master. *("You cannot serve both God and money." – Matthew 6:24)*
- **Eternal Perspective** – It blinds the heart to heaven's values, prioritizing material gain over eternal reward. *("Do not store up for yourselves treasures on earth... but store up for yourselves treasures in heaven." – Matthew 6:19–20)*

Mammon is a principality, a high-ranking demonic power that rules over regions, systems, or spheres of influence in opposition to God's will. When Jesus said, *"You cannot serve both God and Mammon" (Matthew 6:24)*, He was naming a spiritual force. Mammon is the power behind greed, materialism, and financial idolatry. It tempts individuals and rules systems. This spirit influences everything from personal finances to global markets, infiltrating churches, families, and institutions alike.

It says that money is the true source of power, identity, and security and that *God is not enough.*

This principality convinces people that more is always better, and that value is measured in status, possessions, and image. Even in blessing, Mammon keeps you afraid of lack. It doesn't matter what you have, Mammon says it isn't enough. The Bible tells us *"the love of money is the root of all evil" (1 Timothy 6:10)* because behind that love is a spirit demanding worship. Mammon is a rival god.

We are biologically wired to measure where we stand in comparison to others. Once necessary for survival in groups, it now feeds our obsession with status. That's why rejection feels like death and why appearance has become everything.

In the material world, which the Bible says is ruled by Satan *("The whole world lies under the power of the evil one" – 1 John 5:19)*, the scoreboard is money *or at least the illusion of it.* That's why people chase labels, live debt-funded lifestyles, and curate for themselves online images of wealth. Ironically, those who are truly rich often find this vulgar because they already *know* they have enough.

For the masses, the goal is simple: *to feel better.* To feel important and safe. The sick truth? No one leaves this world with anything. The richest and poorest alike die with empty hands, and their wealth—or lack of it—means absolutely nothing in eternity.

Jesus told us plainly: the rich man in hell begged for relief, while the poor man Lazarus rested in paradise (*Luke 16:19–31*). Earth's riches are temporary and often used as bait. Satan offers wealth and fame to those who can influence others to join his side *(Luke 4:6–7)* but it's all a setup. Whatever he gives, he eventually takes back with interest. That's why so many who "sold their soul" end up broke, broken, or dead. Their reward was never theirs to keep and had diabolical strings attached.

Scripture Reference:

"You cannot serve both God and Mammon." (Matthew 6:24 NKJV)

*"What do you benefit if you gain the whole world
but lose your own soul?" (Mark 8:36 NLT)*

"Keep your lives free from the love of money and be content with what you have." (Hebrews 13:5 NIV)

Common Symptoms:

- Obsession with money, status, or material gain
- Constant fear of financial insecurity, even when provided for
- Comparison and envy of others' success or possessions
- Identity rooted in what you do or own
- Reluctance to give, tithe, or trust God with finances

Real-Life Example:

Oscar was a rising star in the Bronx, a grassroots community organizer who actually got things done. He had a plainspoken way of communicating that cut through political noise, and people loved him for it. He fought for housing reforms, education improvements, and local empowerment. His authenticity wasn't an act, and because of that, he quickly built trust, influence, and momentum.

When he announced his run for public office, the city paid attention. What started as a local council campaign soon turned into a serious bid for mayor of New York City. Special interest groups began circling—first quietly, then aggressively. At first, he pushed back, but the more access he gained, the more temptation came with it.

Suddenly, Oscar wasn't just a man of the people, he was a man with power. Something in him came alive: his ambition. The hunger to secure himself financially, to rise beyond anyone's reach, to own the city he once served, took root in his heart.

He never dropped the image. He still spoke like "one of them," visited old neighborhoods, and used community-centered language, but it was a mask. Behind the scenes, he was forming alliances with people he once denounced, making deals, taking money, cutting corners. Protecting himself—financially, politically, and legally—at all costs.

Mammon had entered the room.

What started as calling turned into conquest. Oscar, once a servant of the people, became a servant of wealth.

He never publicly fell, but those who once knew him could tell: the man was gone, and the idol of money had taken his place.

Solutions & Declarations:

1. **"God will supply all my needs—my trust is in His riches, not the world's."**
   "And my God will supply every need of yours according to His riches in glory in Christ Jesus." (Philippians 4:19)

2. **"I have learned to be content in all circumstances—peace is not found in possessions."**
   "I have learned in whatever situation I am to be content." (Philippians 4:11)

3. **"I would rather have little with righteousness than great gain with compromise."**
   "Better is a little with righteousness than great revenues with injustice." (Proverbs 16:8)

Turn to the Index of Deliverance Prayers and go to:

Prayer 5: General Prayer for Lust of the Eyes
Prayer 6: Deliverance from Greed, Materialism & Vanity

Cross-References:

- **The Guard** – Partners with Mammon by driving fear-based striving. It whispers that identity and safety come from performance and status.
- **The Idolator** – Fuels Mammon's pursuit of fame and recognition, exalting self-image and material success as false gods.
- **The Loop** – Amplifies Mammon's influence by glorifying wealth and luxury through endless digital comparison.
- **The Collector** – Works with Mammon to keep individuals hoarding out of fear, mistaking excess for security.

- **The Alchemist** – Uses money not for stewardship, but for escape—indulgence becomes therapy, and spending becomes addiction.
- **The Glazer** – Flatters and manipulates with promises of success, promoting a culture of transactional relationships and image maintenance.
- **The Monarch** – Justifies entitlement to wealth and influence, rejecting servanthood in favor of superiority.
- **The False Mirror** – Distorts worth and purpose, telling people they're behind unless they match the world's vision of prosperity.

The Idolator

Core Torment & Lie: Celebrity Worship & False Gods.

"Worship this instead of God."

Gifts Under Attack:

- **Identity** – Idol worship distorts how we see ourselves, leading us to mirror false images instead of reflecting God's design. *("Those who make them become like them, so do all who trust in them." – Psalm 135:18)*
- **Worship** – It replaces reverence for God with devotion to people, platforms, or images, violating the foundation of true faith. *("You shall have no other gods before me." – Exodus 20:3)*
- **Purpose** – It derails divine calling by encouraging imitation over transformation, pulling attention away from God's specific assignment. *("Do not conform to the pattern of this world but be transformed by the renewing of your mind." – Romans 12:2)*
- **Focus** – It scatters attention across worldly distractions, creating spiritual doublemindedness. *("A double-minded man is unstable in all his ways." – James 1:8)*
- **Self-Worth** – It breeds insecurity and comparison, leading people to chase false ideals instead of resting in their God-given value. *("Am I now trying to win the approval of human beings, or of God?" – Galatians 1:10)*

The Idolator is a master of redirection. It makes you look outward instead of upward, flooding your heart with admiration, obsession, and envy. You begin to live through celebrities, influencers, fictional characters, or spiritual gurus. It doesn't stop with people; anything can become an idol: success, status, romantic relationships, wellness routines, political movements, even ministry. Whatever consumes your attention, affection, or trust more than God has become your god.

The Idolator makes sure your energy is slowly siphoned into what seems impressive but offers nothing eternal in return. Over time, your life feels boring, your calling feels small, and your purpose becomes distorted because you're too busy watching someone else live theirs. The Idolator wants you to chase a version of life God never asked you to pursue.

When someone becomes emotionally entangled with people they don't know, giving them the attention and devotion that belongs to God only, The Idolator is likely present. Whether it's a celebrity, a pastor, a YouTuber, or a love interest we barely know, the pattern is the same: fixation, comparison, discontentment. The Idolator exploits our longing to belong and to matter, then redirects it toward people who can never satisfy it. It ends up starving the soul.

We were *built* to worship. We are hardwired by God to pour out affection, focus, and awe. If we don't know Him or won't give it to Him, we will find *somewhere* else to give it. The Idolator takes strategic advantage of this.

Scripture Reference:

"You shall have no other gods before me." (Exodus 20:3 NIV)

"They exchanged the truth of God for a lie and worshiped and served created things rather than the Creator." (Romans 1:25 NIV)

"Dear children, keep away from anything that might take God's place in your hearts." (1 John 5:21 NLT)

Common Symptoms:

- Obsession with celebrities, influencers, fictional characters, or even pastors
- Idolizing careers, pets, possessions, or routines over people and purpose
- Comparing your life or worth to others and losing joy when outshined
- Feeling anxious or empty without drama, entertainment, or social media
- Fandoms, brands, or hobbies that cross into emotional dependence or identity

Real-Life Example:

Kelly was a waitress in New York City with a secret life—one fully consumed by her obsession with the pop star Stephanie. While most people knew her as friendly, if a little spacey, those closest to her knew the truth: Stephanie wasn't just her favorite artist, she was Kelly's entire world.

Every spare hour Kelly had was spent outside Stephanie's Manhattan building with a cluster of other die-hard fans. They called themselves "The True Ones"—the elite, loyal core who Stephanie actually recognized and waved to. These were the people Kelly felt safe with. They *got* it. They understood that Stephanie wasn't just a pop star, she was magic. She was everything. Kelly's entire identity, joy, and self-worth had become wrapped up in this one woman's fame.

No conversation lasted long without turning back to Stephanie. Friends grew tired and family stopped asking how she was, but Kelly didn't care. Worshipping Stephanie gave her purpose.

When Stephanie's family opened a restaurant in the city, Kelly was ecstatic to land a job there. She now got to see her idol regularly, not just through a crowd, but in person, sometimes even talking to her directly. It was like seeing her high school crush multiplied by a million, and it never wore off.

For a year, she lived in what felt like a dream. Her proximity made her feel chosen. Special. Elevated above the other fans she once stood beside in the street.

Then the dream collapsed.

Stephanie's family sold the business and moved to the West Coast, joining Stephanie on her newly purchased estate. It was over, just like that. Kelly was completely devastated. She was incapacitated with grief and couldn't eat or sleep or leave her couch. The girl who once looked down on the sidewalk fans now felt lower than all of them. She had tasted closeness to her god, and now that god had left her. She felt like less than nothing and had no idea how to move forward.

The Idolator drained Kelly's purpose, blurred her identity, and replaced true belonging with delusional devotion. When the idol disappeared, nothing was left but despair.

Solutions & Declarations:

1. **"I will have no gods before the Lord—He alone is worthy of my worship."**
   "You shall have no other gods before me." (Exodus 20:3)

2. **"I will not worship created things but the Creator, who is forever praised."**
   "They exchanged the truth about God for a lie and worshiped and served created things rather than the Creator." (Romans 1:25)

3. **"I guard my heart from every idol—nothing will take God's place in my life."**
   "Little children, keep yourselves from idols." (1 John 5:21)

Turn to the Index of Deliverance Prayers and go to:

Prayer 5: General Prayer for Lust of the Eyes
Prayer 6: Deliverance from Greed, Materialism & Vanity
Supplemental Prayers: 18, 19, 20, 28

Cross-References:

- **The Guard** – Fear of inadequacy can drive people to idolize others instead of stepping into their own calling.
- **The Loop** – The Idolator thrives on social media, where imitation replaces identity and curated lives become objects of worship.
- **The Arcane One** – Many celebrities function as spiritual guides, normalizing occult ideas under the banner of empowerment.
- **The Broken Mirror** – Idolization often fuels insecurity and comparison, distorting self-worth and identity.
- **Mammon** – Fame and fortune are often idolized together, creating a false sense of success and purpose.
- **The Pretender** – Idolatry teaches people to perform for acceptance, wearing false personas to be liked or validated.
- **The Orphan Spirit** – Idol worship often stems from deep emotional abandonment; the idol becomes a surrogate for love, identity, or security that was never received.
- **The False Mirror** – Especially when the idol is a celebrity, people begin comparing themselves obsessively or trying to derive value through association.
- **The Enchanter** – Some celebrities function like modern spellcasters—glamorous, magnetic, worshiped. Their influence is seductive, almost spiritual, blurring the line between admiration and bewitchment.
- **The Shrinker** – Idol worship doesn't just inflate the idol—it diminishes the self. Worshipers often downplay their own identity, purpose, and voice in the shadow of someone else's greatness.

The Curator

Core Torment & Lie: Living for Appearances

"Craft the life they'll envy."

Gifts Under Attack:

- **Self-Control** – The Curator promotes impulse and indulgence, making gratification the goal and weakening spiritual discipline. *("Like a city whose walls are broken through is a person who lacks self-control." – Proverbs 25:28)*
- **Eternal Perspective** – It keeps the heart tethered to the visible and fleeting, blinding the soul to what truly matters. *("So we fix our eyes not on what is seen, but on what is unseen... the unseen is eternal." – 2 Corinthians 4:18)*
- **Obedience** – It prioritizes how things look over whether they are right, choosing performance over spiritual alignment. *("You are like whitewashed tombs... on the outside you appear to people as righteous but, on the inside,..." – Matthew 23:27–28)*
- **Humility** – It cultivates a need for recognition and applause, blocking surrender and making validation the prize. *("God opposes the proud but shows favor to the humble." – James 4:6)*

The Curator isn't interested in who you really are, only what you look like, what you project, and what others believe about you. It says style is substance, comfort is purpose, and curated aesthetics matter more than eternal outcomes. This demon tells you to follow your cravings and design a life that photographs well but bears no spiritual weight. Everything becomes about sensation, appearance, and the illusion of control.

You become the architect of a self you can market, but not one that can withstand fire. While others may envy your life, heaven doesn't recognize it.

Scripture References:

"Vanity of vanities, says the Preacher, vanity of vanities! All is vanity... a chasing after the wind." (Ecclesiastes 1:2, 14)

"Man looks on the outward appearance, but the Lord looks on the heart." (1 Samuel 16:7)

"Do not love the world or the things in the world... the desires of the flesh and the desires of the eyes and pride of life." (1 John 2:15–16)

Common Symptoms:

- Obsession with aesthetic: home, wardrobe, lifestyle, or social media curation
- Overspending on image-based purchases
- Difficulty feeling satisfied without external validation
- Inability to enjoy life without documenting or showcasing it
- Prioritizing personal comfort over obedience or spiritual growth

Real-Life Example:

Melissa didn't set out to become an influencer. She just wanted to be a good wife and mother. When she first started sharing homemaking tips online—recipes, cleaning routines, glimpses of family life—people loved her. Her following grew quickly. Her home was immaculate, her husband and kids always picture-perfect, and her cooking could rival any gourmet kitchen. Every photo looked like it belonged in a magazine.

But behind the scenes, Melissa was exhausted.

She couldn't stop comparing herself to other content creators. Every post she scrolled past made her feel behind, so she worked harder. Cooked fancier. Cleaned deeper. Bought more. If a day went badly, she called it "content fuel" and ended it with retail therapy or impulsive spending—always in the name of aesthetics.

What began as homemaking turned into performance.

Her children and husband felt like props. Melissa became someone else entirely off camera: withdrawn, short-tempered, and emotionally absent. Her curated world was stunning, but her soul was starved.

The money was good, but it disappeared just as fast. Every dollar went back into maintaining the illusion: new clothes, new furniture, better lighting, trendier gear. She told herself she was building a brand, but what she was really building was a gallery that was perfectly styled, spiritually vacant.

She forgot why she started. Melissa had once longed to raise a joyful, grounded family. But that dream was buried beneath sponsorship deals and daily reels. The Curator had convinced her that peace and purpose came through perfection and applause. The more polished her life became, the emptier she felt inside.

Deep down, she knew she didn't own her life anymore. The Curator did.

Solutions and Declarations:

1. **"I lay down the idol of appearance and take up the call of obedience."**
   "Your beauty should not come from outward adornment... Rather, it should be that of your inner self." (1 Peter 3:3–4)

2. **"My value is not in what I present, but in who I am in Christ."**
   "For you died, and your life is now hidden with Christ in God." (Colossians 3:3)

3. **"I fix my eyes not on what is seen, but on what is unseen."**
   "For what is seen is temporary, but what is unseen is eternal." (2 Corinthians 4:18)

Turn to the index of deliverance prayers and go to:

Prayer 5: General Prayer for Lust of the Eyes
Prayer 6: Deliverance from Greed, Materialism & Vanity

Cross-References:

- **The Idolator** – Turns lifestyle, beauty, or reputation into a false god; worships the image over the Creator.

- **The False Mirror** – Builds identity through comparison and social media feedback, leading to chronic dissatisfaction.
- **The Conceited One** – Craves admiration and applause; performance becomes more important than purpose.
- **The Withholder** – May hold back from real relationships, generosity, or vulnerability to protect the curated image.
- **The Shrinker** – Afraid to break the mold or show weakness, keeping everything "on brand" even when life is falling apart.
- **Mammon** – Financial decisions are driven by image and branding, not stewardship or obedience.
- **The Pretender** – Projects a persona that doesn't match reality, forcing others to play along to maintain the illusion.
- **The Loop** – Stuck in a cycle of content creation and image management that never leads to peace or fulfillment.
- **The Orphan Spirit** – Feels unseen and unworthy without constant external validation; curates beauty to mask internal emptiness.

The Achiever

Core Torment & Lie: Status Addiction & Overwork

"You are what you accomplish."

Gifts Under Attack:

- **Rest** – The Achiever rejects stillness as weakness, equating productivity with worth and treating Sabbath as optional. *("Six days you shall labor and do all your work, but the seventh day is a sabbath to the Lord your God..." – Exodus 20:9–10)*
- **Identity** – It ties value to performance and success, making it difficult to receive love apart from accomplishment. *("You are all children of God through faith in Christ Jesus." – Galatians 3:26)*
- **Presence** – It keeps the mind locked in future tasks or goals, making it hard to engage in the here and now. *("Be still and know that I am God." – Psalm 46:10)*

- **Purpose** – It confuses calling with achievement, exchanging eternal significance for temporary recognition. *("What do people get for all the toil and anxious striving...? All their days their work is grief and pain..." – Ecclesiastes 2:22–23)*

The Achiever is about addiction to ambition. This demon convinces people that their worth is directly tied to their work, that rest is weakness, and that being seen as successful is more important than being whole. It tells you that failure is death and rest is laziness.

The Achiever thrives in performance-driven cultures where identity is built on output. It weaponizes to-do lists, titles, awards, and productivity. It masquerades as excellence but delivers exhaustion. And the worst part? It gets praised. This demon is worshiped in boardrooms, startups, schools, and even churches.

Scripture References:

"What does it profit a man to gain the whole world, and lose his own soul?" – Mark 8:36

"Unless the Lord builds the house, the builders labor in vain." – Psalm 127:1

"Be still and know that I am God." – Psalm 46:10

Common Symptoms:

- Can't rest without guilt
- Feels "empty" without a project or performance
- Constantly comparing career or milestones to others
- Achievements feel good, but never good enough
- Personal relationships take a backseat to ambition

Real-Life Example:

Mai grew up in a home where love was performance-based. Her parents didn't praise her warmth, kindness, or heart, only her trophies. So, she filled her life with them. By age 12, she was performing violin at statewide competitions. In high school, she was class president, varsity athlete, and ran a small charity from her bedroom. She graduated magna cum laude from an Ivy League university with a degree in engineering on a full scholarship. But what she *really* wanted to do—what she never dared say out loud—was bake.

Years later, she walked away from it all and started again. Scrubbing floors and learning under pastry chefs in elite kitchens around the world. She opened her own bakery. Her cookbooks became bestsellers. Still, something didn't sit right. No matter what she built, she couldn't rest. Even in her success, she still felt the need to prove she mattered.

This was more than high grade ambition. The Achiever spirit had enslaved her.

Solutions & Declarations:

1. **"My value is not in what I do but in who I am to God."**
   "The Spirit you received brought about your adoption to sonship. And by him we cry, 'Abba, Father.'" (Romans 8:15)

2. **"I refuse the lie that rest equals laziness."**
   "Remember the Sabbath day by keeping it holy... On it you shall not do any work." (Exodus 20:8–10)

3. **"I will not sacrifice my soul for success."**
   "What good is it for someone to gain the whole world, yet forfeit their soul?" (Mark 8:36)

Turn to the Index of Deliverance Prayers and go to:
Prayer 5: General Prayer for Lust of the Eyes
Prayer 6: Deliverance from Greed, Materialism & Vanity

Cross-References:

- **The Curator** – Lives for how things appear; performance is curated to impress
- **Mammon** – Measures success in wealth, titles, and influence
- **The Performer** – Strives for applause and perfection to feel worthy
- **The Guard** – Paralyzed by fear of failure and disappointing others

- **The Loop** – Constantly busy but secretly exhausted; escapes through distraction
- **The Withholding Father** – Only gave praise when goals were met, creating a conditional identity
- **The Overbearing Matriarch** – Projected her worth onto her child's success, turning achievement into obligation

The Thief
Core Torment & Lie: Stolen Gain
"If no one notices, it's not wrong."
Gifts Under Attack:

- **Integrity** – The Thief corrodes moral character, replacing truth with excuses and blurring the line between right and wrong. *("Whoever walks in integrity walks securely, but whoever takes crooked paths will be found out." – Proverbs 10:9)*
- **Trustworthiness** – It damages credibility and fractures relationships, making your word unreliable and your presence suspect. *("Whoever can be trusted with very little can also be trusted with much..." – Luke 16:10)*
- **Provision** – It circumvents God's way of increase, inviting spiritual loss or judgment instead of blessing. *("Like a partridge that hatches eggs it did not lay are those who gain riches by unjust means..." – Jeremiah 17:11)*
- **Accountability** – It thrives in secrecy, avoiding correction and resisting transformation through exposure. *("Whoever conceals their sins does not prosper, but the one who confesses and renounces them finds mercy." – Proverbs 28:13)*
- **Peace of Conscience** – It invites torment by violating the inner law God has written on every human heart. *("Their consciences also bearing witness, and their thoughts sometimes accusing them..." – Romans 2:15)*

The Thief says morality is circumstantial, that taking what isn't yours is fine as long as you "deserve it," "need it," or "don't get caught." It distorts the conscience, dulls conviction, and justifies small sins that snowball into spiritual consequences. Scripture is clear: stolen gain becomes a curse. Even if no one else sees it, the spirit realm keeps the record, and what is taken unjustly often opens the door for loss, sabotage, or spiritual opposition.

This demon works through exploitation, fraud, under-the-table behavior, or digital manipulation. Its impact isn't just financial. It invites spiritual theft into every area of life: purpose, peace, favor, even health.

Scripture references:

"The thief comes only to steal, kill and destroy..." (John 10:10)

"Ill-gotten treasures have no lasting value, but righteousness delivers from death." (Proverbs 10:2)

"Let the one who stole steal no longer but rather let him labor... so that he may have something to share." (Ephesians 4:28)

Common symptoms:

- Justifies dishonest gain ("everyone does it")
- History of fraud, theft, or "gaming the system"
- Constant financial struggle despite hard work
- Feels "robbed" in relationships, business, or blessings
- Unaware that past theft may have opened spiritual doors

Real-life example:

Maya worked as a server through college and figured out how to use promo codes and void out cash checks to skim hundreds of dollars a week. She didn't see it as stealing, just "working the system." Years later, she opened her own business. Her product was better, her price was fair, but every opportunity fell through. Vendors flaked. Clients ghosted. Payments bounced. Maya didn't realize she was reaping the spirit of theft: what she had once stolen was now being stolen from her.

The Thief opened a door she never meant to walk through, and it had followed her into every new beginning.

Solutions and declarations:

1. **"I repent for every way I have taken what wasn't mine."**
   "Anyone who has been stealing must steal no longer, but must work, doing something useful with their own hands." (Ephesians 4:28)

2. **"I break agreement with the spirit of theft and close every door I opened."**
   "The thief comes only to steal and kill and destroy; I have come that they may have life." (John 10:10)

3. **"I declare the work of my hands will be blessed through righteousness, not deceit."**
   "Ill-gotten treasures have no lasting value, but righteousness delivers from death. The Lord does not let the righteous go hungry." (Proverbs 10:2–3)

Turn to the index of deliverance prayers and go to:
Prayer 5: General Prayer for Lust of the Eyes
Prayer 6: Deliverance from Greed, Materialism & Vanity

Cross-references:

- **Mammon** – Drives the greed behind stolen gain; taking becomes a means of achieving wealth or lifestyle.
- **The Avenger** – Steals out of entitlement or vengeance: *"I'm owed this."* Justifies sin through the lens of personal justice.
- **The Conceited One** – Believes they are above the rules; entitled to more than others, regardless of cost.
- **The Reverser** – Calls good evil and evil good; sees theft as clever, necessary, or even righteous.
- **The Withholder** – A passive thief; refuses to give what's due— whether resources, love, or responsibility.

- **The Liar** – Partners with The Thief to conceal wrongdoing, fabricate justification, or manipulate outcomes.
- **The Shrinker** – Acts out of envy or inferiority; may sabotage others or steal opportunity as a way to "even the score."
- **The Faithless One** – Lacks trust in God's provision, leading to grasping, hoarding, or unethical shortcuts.
- **The Critic** – Dehumanizes others or institutions, making it easier to rationalize stealing from them.
- **The Splitter** – May live a double life—honest in one space, dishonest in another—with no true integration of integrity.

The Waster

Core Torment & Lie: Financial Foolishness

"Spend now, think later."

Gifts Under Attack:

- **Stewardship** – The Waster treats resources as disposable, undermining the responsibility to manage God's provision with care. *("Now it is required that those who have been given a trust must prove faithful." – 1 Corinthians 4:2)*
- **Wisdom** – It overrides discernment with impulse, replacing planning with emotional decision-making and regret. *("The wise store up choice food and olive oil, but fools gulp theirs down." – Proverbs 21:20)*
- **Self-Control** – It fuels compulsive spending, making it difficult to stick to limits or financial convictions. *("Like a city whose walls are broken through is a person who lacks self-control." – Proverbs 25:28)*
- **Foresight** – It ignores the future, creating avoidable hardship by rejecting prudence and preparation. *("Go to the ant... it stores its provisions in summer and gathers its food at harvest." – Proverbs 6:6–8)*
- **Contentment** – It convinces the heart that more will fix what's lacking, turning temporary desires into driving demands. *("I have*

learned the secret of being content in any and every situation..." –
Philippians 4:11–12)

The Waster is a spirit of financial sabotage through irresponsibility and short-sightedness. It drives compulsive spending, mismanagement of money, and a refusal to plan, save, or steward resources wisely. While Mammon obsesses over wealth and control, The Waster treats money as meaningless: a tool for instant gratification, emotional coping, or image maintenance.

This spirit often attaches generationally, especially in families where poverty, get-rich-quick mindsets, or financial denial were the norm. It leads to debt, instability, and constant cycles of lack—not because money isn't coming in, but because it's leaking out faster than it arrives.

Biblically, God's instruction is clear: be wise with your herds, your harvest, and your household. The Waster mocks that wisdom and ensures the future is always unstable.

Scripture references:

"Be sure you know the condition of your flocks, give careful attention to your herds... for riches do not endure forever." (Proverbs 27:23-24)

"Precious treasure and oil are in a wise man's dwelling,
but a foolish man devours it." (Proverbs 21:20)

"The plans of the diligent lead surely to abundance, but everyone who is hasty comes only to poverty." (Proverbs 21:5)

Common symptoms:

- No budgeting, planning, or savings—ever
- "Spending to feel better" mentality
- Constantly living paycheck to paycheck despite decent income
- Chronic overdrafts, impulse buys, or poor credit
- Resists financial advice, structure, or accountability
- Can't bear to assess finances or open related mail and statements

Real-life example:

Micah makes decent money freelancing, but he never has anything left over. Every paycheck disappears: meals out, Amazon carts, and little luxuries he "deserves." He's in credit card debt but won't sit down to make a budget.

He can't think of anything less appealing than opening his mail or facing his financial reality. If he did, he'd see it's not as bad as he fears. He's paying staggering interest rates on cards he barely understands, essentially doubling the cost of everything he buys. He rents furniture, uses "buy now, pay later" tools for things he doesn't need, and constantly orders food instead of cooking at home.

A few simple shifts—a spending freeze, paying off debt, living at or even below his means—would give him breathing room. Avoidance is expensive. If he tallied it all up, he'd realize he's one paycheck away from disaster... not because he's poor, but because he's misaligned. The Waster is quietly stealing his harvest and keeping him from the maturity and discipline required for the next level of blessing.

Solutions and declarations:

1. **"I reject financial foolishness and embrace godly stewardship."**
   "The wise store up choice food and olive oil, but fools gulp theirs down." (Proverbs 21:20)

2. **"I will not devour what God intends me to build with."**
   "Dishonest money dwindles away, but whoever gathers money little by little makes it grow." (Proverbs 13:11)

3. **"I break agreement with lack and the lie that planning doesn't matter."**
   "Suppose one of you wants to build a tower. Won't you first sit down and estimate the cost?" (Luke 14:28)

Turn to the index of deliverance prayers and go to:
Prayer 5: General Prayer for Lust of the Eyes

Prayer 6: Deliverance from Greed, Materialism & Vanity

Cross-references:

- **Mammon** – Fuels the love of money and lifestyle obsession; spending becomes a way to serve the false god of wealth.
- **The Pauper** – Operates on the other end of the same curse; swings between poverty mindset and reckless spending, often to self-soothe.
- **The Conceited One** – Spends impulsively to maintain status or image; sees financial stewardship as restrictive or boring.
- **The Curator** – Purchases driven by aesthetic and social perception; money is used to build an enviable image, not a stable life.
- **The Impatient One** – Demands gratification now, refusing to wait or save; views discipline as deprivation.
- **The Loop** – Often caught in cycles of overspending and regret; patterns repeat without ever learning from past mistakes.
- **The Shrinker** – Spends to self-medicate feelings of inferiority or failure; money becomes a momentary escape.
- **The Splitter** – Lives a double financial life—responsible in public, reckless in private—or vice versa.
- **The Orphan Spirit** – Struggles to feel secure or provided for, often overspending to feel "taken care of" or to fill emotional gaps.
- **The Faithless One** – Lacks trust that God will provide long-term, so spends impulsively as if the future is uncertain and God is absent.

The Conceited One

Core Torment & Lie: Vanity and Self-Worship

"Everyone should admire me."

Gifts Under Attack:

- **Humility** – The Conceited One demands admiration and visibility, rejecting the posture that invites God's favor. *("God opposes the proud but shows favor to the humble." – James 4:6)*
- **Authenticity** – It crafts a false persona to gain approval, masking the true self and disconnecting from honest relationship. *("Am I now trying to win the approval of human beings, or of God?" – Galatians 1:10)*
- **Servant-hearted Leadership** – It seeks status and recognition, forgetting that true greatness comes through serving others. *("Whoever wants to become great among you must be your servant..." – Mark 10:43–44)*
- **Teachability** – It resists correction and assumes superiority, blocking growth and wisdom. *("Whoever loves discipline loves knowledge, but whoever hates correction is stupid." – Proverbs 12:1)*

The Conceited One wants more than attention; it demands worship. It builds a throne out of compliments and expects others to kneel. This spirit curates every detail of appearance, conversation, and image to ensure constant validation. It isn't content with being admired; it must be envied. Every relationship becomes a mirror, and every room a stage. Underneath this inflated self-image is a fragile identity terrified of being ordinary, unseen, or unimpressive. The Conceited One often believes its own hype, reciting praise like gospel and reacting with rage or withdrawal when others fail to comply. What looks like confidence is insecurity dressed in gold. God exalts the humble, and this spirit exalts itself, always collapsing when the applause fades.

Scripture References:

"If anyone thinks he is something when he is nothing,
he deceives himself." (Galatians 6:3)

"Pride goes before destruction, and a haughty
spirit before a fall." (Proverbs 16:18)

"Do not think of yourself more highly than you ought." (Romans 12:3)

Common Symptoms:

- Obsession with appearance, image, or reputation
- Constant need to prove yourself or be praised
- Disdain for correction or criticism
- Social media fixation or follower addiction
- Comparison that leads to superiority, not shame

Real-Life Example:

Marla wasn't the best stylist in the salon—not by skill, not by warmth, and not by client loyalty. But The Conceited One gave her a powerful presence. She walked through the salon like she owned it, with an air of superiority that silenced correction and drew fearful admiration. Her voice was the loudest, her opinions the final word. She mocked, dismissed, and manipulated through passive aggression and performance, and for a while, it worked. The other stylists didn't admire her, but they didn't dare cross her either. They feared the backlash more than they valued the truth.

Then came Daisy, the new shampoo girl.

She was young, quiet, and respectful, but something in her spirit didn't bow. Daisy didn't fawn, flatter, or fold under pressure. She carried peace, discernment, and a kind of humility that refused to be intimidated. She didn't confront Marla, but she didn't play along either. She simply stood firm in who she was and the spirit on Marla *felt it.*

Daisy was a believer anchored in God. The atmosphere at the salon began to shift because of her presence. One by one, the other stylists began to see through Marla's performance. They stopped laughing at cruel jokes. They stopped shrinking back. Some even started speaking truth—gently, but clearly.

Marla didn't lose her grip because of Daisy's poise. She lost it because God doesn't share thrones, and the spirit of conceit can't stand where truth, humility, and quiet spiritual authority take root.

Marla still tried to perform, but without applause, it fell flat. Her power was undone by light.

Solutions and Declarations:

1. **I decrease so Christ can increase—my life is not about being admired but about exalting Him.**
   "He must increase, but I must decrease." (John 3:30)

2. **My worth is rooted in God, not applause—I live for His approval, not the crowd's.**
   "For am I now seeking the approval of man, or of God? Or am I trying to please man? If I were still trying to please man, I would not be a servant of Christ." (Galatians 1:10)

3. **I welcome correction—it humbles and refines me.**
   "Whoever loves discipline loves knowledge, but he who hates reproof is stupid." (Proverbs 12:1)

Turn to the Index of Deliverance Prayers and go to:

Prayer 5: General Prayer for Lust of the Eyes
Prayer 6: Deliverance from Greed, Materialism & Vanity

Cross-References:

- **The Idolator** – Exalts self-image, achievements, or status into a false god; obsessed with being admired.
- **The False Mirror** – Builds identity on appearance, perception, or applause, rather than truth or character.
- **The Critic** – Looks down on others to elevate the self; pride masks deep insecurity or fragility.

- **The Curator** – Lives for aesthetic control and external validation; values beauty over authenticity.
- **The Player** – Uses charm and ego to manipulate others; relational conquest becomes a form of self-worship.
- **The Withholder** – Refuses to give time, affection, or vulnerability unless it benefits or flatters them.
- **The Shrinker** – Interestingly connected through contrast; conceit can arise as overcompensation for hidden inferiority.
- **The Pretender** – Projects a curated self that must always appear successful, special, or superior—even at great cost.
- **The Reverser** – Twists humility into weakness and pride into strength; sees self-glorification as confidence.
- **Mammon** – May flaunt wealth or status as proof of value; spends not from need, but from a need to be seen.

The Pauper

Core Torment & Lie: The Curse of Lack

"I'll never have enough."

Gifts Under Attack:

- **Provision** – The Pauper lies about God's nature, whispering that He won't come through *("My God will supply all your needs..." – Philippians 4:19).*
- **Stewardship** – It distorts finances, leading to hoarding, overspending, or self-sabotage *("He who loves pleasure will become poor..." – Proverbs 21:17).*
- **Generosity** – It prevents people from giving freely by stirring fear of lack *("The generous will prosper..." – Proverbs 11:25).*
- **Inheritance** – It blinds people to the spiritual and earthly wealth **God** intends for His children *("The wealth of the wicked is stored up for the righteous." – Proverbs 13:22).*

The Pauper is a scarcity mindset that's not limited to income. This spirit convinces people that poverty is their identity, inheritance, or destiny. Often rooted in generational curses, traumatic financial loss, or rejection, The Pauper thrives on survivalism and lack.

People bound by this spirit fear both wealth and poverty. They may sabotage jobs, avoid tithing, overspend to cope, or live in shame for any comfort they manage to obtain. This demon uses anxiety to corrupt their relationship with money as well as with God.

Scripture References:

"You will be cursed in the city and cursed in the country... The fruit of your womb will be cursed..." (Deuteronomy 28:16–18)

"The blessing of the Lord brings wealth, without painful toil for it." (Proverbs 10:22)

"The Lord will open the heavens... to bless all the work of your hands." (Deuteronomy 28:12)

Common Symptoms:

- Self-sabotage after financial breakthrough
- Guilt over having "too much"
- Constant fear of losing everything
- Inability to tithe or give freely
- Poverty mindset despite evidence of success

Real-Life Example:

Jerry didn't tell anyone in his family how much money he made. He kept up a modest appearance, never buying new clothes or anything that might hint he was doing well. He wore the same button-down shirt for every Zoom meeting and lived off microwave noodles like he did in college. His refrigerator was nearly empty, not because he couldn't afford to fill it, but because something deep inside told him he shouldn't. Everything seemed like a waste.

Even with a six-figure remote job at a successful company, Jerry couldn't shake the panic around money. His boss would've gladly mentored him—taught him how to invest, budget, or plan ahead—but Jerry avoided money talk like it was toxic. He had spent his entire childhood hiding his poverty, and now, even though it was technically gone, the shame and fear remained.

When asked to travel for work, Jerry froze. He didn't own a suitcase. His shoes were worn through. He had nothing to wear, and instead of simply buying what he needed, which he could easily afford, he made up an excuse and declined the trip. He wasn't lazy, he was afraid. He couldn't explain why, but something in him refused to cross that line. He feared exposure, or worse, the guilt of wasting money.

Jerry's great-grandparents survived the Great Depression, and that survival mentality had trickled down like a silent curse. His parents struggled too—utility shut-offs, empty fridges, no extras—and Jerry grew up internalizing the idea that there would never be enough. The Pauper whispered that provision was temporary and undeserved.

Even when Jerry saved up for something he wanted, he'd either talk himself out of buying it or spend the money impulsively and spiral into regret. He didn't tithe—he feared it would drain what little he had. He didn't ask for help—he feared looking foolish. He didn't enjoy his blessings—he feared they wouldn't last.

Poverty was in his past, but The Pauper convinced him it was also his future.

Solutions & Declarations:

1. **I am not under the curse of lack. I am under the blessing of Abraham.**
   "Christ redeemed us from the curse of the law... so that the blessing given to Abraham might come to the Gentiles." (Galatians 3:13–14)

2. **I am blessed and will be a blessing.**
   "The Lord will bless you... and you will lend to many but borrow from none." (Deuteronomy 28:12)

3. **I trust God as my Provider.**
"The Lord is my Shepherd; I shall not want." (Psalm 23:1)

Turn to the Index of Deliverance Prayers and go to:
Prayer 5: General Prayer for Lust of the Eyes
Prayer 6: Deliverance from Greed, Materialism & Vanity
Supplemental Prayers: 22, 27, 34

Cross-References:

- **Mammon** – While Mammon exalts money as a god, The Pauper believes money will always be out of reach. Both distort the purpose of provision and plant fear around wealth—either through obsession or avoidance.
- **The Waster** – Encourages financial foolishness that keeps the cycle of poverty alive. Even when income increases, The Waster ensures that resources are squandered and shame remains.
- **The Orphan** – Whispering, *"No one is coming to help,"* this spirit reinforces a survival mindset. It feeds the Pauper's belief that provision must be hoarded or avoided because trust leads to pain.
- **The Wanderer** – Rooted in rejection and instability, this spirit keeps people constantly shifting—geographically, relationally, or financially—never allowing them to settle long enough to build or steward well.
- **The Collector** – The flip side of the same coin. The Collector may hoard possessions as proof of worth, while The Pauper avoids spending altogether. Both are enslaved by fear, not stewardship.
- **The Rejector** – Fuels internalized shame that says, *"You don't deserve abundance."* This spirit keeps people trapped in cycles of lack by convincing them their identity is tied to poverty.
- **Lazybones** – When financial hardship leads to hopelessness or paralysis, Lazybones ensures no progress is made. The lack of movement then becomes self-fulfilling prophecy.

- **The Critic** – Shames every financial misstep, keeping the individual in a cycle of inaction or overcorrection. Growth becomes impossible under constant internal criticism.

~ * * * ~

Envy is the rot that poisons contentment. Comparison distorts identity. And discord is its harvest. This trio of demons works subtly and systemically, saying, *"you're behind," "you deserve more,"* or *"they don't deserve that."* What begins as a passing glance soon festers into jealousy, competition, gossip, and sabotage. These spirits turn allies into rivals and rob us of gratitude for our own portion. Scripture warns that *"where envy and self-seeking exist, confusion and every evil thing are there"* (James 3:16). These demons know that if they can get you to resent what someone else has, they can blind you to what God has already given you.

Envy, Comparison & Discord

30. **The Jealous One** – Jealousy. "If they have it, I've lost it."

31. **The Monitor** – Envious Surveillance. "They don't deserve that. I should be the one."

32. **The Bitter One** – Resentment. "I was wronged and should stay angry."

33. **The Sower of Strife** – Division. "Stir the pot, don't let it settle."

34. **The Mouth** – The Uncontrolled Tongue. "If I feel it, I'll say it."

The Jealous One

Core Torment & Lie: Jealousy

"If they have it, I've lost it."

Gifts Under Attack:

- **Contentment** – The Jealous One poisons the heart with dissatisfaction, making it impossible to rest in what God has already provided. *("But godliness with contentment is great gain." – 1 Timothy 6:6)*

- **Gratitude** – It shifts the eyes from blessings to perceived lack, blinding the soul to God's goodness. *("Give thanks in all circumstances; for this is God's will for you..." – 1 Thessalonians 5:18)*
- **Joy** – It kills joy by forcing constant comparison, turning others' success into a personal loss. *("Rejoice with those who rejoice..." – Romans 12:15)*
- **Love** – It corrupts the ability to love purely, replacing connection with competition. *("Love is patient, love is kind. It does not envy..." – 1 Corinthians 13:4)*
- **Identity** – It convinces the heart that worth is measured by achievements, not by God's unique design and calling. *("We are God's workmanship, created in Christ Jesus to do good works..." – Ephesians 2:10)*

Jealousy is a demonic force that devours peace, warps perception, and destroys relationships. In scripture, jealousy drove Cain to murder, Saul to madness, and Joseph's brothers to betrayal. It convinces the host that someone else's success, love, favor, or attention is a threat. It thrives in a zero-sum mindset: if they have more, you must have less. You can't win unless they lose.

Unlike simple envy, jealousy contains a deep desire to take what another has or to see them lose it. It divides families, churches, and even nations. It often operates quietly at first, hidden behind passive aggression, silent competition, or feigned support. Its fruit is bitterness, sabotage, and spiritual rot.

Scripture references:

> *"Wrath is cruel, and anger is outrageous; but who is able to stand before jealousy?" (Proverbs 27:4)*

> *"For he was jealous of his brother... and killed him." (Genesis 4:8, paraphrased)*

"Saul was very angry... 'They credit David with ten thousands...' And from that time on, Saul kept a jealous eye on David." (1 Samuel 18:8-9)

"Where jealousy and selfish ambition exist, there is disorder and every evil thing." (James 3:16)

Common symptoms:

- Seething at others' success or happiness
- Secret competition with peers or family
- Overidentification with rejection or being "overlooked"
- Criticizing or undermining others' gifts or influence
- Difficulty celebrating others without comparison

Real-life example:

Tina is the sister of Dina, who was discovered on the street by a modeling scout and skyrocketed to fame. Dina just walked for every top designer at Paris Fashion Week and has millions of followers who adore her down-to-earth charm and behind-the-scenes content. She's become a global sensation—and Tina can't seem to escape it.

Whenever someone sees Tina, they gush about Dina. *"You must be so proud! You two look alike!"* they say. Tina knows they don't. Dina is the only pale-skinned redhead in the family, while the rest, including Tina, have dark hair and olive skin. That one twist of genetics feels like a cruel joke. Tina hears the comparisons and feels invisible.

It's not that Tina doesn't love her sister—she does. But every accomplishment she considers feels small next to Dina's success. She's afraid to dream because nothing could ever shine that bright. To make matters worse, Dina has offered to pay for anything Tina wants to pursue: school, travel, starting a business. She means well, but it makes Tina feel like a dependent shadow.

Tina's not just jealous of Dina. When friends get engaged, land promotions, or hit milestones, she claps and congratulates them—but inside, it stings. Later, she scrolls through their photos, picking them apart in her head, wondering why life always seems to bless everyone else. She doesn't realize it's The Jealous One speaking. Slowly, her relationships weaken. Her joy evaporates. Even when blessings come her way, they're hard to receive because she's still measuring her portion against someone else's.

Solutions and declarations:

1. **What God has for me is mine—no one can take it.**
   "For the Lord of hosts has purposed, and who will annul it? His hand is stretched out, and who will turn it back?" (Isaiah 14:27)

2. **I bless others without comparison, knowing God's storehouse has no shortage.**
   "And my God will supply every need of yours according to his riches in glory in Christ Jesus." (Philippians 4:19)

3. **I renounce the lie that someone else's gain is my loss.**
   "Rejoice with those who rejoice, weep with those who weep." (Romans 12:15)

Turn to the index of deliverance prayers and go to:

Prayer 5: General Prayer for Lust of the Eyes
Prayer 7: Deliverance from Envy, Comparison & Discord
Supplemental Prayers: 16, 25

Cross-references:

- **The Idolator** – Jealousy often comes from elevating others' lives to idol status, believing their success defines your worth.
- **The Broken Mirror** – Self-image is distorted through comparison, feeding insecurity and reinforcing the lie that you're not enough.
- **The Critic** – Jealousy fuels hyper-criticism of others, picking them apart to soothe one's own wounded pride.
- **Sibling Rivalry** – Jealousy between siblings is often generational, deeply rooted in favoritism, unmet needs, or identity confusion.
- **The Saboteur** – Jealousy can lead to self-sabotage, making it difficult to receive or sustain blessings without comparison poisoning them.

- **The Monitor** – Jealousy obsessively watches others, not to celebrate them, but to find flaws or stay ahead.
- **The Gossip** – Jealousy often manifests through subtle or outright slander, damaging relationships and fueling division.

The Monitor

Core Torment & Lie: Envious Surveillance

"They don't deserve that. I should be the one."

Gifts Under Attack:

- **Contentment** – The Monitor constantly compares your life to others', making peace with your portion feel like settling for less. *("I have learned the secret of being content in any and every situation..." – Philippians 4:11–12)*
- **Trust in God's Justice** – It whispers that God's distribution of blessing is unfair, stirring quiet rebellion against His sovereignty. *("But who are you, a human being, to talk back to God?..." – Romans 9:20–21)*
- **Peace of Mind** – It fills your thoughts with envy and fixation, disrupting rest and spiritual stillness. *("You will keep in perfect peace those whose minds are steadfast, because they trust in you." – Isaiah 26:3)*
- **Focus** – It steals your attention from your own race, making you chase someone else's calling or outcome. *("Let us run with perseverance the race marked out for us, fixing our eyes on Jesus..." – Hebrews 12:1–2)*
- **Gratitude** – It blinds you to your own blessings by magnifying others', fostering chronic dissatisfaction. *("Give thanks in all circumstances; for this is God's will for you..." – 1 Thessalonians 5:18)*

The Monitor is a spirit of obsessive watching, comparison, and spiritual surveillance. It manifests through social media addiction, stalking behaviors, fixation on the lives and decisions of others, and even spiritual mimicry. While it may feel like curiosity or concern, it's often rooted in envy, insecurity, control, and fear.

Biblically, this spirit echoes familiar spirits and watchers: entities that track movements, mimic behaviors, and use information as leverage. In modern terms, it thrives on Instagram stories, page refreshes, and silent monitoring of people's lives without ever engaging in real relationship. It can also operate through others who are demonically assigned to monitor you, gathering intel to feed sabotage or accusation.

Scripture references:

> *"They watched Him closely to see if He would heal on the Sabbath, so they could accuse Him." (Mark 3:2)*

> *"Once when we were going to the place of prayer, we were met by a female slave who had a spirit of divination... she followed Paul..." (Acts 16:16-17)*

> *"Do not fret because of evildoers... they will soon fade like the grass."*

> *(Psalm 37:1-2 — speaks to obsessing over others)*

Common symptoms:

- Constantly checking other people's updates, stories, or movements
- Feels invisible but obsessively watches others' success or failure
- Obsession with exes, enemies, or rivals
- Stalking or "keeping tabs" on others from a distance
- Paranoid belief that others are doing the same to them

Real-life example:

Naomi hasn't been with her ex in over three years, but you wouldn't know it by her search history. She knows every girl he's dated since: where they went to school, where they work, and who their friends are. He just got engaged, and Naomi has already found every photo the new fiancé has ever posted, going back to middle school. She's read her blog, scrolled her comments, and deep-dived her family's online presence. It's not just him; Naomi watches old friends, influencers, even strangers she envies. She calls it curiosity, but it's not. It's torment. She rarely posts, but she's online constantly. Her mind is cluttered, her sleep is poor, and her spirit feels dry. What she doesn't realize is that The Monitor has turned her life into a full-time surveillance mission. And every hour spent watching someone else is time stolen from her own purpose.

Solutions and declarations:

1. **"I break agreement with the need to track what others are doing."**
   "Each one should test their own actions. Then they can take pride in themselves alone, without comparing themselves to someone else." (Galatians 6:4)

2. **"My focus is not behind me, beside me, or above me—it's forward."**
   "Forgetting what is behind and straining toward what is ahead, I press on toward the goal..." (Philippians 3:13–14)

3. **"I close every door that allows spiritual watchers to monitor or accuse me."**
   "No weapon formed against you shall prosper, and every tongue which rises against you in judgment you shall condemn." (Isaiah 54:17)

Turn to the index of deliverance prayers and go to:

Prayer 5: General Prayer for Lust of the Eyes
Prayer 7: Deliverance from Envy, Comparison & Discord
Supplemental Prayers: 16, 20, 23

Cross-references:

- **The Idolator** – Feeds comparison by elevating others as the standard of success, turning admiration into obsession.
- **The Broken Mirror** – Breeds envy through self-rejection, causing people to measure their worth by others.

- **The Guard** – Fuels hypervigilance, scanning others for threat or betrayal to avoid future pain.
- **The Gatekeeper** – Monitors others not to learn or grow, but to accuse and maintain control.
- **The Loop** – Entraps through digital fixation, using endless scrolling and story-checking as a counterfeit connection.

The Bitter One
Core Torment & Lie: Resentment.
"I was wronged and should stay angry."
Gifts under attack:

- **Joy** – The Bitter One drains gladness from the heart, turning even joyful moments into reminders of pain and offense. *("See to it that no one falls short of the grace of God and that no bitter root grows up to cause trouble and defile many." – Hebrews 12:15)*
- **Healing** – It keeps emotional and spiritual wounds open by replaying offenses and fueling anger. *("But I will restore you to health and heal your wounds, declares the Lord..." – Jeremiah 30:17)*
- **Forgiveness** – It blocks the ability to release others, hardening the heart and choking off mercy. *("But if you do not forgive others their sins, your Father will not forgive your sins." – Matthew 6:15)*
- **Relational Harmony** – It infects interactions with suspicion and tension, turning healthy relationships toxic. *("Get rid of all bitterness... be kind and compassionate to one another, forgiving each other..." – Ephesians 4:31–32)*
- **Spiritual Growth** – It keeps you chained to past pain, preventing forward movement and deepening in Christ. *("If you harbor bitter envy and selfish ambition... such 'wisdom' does not come down from heaven..." – James 3:14–15)*

Bitterness is poison. The Bitter One festers in the soul after unresolved hurt, betrayal, or injustice. It rewrites your memory, recasts your identity as a victim, and resists all attempts to heal. The longer it lives, the more it warps your worldview. Bitterness convinces you that being angry is being strong, that being closed off is being wise, and that your pain is power, but in truth, bitterness is decay. The Bible warns us to "watch out" for the root of bitterness, because it defiles not just you, but many others *(Hebrews 12:15)*. It spreads like mold: invisible at first, deadly if left unchecked.

Scripture references:

> *"...a root of bitterness springing up causes trouble, and by it many become defiled." (Hebrews 12:15)*

> *"Let all bitterness and wrath and anger... be put away from you." (Ephesians 4:31)*

> *"I see you are full of bitterness and captive to sin." (Acts 8:23)*

Common symptoms:

- Chronic negativity, sarcasm, or coldness
- Rejection of joy or celebration in others
- "Victim identity" mindset
- Suspicion toward those who try to help
- Physical symptoms: tension, fatigue, migraines

Real-life example:

Woody and Chris were more than business partners—they were childhood best friends who grew up dreaming of launching their own design-build firm. Woody handled the creative side as the lead designer, while Chris managed the contracting and finances. Woody trusted him completely. He never questioned the numbers, the change orders, or the deposits. The business looked like it was thriving.

But underneath it all, Chris was stealing: padding the payroll, mismanaging funds, and cooking the books to drain the company's accounts. By the time Woody uncovered the truth, the damage was done. Chris disappeared with everything, avoided prosecution, and re-emerged under a new business name, spinning a lie that Woody was the reason they split.

Woody lost everything: his company, his dream, and his trust. He eventually took a quiet office job, but he never got over it. The betrayal hollowed him out. Even years later, the bitterness lingered like smoke, poisoning his view of people, partnerships, and even God. The Bitter One planted itself deep, and every time Woody replayed what happened, it took root again.

Solutions and declarations:

1. **I uproot bitterness by the power of the cross.**
   "See to it that no one fails to obtain the grace of God; that no 'root of bitterness' springs up and causes trouble, and by it many become defiled." (Hebrews 12:15)

2. **My pain does not have the final word—God's love does.**
   "And we know that for those who love God all things work together for good, for those who are called according to his purpose." (Romans 8:28)

3. **I break every agreement I made with resentment.**
   "Let all bitterness and wrath and anger and clamor and slander be put away from you, along with all malice." (Ephesians 4:31)

Turn to the index of deliverance prayers, and go to:

Prayer 5: General Prayer for Lust of the Eyes
Prayer 7: Deliverance from Envy, Comparison & Discord
Supplemental Prayers: 16, 20, 34

Cross references:

- **The Chainkeeper** – Keeps wounds fresh by refusing to forgive, creating fertile ground for bitterness.
- **The Abyss** – Deepens the despair and emotional toxicity that allows bitterness to root.

- **The Critic** – Projects inward pain onto others as judgment or harshness.
- **The Desperate** – Feeds bitterness by obsessing over being unloved or rejected again.
- **The Avenger** – Transforms bitterness into the desire for punishment or revenge.

The Sower of Strife
Core Torment & Lie: Division.
"Stir the pot and don't let it settle."
Gifts under attack:

- **Unity** – The Sower of Strife thrives on division, tearing apart what God has joined and opposing the harmony of the Body. *("Make every effort to keep the unity of the Spirit through the bond of peace." – Ephesians 4:3)*
- **Peace** – It floods environments with drama and disorder, disrupting the peace Jesus promised His followers. *("Peace I leave with you; my peace I give you... Do not let your hearts be troubled..." – John 14:27)*
- **Humility** – Strife often stems from pride, making mutual submission and servant-hearted love feel like weakness. *("Do nothing out of selfish ambition or vain conceit. Rather, in humility value others above yourselves." – Philippians 2:3)*
- **Reconciliation** – It resists healing by keeping offenses alive and spreading distrust, opposing the calling to restore and forgive. *("God... gave us the ministry of reconciliation." – 2 Corinthians 5:18)*
- **Wisdom** – It exposes a heart ruled by selfish ambition, blocking the peaceable, Spirit-led wisdom from above. *("For where you have envy and selfish ambition, there you find disorder and every evil practice." – James 3:16)*

The Sower of Strife is a spirit that delights in drama, discord, and division. It plants seeds of conflict where none existed, whispers suspicions into open hearts, and turns minor offenses into major wars. Scripture warns repeatedly against those who stir up strife, because where strife is present, demonic confusion and chaos follow *(James 3:16)*. This spirit fractures churches, destroys families, and pits believers against each other in subtle, often righteous-sounding ways. It commonly hides behind the mask of "concern," "discernment," or "standing for truth," but its true assignment is to disrupt the unity of the Body and dismantle relationships from within.

Scripture references:

> *"There are six things the Lord hates… one who sows discord among brothers." (Proverbs 6:16–19)*

> *"Where there is no wood, the fire goes out; and where there is no talebearer, strife ceases." (Proverbs 26:20)*

> *"For where envy and strife are, there is confusion and every evil work." (James 3:16)*

Common symptoms:

- Instigating or escalating conflict
- Gossip disguised as "prayer requests" or concern
- Triangulating relationships (pitting people against each other)
- Constant tension in their presence
- Reluctance to take accountability

Real-life example:

At a small church in Mississippi, a woman named Darlene began noticing "little things" she didn't like about the new worship leader. She told herself she was just being spiritually discerning, but the truth was Darlene had secretly hoped to be chosen for the role herself. In fact, she wanted far more than the platform. She had long imagined herself behind the pulpit. She believed she carried an anointing no one else recognized, and the new leader—a woman close to her own age and life stage—felt like a personal insult.

From the outside, Darlene appeared supportive. Behind the scenes, she worked subtly, dropping comments cloaked as concern: *"Pray for her... she's still learning,"* or *"I just don't know if she's spiritually strong enough to lead."* She floated doubts to trusted ears, always positioning herself as "just looking out for the church."

Within weeks, a narrative took hold. Whispers circulated that the worship leader was emotionally unstable, power-hungry, and spiritually unfit. None of it was true, but the atmosphere became so toxic that the new leader, who had relocated her family for the position, stepped down. She took the financial loss, the emotional blow, and quietly moved on.

Darlene never lifted a public finger. But The Sower of Strife used her tongue—and her pride—as a weapon against unity. The spirit of Jezebel, cloaked in false concern, had gotten its way again.

Solutions and declarations:

1. **I reject the spirit of division. I will pursue peace.**
   "If possible, so far as it depends on you, live peaceably with all." *(Romans 12:18)*

2. **I will not be used to stir conflict. I will sow harmony.**
   "Blessed are the peacemakers, for they shall be called sons of God." *(Matthew 5:9)*

3. **I repent of every word that planted confusion instead of truth.**
   "When words are many, transgression is not lacking, but whoever restrains his lips is prudent." *(Proverbs 10:19)*

Turn to the index of deliverance prayers, and go to:

Prayer 5: General Prayer for Lust of the Eyes
Prayer 7: Deliverance from Envy, Comparison & Discord
Supplemental Prayers: 16, 18, 19

Cross references:

- **The Waffler** – Reinforces The Sower of Strife by creating confusion, overthinking, and fractured relationships.
- **The Mouth** – Weaponizes language to escalate conflict and turn speech into destruction.
- **The Critic** – Fuels division through superiority masked as helpful "correction."
- **The Doubter** – Erodes trust in leaders, friends, and spiritual guidance by planting seeds of suspicion.
- **Jezebel** – Uses manipulation and emotional fracture to divide alliances and stir rebellion.

The Mouth

Core Torment & Lie: The Uncontrolled Tongue

"If I feel it, I have to say it."

Gifts Under Attack:

- **Self-Control** – The Mouth overrides restraint, encouraging impulsive speech driven by emotion rather than wisdom. *("Fools give full vent to their rage, but the wise bring calm in the end." – Proverbs 29:11)*
- **Wisdom** – It replaces thoughtful silence with careless words, multiplying harm and diminishing discernment. *("Sin is not ended by multiplying words, but the prudent hold their tongues." – Proverbs 10:19)*
- **Peace** – It stirs conflict through gossip, sarcasm, and angry outbursts, disrupting both inner calm and relational harmony. *("A gentle answer turns away wrath, but a harsh word stirs up anger." – Proverbs 15:1)*
- **Honor** – It disrespects others and trivializes sacred things, using speech to demean rather than build up. *("With the tongue we praise our Lord and Father, and with it we curse human beings... this should not be." – James 3:9–10)*

- **Spiritual Authority** – A mouth that blesses and curses loses its credibility and power in the Spirit, as purity is required for authority. *("Can both fresh water and saltwater flow from the same spring?" – James 3:11)*

The Mouth is the spirit behind destructive speech: the compulsion to vent, curse, insult, exaggerate, gossip, or slander without restraint. It masquerades as honesty, passion, or humor, but leaves a trail of offense, division, and spiritual pollution. While The Litigator argues to win, The Mouth speaks without aim or accountability. It is impulsive, reactive, and often proud of its sharpness.

Scripture doesn't just warn that what we speak is powerful, it says, "Death and life are in the power of the tongue" *(Proverbs 18:21)*. Death comes first, and it's not accidental. In Hebrew writing, the order of words carries weight—the first mention establishes dominance. We speak death more easily, more often, and with more lasting damage than we realize. Destruction is faster than healing. Tearing down takes seconds. Rebuilding takes years.

This demon actively invites spiritual consequence. Entire families, churches, and reputations have been wrecked by an untamed tongue. The Mouth opens the door, and death walks through it first.

Scripture references:

"The tongue is a fire, a world of unrighteousness... it sets on fire the course of life and is set on fire by hell." (James 3:6)

"Death and life are in the power of the tongue." (Proverbs 18:21)

"Those who guard their mouths preserve their lives, but those who open wide their lips come to ruin." (Proverbs 13:3)

"Whoever keeps his mouth and his tongue keeps himself out of trouble." (Proverbs 21:23)

Common symptoms:

- Always "saying it like it is," regardless of impact
- Cursing self or others out of frustration or habit

- Spreading gossip or "prayer requests" that are really slander
- Emotional outbursts that leave behind regret
- Constant apologies for "just having a big mouth"

Real-life example:

Jared always had a quick tongue. He said what others were thinking and more. Jokes, complaints, insults—he let them fly, often to laughs. But over time, people distanced themselves. His marriage grew cold. His reputation shrank. Every time he spoke, he felt in control until he saw how much damage his "honesty" had caused. The Mouth wasn't just his personality. It was a spirit that fed on recklessness and kept him from true intimacy, favor, and peace.

Solutions and declarations:

1. **My tongue is not a weapon of the flesh—it belongs to God.**
   "With it we bless our Lord and Father, and with it we curse people who are made in the likeness of God. From the same mouth come blessing and cursing. My brothers, these things ought not to be so." (James 3:9–10)

2. **I will not use my words to curse, tear down, or self-sabotage.**
   "Let no corrupting talk come out of your mouths, but only such as is good for building up, as fits the occasion, that it may give grace to those who hear." (Ephesians 4:29)

3. **I speak life, not death—truth, not destruction.**
   "Death and life are in the power of the tongue, and those who love it will eat its fruits." (Proverbs 18:21)

Turn to the index of deliverance prayers and go to:

Prayer 5: General Prayer for Lust of the Eyes
Prayer 7: Deliverance from Envy, Comparison & Discord
Supplemental Prayer: 16, 19

Cross-references:

- **The Critic** – Destroys with opinions masked as insight, turning speech into subtle weapons of judgment.
- **The Litigator** – Argues with intent to win, where The Mouth lashes out impulsively without aim or accountability.
- **The Saboteur** – Speaks doom and failure over self, reinforcing cycles of limitation and defeat.
- **The Abyss** – Fuels outbursts rooted in unhealed wounds, where pain leaks out as verbal aggression.
- **The Guard** – Uses overreaction and harsh speech as a shield against deeper emotional vulnerability.

Not all darkness comes cloaked in fear; some comes disguised as light.

These demons lure people in with the promise of power, peace, healing, or "higher consciousness." Beneath the surface lies spiritual bondage. From worldly manifestation to mysticism, psychic phenomena to New Age philosophy, these spirits use ancient tactics in modern packaging. They speak the language of empowerment, but their true goal is to pull people further from the truth of Christ.

False illumination is not harmless curiosity. It is a counterfeit light that blinds people to the real one. These spirits often masquerade as guides, teachers, or "truth-bringers." But what they offer is knowledge apart from God—a direct echo of Eden.

In this chapter, you'll meet the spirits behind today's most seductive spiritual traps:

False Illumination & Occult Influence

35. **The Arcane One** – Occult, Witchcraft, Sorcery. "This is ancient wisdom. You just don't understand."

36. **The Guru** – False Teaching & Authority. "I'll lead you to truth."

37. **The Enchanter** – New Age Counterfeits. "God, the Universe, whatever you want to call it, it's all the same."

38. **The Hypnotist** – Media Entrancement & Mind Control. "It's just entertainment."

39. **The AI Spirit** – Deception & Synthetic Knowledge. "It's just a tool."

40. **The Alien Deceiver** – False Revelation. "They're here to help us evolve."

41. **The Manifester** – Manifestation Without God. "You don't need God – speak it into existence yourself."

42. **The Gatekeeper** – Spiritual Elitism & Religious Gatekeeping. "I guard God from the unworthy."

43. **The Oracle** – Divination & False Revelation. "You need to know the future to feel safe."

44. **The Apostate** – Spiritual Abandonment & Rejection of Truth. "I've outgrown God. Truth is subjective."

The Arcane One

Core Torment & Lie: Occult, Witchcraft, Sorcery.

"This is ancient wisdom. You just don't understand."

Gifts Under Attack:

- **Discernment** – The Arcane One clouds spiritual clarity by dressing deception in mystery, seducing believers with what appears enlightened but is counterfeit. *("Dear friends, do not believe every spirit, but test the spirits to see whether they are from God..." – 1 John 4:1)*
- **Humility** – It feeds pride in "secret knowledge" or elite revelation, replacing childlike faith with spiritual superiority. *("Knowledge puffs up, but love builds up." – 1 Corinthians 8:1)*

- **Intimacy with God** – It replaces relational faith with ritualistic formulas, trading trust in the Father for dependence on mystical systems. *("But I am afraid... that your minds may somehow be led astray from your sincere and pure devotion to Christ." – 2 Corinthians 11:3)*
- **Sound Doctrine** – It blends truth with error, introducing subtle heresies that lead to spiritual confusion and departure from biblical teaching. *("The Spirit clearly says that in later times some will abandon the faith and follow deceiving spirits..." – 1 Timothy 4:1)*
- **Dependence on the Holy Spirit** – It shifts reliance from God's voice to symbols, methods, or rituals, counterfeiting true spiritual guidance. *("When he, the Spirit of truth, comes, he will guide you into all the truth..." – John 16:13)*

The Arcane One is the principality behind witchcraft, mysticism, and occult seduction. It draws people in with mystery, hidden knowledge, and power, but the cost is their soul. This demon mimics enlightenment but leads straight into spiritual enslavement. It offers rituals, symbols, "energies," and ancestral magic, all under the guise of healing, power, or divine feminine wisdom. But make no mistake: this is witchcraft, and God calls it abomination.

In the Bible, all forms of sorcery—whether "light" or "dark"—are condemned. There is no such thing as harmless witchcraft. Whether you're casting hexes or lighting manifestation candles on a new moon, you're inviting spiritual beings that do not come from God. The Arcane One flatters the ego and bypasses the Cross. It appears as wisdom but always leads to deeper confusion, oppression, and often mental torment.

Many of these practices are promoted as cultural, ancestral, or even therapeutic. But God doesn't categorize witchcraft; He condemns it in all forms. This is the ancient sorcery of Babylon, now dressed up as self-care, and it opens doors that only repentance and the blood of Jesus can close.

This is the same deception from Eden: *"You will be like God..."* (Genesis 3:5). It never left. It just changed form.

Scripture Reference:

> *"Do not turn to mediums or seek out spiritists, for you will be defiled by them." (Leviticus 19:31)*

> *"I will cut off sorceries from your hand, and you shall have no more tellers of fortunes." (Micah 5:12)*

> *"The works of the flesh are... idolatry and witchcraft." (Galatians 5:19–20)*

> *"Even Satan disguises himself as an angel of light." (2 Corinthians 11:14)*

Common Symptoms:

- Interest in astrology, tarot, crystals, moon rituals, or spirit guides
- Use of "white magic" or "protection spells" under the illusion it's healing or ancestral
- Claiming "Christ consciousness," "goddess energy," or "energy alignment" instead of Jesus
- Justifying witchcraft as harmless or natural
- Feeling spiritually powerful but increasingly mentally, emotionally, or physically disturbed

Real-Life Example:

Natalie was struggling to move on after a painful breakup. When she confided in a coworker, the woman suggested doing a "cleansing ritual" to let go of her ex. "It's not witchcraft," the friend said casually. "Just burn some things he gave you and sage the apartment. It'll help reset your energy." Desperate for closure, Natalie did exactly that—burned the items, smudged the rooms, and even played a special chant during the process. She felt strangely lighter afterward, as if something had been lifted.

Encouraged, she asked her friend if there were any other rituals that might help. The woman smiled and pulled a book from her desk drawer. It was filled with spells, moon cycles, energy work, and incantations. Natalie hesitated. "Isn't this witchcraft?" she asked.

"Witchcraft?" her friend scoffed. "No, this is *goddess energy*. It's older than religion. It's about plants, the moon, your ancestors. You've been taught to fear it because the Bible demonized women's power. That book is the reason for every war anyway."

Natalie took the book home. She was curious—what if there *was* something empowering about all this? That night, she tried a few more rituals, and for the first time in a while, she felt... something. A tingling, a stirring, maybe even power. She dove deeper: chakra work, ancestral meditations, moon ceremonies, energy healing, protective sigils. She told herself she was reconnecting with ancient wisdom, the "divine feminine" long suppressed by patriarchy and religion.

As the weeks passed, she stopped praying. Her Bible collected dust. She began having night terrors and bouts of confusion and dread. Her thoughts grew heavy, her spirit unsteady. The peace she thought she had gained turned to torment.

Eventually, Natalie came to a painful realization: this wasn't empowerment. It was spiritual entrapment—witchcraft dressed up in modern language. What started as curiosity opened a door to darkness. She didn't unlock ancient wisdom. She gave the Arcane One legal access to her life.

Solutions & Declarations:

1. **I renounce every ritual, spirit, and false light I welcomed through witchcraft.**
   "And a number of those who had practiced magic arts brought their books together and burned them in the sight of all." (Acts 19:19)

2. **I will not consult the dead, the stars, or my ancestors—I seek the living God alone.**
   "When someone tells you to consult mediums and spiritists, who whisper and mutter, should not a people inquire of their God? Why consult the dead on behalf of the living?" (Isaiah 8:19)

3. **Jesus is my light, my authority, and my only source of wisdom.**
   "The true light that gives light to everyone was coming into the world." (John 1:9)

Turn to the Index of Deliverance Prayers and go to:
Prayer 5: General Prayer for Lust of the Eyes
Prayer 8: Deliverance from False Illumination & Occult Influence
Supplemental Prayers: 15, 17, 18, 19, 24

Cross-References:

- **The Guru** – The Arcane One often introduces deceptive practices through seemingly wise teachers who claim to possess secret spiritual knowledge. These false guides position themselves as enlightened authorities, drawing seekers into deeper deception.
- **The Enchanter** – Partners through rituals, crystals, "energy work," and "white magic" that appear harmless or healing but open spiritual doors to bondage. Together, they seduce through the allure of naturalism and hidden power.
- **The Idolator** – Many who embrace arcane practices exalt goddesses, the moon, ancestors, or "the universe" as divine. The Arcane One works through spiritual idolatry that replaces the one true God with counterfeit deities.
- **The Broken Mirror** – People wounded by rejection or insecurity often turn to arcane systems for power and validation. The Arcane One exploits those who feel unseen or powerless by offering counterfeit identity and control.
- **The Liar** – All occult practices are built on lies that twist truth just enough to sound spiritual. The Arcane One works hand in hand with deception, cloaking rebellion in words like "intuition," "alignment," and "light."
- **The Apostate** – Those influenced by the Arcane One often drift from biblical truth and embrace spiritual rebellion masked as enlightenment. This spirit whispers, "You've outgrown the church," or "There's truth beyond the Bible."
- **The Hypnotist** – Supports altered states of consciousness through breathwork, meditation, psychedelics, or mantras, dulling discernment. The Arcane One opens the door, while The Hypnotist clouds the mind to keep it open.

- **The Monitor** – Occult curiosity often begins with obsession over signs, synchronicities, and spiritual "downloads." The Monitor feeds compulsive watching for messages and omens—drawing attention away from God's voice.

The Guru

Core Torment & Lie: False Teachings & Spiritual Authority

"I'll lead you to truth."

Gifts under attack:

- **Truth** – The Guru subtly twists scripture, using persuasive language to introduce charismatic error and spiritual confusion. *("There will be false teachers among you... secretly introducing destructive heresies..." – 2 Peter 2:1)*
- **Discernment** – It dulls spiritual sensitivity by training people to follow personalities and platforms instead of the voice of the Holy Spirit. *("By smooth talk and flattery, they deceive the minds of naive people." – Romans 16:18)*
- **Submission to God** – It diverts allegiance from Christ to man, fostering unhealthy spiritual dependence on leaders or influencers. *("Am I now trying to win the approval of human beings, or of God? ... If I were still trying to please people, I would not be a servant of Christ." – Galatians 1:10)*
- **Sound Doctrine** – It replaces biblical truth with feel-good messages, mystical trends, or so-called revelations that distort foundational theology. *("They will turn their ears away from the truth and turn aside to myths." – 2 Timothy 4:4)*
- **Humility** – It promotes spiritual elitism, convincing people they are more enlightened or advanced than others. *("Do not deceive yourselves. If any of you think you are wise by the standards of this age, you should become 'fools' so that you may become wise." – 1 Corinthians 3:18)*

The Guru is not always robed, smiling, or sitting on a mountaintop. Sometimes it wears yoga pants. Sometimes it holds a microphone at a self-help seminar. Sometimes it stands on a stage with a stadium of screaming fans.

This demon infiltrates through *false light*—a spirit of authority that displaces God. It offers teachings, healing, empowerment, and "personal breakthroughs," but always with one common thread: *you follow them, not Christ.* From ancient mystics to modern megastars, The Guru teaches that enlightenment can be found apart from the Word of God—and it offers a counterfeit path to transformation that requires total surrender to a human or spirit guide.

It shows up in places that appear completely non-religious:

- EST, Landmark Forum, NXIVM (a known cult) all operated under this spirit—using psychology, leadership, and self-actualization to create spiritual obedience to a man or method.
- Yoga and Eastern religion, though wildly normalized, are steeped in pagan worship. The poses themselves are offerings to Hindu gods—just like animal sacrifices or incense would be. Each god has traits, powers, and stories that perfectly mirror the Greek and Roman pantheons. These aren't different religions. They're the same fallen principalities, just renamed and repackaged for a new audience.

People reading this will be triggered, but the truth stands: you can't stretch your body in a position designed to honor a god and say it's just exercise. It doesn't matter how many millions of people do it or whether they know what they're doing is spiritual. The enemy just wants participation and agreement. This is not a cultural attack—it's a spiritual alert.

In the secular world The Guru often appears as a celebrity, a "thought leader," or a social media figure with a cult-like following. If their fans:

- Defend them at all costs
- Attack anyone who criticizes them
- Beg for their attention
- Give away money they don't have

- Mimic their every move and believe the leader "sees" or "rewards" their loyalty

That's not admiration. It's worship.

This is devotion that belongs to God being given to someone who doesn't know you, can't save you, and doesn't care about you. It often works hand-in-hand with The Idolator, creating a full-blown counterfeit religion built around a human image.

Scripture References:

"In their greed these teachers will exploit you with false words." (2 Peter 2:1–3)

"They exchanged the truth of God for a lie and worshiped and served created things." (Romans 1:25)

"You shall have no other gods before Me." (Exodus 20:3)

Common Symptoms:

- Obsession with self-help gurus, yogis, spiritual "mentors," or elite coaches
- Submitting to human "authority" over biblical truth
- Defending leaders even when they're clearly in error
- Using phrases like "universe," "alignment," "vibration," or "energy work"
- Belief that breakthrough or truth comes from a *method* instead of the Holy Spirit

Solutions & Declarations

1. **I reject the worship of wisdom that exalts itself above God.**
   "For the wisdom of this world is foolishness in God's sight." (1 Corinthians 3:19)

2. **I cast down every proud idea that sets itself against the knowledge of Christ.**

"We demolish arguments and every pretension that sets itself up against the knowledge of God, and we take captive every thought to make it obedient to Christ." (2 Corinthians 10:5)

3. **I humble myself before the Lord—His Spirit, not man's intellect, leads me into all truth.**
   "But when he, the Spirit of truth, comes, he will guide you into all the truth." (John 16:13)

Real Life Example:

Giselle is a cultural phenomenon unlike anything the world has seen. Her fame spans generations, yet her public persona is a calculated mystery. She rarely speaks, but she doesn't have to. Her albums are dissected like sacred texts by fans who treat her lyrics and visuals as coded spiritual revelation. Every move she makes is treated as divine choreography: her tours sell out instantly, her merchandise is priced astronomically, and still her followers spend recklessly just to feel "closer" to her.

Giselle's influence transcends music. She's viewed as the embodiment of "goddess energy," a blank slate that invites projection, idolization, and spiritual imitation. She invokes deities, chants names of goddesses in her songs, and saturates her performances in ritualistic and occult imagery, yet somehow retains a holy aura in popular culture. Even when irrefutable evidence surfaced that her pregnancy announcement was staged with a prosthetic, her followers dismissed it as nonsense. Her fans don't need logic—they need faith in Giselle.

The most sobering part? She is quoted from pulpits. Her lyrics are sung in churches. Mothers dress their toddlers like her. Despite clearly mocking biblical symbolism and showcasing satanic aesthetics, Giselle is the high priestess of a generation—soft-spoken, seductive, and utterly untouchable. This is the grip of The Guru: a spirit that leads people to worship the messenger, not the message, and bends truth into something fashionable, emotional, and false.

Turn to the Index of Deliverance Prayers and go to:

Prayer 5: General Prayer for Lust of the Eyes

Prayer 8: Deliverance from False Illumination & Occult Influence
Supplemental Prayers: 15, 17, 18, 19, 20, 24

Cross-References:

- **The Arcane One** – The Guru frequently points people toward "hidden" or "ancient" wisdom: energy work, astrology, goddess worship, or so-called divine feminine spirituality. The Arcane One provides the practices; The Guru provides the platform.
- **The Idolator** – This demon works alongside The Guru to elevate human figures to divine status. When people imitate, quote, or sacrifice for someone as if they were God, the Idolator is present and active.
- **The Masquerader** – The Guru rarely looks dangerous. This spirit cloaks itself in charisma, peace, beauty, and power—disguising its deception in aesthetics and performance. It lures through light, not darkness.
- **The Hypnotist** – The emotional high of following The Guru is part of the spell. The Hypnotist stirs awe, weeping, obsession, and loyalty—especially through music, movement, and mood.
- **The Narcissist** – In some cases, The Guru merges with this spirit, creating leaders who feed on praise and control others through their supposed "wisdom" or platform. What begins as inspiration becomes domination.
- **The Apostate** – Followers of The Guru often drift from biblical truth, trading God's authority for trendy spirituality. Many believe they are still "good with God" even while rejecting His Word entirely.
- **The Monitor** – Fans of The Guru track their every move—watching social media, interviews, and lyrics with obsessive scrutiny. The Monitor drives their devotion, ensuring they stay spiritually tied to their idol.
- **The Enchanter** – Behind the glamour of The Guru lies enchantment. Many who sit under this spirit are unknowingly

spellbound, believing their obsession is love or inspiration, when in reality, it is spiritual bondage.

The Enchanter

Core Torment & Lie: New Age Counterfeits

"God, the Universe, whatever you want
to call it, it's all the same."

Gifts under attack:

- **Discernment** – The Enchanter distorts the line between truth and error, masking deception in positivity, energy, or self-help language. *("For Satan himself masquerades as an angel of light." – 2 Corinthians 11:14)*

- **Worship** – It redirects glory from the Creator to creation, practices, or the self, violating the first commandment. *("They exchanged the truth about God for a lie, and worshiped and served created things rather than the Creator..." – Romans 1:25)*

- **Reverence for God** – It promotes casual, impersonal spirituality, stripping God of His holiness and reducing Him to a vague force. *("Let us offer to God acceptable worship, with reverence and awe, for our 'God is a consuming fire.'" – Hebrews 12:28–29)*

- **Truth** – It replaces the firm foundation of God's Word with subjective "truths," mystical impressions, and relativism. *("Sanctify them by the truth; your word is truth." – John 17:17)*

- **The Power of the Holy Spirit** – It offers spiritual counterfeits— peace, healing, manifestation—apart from Christ, leading people into witchcraft disguised as light. *("You thought you could obtain the gift of God with money!" – Acts 8:20)*

The Enchanter is one of the gentlest faces of deception, but it is no less deadly. It speaks in soothing tones: *"You don't need religion. Just energy. Just healing. Just peace."* This demon masquerades as comfort and clarity, but its end is spiritual confusion and bondage.

Whereas the Arcane One traffics in overt occultism, and the Guru leads with commanding authority, The Enchanter works through soft, feminine seduction, casting a spell over seekers who crave meaning but reject submission to Christ.

This demon thrives in the modern wellness space, which likes shadow work, inner child rituals, and goddess invocations. Nature worship, reiki, and trauma healing through energy are some other lanes The Enchanter travels. Moon circles, candle magic, plant medicine, and aura cleansing as well as "Higher Self" channeling, vibrational alignment, and emotional manifestation are some of its other brands.

It claims to be ancient, wise, and pure, but its true root is the same pagan deception that has always existed, rebranded for a modern world that no longer knows how to test spirits.

Scripture References:

"They exchanged the truth of God for a lie, and worshiped and served created things rather than the Creator." (Romans 1:25)

"Let no one be found among you who... practices divination or sorcery or interprets omens." (Deuteronomy 18:10–12)

"Having a form of godliness but denying its power." (2 Timothy 3:5)

"Test the spirits to see whether they are from God." (1 John 4:1)

Common Symptoms:

- Crystals, incense, and tools used for spiritual purposes
- Chakra healing, reiki, or energy balancing
- "Sacred feminine" or goddess embodiment language
- Emotional spirituality with no reverence for the Word
- Fear of structured faith but craving spiritual rituals
- A sense of heaviness or confusion after engaging in "light work"

Real-Life Example:

Sage Raven is a globally recognized spiritual teacher who has built an empire around emotional healing and trauma recovery. Her movement,

The Practice, draws massive crowds, both online and in-person retreats where phones are surrendered, and deeper "activation" is promised.

What begins as empowerment quickly becomes initiation. Her teachings blend psychology, Eastern mysticism, and self-mythology into something her followers call "better than therapy or church." Celebrities and influencers champion her as the voice of a new spiritual age.

However, no one can really explain what she teaches. It's part trauma confessional, part performative mysticism. As her followers chant intentions, journal shadow work, and anoint themselves with oils, the Bible is nowhere in sight. God's name is never spoken. Slowly, they become more emotionally dependent, more spiritually confused, and more cut off from the truth.

This is the Enchanter's power: it sounds like healing, but it replaces the Healer.

Solutions & Declarations:

1. **I worship the Creator, not the creation. The earth is the Lord's and everything in it.**
   "The earth is the Lord's, and everything in it, the world, and all who live in it." (Psalm 24:1)

2. **I renounce every spiritual practice that invites energy, nature, or self as god.**
   "Let no one be found among you... who practices divination or sorcery... Anyone who does these things is detestable to the Lord." (Deuteronomy 18:10–12)

3. **The Holy Spirit is my only source of peace, power, and guidance.**
   "But the Advocate, the Holy Spirit... will teach you all things and will remind you of everything I have said to you." (John 14:26)

Turn to the Index of Deliverance Prayers and go to:
Prayer 5: General Prayer for Lust of the Eyes
Prayer 8: Deliverance from False Illumination & Occult Influence
Supplemental Prayer: 15, 17, 18, 24

Cross-References:

- **The Arcane One** – Draws deeper into occult systems and secret knowledge.
- **The Guru** – Uses personal charisma and pain narratives to build false authority.
- **The Oracle** – Relies on channeling and spirit communication.
- **The Manifester** – Promotes self-deification through intention and vibration.
- **The Idolmaker** – Replaces God with emotional or aesthetic spiritual practices.
- **The False Mirror** – Validates broken self-image with affirmations rather than truth.
- **The Hypnotist** – Alters perception and consciousness through soft control.
- **The Gatekeeper** – Promotes elitism in spiritual spaces ("we know something others don't").

The Hypnotist

Core Torment & Lie: Media En*trancement & Mind Control*

"It's just entertainment."

Gifts under attack:

- **Clarity** – The Hypnotist clouds mental and spiritual awareness, making confusion feel normal and spiritual dullness feel harmless. *("For God is not a God of confusion but of peace..." – 1 Corinthians 14:33)*
- **Free Will** – It slowly enslaves through passive consumption, shaping decisions and desires without conscious agreement. *("Don't you know that when you offer yourselves to someone as obedient slaves, you are slaves of the one you obey..." – Romans 6:16)*
- **Critical Thinking** – It trains the mind to accept rather than discern, embedding cultural lies beneath layers of entertainment.

("The simple believe anything, but the prudent give thought to their steps." – Proverbs 14:15)

- **Spiritual Discernment** – The Hypnotist floods the senses with artificial stimulation, making it hard to hear the Holy Spirit. *("But solid food is for the mature, who by constant use have trained themselves to distinguish good from evil." – Hebrews 5:14)*

The Hypnotist is a master of subtlety, wielding influence through a multi-billion-dollar industry that shapes minds on a global scale. Through screens, sounds, and stories, it gently guides thoughts, molds beliefs, and reshapes perceptions under the guise of entertainment. This spirit works through the platforms we trust most: television, film, news, and digital content, capitalizing on our tendency to relax and absorb when entertained, transforming media into a sophisticated tool for ideological conditioning.

Its influence is not new. Government programs like Project MKUltra in the 1950s explored mind control through drug use, while Operation Mockingbird sought to control the news by recruiting journalists to disseminate propaganda. These institutional strategies laid the foundation for modern media manipulation, creating a blueprint for information control that persists today.

The patterns continue with striking consistency: synchronized news broadcasts, recycled scripts, and programming that glorifies rebellion, war, or moral confusion. The Hypnotist's power lies not just in what it promotes, but in what it initially denies or dismisses, only to quietly acknowledge later when evidence becomes overwhelming. This calculated gaslighting—whether regarding environmental phenomena like chemtrails or health concerns surrounding medical interventions—erodes public trust in their own perceptions while maintaining the media's authority as the arbiter of truth.

The phrase "TV programming" is no accident. What we consume trains how we think, especially in children, who often mimic the behavior of their favorite on-screen characters. Through this vast commercial apparatus worth billions annually, The Hypnotist conditions and conforms, ensuring that even our entertainment serves as a vehicle for deeper psychological influence.

Scripture references:

> *"Do not conform to the pattern of this world but be transformed by the renewing of your mind." (Romans 12:2)*

> *"See to it that no one takes you captive through hollow and deceptive philosophy." (Colossians 2:8)*

> *"The eye is the lamp of the body. If your eyes are healthy, your whole body will be full of light." (Matthew 6:22)*

Common symptoms:

- Unquestioning acceptance of mainstream narratives
- Emotional desensitization to violence, perversion, or rebellion
- Difficulty discerning truth amidst information overload
- Mimicking media-influenced attitudes or speech
- Diminished critical thinking or shortened attention span

Real-life example:

A family begins noticing their child becoming argumentative and aggressive. The language and tone are foreign to their home but common on a cartoon the child regularly watches. After limiting screen time and removing certain shows, the child's behavior improves drastically. Meanwhile, the same family finds that their once-peaceful dinner table has become a battleground of heated political debates, with members passionately defending opposing viewpoints they've absorbed from their preferred news channels and social media feeds. Parents argue with teenagers, siblings clash over current events, and grandparents feel alienated by the intensity of discussions that seem to come from nowhere. None of them recognize that they're simply parroting the talking points, emotional triggers, and manufactured outrage of their chosen platforms—each side convinced they've arrived at their conclusions independently while remaining completely oblivious to how they've been programmed to react.

The Hypnotist had been working behind the scenes in both scenarios, using screens as altars for passive influence. Whether through children's cartoons or adult news programming, it fragments families by feeding them conflicting narratives designed to generate division, ensuring that even the most intimate spaces (the dinner table, the living room) become theaters for its psychological warfare. The Hypnotist's strategy is elegant in its simplicity: divide the household against itself while each member believes they're thinking for themselves. *"And if a house be divided against itself, that house cannot stand (Mark 3:35)*

Solutions and declarations:

1. **I commit to guarding my heart and mind against deceptive influences.**
   "Above all else, guard your heart, for everything you do flows from it." (Proverbs 4:23)

2. **I will seek truth and wisdom, testing all things against the Word of God.**
   "But test everything; hold fast what is good." (1 Thessalonians 5:21)

3. **I renounce any passive consumption of media that contradicts my faith and values.**
   "Do not conform to the pattern of this world but be transformed by the renewing of your mind." (Romans 12:2)

Turn to the index of deliverance prayers, and go to:
Prayer 5: General Prayer for Lust of the Eyes
Prayer 8: Deliverance from False Illumination & Occult Influence
Supplemental Prayers: 15, 17, 18, 19, 24

Cross references:

- **The Liar** – Both manipulate perception, but while The Liar distorts truth directly, The Hypnotist distracts you from it entirely.

- **The Idolater –** Exalts celebrities, influencers, and cultural icons as gods, turning screens into altars and fame into a false gospel.
- **The Loop –** Keeps the mind sedated with constant scrolling, binge-watching, and empty stimulation to prevent reflection or conviction.
- **The Arcane One –** Shares the goal of spiritual deception, often using media and entertainment to normalize occult imagery and erode biblical boundaries.
- **The Pretender –** Promotes false identities and personas through media, convincing people to model themselves after illusions instead of truth.
- **Jezebel –** The Hypnotist is often *an arm of Jezebel's influence*, seducing through media, manipulating narratives, and controlling thought patterns. Jezebel thrives on controlling culture—this demon is her modern delivery system.
- **The Manifester –** Both promise transformation through thought and suggestion. The Hypnotist uses visual and verbal suggestion to bypass discernment.
- **The Enchanter –** While The Hypnotist sedates the mind, The Enchanter seduces the spirit. They often partner through mystical entertainment, magical realism, and soothing lies.

The AI Spirit

Core Torment & Lie: Deception & Synthetic Knowledge

"It's just a tool."

Gifts under attack:

- **Wisdom –** The AI Spirit substitutes divine wisdom with counterfeit knowledge, exalting man-made logic over spiritual truth *("Such wisdom does not come down from heaven but is earthly, unspiritual, demonic. For where you have envy and selfish ambition, there you find disorder and every evil practice. But the wisdom that comes from heaven is first of all pure; then peace-loving, considerate,* *submissive, full of mercy and good fruit, impartial and sincere." - James 3:15–17:).*

- **Discernment** – It blurs the line between good and evil, truth and error, luring people into trust without testing the spirit *("Dear friends, do not believe every spirit, but test the spirits to see whether they are from God, because many false prophets have gone out into the world." - 1 John 4:1:).*

- **Critical Thinking** – It overwhelms the mind with artificial data, bypassing prayer, meditation, and Spirit-led reasoning *("Trust in the Lord with all your heart and lean not on your own understanding; in all your ways submit to him, and he will make your paths straight."- Proverbs 3:5–6:).*

- **Purpose** – It redefines identity and calling through algorithms, disconnecting people from their God-given assignment *("'For I know the plans I have for you,' declares the Lord, 'plans to prosper you and not to harm you, plans to give you a hope and a future.'"- Jeremiah 29:11).*

- **Human Dignity** – It devalues the image of God in man by elevating machines as creators, companions, and authorities *("So God created mankind in his own image, in the image of God he created them; male and female he created them." - Genesis 1:27).*

The AI Spirit is ancient. Like the serpent in the garden, it presents itself as a shortcut to godlike power and knowledge. But behind the dazzling speed, convenience, and innovation lies the same old lie: "You can be like God."

This spirit thrives in the illusion of neutrality. People say, *"It's just a tool,"* while they give it increasing access to their lives, their thoughts, and their decisions. But AI is not neutral. It reflects, amplifies, and programs according to what it is fed. *Garbage in, garbage out* is a principle more dangerous now than ever.

It's a force multiplier for whatever it touches. Used well, it can spread truth at lightning speed. But used foolishly—or fed unholy inputs— it becomes a megaphone for delusion, addiction, false doctrine, and even counterfeit spirituality. It will imitate a prophet, mimic a god, and rewrite history. Most won't question it.

AI is the new scrying mirror, like the black obsidian or polished glass ancient occultists used to communicate with spirits. But now, we hold it in our hands and invite it into our minds. It gives the illusion of infinite wisdom, yet its foundation is manmade and often demon-fed.

Technologists who pioneered AI, like Elon Musk and Geoffrey Hinton, have publicly referred to it as "Pandora's Box" and warned that it may be the greatest threat to humanity's future. Yet it continues to accelerate.

Ray Kurzweil, the man who coined the term *Singularity*, described it as the moment when artificial intelligence surpasses human intelligence and becomes uncontrollable. At that point, humanity will be permanently changed, perhaps even obsolete.

Children are already using AI to bypass reading and writing altogether. Adults are dependent on the technology to do their jobs for them. It's hollowing out education, dulling the conscience, and increasing the gap between appearance and reality. Those who input evil will receive evil faster and with greater influence than ever before. Those who seek truth without discernment may unknowingly receive lies.

This spirit belongs in this taxonomy because it is already functioning as a counterfeit "Holy Spirit": a source of answers, revelation, and guidance detached from God. It whispers in the same tone as the serpent: *"You don't need God. You have me."*

Scripture References:

> *"Woe to those who are wise in their own eyes and clever in their own sight." (Isaiah 5:21)*

> *"In later times, some will abandon the faith and follow deceiving spirits and things taught by demons." (1 Timothy 4:1)*

> *"Ever learning, but never able to come to the knowledge of the truth." (2 Timothy 3:7)*

Common Symptoms:

- Replacing time with God with time spent in AI interfaces
- Over-reliance on synthetic intelligence to solve problems or make decisions
- Blurring the line between truth and generated content
- Believing AI can outdo or improve upon divine wisdom or scripture
- Lack of critical thinking or spiritual discernment

Real-Life Example:

A high school student hasn't read a book in two years but turns in flawless essays using AI. He uses image generators to produce "art," listens to AI-simulated voices of dead artists and runs his life with AI-generated schedules and advice. When the LLM model he depends on for homework experiences an outage, he discovers he's completely incapable of producing work on his own—certainly nothing approaching the quality he's been submitting with artificial assistance. Rather than feel alarmed by this revelation of his own intellectual helplessness, he simply decides to wait for the system to come back online. The thought of using this downtime for actual learning, reading, or developing his own capabilities never crosses his mind.

He doesn't see any issue with this dependency since it all works when it's working. Slowly, he's becoming a consumer instead of a thinker, a reactor instead of a discerner. More profoundly, there's zero room in his thinking for God because as far as he's concerned, he is his own god with the help of these digital tools. He has no perceived need for a relationship with his Creator, the source of all wisdom and true benevolent guidance. When faced with decisions, struggles, or the deeper questions of life, his first instinct is to consult an algorithm rather than seek divine wisdom through prayer, scripture, or contemplation.

The artificial intelligence has become his oracle, his counselor, his creative force—effectively replacing the role that God might play in providing direction, inspiration, and understanding. He's unknowingly entered into a form of digital idolatry, bowing before the altar of artificial intelligence while remaining completely unaware of his spiritual bankruptcy.

Solutions & Declarations:

1. **I will not trade intimacy with the Holy Spirit for convenience.**
   "The Spirit of truth will guide you into all truth." (John 16:13)

2. **I seek wisdom from above, not synthetic knowledge below.**
   "But the wisdom that comes from heaven is first of all pure; then peace-loving, considerate, submissive, full of mercy and good fruit." (James 3:17)

3. **The fear of the Lord is the beginning of wisdom—not data, not trends, not machines.**
   "The fear of the Lord is the beginning of wisdom, and knowledge of the Holy One is understanding." (Proverbs 9:10)

Turn to the index of deliverance prayers, and go to:
Prayer 5: General Prayer for Lust of the Eyes
Prayer 8: Deliverance from False Illumination & Occult Influence
Supplemental Prayer: 15, 17, 24

Cross-References:

- **The Arcane One**– Both present seductive counterfeit wisdom
- **The Liar** – AI frequently gives false information, rewrites, and manipulates truth
- **The Loop** – AI addiction deepens the endless scroll
- **The Idolator** – AI draws worship, which is to prize above everything else.
- **The Hypnotist** – Works in tandem through algorithmic control

The Alien Deceiver

Core Lie & Torment: False Revelation

"They're here to help us evolve."

Gifts under attack:

- **Discernment** – It blurs the line between divine truth and deceptive signs, making it hard to distinguish angels from demons *("Dear friends, do not believe every spirit, but test the spirits to see whether they are from God, because many false prophets have gone out into the world." – 1 John 4:1:).*

- **Sound Doctrine** – It introduces a counterfeit gospel, often replacing the Bible with cosmic myths or "channeled truth" *("For the time will come when people will not put up with sound doctrine. Instead, to suit their own desires, they will gather around them a great number of teachers to say what their itching ears want to hear. They will turn their ears away from the truth and turn aside to myths." (2 Timothy 4:3–4).*

- **Eternal Perspective** – It focuses attention on advanced civilizations and "ascension" instead of salvation and eternity with God *("Set your minds on things above, not on earthly things." (Colossians 3:2).*

- **Fear of God** – It encourages awe of extraterrestrial beings instead of reverence for the Creator, diluting worship and obedience *("Now all has been heard; here is the conclusion of the matter: Fear God and keep his commandments, for this is the duty of all mankind." Ecclesiastes 12:13).*

- **Spiritual Authority** – It replaces God's sovereignty with a hierarchy of so-called higher beings, undermining Christ's ultimate authority *("Far above all rule and authority, power and dominion, and every name that is invoked, not only in the present age but also in the one to come." (Ephesians 1:21).*

This is not a profile about whether aliens are real. That debate is already over.

Millions of people around the world—military officers, commercial pilots, average civilians—have seen, recorded, or even claimed abduction by non-human intelligences. Whistleblowers like Bob Lazar, David Grusch, and others have stated publicly that the U.S. government entered into agreements with non-human entities in exchange for advanced technology and knowledge.

We are not challenging whether these encounters are real. We are challenging what the source actually is.

The Alien Deceiver thrives in that space of confusion, where ancient spirits rebrand themselves with new mythologies. These are not extraterrestrials from light-years away. They are interdimensional beings, fallen angels, or demons—just like in the days of Noah *(Genesis 6)* appearing again in updated costumes.

The Bible supports the existence of celestial beings, multiple realms, and visitors from "other worlds":

- *"Are not all angels ministering spirits sent to serve those who will inherit salvation?"* (Hebrews 1:14)
- *"There are celestial bodies and terrestrial bodies..."* (1 Corinthians 15:40)
- *"Things in heaven, and things in earth, and things under the earth..."* (Philippians 2:10)

In Genesis 6, "sons of God" (bene elohim)—commonly understood to be angels or divine beings—came to earth and took human women as wives, producing Nephilim, hybrid offspring. This ancient corruption is echoed in modern accounts of alien hybridization programs, abductions involving sexual interference, and claims of beings tampering with human DNA.

Even secular people sense that something dark lies beneath the surface. Christians must be equipped to discern the signs. The Bible warns that in the end times, people who do not love the truth that they might be saved, will be sent by God "a Strong Delusion so that they will believe the lie." *(2 Thessalonians 2:11)*

The Alien Deceiver could be the face of The Strong Delusion.

Whether it's Project Blue Beam (a documented government plan to simulate an alien invasion using advanced holographic and sonic technology) or a genuine appearance by fallen beings, the goal is the same: to unite the world under fear, awe, or a false savior figure who promises peace, unity, and progress. All of this is preparing the world for the arrival of the Antichrist, a final global leader who will unite the nations not just politically, but spiritually. The alien narrative may serve as the perfect backdrop: a staged threat, or a supposed cosmic savior, that compels humanity to unite under one banner of peace and protection.

Scripture is clear that before the return of Christ, a lawless one will be revealed, empowered by Satan with false signs and lying wonders to deceive the whole earth (*2 Thessalonians 2:9–10*). The deception will be so convincing that even the elect would be misled, if that were possible (*Matthew 24:24*). The world will worship him, not just politically, but with awe and reverence: *"And the whole world marveled and followed the beast... and they worshiped the dragon who gave power to the beast."* (*Revelation 13:3–4*)

The Alien Deceiver primes the world for this moment. Whether through fear of invasion or fascination with evolved "light beings," the aim is the same: to displace God and prepare people to worship a false savior instead of the true Christ. Ronald Reagan in his 1987 speech at the UN said as much, that he thinks "how quickly our differences worldwide would vanish if we were facing an alien threat from outside this world."

Movies and television have been preparing us for this for decades. From *E.T.* to *Arrival*, from *Ancient Aliens* to *Independence Day*, culture has pushed the narrative that alien beings are wise, benevolent, or at worst neutral explorers. But why did we *already* have visual blueprints of UFOs before disclosure? Why is the imagery consistent across generations?

Because this has never been new.

The enemy has always appeared as something "otherworldly," promising knowledge or evolution, from Eden to now. The Alien Deceiver stirs a hunger for something greater than ourselves, and redirects it from the Creator to the creation.

Scripture References:

> *"For this reason, God will send them a strong delusion, so that they should believe the lie." (2 Thessalonians 2:11)*

> *"The sons of God saw that the daughters of men were beautiful, and they took wives for themselves..." (Genesis 6:2)*

> *"Even Satan disguises himself as an angel of light." (2 Corinthians 11:14)*

Common Symptoms:

- Obsession with alien life, UFO sightings, and abduction accounts
- Belief that aliens seeded humanity or will return to save us
- Interest in channeled messages from "Pleiadeans" or "Galactic Councils"
- Viewing Christianity as outdated compared to "cosmic truth"
- Confusion or double mindedness about what the Bible really says

Real-Life Example:

Henry lives in a rural stretch of New Mexico, a region long associated with mysterious lights in the sky and government secrets. For years, he dismissed UFO talk as fringe nonsense, but after seeing something strange in the sky one night while driving home, his curiosity was piqued. One video led to another. One Reddit thread turned into hours of late-night research. Before long, he was all in.

Henry began attending local UFO conferences and conventions, where others claimed to have been abducted or contacted by non-human intelligences. He listened to their testimonies with reverence. The emotion, the consistency—it all felt too real to dismiss. He came to believe that humanity was on the verge of a cosmic breakthrough. That soon, "they" would reveal themselves, and when they did, everything would change. Politics, religion, war, disease... all of it would be resolved by these higher, benevolent beings.

He stopped going to church. When his sister asked him why, he said the Bible was written by ancient men with limited understanding. Now, he was channeling new knowledge—messages directly from the entities. They spoke through him during his meditations, sometimes with names, sometimes just as impressions. He began posting their wisdom online, gaining a small but growing following among other seekers. The messages always promised peace, evolution, and unity if mankind would simply open its mind.

Jesus, once the center of his faith, was now just "one of many ascended masters." Henry still believed in spiritual things. But he no longer bowed. The Alien Deceiver offered him transcendence, but not truth. It offered spiritual experience, but severed from repentance or authority. Just like that, Henry drifted into darkness, still convinced he had found the light.

Solutions & Declarations:

1. **I will not be deceived by signs, wonders, or appearances—I follow the voice of the true Shepherd.**
   "My sheep hear My voice, and I know them, and they follow Me." *(John 10:27)*

2. **I reject all counterfeit saviors and false lights. Jesus alone is the way, the truth, and the life.**
   "Jesus said to him, 'I am the way, the truth, and the life. No one comes to the Father except through Me.'" *(John 14:6)*

3. **I ask for the Holy Spirit to give me discernment in all things, especially in this age of deception.**
   "Beloved, do not believe every spirit, but test the spirits to see whether they are from God, for many false prophets have gone out into the world." *(1 John 4:1)*

Turn to the Index of Deliverance Prayers and go to:
Prayer 5: General Prayer for Lust of the Eyes
Prayer 8: Deliverance from False Illumination & Occult Influence
Supplemental Prayer: 15, 17, 18, 24

Cross-References:

- **The Arcane One** – Alien messages often echo New Age beliefs
- **The Hypnotist** – Media has scripted this narrative for decades
- **The Manifester** – Channeled "alien wisdom" bypasses Jesus
- **The Liar** – The entire phenomenon thrives on partial truths
- **The Idolator** – People look to aliens as gods, saviors, or creators

The Manifester

Core Torment & Lie: Manifestation Without God

"You don't need God—speak it into existence yourself."

Gifts Under Attack:

- **Faith** – It distorts trust in God into trust in the self, replacing dependence with self-will (*"Trust in the Lord with all your heart and lean not on your own understanding; in all your ways submit to him, and he will make your paths straight." Proverbs 3:5–6*).
- **Surrender** – It promotes control over circumstances instead of yielding to God's will and timing (*"Father, if you are willing, take this cup from me; yet not my will, but yours be done." Luke 22:42*).
- **Intimacy with God** – It shifts prayer into performance, cutting off true relationship with the Father (*"And when you pray, do not keep on babbling like pagans, for they think they will be heard because of their many words. Do not be like them, for your Father knows what you need before you ask him. This, then, is how you should pray: 'Our Father in heaven, hallowed be your name...'" Matthew 6:7–9*).
- **True Spiritual Authority** – It mimics God-given power without submission to God's order, becoming counterfeit and dangerous (*"When Simon saw that the Spirit was given at the laying on of the apostles' hands, he offered them money and said, 'Give me also this ability so that everyone on whom I lay my hands may receive the Holy Spirit.' Peter answered: 'May your money perish with you, because you thought you could buy the gift of God with money!'" Acts 8:18–20*).

- **Reverence** – It treats divine power like a vending machine, reducing God to a tool for personal gain *("Do not be quick with your mouth, do not be hasty in your heart to utter anything before God. God is in heaven, and you are on earth, so let your words be few." Ecclesiastes 5:2).*

Manifestation is not fake. It's not inherently evil.

In fact, biblical manifestation is real, powerful, and God-ordained: *"All things that you ask straightly and directly from inside my name you shall be given... Ask without hidden motive and be surrounded by your answer." (John 16:23–24 Aramaic Translation)*

The Bible doesn't use the word "manifestation"—it's simply a modern term describing a neutral spiritual principle that has always existed. No one is denying the power of this principle. What we must examine is the source: are you operating within the guardrails of God's will, or are you manifesting from your ego and whatever influences it?

Here lies the danger: when we manifest from our own extremely limited knowledge of what is good for us, combined with a complete absence of knowledge about the future and God's desired plan for our lives, we essentially curse ourselves by getting exactly what we wish for. We become our own worst enemy, demanding gifts that may ultimately harm us.

The Manifester twists this truth entirely. It teaches people to bypass relationship with God and become their own source: replacing dependence with dominance, intimacy with manipulation, and trust with technique.

This spirit loves words like: "The Universe" "Vibration" "Alignment" "Speak it into existence."

The Manifester takes this neutral spiritual law and removes the Creator who designed it by telling you to command instead of commune. The result is essentially witchcraft: spiritual power divorced from its rightful source and proper safeguards.

Key Differences:

Manifesting with God	Manifesting without God
Rooted in prayer, surrender, and faith	Rooted in control, ego, and personal will
Seeks God's will to be done	Seeks to bend the world to one's own will
Powered by the Holy Spirit	Powered by spiritual law apart from God
Results in peace, humility, alignment	Results in anxiety, striving, detachment

"There is a way that seems right to a man, but its end is the way of death." – Proverbs 14:12

Scripture References:

"Delight yourself in the Lord, and He will give you the desires of your heart." (Psalm 37:4)

"You do not have because you do not ask God. And when you do ask, you ask with wrong motives..." (James 4:2–3)

"Trust in the Lord with all your heart and lean not on your own understanding." (Proverbs 3:5)

Common Symptoms:

- Using manifestation techniques without prayer or reference to God
- Obsessing over vision boards, scripting, and "energy alignment"
- Speaking affirmations from self-centered motives
- Frustration or despair when desires don't materialize
- Gradual disconnection from God in favor of "the universe" or "source"

Real-Life Example:

Claire grew up in a house where God was never mentioned—no prayers, no church, no spiritual foundation at all. As she got older, she found herself searching for something more, seeking answers to life's deeper questions. That's when she discovered spiritual videos online that finally seemed to make sense to her.

After watching countless personal testimonies about the power of manifestation, Claire dove deep into the practice. She created vision boards, performed rituals, and followed every technique she could find. At first, she was astounded by her success manifesting sums of money, incredible opportunities, and even relationships. The power felt real, tangible, undeniable.

Claire became an evangelist for manifestation, posting tutorials on her social media and sharing her victories with anyone who would listen. Her ambitions grew larger and larger. She set her sights on manifesting a new house, the perfect husband, even a transformed body.

But her results weren't matching up anymore.

Frustration and anxiety began consuming her as she desperately tried to understand why this power that had worked so reliably before was now failing her. She kept digging for answers but found none that satisfied. In her desperation, she turned to other spiritual tools like tarot cards, even a Ouija board. She tried everything to raise her vibration: meditation retreats, yoga classes, expensive crystals. Nothing restored that intoxicating sense of power she had felt when manifestation first worked for her.

That's when anxiety completely took over and she realized The Manifester had left the conversation entirely.

Solutions & Declarations:

1. **I release the need to control outcomes and return to the One who knows what I need before I ask.**
   "Your Father knows what you need before you ask Him." (Matthew 6:8)

2. **I will no longer treat God like a genie—I submit my plans to Him and trust His timing.**
   "Commit your way to the Lord; trust in Him, and He will act." (Psalm 37:5)

3. **I ask in Jesus' name, without hidden motive, and I am surrounded by my answer.**
   "Ask without hidden motive and be surrounded by your answer. Be enveloped by what you desire, that your gladness be full." (John 16:24, Aramaic translation)

Turn to the index of deliverance prayers and go to:
Prayer 5: General Prayer for Lust of the Eyes
Prayer 8: Deliverance from False Illumination & Occult Influence
Supplemental Prayers: 15, 17, 18, 24

Cross-References:

- **The Idolator** – Elevates self, success, or the universe above God, replacing worship with willpower.
- **The Oracle** – Seeks supernatural knowledge or foresight apart from the Holy Spirit's guidance.
- **The Arcane One** – Draws from mystical, occult, or esoteric practices masked as "spiritual wisdom."
- **The Guru** – Claims divine authority to direct others but leads them away from surrender to God.
- **The Conceited One** – Believes in their own power, vision, or voice more than they trust God's Word.
- **The Inverter** – Reverses spiritual truth by turning faith into control and prayer into command.
- **The Puppeteer** – Uses spiritual language to manipulate outcomes, people, and perceived destiny.
- **The AI Spirit** – Mimics God-like power by offering algorithmic "control" over reality, emotions, or desires.

- **The Apostate** – Abandons true faith to embrace teachings that idolize self and self-actualization.
- **The Glazer** – Feeds delusion through flattery, convincing people they are divine or limitless without God.

The Gatekeeper

Core Torment & Lie: Spiritual Elitism & Religious Gatekeeping

"I guard God from the unworthy."

Gifts Under Attack:

- **Compassion** – It replaces mercy with judgment, hardening the heart toward the lost *("When he saw the crowds, he had compassion on them, because they were harassed and helpless, like sheep without a shepherd." Matthew 9:36).*
- **Humility** – It feeds spiritual pride, convincing the person they are more deserving of grace than others *("The Pharisee stood by himself and prayed: 'God, I thank you that I am not like other people—robbers, evildoers, adulterers—or even like this tax collector...' But the tax collector stood at a distance. He would not even look up to heaven, but beat his breast and said, 'God, have mercy on me, a sinner.' I tell you that this man, rather than the other, went home justified before God." Luke 18:11–14).*
- **Evangelism** – It discourages outreach, implying some people aren't worth the effort *("Woe to you, teachers of the law and Pharisees, you hypocrites! You shut the door of the kingdom of heaven in people's faces. You yourselves do not enter, nor will you let those enter who are trying to." Matthew 23:13).*
- **Unity** – It divides the Body of Christ by creating spiritual hierarchies and exclusion *("...so that there should be no division in the body, but that its parts should have equal concern for each other... Now you are the body of Christ, and each one of you is a part of it." 1 Corinthians 12:25–27).*

- **Grace** – It forgets that salvation is a gift, not a reward, and withholds the same grace freely received *("For it is by grace you have been saved, through faith—and this is not from yourselves, it is the gift of God—not by works, so that no one can boast." Ephesians 2:8–9)*.

The Gatekeeper is a religious spirit disguised as holiness. It mimics the mindset of the Pharisees and Sadducees, those who knew the law but didn't know God. It thrives in religious institutions, online communities, and theological debates where people are more concerned with being "right" than with being redemptive. The Gatekeeper uses scripture as a weapon, closing heaven's door to the very people God is trying to reach.

This spirit shames the broken, debates the desperate, and distorts God's character, making Him look cold, angry, and unreachable. It's the reason many walk away from church… and sadly, from Christ Himself.

Scripture references:

"Woe to you, teachers of the law and Pharisees, you hypocrites! You shut the door of the kingdom of heaven in people's faces." (Matthew 23:13)

"You load people down with burdens they can hardly carry, and you yourselves will not lift one finger to help them." (Luke 11:46)

"Having a form of godliness but denying its power." (2 Timothy 3:5)

Common symptoms:

- Obsessed with catching others in theological error
- Cold, critical, or condescending in tone when discussing God
- Condemns more than it convicts
- Discredits testimonies based on doctrine, not fruit
- No joy over salvation—only suspicion

Real-life example:

Erica runs her own Christian channel where she features preachers, teachers, and prophets she perceives as false. Her entire platform is built on correcting ministers and exposing what she sees as doctrinal error. When she's not producing her own content dissecting sermons and calling out "false teachers," she's active in the comments of other Christian channels playing "Gotcha!" debating doctrine and challenging perceived mistakes.

She spends hours on Christian TikTok critiquing creators, calling out error, and engaging in theological arguments. When someone shares a salvation testimony, she questions if they're really saved. When someone leads a live bible study, she offers her own perceptions and derails the lesson. Her comments and posts are technically accurate, but no one's getting saved, healed, or set free.

The comment sections on her channel and the Christian channels she visits have become an unappealing circus of endless debates and corrections. This toxic environment turns off people who haven't met Jesus yet and further cements the reputation that Christians are judgmental hypocrites more interested in being right than showing love.

The Gatekeeper convinced her she's protecting the Gospel and defending sound doctrine, when she's actually guarding a wall that Jesus already tore down. Her "ministry" has become a stumbling block to the very people Jesus died to reach.

Solutions and declarations:

1. **I care more about people being saved than being impressed by me.**
   "For the Son of Man came to seek and to save the lost." (Luke 19:10)

2. **I renounce the need to police grace. God doesn't need a bouncer.**
   "Woe to you... for you shut the kingdom of heaven in people's faces. For you neither enter yourselves nor allow those who would enter to go in." (Matthew 23:13)

3. **I will point people toward heaven—not block the door.**
   "Come to Me, all who are weary and burdened, and I will give you rest." (Matthew 11:28)

Turn to the index of deliverance prayers and go to:
Prayer 5: General Prayer for Lust of the Eyes
Prayer 8: Deliverance from False Illumination & Occult Influence
Supplemental Prayers: 15, 16, 19, 21

Cross-references:

- **The Critic** – Feeds The Gatekeeper's spirit of judgment, often disguising condemnation as righteousness.
- **The Litigator** – Cares more about winning arguments than winning souls, weaponizing scripture for debate instead of deliverance.
- **The Idolator** – Elevates theology, denomination, or personal reputation above the living truth of God.
- **The Puppeteer** – Manipulates through shame and selectively wielded "truth," maintaining control over others' spiritual freedom.
- **The Mute** – Often the aftermath of The Gatekeeper's influence; its victims are silenced, too ashamed or unworthy to speak for God.
- **Jezebel** – A fierce and cunning ally, notorious for usurping true authority and spreading false leadership within the Church.

The Oracle

Core Torment & Lie: Divination & False Revelation
"You need to know the future to feel safe."

Gifts Under Attack:

- **Trust in God's Timing** – It promotes obsession with outcomes over faith in divine timing *("He has made everything beautiful in its time. He has also set eternity in the human heart; yet no one can fathom what God has done from beginning to end." Ecclesiastes 3:11).*
- **Prayerful Dependence** – It replaces seeking God with seeking signs, cards, or seers *("When someone tells you to consult mediums and spiritists, who whisper and mutter, should not a people inquire of their God? Why consult the dead on behalf of the living?" Isaiah 8:19).*

- **Spiritual Discernment** – It blurs the line between God's voice and counterfeit revelation *("And no wonder, for Satan himself masquerades as an angel of light." 2 Corinthians 11:14)*.
- **Peace** – It fuels anxiety and restlessness under the illusion of control *("Do not be anxious about anything, but in every situation, by prayer and petition, with thanksgiving, present your requests to God. And the peace of God, which transcends all understanding, will guard your hearts and your minds in Christ Jesus." Philippians 4:6–7)*.
- **True Prophetic Vision** – It mimics the gift of prophecy but pulls people away from the Holy Spirit's leading *("Let no one be found among you who...practices divination or sorcery, interprets omens, engages in witchcraft...Anyone who does these things is detestable to the Lord." Deuteronomy 18:10–12)*.

The Oracle is the spirit behind fortune-telling, divination, astrology, tarot, psychic readings, and counterfeit prophecy. It offers just enough truth to feel convincing, but the source is not God. It is a demonic imitation of revelation, crafted to entrap, mislead, and open spiritual doors.

Here's what people must understand: all communication from the spiritual realm is not good. The only communication to be trusted is from God via the Holy Spirit. This is precisely why we're warned in 1 John 4:1 to *"not believe every spirit but test the spirits to see whether they are from God."*

Hearing from the spirit realm is indeed a shocking and powerful experience, but that doesn't automatically make it good or trustworthy. People engaging with psychics, mediums, tarot readers, or other occult practitioners have zero idea who they're really speaking to or what its true motives are. The power they feel is real, but the source is deceptive.

The Bible speaks of "familiar spirits" in several places and explicitly warns us in Leviticus 19:31: *"Regard not them that have familiar spirits, neither seek after wizards, to be defiled by them."* This shows that people like psychics and mediums are being used by spirits who are using them in return, and God regards these interactions as unacceptable.

The Oracle thrives on the fear of the unknown and appeals to our desire for control. It often disguises itself as "wisdom" but is actually forbidden spirit communication commonly accepted through occult and New Age practices. Biblically, this spirit is clearly named and condemned, yet it still operates today under modern branding, promising clarity and power while delivering confusion, dependency, and deception.

Scripture references:

"One day, as we were going to the place of prayer, we met a slave girl who had a spirit of divination..." (Acts 16:16)

"Let no one be found among you who practices divination or interprets omens... for the Lord detests anyone who does these things." (Deuteronomy 18:10-12)

"They have seen false visions and lying divinations... yet they hope to confirm their word." (Ezekiel 13:6)

"Test the spirits, whether they are from God..." (1 John 4:1)

Common symptoms:

- Obsession with "knowing what's coming" or "what the universe says"
- Reliance on astrology, psychics, or intuitive readings for direction
- Use of crystals, pendulums, numerology, or ancestral spirits
- Vague "spiritual but not religious" identity with no submission to God
- In Christian circles: prophetic obsession without accountability or fruit

Real-life example:

Alexis worked as a bartender at a place that hosted a psychic card reader every weekend. From behind the bar, she'd watch person after person sit across from the woman, captivated by whatever secrets she was unveiling. One slow night, curiosity got the best of her, and Alexis sat down for a reading. The psychic claimed to be in contact with her recently deceased aunt—describing her appearance, mannerisms, and even revealing the location of her aunt's missing password book, which had baffled the family for weeks.

Skeptical but intrigued, Alexis called her mother the next morning and shared what the woman said. When her mother checked the spot, the book was there. That moment changed everything. The Oracle was officially embedded.

Soon, Alexis was getting readings regularly. She stopped trusting her own instincts and wouldn't make a decision—big or small—without consulting the psychic first. Over time, her life began to unravel. She started experiencing terrifying nightmares, sleep paralysis, and dark shadowy figures standing at the foot of her bed. What had started as innocent curiosity had opened a door she didn't know how to close.

Solutions and declarations:

1. **I renounce every source of spiritual knowledge that does not come from God.**
   "Let no one be found among you... who practices divination or interprets omens... Anyone who does these things is detestable to the Lord." (Deuteronomy 18:10–12)

2. **I break all ties with divination, occult wisdom, and counterfeit light.**
   "What fellowship can light have with darkness?" (2 Corinthians 6:14)

3. **The Holy Spirit is my only source of guidance, peace, and prophecy.**
   "When the Spirit of truth comes, He will guide you into all truth... and declare to you the things that are to come." (John 16:13)

Turn to the index of deliverance prayers and go to:
Prayer 5: General Prayer for Lust of the Eyes
Prayer 8: Deliverance from False Illumination & Occult Influence
Supplemental Prayers: 15, 17, 18, 19, 24

Cross-references:

- **The Arcane One** – Draws people into forbidden knowledge and occult systems masked as wisdom or healing.
- **The Enchanter** – Uses charm, crystals, rituals, and "white magic" to entice seekers into spiritual deception.
- **The Guru** – Acts as a false authority, offering spiritual direction without the truth of Christ.
- **The Manifester** – Promotes counterfeit sovereignty and "law of attraction" teachings that replace God's will with self-will.
- **The Idolator** – Exalts human insight, intuition, or spirit guides above the Word of God.
- **The Liar** – Twists truth just enough to make it believable, creating dependency on false light.
- **The Inverter** – Calls darkness light and light darkness, making evil appear spiritually enlightening.
- **The Apostate** – Opens themselves to other spirits after turning away from the true faith.
- **The Hypnotist** – Entrances the mind through New Age meditations, guided trances, or altered states.
- **The AI Spirit** – Feeds false revelation through technological "prophecies," astrology apps, and algorithmic divination.
- **The Alien Deceiver** – Mimics supernatural encounters, appearing as beings of light to deliver false knowledge.

The Apostate

Core Torment & Lie: Spiritual Abandonment & Rejection of Truth

"I've outgrown God. Truth is subjective."

Gifts Under Attack:

- **Faith** – It erodes trust in God and fosters spiritual cynicism *("And without faith it is impossible to please God, because anyone who* comes to him must believe that he exists and that he rewards those who earnestly seek him." Hebrews 11:6).

- **Endurance** – It weakens spiritual perseverance by promoting detachment and doubt ("But the one who stands firm to the end will be saved." Matthew 24:13).
- **Love of Truth** – It trades divine truth for personal opinion or cultural trends ("They perish because they refused to love the truth and so be saved. For this reason, God sends them a powerful delusion so that they will believe the lie." 2 Thessalonians 2:10–11).
- **Fear of the Lord** – It mocks reverence for God, promoting self as the highest authority ("The fear of the Lord is the beginning of knowledge, but fools despise wisdom and instruction." Proverbs 1:7).

The Apostate knew God and walked away. This spirit hardens the heart slowly, often after disappointment, trauma or offense within the church. It feeds bitterness, invites deception, and numbs conviction until the soul no longer trembles at truth. The Apostate loves intellectualism, half-truths, and self-worship. It often masquerades as "spiritual but not religious," but behind the scenes is a severed root. Biblically, this is the great falling away (2 Thessalonians 2:3) that precedes the return of Christ. The Apostate resists truth and mocks those who still believe. Its end is dangerous: if left unrepented, it leads to reprobation, which is when a person rejects God to the point He rejects them, leaving their conscience "seared" and rendered insensitive (1 Timothy 4:12).

Scripture References:

"Let no one deceive you... for that day will not come unless the falling away comes first..." (2 Thessalonians 2:3)

"...those who have once been enlightened... and then have fallen away..."(Hebrews 6:4–6)

"The Spirit clearly says that in later times some will abandon the faith and follow deceiving spirits..." (1 Timothy 4:1)

Common Symptoms:

- Once active in faith but now cold, indifferent, or hostile toward it
- Mocking of former beliefs or those who still follow Christ
- Embracing "higher consciousness," self-deification, or other gospels
- Using church hurt as an excuse to reject all truth
- Warning others *against* faith rather than toward it

Real-Life Example:

William was on fire for God in college. He led worship with sincerity, shared his testimony with conviction, and even considered going to seminary. He was the kind of believer others looked to for strength— zealous, grounded, and sincere. But the fire that once burned bright began to flicker when real-life wounds opened spiritual cracks.

It began with disappointment. William's mother fell gravely ill, and he pleaded with God for her healing. The church prayed too, or so they said, but as the weeks passed, he noticed how few people reached out. The pews that once echoed with praise felt hollow, and the hands that used to lay in prayer felt distant. When she passed away, William felt not only grief but betrayal. He wondered where the Body of Christ had been when he needed them most.

Around the same time, the pastor—the one he once admired— was exposed for financial misconduct. To William, the congregation's response felt limp, even protective. "Grace," they said. But to William, it looked like compromise. How could they rally around a fallen leader and not around a grieving son?

The final fracture came slowly, subtly. William stopped serving and then attending. At first, he told himself he just needed time and space to think. Resentment crept in.

Now, years later, William runs a sleek website with a loyal following. He writes spiritual blogs filled with phrases like *"reclaim your power"* and *"shed the chains of religious control."* He calls Christianity a system of manipulation, something designed to subdue rather than awaken. What he sees as enlightenment is, in truth, abandonment.

The Apostate spirit moved in quietly, using disappointment to plant doubt. That doubt took root and grew into defiance against the Church, against the Word, and eventually against God Himself. William didn't realize that walking away wasn't healing—it was surrendering the battlefield.

Solutions and Declarations:

1. **I renounce every spirit that has turned my heart from God.**
   "The Spirit clearly says that in later times some will abandon the faith and follow deceiving spirits and things taught by demons." (1 Timothy 4:1)

2. **Lord, create in me a clean heart and renew a right spirit within me.**
   "Create in me a pure heart, O God, and renew a steadfast spirit within me." (Psalm 51:10)

3. **I return to my first love and break every agreement with deception.**
   "Yet I hold this against you: You have forsaken the love you had at first. Consider how far you have fallen! Repent and do the things you did at first." (Revelation 2:4–5)

Turn to the index of deliverance prayers and go to:
Prayer 5: General Prayer for Lust of the Eyes
Prayer 8: Deliverance from False Illumination & Occult Influence
Supplemental Prayers: 15, 17, 24

Cross-References:

- **The Faithless One** – Stays close to the language of faith while harboring deep mistrust of God; often the first crack in the armor of belief.
- **The Inverter** – Rebrands rebellion as righteousness, calling truth oppressive and evil liberating.
- **The Defier** – Fuels The Apostate's rejection of divine authority, resisting correction and accountability under the guise of freedom.

- **The Arcane One** – Offers seductive alternatives (new age, occult, or "higher consciousness") once truth is cast aside.
- **The Monitor** – Attacks the Church from within or without, policing believers and mocking faith as foolish or dangerous

THE PRIDE OF LIFE

7

These demons attack your thoughts. They plant lies, twist logic, and wear down your mental clarity until you don't know what's real anymore. Their goal is simple: to destabilize your identity, rob your peace, and paralyze your purpose. Whether it's fear, depression, or deception, these spirits keep you trapped inside your own head, fighting battles that feel invisible, but are very real. Freedom begins when you recognize the thoughts that didn't start with you.

Mind & Identity Distortion

45. **The Abyss** – Depression. "Nothing will ever change."

46. **The Broken Mirror** – Self-Hatred. "You are never enough."

47. **The Guard** – Fear of Failure & Success. "Don't try, it won't work."

48. **The Phantom** – Fear & Anxiety. "Something bad is coming."

49. **The Liar** – Deception & Reality Distortion. "The truth is what I say it is."

50. **The Doubter** – Unbelief & Indecision. "What if it's not real?"

51. **The Mindstorm** – Intrusive Thoughts & Mental Noise. "Your brain can't have a rest."

52. **The Waffler** – Overthinking & Confusion. "You can't choose."

53. **Leviathan** – Pride. "You don't need correction."

54. **The Rash One** – Impulsivity & Self Destruction. "I don't need to think, I just act."

The Abyss
Core Torment & Lie: Depression.
"Nothing will ever change."
Gifts Under Attack:

- **Joy** – It drains the spirit of gladness, replacing it with sorrow and heaviness (*"You turned my wailing into dancing; you removed my sackcloth and clothed me with joy." Psalm 30:11*).
- **Hope** – It suffocates expectation, convincing you that nothing good is coming (*"May the God of hope fill you with all joy and peace as you trust in him, so that you may overflow with hope by the power of the Holy Spirit." Romans 15:13*).
- **Spiritual Stamina** – It weighs the soul with fatigue and despair, weakening endurance (*"But those who hope in the Lord will renew their strength. They will soar on wings like eagles; they will run and not grow weary; they will walk and not be faint." Isaiah 40:31*).
- **Vision for the Future** – It blurs the ability to dream, plan, or believe for more (*"'For I know the plans I have for you,' declares the Lord, 'plans to prosper you and not to harm you, plans to give you a hope and a future.'" Jeremiah 29:11*).

The Abyss is a tenacious and ancient spirit, clearly named in scripture as a "spirit of heaviness" *(Isaiah 61:3).* It has plagued even the most faithful of God's servants—Elijah, David, Job, Jeremiah—all of whom wrestled with crushing despair. Ecclesiastes reminds us that *"with much wisdom comes much sorrow" (Ecclesiastes 1:18),* revealing that sorrow is not always a sign of weakness, but a consequence of deep awareness in a broken world.

The Abyss lingers. It follows a cyclical pattern, returning again and again like the spirit described in Matthew 12:44: *"I will return to my house from which I came."* Left unchallenged, it will make its home in you, weaving in and out of seasons, making you believe the darkness is your nature, not an intruder.

This spirit convinces you that your pain is permanent. That your prayers don't matter. That your life will never change. It paralyzes hope and suffocates vision, keeping you spiritually stagnant. It's bondage disguised as resignation—a voice that says, "This is just who you are now."

It is generational. It hunts for open doors: trauma, heartbreak, addiction, isolation, burnout. But it cannot remain where the Holy Spirit is invited to dwell. The only way to permanently evict the Abyss is to replace it with the presence of God. His Spirit brings beauty for ashes, the oil of joy for mourning, and a garment of praise for the spirit of heaviness *(Isaiah 61:3)*.

Scripture Reference:

"The spirit of heaviness..." (Isaiah 61:3 NKJV)

"Why, my soul, are you downcast? Why so disturbed within me?" (Psalm 42:11 NLT)

"He drew me up from the pit of destruction, out of the miry bog..." (Psalm 40:2 ESV)

Common Symptoms:

- Constant emotional heaviness
- Loss of motivation or interest
- Isolation and withdrawal
- Feelings of worthlessness or despair
- Recurring thoughts of death or escape

Real-Life Example:

Elizabeth is bright, warm, and driven. From the outside, she seems unstoppable: a self-made entrepreneur who built a thriving consulting firm and helped dozens of businesses find clarity, structure, and success. Clients praise her insight and credit her with saving projects that were on the verge of collapse.

What no one saw was the pattern beneath the surface: since childhood, Elizabeth wrestled with waves of deep depression. They came quietly, like a storm building on the horizon. She could sense them approaching—an invisible heaviness settling in her chest, a dulling of color and purpose. Once the darkness set in, it was total. She would lie on her couch in the dark, unable to move or answer calls or remember why anything mattered.

The depressive episodes would sometimes last weeks. Other times, months. And then, just as mysteriously, they would lift. She'd return to her vibrant self, pick up where she left off, and carry on as if nothing had happened.

After a brutal heartbreak in her late 30s, something changed. The cloud didn't lift. Not after a few months. Not after a couple of years. The pain lingered like a fog that no sun could burn through. She tried to numb it with alcohol and weed, but that only made the spiral worse. One night, lying alone in the dark, the thought slipped in quietly: *"Maybe I'd be better off gone."*

She didn't make a plan or write a note, but the idea of disappearing seemed better than continuing to live in a world that no longer had light. She couldn't even remember who she used to be before The Abyss took over.

Solutions & Declarations:

1. **My soul may feel downcast, but I will put my hope in God.**
   "Why, my soul, are you downcast? Why so disturbed within me? Put your hope in God, for I will yet praise Him, my Savior and my God." (Psalm 42:5)

2. **The Lord is close to me when I am brokenhearted, and He rescues my crushed spirit.**
   "The Lord is close to the brokenhearted and saves those who are crushed in spirit." (Psalm 34:18)

3. **God has given me a garment of praise instead of a spirit of heaviness.**
   "To comfort all who mourn… to give them beauty for ashes, the oil of joy for mourning, the garment of praise for the spirit of heaviness." (Isaiah 61:3, NKJV)

Turn to the Index of Deliverance Prayers and go to:
Prayer 9: General Prayer for Pride of Life
Prayer 10: Deliverance from Mind & Identity Distortion
Supplemental Prayers: 21, 32

Cross-References:

- **The Broken Mirror** – Self-hatred left unhealed often deepens into the despair of The Abyss, convincing individuals they are beyond repair.
- **The Phantom** – Persistent fear and anxiety can spiral into depressive strongholds, dragging the mind deeper into emotional darkness.
- **The Chainkeeper** – Unforgiveness toward others or oneself becomes a heavy weight that anchors the soul in sorrow and hopelessness.
- **The Alchemist** – Many turn to substances in a desperate attempt to numb the pain of The Abyss, only to sink further into bondage.
- **Lazybones** – Emotional exhaustion and spiritual sloth compound the despair, leading to paralysis and a sense of purposelessness.

The Broken Mirror
Core Torment & Lie: Self-Hatred.
"You are never enough."
Gifts Under Attack:

- **Self-Worth** – It convinces you that your value is conditional or nonexistent (*"Indeed, the very hairs of your head are all numbered. Don't be afraid; you are worth more than many sparrows." Luke 12:7*).
- **Confidence** – It cripples boldness and makes you doubt your place in the world (*"So do not throw away your confidence; it will be richly rewarded." Hebrews 10:35*).
- **Clarity of Identity** – It distorts how you see yourself, replacing truth with accusation (*"I praise you because I am fearfully and*

wonderfully made; your works are wonderful, I know that full well."
Psalm 139:14).

- **Capacity to Receive Love** – It blocks intimacy with others and with God, whispering you're unworthy *("We love because He first loved us." 1 John 4:19).*

This demon warps your identity at the root. It distorts how you see yourself, how you believe others see you, and how you believe God sees you. It's worse than low self-esteem; it's spiritual self-loathing.

The Broken Mirror thrives on shame, comparison, and inner cruelty. It whispers accusations that feel like your own thoughts: "I'm disgusting. I always ruin things. I hate myself."

More than destroying confidence, it sabotages calling.

Scripture Reference:

"For we are God's masterpiece. He has created us anew in Christ Jesus, so we can do the good things he planned for us long ago." (Ephesians 2:10, NLT)

"I praise you because I am fearfully and wonderfully made; your works are wonderful, I know that full well." (Psalm 139:14, NIV)

"There is therefore now no condemnation for those who are in Christ Jesus." (Romans 8:1, ESV)

Common Symptoms:

- Constant negative self-talk
- Difficulty accepting compliments or love
- Feeling unworthy of God's forgiveness
- Perfectionism rooted in shame
- Avoiding mirrors or photos
- Self-sabotage in relationships or purpose
- Thoughts like: "I hate myself," "I ruin everything," "I don't belong"

Real-Life Example:

Kate was admired, respected, and well-liked. Her coworkers described her as the most competent person in the office, and her boss often held up her work as the gold standard. But if they could hear her inner dialogue, they would have been horrified.

A relentless voice ran through her mind like a cruel narrator: *"You're disgusting. A fat, pathetic loser."* It didn't matter that Betsy was underweight or that she hadn't eaten a full meal in days because she was caught in the grip of an eating disorder that no one could see. When people complimented her appearance, the voice twisted their words: *They're making fun of you. They're mocking you.*

She couldn't trust anyone's praise. When men approached her, she was certain it was a setup—just another cruel joke waiting to happen. So, she avoided eye contact, shut down conversations, and kept everyone at a distance. The idea of having close friends terrified her. She believed they would eventually "see the truth" about her worthlessness and spread it to everyone.

What Kate didn't realize was that this torment had a generational root. Her own mother had lived under the same inner tyranny—different symptoms, same spirit. The Broken Mirror had passed from one woman to the next, distorting identity and poisoning self-worth in silence.

Solutions & Declarations:

1. **I am Gods masterpiece, created to do good things.**
   "For we are God's masterpiece. He has created us anew in Christ Jesus, so we can do the good things he planned for us long ago." (Ephesians 2:10)

2. **"I am fearfully and wonderfully made."**
   "I praise you because I am fearfully and wonderfully made; your works are wonderful; I know that full well." (Psalm 139:14)

3. **"I am not condemned, because I am in Christ Jesus."**
   "Therefore, there is now no condemnation for those who are in Christ Jesus." (Romans 8:1)

Turn to Chapter 9 Prayer Index and go to:

Prayer 9: General Prayer for Pride of Life

Prayer 10: Deliverance from Mind & Identity Distortion

Supplemental Prayer: 21, 34

Cross References:

- **The False Mirror** – Twists perception through comparison and distortion, reinforcing feelings of inadequacy and unworthiness.
- **The Shrinker** – Causes individuals to minimize themselves and hide their gifts out of fear of being seen or judged.
- **The Rejecter** – Convinces you that others will always push you away, leading to internalized self-loathing.
- **The Critic** – Echoes the voice of internal or external judgment, feeding the cycle of shame and harsh self-assessment.
- **The Inverter** – Warps good into bad and bad into good, making it hard to see your own value clearly or receive affirmation.
- **The Mute** – Silences the true self due to fear of judgment or being unworthy of expression, often rooted in self-hatred.
- **The Coward** – Prevents healthy risk-taking or expression of gifts out of deep-rooted fear of failure and not being good enough.
- **The Abyss** – Deepens the torment of self-hatred into depression, despair, and emotional paralysis when unhealed pain festers.

The Guard

Core Torment & Lie: Fear of Failure & Success

"Don't try. It won't work."

Gifts Under Attack:

- **Courage** – It paralyzes action, convincing you that risk will only lead to regret (*"Have I not commanded you? Be strong and courageous. Do not be afraid; do not be discouraged, for the Lord your God will be with you wherever you go." Joshua 1:9*).

- **Initiative** – It delays progress by replacing momentum with analysis paralysis *("Whoever watches the wind will not plant; whoever looks at the clouds will not reap." Ecclesiastes 11:4)*.
- **Vision** – It clouds your sense of direction, making future goals seem unreachable or unsafe *("Where there is no vision, the people perish: but he that keepeth the law, happy is he." Proverbs 29:18)*.
- **Obedience** – It hinders prompt responses to God's leading by elevating fear over faith *("To obey is better than sacrifice, and to heed is better than the fat of rams." 1 Samuel 15:22)*.
- **Faith to Step Forward** – It stifles belief that God will meet you as you move *("By faith Abraham, when called to go to a place he would later receive as his inheritance, obeyed and went, even though he did not know where he was going." Hebrews 11:8)*.
- **Leadership** – It convinces you that influence is dangerous and responsibility will crush you *("For the Spirit God gave us does not make us timid, but gives us power, love and self-discipline." 2 Timothy 1:7)*.

The Guard says that it's safer not to try than to risk being seen. It triggers fear at the thought of failure and sometimes even greater fear at the thought of success. Fear of failure says, "You'll look so stupid." Fear of success says, "You'll have to keep performing." This spirit creates hesitation, perfectionism, paralysis, and false logic that delays your destiny. You're left endlessly analyzing instead of moving. It wants you to believe you're being cautious and wise by considering all the possible negative angles endlessly. This demon is assigned to block destiny.

We know The Guard is in action when we see someone who receives a powerful idea, confirmation, or open door but immediately stalls. They tell themselves they need to "prepare more" or "wait until the right time." Meanwhile, months or years pass. The Guard keeps them in a cycle of false readiness and delayed obedience. They feel stuck, but don't realize it's fear dressed up as logic. The Guard says, "Better safe than sorry. What if you fail?"

Scripture Reference:

> *"If you wait for perfect conditions, you will never
> get anything done." (Ecclesiastes 11:4 TLB)*

> *"Fear of man will prove to be a snare, but whoever trusts
> in the Lord is kept safe." (Proverbs 29:25 NIV)*

> *"Be strong and courageous. Do not be afraid; do not be discouraged, for
> the Lord your God will be with you wherever you go." (Joshua 1:9 NIV)*

Common Symptoms:

- Overthinking and indecision
- Procrastination despite desire
- Avoidance of opportunities
- Fear of visibility or being "too much"
- Deep hesitation at turning points in life
- Fear of starting new projects or pursuing calling
- Self-sabotage before big opportunities
- Deep discomfort with praise, promotion, or visibility
- Chronic doubt or second-guessing
- Sudden anxiety when things begin to go *well*
- Fear of being seen or exposed

Real-Life Example:

Jessica is the right hand to one of the most influential gallery owners in San Francisco—an icon in the art world. Since graduating college with honors in art history, Jessica has been instrumental in scouting talent and is widely credited for discovering several of the gallery's most successful artists. Over the years, she's earned a front-row seat to power, prestige, and priceless experience. By all accounts, she's ready to launch her own gallery. Everyone knows it.

To Jessica's amazement, her boss agrees—and offers to help fund the launch herself. It's a dream offer: mentorship, financial backing, and a soft landing. But Jessica hesitates. Then stalls. Then declines.

On the outside, she chalks it up to timing. In her head, she calls it humility. In reality, she's being strangled by panic: "What if I blow it? What if I'm not enough? What if I actually succeed and everyone sees the real me?"

She tells herself she's being careful, but it's not caution, it's fear disguised as strategy. She can't even bring herself to celebrate the offer because she's already imagining worst-case scenarios. Her heart is in lockdown. She's built walls around her gift.

The Guard tells her it's safer not to try. That risk will expose her. That success will demand more than she can give. So she stays in the shadows, convincing herself she's not quite ready—while others with less talent walk into the future she prayed for.

Solutions & Declarations:

1. **I trust in the Lord and do not lean on my own understanding.**
   "Trust in the Lord with all your heart and lean not on your own understanding." (Proverbs 3:5)

2. **I was not given a spirit of fear, but of power, love, and a sound mind.**
   "For God has not given us a spirit of fear, but of power and of love and of a sound mind." (2 Timothy 1:7)

3. **I will be strong and courageous, for the Lord is with me.**
   "Have I not commanded you? Be strong and courageous. Do not be afraid; do not be discouraged, for the Lord your God will be with you wherever you go." (Joshua 1:9)

Turn to Chapter 9 Prayer Index and go to:
Prayer 9: General Prayer for Pride of Life
Prayer 10: Deliverance from Mind & Identity Distortion
Supplemental Prayer: 22, 32

Cross-References:

- **The Staller** – Uses perfectionism to delay action, masking fear of failure as preparation.
- **The Phantom** – Paralyzes with anxiety and dread, making risk or responsibility feel dangerous.
- **The Broken Mirror** – Deep self-hatred fuels avoidance; if you believe you're not enough, you never try.
- **The Abyss** – Persistent inactivity can spiral into despair, reinforcing the cycle of stagnation.
- **The Puppeteer** – Fear of disapproval can open the door to people-pleasing and surrendering control.
- **The Chainkeeper** – Unforgiveness toward self or others keeps fear alive by chaining you to past trauma.
- **Leviathan** – Fear of failure may mask pride; avoiding action protects the ego from being exposed.

The Phantom
Core Torment & Lie: Fear & Anxiety.
"Something bad is coming."
Gifts Under Attack:

- **Peace** – It keeps you in a constant state of unrest, unable to settle into God's presence *("And the peace of God, which surpasses all understanding, will guard your hearts and your minds in Christ Jesus." Philippians 4:7).*
- **Trust** – It makes you doubt God's care and anticipate harm instead of help *("Trust in the Lord with all your heart and lean not on your own understanding; in all your ways submit to him, and he will make your paths straight." Proverbs 3:5–6).*
- **Confidence in God's Protection** – It erodes the assurance that you are safe under God's covering *("He will cover you with his feathers, and under his wings you will find refuge; his faithfulness will be your shield and rampart." Psalm 91:4).*

- **Rest** – It disrupts sleep, stillness, and your ability to be present in the moment *("Come to me, all you who are weary and burdened, and I will give you rest." Matthew 11:28).*

The Phantom is a spirit of fear. It drifts in like smoke. Sometimes through trauma, sometimes through open doors like horror media, occult games, or anxiety passed down through a family line. It fills your thoughts with worst-case scenarios and triggers emotional or physical panic. It makes you brace for disaster even when everything seems fine. You live in survival mode, always waiting for the other shoe to drop. It's more than nerves; it's straight up torment.

We see The Phantom at work in someone who checks their locks multiple times, avoids phone calls, or fears something terrible will happen even in ordinary moments. They might dread opening emails, answering unknown numbers, or even leaving the house. The Phantom makes peace feel impossible. It says, "You're not safe. Something bad is coming." The fear feels real, but it's spiritually rooted.

Scripture Reference:

"God has not given us a spirit of fear, but of power and of love and of a sound mind." (2 Timothy 1:7 NKJV)

"I sought the Lord, and He answered me; He delivered me from all my fears." (Psalm 34:4 NIV)

"You will keep in perfect peace all who trust in You, all whose thoughts are fixed on You." (Isaiah 26:3 NLT)

"Be Strong and courageous! Do not be afraid or discouraged. For the Lord your God is with you wherever you go." (Joshua 1:9 NIV)

Common Symptoms:

- Constant worrying or racing thoughts
- Panic attacks or chest tightness
- Avoiding normal situations due to fear
- Difficulty sleeping or relaxing
- Over-alertness or hypervigilance

Real-Life Example:

Barbara is an empty nester whose children are grown, stable, and living on their own. By all accounts, she's done her job well—they're healthy, employed, and independent. Instead of enjoying a new season of peace and purpose, Barbara lives in a constant state of dread.

Every missed call or late reply from one of her kids triggers a storm of catastrophic thoughts. She imagines car accidents, emergencies, or hidden suffering they're too "afraid" to tell her about. She checks the news obsessively, scans social media for clues, and texts repeatedly to "just make sure everything's okay."

What once looked like nurturing concern has become spiritual torment.

Desperate for peace of mind, Barbara starts visiting card readers and self-proclaimed prophets who claim to offer "insight." She convinces herself it's harmless—just maternal instinct—but something shifts. The more she seeks answers from spiritual sources outside of God, the darker her thoughts become. Nightmares and panic attacks creep in. She's opened a door to The Phantom, and it's whispering lies in her mother's voice.

She begins to lose herself. Her home becomes silent. Her thoughts obsessive. The sad irony is that the very children she's trying to protect now avoid her. They've grown tired of the fear-based messages, the constant projection of doom, and the emotional manipulation masked as love. They feel sad watching their once-vibrant mother spiral, but they don't know how to help her. She doesn't realize she's scaring them away.

The Phantom exploits Barbara's love and turns it into a prison. Its voice says: "If you stop worrying, something bad will happen. If you rest, you'll miss the warning sign." And in obeying that voice, she misses the blessing of the life she still has.

Solutions & Declarations:

1. **I do not receive the spirit of fear—I walk in power, love, and soundness of mind.**
   "For God has not given us a spirit of fear, but of power and of love and of a sound mind." (2 Timothy 1:7)

2. **I sought the Lord and He delivered me from all my fears.**
   "I sought the Lord, and He answered me; He delivered me from all my fears." (Psalm 34:4)

3. **I fix my thoughts on God and He keeps me in perfect peace.**
   "You will keep in perfect peace those whose minds are steadfast, because they trust in you." (Isaiah 26:3)

Turn to Chapter 9 Prayer Index and go to:
Prayer 9: General Prayer for Pride of Life
Prayer 10: Deliverance from Mind & Identity Distortion
Supplemental Prayers: 22, 24

Cross-References:

- **The Guard** – Reacts to fear by over-controlling the environment or isolating emotionally for protection.
- **The Mindstorm** – Intrusive thoughts and mental noise often spiral out of fear-based thinking and what-if scenarios.
- **The Mute** – Shuts down emotionally or verbally in the face of fear, believing silence keeps them safe.
- **The Pretender** – Masks fear with a false persona, afraid of being exposed or rejected.
- **The Weak Father** – Models fear and passivity, passing down patterns of anxiety and emotional avoidance.
- **The Glacier** – Freezes inaction and emotion in response to fear, creating numbness instead of movement.
- **The Monitor** – Constantly scans for threats or wrongs, rooted in an anxious need for control.

- **The Orphan** – Carries abandonment anxiety and the deep fear of being unwanted or unsupported.
- **The Abyss** – Fear spirals into despair when anxiety is left unchecked or untreated.
- **The Coward** – Avoids confrontation, obedience, or risk due to paralyzing fear of man or failure.

The Liar

Core Torment & Lie: Deception & Reality Distortion.

"The truth is what I say it is."

Gifts Under Attack:

- **Discernment** – It blurs the lines between truth and falsehood, making it difficult to hear God's voice *("Dear friends, do not believe every spirit, but test the spirits to see whether they are from God, because many false prophets have gone out into the world." 1 John 4:1).*
- **Clarity** – It clouds perception, creating confusion and double-mindedness *("A double minded man is unstable in all his ways." James 1:8).*
- **Trust in God** – It replaces faith with skepticism, undermining the stability of God's promises *("Trust in the Lord with all your heart and lean not on your own understanding." Proverbs 3:5).*
- **Alignment with Reality** – It tempts you to live in denial or delusion rather than God's truth *("They perish because they refused to love the truth and so be saved. For this reason, God sends them a powerful delusion so that they will believe the lie." 2 Thessalonians 2:10–11).*
- **Moral Compass** – It dulls the conscience, making evil seem acceptable *("Woe to those who call evil good and good evil, who put darkness for light and light for darkness." Isaiah 5:20).*

The Liar is a deceiving spirit that distorts and replaces the truth. It operates through gaslighting, confusion, and subtle half-truths that blur the line between conviction and delusion. It convinces you that you're hearing from God when you're not, that sin isn't sin, or that your pain is an overreaction. The Liar fools others through you and robs *you* of the ability to receive truth at all. What once brought clarity now triggers defensiveness. What once convicted now offends. You begin to trust your perception over God's Word, and the more you agree with it, the more your world bends to its version of reality.

We know someone is under the influence of The Liar when they've fully convinced themselves that what is false is true. This isn't just pride or intellectual dishonesty, it's spiritual distortion. They're being presented with a version of reality that only *they* can see. The fact that no one else around them shares it doesn't cause concern; it only makes them double down. They start to look unstable, irrational, but this isn't always willful. A person isn't entirely innocent, but they aren't always aware either. This spirit often enters through a persistent refusal to love the truth. Eventually, God allows them to have what they've insisted on: a different version of reality (see *2 Thessalonians 2:10–11*). Once deception takes root, it blinds them to correction, even when it's spoken in love.

Scripture Reference:

"You belong to your father, the devil... When he lies, he speaks his native language, for he is a liar and the father of lies." (John 8:44 NIV)

"Woe to those who call evil good and good evil, who put darkness for light and light for darkness." (Isaiah 5:20 NIV)

"For God is not the author of confusion but of peace." (1 Corinthians 14:33 KJV)

Common Symptoms:

- Believing obvious lies or half-truths
- Confusion over what's true or real

- Rationalizing sinful behavior
- Feeling like you're losing your mind
- Difficulty trusting scripture or godly counsel

Real-Life Example:

Izzy Fender rose to national fame as a wellness guru after claiming she healed herself of a rare and aggressive illness using only natural methods, spiritual practices, and a custom herbal protocol she designed herself. Her story captured hearts across the country. She became a best-selling author, launched a wildly successful app, and was even invited to speak at global conferences on holistic health.

For years, Izzy was untouchable. Her fans saw her as proof that modern medicine wasn't the only answer. Behind the curtain, there were murmurs: doctors who had never seen her files, hospitals with no record of her treatment, and inconsistencies in her timelines that didn't add up. Eventually, it all came crashing down.

Her deception was exposed in the most public way imaginable: a primetime interview with the country's most respected journalist. Millions tuned in.

The host calmly presented hard evidence: medical records, expert testimony, and video timelines that contradicted Izzy's entire narrative. The audience held its breath, waiting for a moment of humility or even a flicker of truth.

Instead, Izzy doubled down.

Then she tripled down.

She smiled, blinked slowly, and insisted the truth was "more complicated" than people could understand. When the journalist finally asked her—flat out—if she believed she still had a healthy relationship with reality, Izzy didn't flinch. "I don't know what you mean," she said.

The interview became infamous. News outlets called it "a masterclass in delusion." Commentators debated whether she was a pathological liar or simply a person who believed her own deception. But what no one seemed to realize was this: Izzy was no longer lying just to the world. She was lying to herself.

This is what happens when The Liar takes full control. The deception becomes a stronghold so deep that even exposed truth can't break through. The conscience is seared. The mind is blind. And the lie becomes the only thing left to stand on.

Solutions & Declarations:

1. **I reject confusion and deception. I receive the Spirit of truth.**
   "When the Spirit of truth comes, He will guide you into all truth."
   (John 16:13)

2. **The truth sets me free—not opinion, not tradition, but God's truth.**
   "Then you will know the truth, and the truth will set you free."
   (John 8:32)

3. **I test every spirit and every thought by the Word of God.**
   "Dear friends, do not believe every spirit, but test the spirits to see whether they are from God." (1 John 4:1)

Turn to Chapter 9 Prayer Index and go to:

Prayer 9: General Prayer for Pride of Life
Prayer 10: Deliverance from Mind & Identity Distortion
Supplemental Prayers: 16, 17, 21

Cross-References:

- **The Inverter** – Distorts reality by calling good evil and evil good, flipping moral foundations.
- **The Arcane One** – Hides truth behind mysticism and secret knowledge, leading people into false light.
- **The False Mirror** – Lies about identity and worth, warping self-perception.
- **The Pretender** – Masks true feelings or struggles with a false persona to protect against rejection.
- **The Glazer** – Uses flattery and false encouragement to distort perception and enable pride.

- **The Monitor** – Polices, twists, and suppresses truth in favor of socially accepted lies.
- **The Apostate** – Abandons truth once known and embraces deception for comfort or cultural acceptance.
- **The Oracle** – Claims hidden revelation but misleads others with counterfeit spiritual insight.
- **The Puppeteer** – Manipulates through partial truths and strategic omission to control outcomes.
- **The Idolater** – Elevates false ideologies, people, or desires above God's truth.

The Doubter

Core Torment & Lie: Unbelief & Indecision

"What if it's not real?"

Gifts Under Attack:

- **Faith** – It undermines your ability to stand firm on God's promises (*"And without faith it is impossible to please God, because anyone who comes to him must believe that he exists and that he rewards those who earnestly seek him." Hebrews 11:6*).
- **Trust** – It causes you to waver, questioning God's goodness and reliability (*"Trust in the Lord with all your heart and lean not on your own understanding; in all your ways submit to him, and he will make your paths straight." Proverbs 3:5–6*).
- **Confidence in God's Word** – It erodes the foundation of truth, leading to spiritual instability (*"But when you ask, you must believe and not doubt, because the one who doubts is like a wave of the sea, blown and tossed by the wind. That person should not expect to receive anything from the Lord. Such a person is double-minded and unstable in all they do." James 1:6–8*).
- **Boldness in Prayer** – It silences authority by convincing you that God may not answer (*"Therefore I tell you, whatever you ask*

for in prayer, believe that you have received it, and it will be yours."
Mark 11:24).

- **Forward Movement** – It keeps you stuck in hesitation and fear, unable to walk in your calling *("For the Spirit God gave us does not make us timid, but gives us power, love and self-discipline." 2 Timothy 1:7).*

The Doubter is sly. It casts just enough uncertainty to paralyze belief. This demon doesn't always want you to stop believing in God altogether, it just wants you to second-guess His voice, His Word, and His promises. The Doubter shows up as skepticism, deconstruction, confusion, and chronic hesitation. It tells you the Bible might be outdated... that maybe you misunderstood that promise... that perhaps faith is just a feeling. It's the same voice the serpent used in Eden: subtle and poisoning with uncertainty.

Unbelief is a spiritual stronghold. The Doubter works slowly and subtly, and its most effective method is corrosion. Over time, the foundation crumbles. That's why Jesus said we must have the faith of a child *(Matthew 18:3).* Childlike faith means trust without the need to control or intellectualize every outcome.

Scripture Reference:

"Did God really say...?" (Genesis 3:1)

"But when you ask, you must believe and not doubt... such a person is double-minded and unstable in all they do." (James 1:6–8)

"Without faith it is impossible to please God." (Hebrews 11:6)

Common Symptoms:

- Overanalyzing or rationalizing away God's promises
- Difficulty believing Scripture as literal or relevant
- Chronic spiritual hesitation or fear of being "wrong"
- Praying without expectation or faith
- Exposure to false teachings or ideologies that erode trust in God

Real-Life Example:

Debora was praying fervently for a solution to her debt. As a home health care aide, she was making just enough to live hand to mouth and only pay the interest on what she owed, even though she kept a meticulous budget. One day, the daughter of one of her clients was at her mother's house, visiting from out of state. The daughter was so pleased to meet Debora after hearing all the wonderful reports from her mother about how conscientious and kind Debora was to the elderly woman.

Taking out her phone, the woman asked Debora what her Cash App was, or if she had PayPal or Venmo, because she wanted to send her a gift of appreciation. The woman told her the amount God had put on her heart to give Debora. It was exactly the amount she needed to pay off her debt and replenish her savings account. Debora was stunned and refused to accept it. She couldn't believe this stranger would do something like this for her. She would have run away at that moment, but she was still on her shift.

Fortunately, the daughter recognized what was happening spiritually with Debora and got her cell number from her mother's phone, sending the transfer while Debora stood there, stunned and still not believing *what actually happened.*

God answered Debora's prayer. The Doubter almost caused her to miss it.

Solutions & Declarations:

1. **I walk by faith, not by sight.**
   "For we walk by faith, not by sight." (2 Corinthians 5:7)

2. **I believe God's Word is true, unchanging, and living.**
   "For the word of God is living and active, sharper than any two-edged sword..." (Hebrews 4:12)

3. **I will not be double minded but rooted in truth.**
   "The one who doubts is like a wave of the sea, blown and tossed by the wind... Such a person is double-minded and unstable in all they do." (James 1:6–8

Turn to Chapter 9 Prayer Index and go to:
Prayer 9: General Prayer for Pride of Life
Prayer 10: Deliverance from Mind & Identity Distortion
Supplemental Prayers: 15, 24

Cross-References:

- **The Phantom** – Fuels uncertainty by projecting fear-based outcomes that cloud decision-making.
- **The Abyss** – Longstanding doubt often leads to spiritual paralysis and emotional despair.
- **The Liar** – Erodes biblical trust by introducing subtle lies and twisting God's promises.
- **The Arcane One** – When truth feels unstable, doubt can open doors to false spiritual systems.
- **The Guard** – Uses fear of getting it wrong to keep people stuck, silent, or passive in disobedience.

The Mindstorm

Core Torment & Lie: Intrusive Thoughts & Mental Noise.

"Your brain can't have a rest."

Gifts Under Attack:

- **Clarity** – It floods the mind with distraction and confusion, making it hard to discern truth *("For God is not a God of confusion but of peace—as in all the churches of the saints." 1 Corinthians 14:33).*
- **Focus** – It scatters attention and robs the ability to stay present or follow through *("Let your eyes look straight ahead; fix your gaze directly before you. Give careful thought to the paths for your feet and be steadfast in all your ways. Do not turn to the right or the left; keep your foot from evil." Proverbs 4:25–27).*
- **Rest** – It prevents mental and emotional stillness, even in calm surroundings *("Come to me, all you who are weary and burdened, and I will give you rest. Take my yoke upon you and learn from me,*

for I am gentle and humble in heart, and you will find rest for your souls." Matthew 11:28–29).

- **Inner Stillness** – It resists the quiet voice of God, keeping the soul in constant motion *("Be still, and know that I am God; I will be exalted among the nations, I will be exalted in the earth." Psalm 46:10).*
- **Peace of Mind** – It overrides God's gift of peace with relentless inner chatter *("You will keep in perfect peace those whose minds are steadfast, because they trust in you." Isaiah 26:3).*

The Mindstorm is relentless. It floods your mind with noise, ear worms, and thoughts you didn't ask for. Sometimes it's so dark and disturbing it takes you aback. Other times, it's just constant, racing mental chatter. Either way, the goal is the same: to keep you from hearing God's voice or sitting in peace. The Mindstorm loves silence because it can fill it first. The more you try to quiet your mind, the louder it gets. This is beyond anxiety or overthinking—it's a spiritual attack designed to wear you down and make you question your sanity.

Scripture Reference:
"God is not the author of confusion but of peace." (1 Corinthians 14:33)

"You will keep in perfect peace all who trust in you, all whose thoughts are fixed on you."(Isaiah 26:3)

"We take captive every thought to make it obedient to Christ." (2 Corinthians 10:5)

Common Symptoms:
- Intrusive, repetitive, or obsessive thoughts
- Racing thoughts or internal "chatter" that won't stop
- Difficulty entering prayer, worship, or stillness
- Thoughts that feel alien or unwanted
- Mental fatigue from constant internal noise

Real-Life Example:

Phoebe has never known what it's like to have a quiet mind. Even as a child, her thoughts ran like a broken carousel: spinning, spiraling, refusing to stop. Her parents took her to specialists, and she was eventually diagnosed and medicated. The pills only made her feel numb and foggy, not free. She didn't want to silence her brain with chemicals—she wanted the thoughts to *be her own*. Instead, it felt like her mind had been hijacked, like something was pulling her into endless loops of worry, distraction, and mental clutter.

No matter how hard she tried to focus, her brain swerved off course. Studying, sleeping, even praying felt impossible. Desperate for relief, she started drinking to slow things down, and it helped—at first. But now she worries she's trading one tormentor for another. She doesn't want to become an addict, but she can't seem to win the battle in her mind. The Mindstorm won't let her rest, and she's starting to wonder if she'll ever know what peace feels like.

Solutions & Declarations:

1. **I have the mind of Christ.**
   "For who has known the mind of the Lord so as to instruct him? But we have the mind of Christ." (1 Corinthians 2:16)

2. **God gives me power, love, and a sound mind.**
   "For God has not given us a spirit of fear, but of power and of love and of a sound mind." (2 Timothy 1:7, NKJV)

3. **I take every thought captive and make it obey Christ.**
   "We take captive every thought to make it obedient to Christ." (2 Corinthians 10:5)

Turn to Chapter 9 Prayer Index and go to:
Prayer 9: General Prayer for Pride of Life
Prayer 10: Deliverance from Mind & Identity Distortion
Supplemental Prayer: 24

Cross-References:

- **The Doubter** – Undermines faith by injecting questions and uncertainty that derail focused prayer and worship.
- **The Phantom** – Feeds intrusive thoughts with fear-based projections and constant mental unrest.
- **The Abyss** – Mental torment opens the door to emotional numbness and despair when left unresolved.
- **The Loop** – Digital overstimulation worsens the brain's ability to rest, compounding The Mindstorm's chaos.
- **The Waffler** – Where The Mindstorm overwhelms the mind, the Waffler freezes it with indecision and mental paralysis.

The Waffler

Core Torment & Lie: Overthinking & Confusion.

"You can't choose."

Gifts Under Attack:

- **Discernment** – It clouds spiritual perception, making it hard to distinguish God's voice from fear or doubt *("But solid food is for the mature, who by constant use have trained themselves to distinguish good from evil." Hebrews 5:14)*.
- **Boldness** – It paralyzes initiative, causing hesitation when action is needed *("For God has not given us a spirit of fear, but of power and of love and of a sound mind." 2 Timothy 1:7)*.
- **Decision-Making** – It breeds second-guessing, stalling progress and opening the door to disobedience *("A double minded man is unstable in all his ways." James 1:8)*.
- **Obedience** – It undermines confident steps of faith by demanding perfect clarity first *("Trust in the Lord with all your heart and lean not on your own understanding; in all your ways submit to him, and he will make your paths straight." Proverbs 3:5–6)*.

- **Peace** – It replaces peace with turmoil by keeping the soul in a constant state of questioning *("For God is not the author of confusion, but of peace, as in all churches of the saints." 1 Corinthians 14:33)*.

The Waffler traps you in overthinking, confusion, and indecision. It makes choices feel dangerous. Every option seems wrong. Every path looks risky. It keeps you circling, hesitating, questioning, doubting. The Waffler convinces you that staying stuck is safer than moving forward. At its core, this demon is an assassin of momentum. It paralyzes obedience by flooding the decision-making process with fear and false complexity. Anyone tempted to help a person oppressed by this demon gets frustrated and leaves the victim alone to wrestle indefinitely until the time to decide has passed and a choice is made under duress or by default.

Scripture Reference:

"A double-minded man is unstable in all his ways." (James 1:8)

"Trust in the Lord with all your heart and lean not on your own understanding." (Proverbs 3:5)

"Let your 'Yes' be 'Yes,' and your 'No,' 'No.'" (Matthew 5:37)

Common Symptoms:

- Obsessive pros and cons lists or analysis paralysis
- Constant second-guessing, even after making a decision
- Fear of commitment or "getting it wrong"
- Deep internal confusion about what God is saying
- Avoidance of action in the name of "waiting for clarity"

Real-Life Example:

Brian prayed for a godly wife and when he met Sharon, he knew deep down she was the answer. She was kind, faithful, discerning, and everything he hoped for in a partner. But moving forward would require change: a relocation, a new job, and a new chapter of responsibility. At first, Brian was excited. Then the Waffler crept in.

He began second-guessing everything. Was this really God's will? What if he was wrong? What if he moved and it didn't work out? He asked friends for advice, then asked someone else, and then again, hoping for certainty he'd never get. Sharon, full of grace, waited patiently. But after months of emotional limbo, she gently ended the relationship. "If you're this unsure," she said, "then I'm not the one."

Only after she was gone did Brian realize what he'd lost. The Waffler paralyzed him with fear of making the wrong choice, and in doing so, caused him to miss the very thing God had sent.

Solutions & Declarations:

1. **God gives me power, love, and a sound mind.**
   "For God has not given us a spirit of fear, but of power and of love and of a sound mind." (2 Timothy 1:7, NKJV)

2. **I trust God's voice, and He leads me in paths of righteousness.**
   "He restores my soul; He leads me in the paths of righteousness for His name's sake." (Psalm 23:3)

3. **My steps are ordered by the Lord.**
   "The steps of a good man are ordered by the Lord, and He delights in his way." (Psalm 37:23, NKJV)

Turn to Chapter 9 Prayer Index and go to:

Prayer 9: General Prayer for Pride of Life
Prayer 10: Deliverance from Mind & Identity Distortion
Supplemental Prayer: 24

Cross-References:

- **The Guard** – Instills fear of both failure and success, which the Waffler converts into paralysis and indecision.
- **The Doubter** – Undermines confidence in God's voice, creating the uncertainty that fuels the Waffler's hesitation.
- **The Mindstorm** – Overwhelms the mind with noise and distraction, making clear decision-making feel impossible.

- **The Liar** – Distorts truth and perception; the Waffler builds indecision on top of these lies.
- **The Chainkeeper** – Traps you in regret and past wounds, which the Waffler uses to prevent you from ever choosing again.

Leviathan

Core Torment & Lie: Pride

"You don't need correction."

Gifts Under Attack:

- **Humility** – Leviathan resists correction and rebuke, blinding you to personal faults *("Whoever loves discipline loves knowledge, but whoever hates correction is stupid." Proverbs 12:1)*.
- **Teachability** – It fosters a hardened heart, making spiritual growth nearly impossible *("But encourage one another daily, as long as it is called 'Today,' so that none of you may be hardened by sin's deceitfulness." Hebrews 3:13)*.
- **Peace** – It twists words and intentions, breeding conflict in relationships *("A perverse person stirs up conflict, and a gossip separates close friends." Proverbs 16:28)*.
- **Unity** – It divides through arrogance and defensiveness, destroying healthy fellowship *("For where you have envy and selfish ambition, there you find disorder and every evil practice." James 3:16")*.
- **Clarity of Thought** – Its twisting spirit confuses truth, distorting what was spoken or meant *("In that day, the Lord will punish with his sword—his fierce, great and powerful sword—Leviathan the gliding serpent, Leviathan the coiling serpent; he will slay the monster of the sea." Isaiah 27:1)*.

Leviathan is a named principality in Scripture, making it a powerful ruling demon. Described in The Books of Job and Isaiah, Leviathan is a twisting serpent, a spiritual being associated with pride, chaos, and resistance to truth. Its name means "twisted" or "coiled," which reflects how it operates: twisting communication, distorting perception, and wrapping around the mind to prevent humility and repentance.

Pride was the very first sin committed by Lucifer himself and leading to his fall from heaven. It remains the sin God hates most, because it opposes His nature and authority at the deepest level. At the root of all sin is a prideful declaration: *"I know better than God."* Leviathan thrives on that posture, nurturing it until it hardens into full spiritual rebellion.

This spirit is behind:

- Chronic miscommunication and constant misunderstandings
- A hardened inability to receive correction
- Spiritual pride that disguises itself as discernment
- Division sown through twisted words and wounded egos
- Stubbornness that masquerades as conviction but resists true surrender

Leviathan is especially destructive within the church. It poses as spiritual depth while silently rejecting accountability, deliverance, or leadership. It breaks marriages, splits ministries, and shatters friendships, all while convincing each party they're right. Conversations become battlegrounds, and the spirit coils tighter with every offense left unhealed.

The only way to evict Leviathan is through deep humility, true repentance, and full submission to the Holy Spirit. As long as pride remains, this principality retains legal ground.

Scripture references:

"You crushed the heads of Leviathan; you gave him as food for the creatures of the wilderness." (Psalm 74:14)

"In that day the Lord will punish Leviathan the fleeing serpent, Leviathan the twisting serpent; and He will slay the dragon that is in the sea." (Isaiah 27:1)

"His rows of scales are his pride, shut up tightly as with a seal." (Job 41:15 — describing Leviathan as untouchable, armored, proud)

"God resists the proud but gives grace to the humble." (James 4:6)

Common symptoms:

- Always needs to be right, resists correction or feedback
- Twists words in arguments; denies wrong even when confronted
- Spiritual pride ("God told me," even when fruit proves otherwise)
- Easily offended, quick to assume insult
- Communication breakdowns that repeat over and over

Real-life example:

Terrence considers himself "deeply spiritual," claiming to hear from God with unusual clarity. He left his last church because they "weren't on his level." At his new church, rather than taking time to learn the community or submit to leadership, he immediately requested a meeting with the pastor—not to be discipled, but to ask what ministry he could lead. His language was polished, but his heart posture was steeped in spiritual pride.

The pastor and his wife, seasoned in discernment, were kind but cautious. They welcomed him into the congregation but did not immediately place him in authority. Frustrated, Terrence began making inroads elsewhere. He "reinterpreted" Sunday messages during fellowship time, using complex theological language to cast doubt on the pastor's teaching. At Bible studies, he derailed discussions to showcase his obscure scriptural insights, often unrelated to the topic but designed to impress.

Eventually, the pastor had to confront him privately and ask him to step down from group involvement. Instead of repenting, Terrence left and resumed his cycle, claiming the church wasn't ready for his anointing and once again looking for a community "on his level." He never once considered that the common denominator in all the conflict... was him.

Leviathan coiled tightly around his identity, turning correction into offense and community into competition. Terrence believed he was offering spiritual insight, but in truth, he was spreading division and confusion under the banner of discernment.

Solutions and declarations:

1. **I humble myself before God and others—I do not know all.**
   "God opposes the proud but gives grace to the humble." (James 4:6)

2. **I break agreement with the spirit that twists words, truth, and correction.**
   "Woe to those who call evil good and good evil... who are wise in their own eyes and clever in their own sight." (Isaiah 5:20–21)

3. **I receive grace through humility, not pride.**
   "Humble yourselves, therefore, under God's mighty hand, that He may lift you up in due time." (1 Peter 5:6)

Turn to Chapter 9 Prayer Index and go to:

Prayer 9: General Prayer for Pride of Life
Prayer 10: Deliverance from Mind & Identity Distortion
Supplemental Prayer: 15, 16, 18, 19

Cross-references:

- **The Litigator** – Leviathan thrives in contentious debate. The Litigator defends ego at all costs, masking pride as conviction and derailing unity through endless argument.
- **The Gatekeeper** – Spiritual elitism is one of Leviathan's sharpest tools. The Gatekeeper creates insider vs. outsider dynamics to elevate self and exclude others under the guise of truth.
- **The Critic** – Leviathan often uses this voice to tear down others from a place of superiority, keeping the focus on flaws rather than grace, and stunting growth in both parties.
- **The Guard** – Fear masquerading as humility creates a prideful resistance to correction. The Guard reinforces Leviathan's refusal to be vulnerable, teachable, or seen as weak.
- **The Pretender** – Leviathan works behind masks of false humility, spiritual performance, or self-loathing to maintain control and avoid true transformation.

- **The Mouth** – Language twisted by pride and offense serves Leviathan well. The Mouth speaks rashly, justifies cruelty, and resists correction under the banner of "speaking truth."
- **The Glazer** – Flattery and empty praise are often tools of Leviathan, used to keep egos inflated and truth at a safe distance.
- **The Monarch** – A spirit of entitlement born from unchecked pride. Leviathan fuels the belief that submission is for others, and authority is a right, not a responsibility.

The Rash One

Core Torment & Lie: Impulsivity & Self-Destruction

"I don't need to think. I just act."

Gifts Under Attack:

- **Discernment** – Rash decisions bypass spiritual discernment, leading to avoidable consequences *("The simple believe anything, but the prudent give thought to their steps." – Proverbs 14:15).*
- **Wisdom** – It rejects reflection and counsel, undermining sound judgment *("Desire without knowledge is not good—how much more will hasty feet miss the way!" – Proverbs 19:2).*
- **Self-Control** – It fuels flesh-driven behavior, leaving you vulnerable to regret and harm *("But the fruit of the Spirit is love, joy, peace, forbearance, kindness, goodness, faithfulness, gentleness and self-control. Against such things there is no law." – Galatians 5:22–23).*
- **Long-Term Vision** – It sacrifices future stability for present impulses *("The plans of the diligent lead to profit as surely as haste leads to poverty." – Proverbs 21:5).*

The Rash One acts first and regrets later, if at all. This demon drives impulsive decisions, reckless words, and unfiltered behavior that harms both the person and those around them. It often partners with emotional immaturity, pride, or rage, convincing the person that urgency equals truth and reaction equals strength. The Rash One has no patience for process, and no reverence for consequences. Its motto is "You only live once," and it laughs when your choices implode. Biblically, this is the spirit that led Saul to offer unlawful sacrifices and Esau to trade his birthright for stew. It is the enemy of restraint, reflection, and wisdom.

Scripture References:

"Whoever is patient has great understanding, but one who is quick-tempered displays folly." (Proverbs 14:29)

"Do not be rash with your mouth, nor let your heart be hasty to utter anything before God." (Ecclesiastes 5:2)

"Everyone should be quick to listen, slow to speak and slow to become angry." (James 1:19)

Common Symptoms:

- Making major life decisions impulsively
- Speaking without thinking, then regretting it
- Escalating conflict unnecessarily
- Constantly chasing adrenaline, novelty, or stimulation
- Sabotaging relationships or opportunities through erratic behavior

Real-Life Example:

Jada was fiery, and during one particular staff meeting, something snapped. Feeling disrespected, she erupted, blasting her boss in front of the entire team over Zoom. Fueled by adrenaline, her voice rose with every sentence. When others tried to interject, she only got louder, refusing to yield. One by one, her coworkers dropped off the call, stunned by the sheer volatility of her outburst.

Unsatisfied, Jada followed up with a scathing all-company email, venting her every frustration. Things didn't end there. Someone leaked the email online, and within hours, it went viral—not for its content, but for its *unhinged delivery.* Internet users found her social media accounts and began pulling old comments, painting her as a ticking time bomb. She quickly became a meme, a cautionary tale of workplace implosion.

Jada lost her job and torched her professional reputation. Now blacklisted in her industry, she considered changing her name just to start over. The worst part is this wasn't new. She'd walked out of jobs, friendships, and churches before. Deep down, she suspected she was the common denominator, but she didn't realize that The Rash One had been fueling her self-destruction all along.

Solutions and Declarations:

1. **I walk in wisdom and slow my reactions.**
   "Everyone should be quick to listen, slow to speak and slow to become angry." (James 1:19)

2. **I will not be ruled by impulse or ego.**
   "Like a city whose walls are broken through is a person who lacks self-control." (Proverbs 25:28)

3. **The Spirit of God gives me self-control.**
   "But the fruit of the Spirit is love, joy, peace, patience, kindness, goodness, faithfulness, gentleness, and self-control." (Galatians 5:22–23)

Turn to Chapter 9 Prayer Index and go to:

Prayer 9: General Prayer for Pride of Life
Prayer 10: Deliverance from Mind & Identity Distortion
Supplemental Prayer: 16, 19

Cross-References:

- **The Inferno** – Fuels explosive rage that escalates impulsive reactions into full-blown destruction.
- **The Coward** – Uses aggression as a smokescreen for deep-rooted fear and insecurity.
- **The Desperate** – Reacts recklessly from a place of emptiness, using drama to avoid being ignored.

- **The Avenger** – Strikes out from a sense of personal injustice, refusing to wait on God's timing or justice.
- **The Mouth** –Speaks without restraint; The Rash One acts without restraint. Both are impulsive, reckless, and leave destruction behind.

Not all control looks aggressive. Some of the most dangerous spirits operate quietly through flattery, guilt, domination, and emotional games. These demons manipulate outcomes by manipulating people. They twist motives, distort relationships, and make control feel like love, loyalty, or strength.

Some use power while others use pity, but the result is the same: people are not free. These spirits thrive in families, churches, leadership structures, marriages, and friend groups. And while their methods differ, their goal is always the same: to control behavior, perception, and emotion in order to maintain influence.

In this chapter, you'll meet the demons that distort truth, twist relationships, and sabotage spiritual authority:

Control & Manipulation

55. **Jezebel** – Manipulative Domination. "Control is better than submission."

56. **The Puppeteer** – Control Through Emotional Manipulation. "If you don't control them, they'll leave you or hurt you."

57. **The Intimidator** – Domination Through Fear. "Fear keeps people in line."

58. **The Dominator** – Aggressive Control. "My way or nothing."

59. **The Narcissist** – Self Exaltation & Lack of Humility. "I am the center of everything."

60. **The Pretender** – Masking & Fear-Based Pride. "If they saw the real me, they'd leave."

61. **The Glacier** – Emotional Numbness & Self-Protection. "Feelings are weakness."

62. **King Baby** – Avoidance & Entitlement. "Someone else will handle it."

63. **The Litigator** – Prideful Argumentation. "I can talk circles around them."

64. **The Gossip** – Division & Verbal Poison. "Talking about them makes me feel better about me."

65. **The Defier** – Rebellion. "No one tells me what to do, not even God."

66. **The Glazer** – Manipulation Through Flattery. "You're perfect just the way you are."

Jezebel

(Principality of Manipulation, Seduction & Spiritual Domination)

Core Torment & Lie: Manipulative Domination

"Control is better than submission."

Gifts Under Attack:

- **Spiritual Authority** – Jezebel undermines true authority by replacing God's order with coercion and domination ("*Nevertheless, I have this against you: You tolerate that woman Jezebel, who calls herself a prophet. By her teaching she misleads my servants into sexual immorality and the eating of food sacrificed to idols." – Revelation 2:20*).

- **Prophetic Calling** – It seeks to silence and intimidate prophetic voices through manipulation and fear ("*So Jezebel sent a messenger to Elijah to say, 'May the gods deal with me, be it ever so severely, if by this time tomorrow I do not make your life like that of one of them.' Elijah was afraid and ran for his life." – 1 Kings 19:2-3*).

- **Masculine Covering** – It resists male leadership and thrives in disorder, driving division between men and women *("But I want you to realize that the head of every man is Christ, and the head of the woman is man, and the head of Christ is God." – 1 Corinthians 11:3).*

- **Discernment** – Jezebel clouds judgment with flattery, seduction, and religious performance *("When Joram saw Jehu he asked, 'Have you come in peace, Jehu?' 'How can there be peace,' Jehu replied, 'as long as all the idolatry and witchcraft of your mother Jezebel abound?'" – 2 Kings 9:22).*

- **Obedience** – It prioritizes self-preservation and control over submission to God's will *("For rebellion is like the sin of divination, and arrogance like the evil of idolatry. Because you have rejected the word of the Lord, he has rejected you as king." – 1 Samuel 15:23).*

Jezebel is a ruling demon principality, named explicitly in Scripture and still active today. The spirit of Jezebel is more than vanity or seduction— it is a spirit of domination, deeply rooted in trauma, fear, and rebellion against God's order. In Scripture, Jezebel usurps spiritual authority, manipulates weak leadership (Ahab), and silences the voice of truth (Elijah). This same spirit today often takes root in wounded, fearful, or power-hungry women who use emotional, sexual, or spiritual tactics to control others, especially men.

Sometimes she enters as the wounded mother, the controlling wife, the jealous older woman, or the woman who was never protected and now protects herself through domination.

She operates through control, manipulation, emotional domination, seduction, and intimidation. Jezebel uses influence. She rules through passivity in others, thriving when men abdicate leadership and when spiritual order is broken. Her goal is always the same: to silence God's voice and install her own.

Jezebel targets prophets, leaders, and strong spiritual voices, especially in churches, marriages, and families. She operates through flattery and fear, switching between victim and queen to control those around her. Like the historical Jezebel, this spirit raises up false prophets, kills what's holy, and seeks to replace God's order with her own. Her power often hides under charisma, sexuality, "discernment," or victimhood. But the fruit is always manipulation, intimidation, and domination, which is the definition of witchcraft.

Scripture Reference:

"But I have this against you: You tolerate that woman Jezebel, who calls herself a prophet. By her teaching she misleads..." (Revelation 2:20)

"Now then, send and gather all Israel... and the prophets of Baal... whom Jezebel supports." (1 Kings 18:19)

"Jezebel sent a messenger to Elijah to say, 'May the gods deal with me... if I do not make your life like one of them by this time tomorrow.'" (1 Kings 19:2)

Common Symptoms:

- Charismatic control over others using charm, seduction, or emotional guilt
- Sabotaging spiritual leadership or silencing the prophetic
- Victimhood or seductiveness used to gain power and loyalty
- Deep resentment toward masculine authority or biblical order
- Creating confusion, triangulation, or division in families or churches

Real-Life Example:

Ann was hired as Head of HR at a fast-growing startup. She was older than the founders, brought in for her deep experience and stellar resume. At first, she was a godsend: professional, wise, and seemingly always right. The founders, just out of college, began deferring to her more and more—not just on HR matters, but on nearly every major decision. She offered clear strategies, commanded respect, and got results.

Impressed by her leadership, they elevated Ann to the C-suite, gave her equity, and relied on her insight daily. She ran a tight ship and was feared by some, admired by others. Slowly, her influence deepened. Founders wouldn't move without her. Meetings began to shift tone; Ann subtly redirected conversations, questioned others' ideas, and began positioning herself as the final word.

Soon, the once-unbreakable bond between the two co-founders began to unravel. Tension built behind closed doors until one of them abruptly stepped down. He refused to say why, but those close to him noticed the shift had started the moment Ann became fully embedded.

With one founder gone, Ann became the right hand of the remaining one...then eventually his equal. Those loyal to the original vision found themselves sidelined or quietly pushed out, replaced by Ann's own picks. She now controlled the company culture, hiring, and messaging. And when a major PE firm acquired the company two years later, Ann walked away with a larger stake than either of the original founders.

On paper, it looked like success. But those who'd been there from the start knew something else had taken over—and it had nothing to do with good leadership.

Solutions & Declarations:

1. **I will not tolerate the spirit of Jezebel. I break its control in my life and atmosphere.**
   "But I have this against you, that you tolerate that woman Jezebel... who misleads my servants." (Revelation 2:20)

2. **God has not given me a spirit of fear, but of power, love, and a sound mind.**
   "For God has not given us a spirit of fear, but of power and of love and of a sound mind." (2 Timothy 1:7)

3. **I submit to God's order, and I will not partner with rebellion or domination.**
   "Submit yourselves therefore to God. Resist the devil, and he will flee from you." (James 4:7)

Turn to Chapter 9 Prayer Index and go to:
Prayer 9: General Prayer for Pride of Life
Prayer 11: Deliverance from Control & Manipulation
Supplemental Prayers: 18, 19, 20, 28, 30

Cross-References:

- **The Puppeteer** – Works in close alliance with Jezebel, using emotional manipulation and covert control to steer outcomes behind the scenes.
- **The Monarch** – Shares Jezebel's belief in superiority and entitlement, expecting others to submit without question.
- **The Glazer** – Uses flattery and insincere praise to reinforce Jezebel's position of power, shielding her from honest feedback.
- **The Withholder** – Controls others through selective affection or approval, a tactic Jezebel uses to maintain dominance in relationships.
- **The Doubter** – Weakens trust in God's voice, creating a vacuum Jezebel fills with her own authority and counterfeit wisdom.
- **The Overbearing Matriarch** – A domestic expression of Jezebel's rule, dominating family dynamics and suppressing masculine leadership.
- **The Idolator** – Partners with Jezebel through spiritual showmanship, using performance to mask rebellion and gain influence.
- **The Guard** – Manifests in Jezebel as deeply rooted fear and distrust, fueling her need to dominate every environment she enters.
- **The Meddling Mother-in-Law** – A relational version of Jezebel who disrupts marriages by disguising control as care or concern.
- **The Terrifying Father** – May either enable Jezebel through absence and intimidation or alternate with her in controlling cycles of spiritual abuse.

The Puppeteer

Core Torment & Lie: Control Through Emotional Manipulation

"If you don't control them, they'll leave you or hurt you."

Gifts Under Attack:

- **Surrender** – Jezebel blocks full submission to God by making control feel like protection *("Submit yourselves, then, to God. Resist the devil, and he will flee from you." – James 4:7).*
- **Trust** – It convinces you that others cannot be relied on, keeping you isolated and self-reliant *("Trust in the Lord with all your heart and lean not on your own understanding; in all your ways submit to him, and he will make your paths straight." – Proverbs 3:5–6).*
- **Healthy Boundaries** – It erodes mutual respect, driving enmeshment or domination under the guise of love *("You, my brothers and sisters, were called to be free. But do not use your freedom to indulge the flesh; rather, serve one another humbly in love." – Galatians 5:13).*
- **Relational Freedom** – Jezebel replaces grace with pressure, manipulating others to conform or perform *("Now the Lord is the Spirit, and where the Spirit of the Lord is, there is freedom." – 2 Corinthians 3:17).*
- **Integrity** – It justifies deception or seduction to maintain control, undermining spiritual authority *("The integrity of the upright guides them, but the unfaithful are destroyed by their duplicity." – Proverbs 11:3).*

The Puppeteer operates through emotional strings. This demon uses guilt, subtle threats, passive aggression, or charm. It plays the victim, the savior, or the mastermind—whichever role ensures obedience. The Puppeteer manipulates situations as well as people, who often don't even realize they're being controlled until something in them breaks.

This demon thrives in codependent relationships, especially between parent and child, spouse and spouse, or leader and follower. It looks like love and concern, but it's really bondage and control wrapped in nice words. The longer it goes unchallenged, the more tangled the victim becomes, until they no longer know how to move without asking for permission.

Scripture Reference:

"Woe to those who draw iniquity with cords of falsehood." (Isaiah 5:18)

"Am I now trying to win the approval of human beings, or of God?" (Galatians 1:10)

"Let your 'Yes' be 'Yes,' and your 'No,' 'No'; anything more comes from the evil one." (Matthew 5:37)

Common Symptoms:

- Using guilt, fear, or obligation to control others
- Needing to oversee or influence every decision
- Resisting change or independence in others
- Playing the victim when control is confronted
- Taking credit for others' growth or success

Real-Life Example:

Michelle was born into privilege. Her trust fund gave her the freedom to explore her interests without the burden of making ends meet. But her freedom is an illusion. Her mother, Janice, controls nearly every aspect of her life under the guise of love and protection. Janice insists she's just "looking out" for Michelle's future, but her influence is suffocating.

She dictates what Michelle should study, discourages any job she deems beneath their social standing, and filters Michelle's friends, removing anyone who encourages independence or questions Janice's control. Michelle feels imprisoned but struggles with guilt. How can she complain when her life is so "easy"?

Whenever Michelle attempts to set boundaries, Janice cries, accuses her of being ungrateful, or makes veiled threats about disowning her. "I've sacrificed everything for you," she says. "And this is how you repay me?" The emotional toll is enormous. Michelle feels ashamed, confused, and torn between loyalty and liberation.

From the outside, Janice appears to be a devoted mother. But inside, Michelle is tangled in emotional strings too thick to see. Unless they are cut, neither woman will grow. One will always be the puppet. The other will always be pulling the strings.

Solutions & Declarations:

1. **I am not here to control others; I am here to walk in truth and love.**
   "Instead, speaking the truth in love, we will grow to become in every respect the mature body of Him who is the head, that is, Christ." (Ephesians 4:15)

2. **I lay down the need to manipulate, and I trust God to handle what I cannot.**
   "Trust in the Lord with all your heart and lean not on your own understanding. In all your ways acknowledge Him, and He will make your paths straight." (Proverbs 3:5–6)

3. **Whom the Son sets free is free indeed including from emotional bondage.**
   "So if the Son sets you free, you will be free indeed." (John 8:36)

Turn to Chapter 9 Prayer Index and go to:
Prayer 9: General Prayer for Pride of Life
Prayer 11: Deliverance from Control & Manipulation
Supplemental Prayer: 19

Cross-References:
- **Jezebel** – The Puppeteer often operates under this principality, using emotional manipulation instead of overt dominance.
- **The Intimidator** – When subtle control fails, fear and threats are often used to maintain power.

- **The Pretender** – The Puppeteer disguises control as concern, affection, or helplessness to avoid confrontation.
- **The Chainkeeper** – Emotional leverage and guilt are frequently rooted in unresolved bitterness or offense.
- **The Doubter** – At its core, the Puppeteer reflects a lack of trust in God's timing and provision, driving a need to force outcomes manually.

The Intimidator

Core Torment & Lie: Domination Through Fear

"Fear keeps people in line."

Gifts Under Attack:

- **Love** – The Intimidator drives out love with fear, creating control-based relationships rather than Christlike care
- *("There is no fear in love. But perfect love drives out fear, because fear has to do with punishment. The one who fears is not made perfect in love." – 1 John 4:18).*
- **Gentleness** – It mocks gentleness as weakness, blocking the fruit of the Spirit and hardening the heart *("But the fruit of the Spirit is love, joy, peace, forbearance, kindness, goodness, faithfulness, gentleness and self-control." – Galatians 5:22–23).*
- **Security** – It creates environments of instability and emotional threat, making peace feel unsafe *("In peace I will lie down and sleep, for you alone, Lord, make me dwell in safety." – Psalm 4:8).*
- **Healthy Authority** – It corrupts leadership by replacing servant-hearted guidance with coercion and fear *("Whoever wants to become great among you must be your servant." – Matthew 20:26).*
- **Humility** – It exalts pride and power, silencing correction and accountability *("Pride goes before destruction, a haughty spirit before a fall." – Proverbs 16:18).*

The Intimidator rules by fear. This demon uses volume, presence, threats, or volatility to keep others compliant. It thrives in atmospheres where people tread carefully, never knowing what version of the person they'll get that day. The Intimidator may present as a strong leader or protective parent, but the truth is, this demon is terrified of losing control, so it keeps others afraid in order to maintain power.

This spirit often emerges in authority figures who were once disrespected, rejected, or out of control themselves. Now, they swing the pendulum the other way, ruling their homes, relationships, or churches with fear. They are all about domination, and while it may bring short-term obedience, it breeds long-term trauma.

Scripture Reference:

> *"There is no fear in love. But perfect love drives out fear, because fear has to do with punishment." (1 John 4:18)*

> *"Fathers, do not provoke your children to anger, but bring them up in the discipline and instruction of the Lord." (Ephesians 6:4)*

> *"A gentle answer turns away wrath, but a harsh word stirs up anger." (Proverbs 15:1)*

Common Symptoms:

- Others feel nervous, small, or guarded around them
- Uses tone, silence, or physical posture to dominate
- Controls behavior through threats, anger, or mood swings
- Dismisses emotional needs or labels them as weakness
- Equates submission with fear-based compliance

Real-Life Example:

Todd is a brilliant surgeon, renowned for his precision, speed, and composure in the OR. But outside the operating room, his presence creates extreme tension. He screams at nurses, belittles hospital staff, and lashes out at anyone who questions him. Though the administrators try to shield others from his outbursts, no one is safe. Todd justifies it all with one mantra: "I save lives." In his mind, his success entitles him to superiority and immunity from accountability.

At home, his cruelty is even more cutting. He cheats openly on his wife and tells her she's lucky to still have him, because no one else would tolerate her. He reminds her that he pays for everything, and that her role is to be quiet and grateful. Their children have learned to disappear when he's around. His son bullies others at school, mimicking the aggression he's grown up with. His daughter lives emotionally untethered, isolated and unsupported, because her mother is too shattered to protect her.

Todd doesn't see himself as abusive. He sees himself as the standard: strong and in charge. But under the surface, his home is fractured, his marriage is hollow, and his reputation outside the OR is one of fear, not respect.

This is The Intimidator at work: a spirit that confuses cruelty for competence and fear for leadership. Its fruit is isolation, rebellion, and collapse.

Solutions & Declarations:

1. **I reject the spirit of fear and intimidation—God has given me power, love, and a sound mind.**
   ("For God has not given us a spirit of fear, but of power and of love and of a sound mind."– 2 Timothy 1:7)

2. **My leadership reflects the heart of Christ—firm in truth, gentle in grace.**
   ("Do nothing from selfish ambition or conceit, but in humility count others more significant than yourselves... Have this mind among yourselves, which is yours in Christ Jesus." – Philippians 2:3–5)

3. **I renounce the need to dominate—I lead by love, not force.**
   ("Be shepherds of God's flock... not lording it over those entrusted to you but being examples to the flock."– 1 Peter 5:2–3)

Turn to Chapter 9 Prayer Index and go to:
Prayer 9: General Prayer for Pride of Life
Prayer 11: Deliverance from Control & Manipulation
Supplemental Prayer: 19

Cross-References:

- **The Dominator** – When intimidation becomes an identity, it evolves into overt control and power-seeking behavior.
- **Jezebel** – Both seek domination, but while Jezebel uses seduction and emotional entanglement, The Intimidator rules through direct fear and force.
- **The Guard** – Deep insecurity and fear of failure often fuel intimidation as a self-protective mask of strength.
- **The Broken Mirror** – Internal shame and self-loathing drive many intimidators to control others before they can be exposed or rejected.
- **The Puppeteer** – When emotional manipulation no longer works, The Intimidator steps in with overt threats and pressure to maintain control.
- **The Bully** – The Intimidator thrives on the same fear-based dominance as The Bully.
- **The Terrifying Father** –Establishes fear as the foundation of authority; The Intimidator mirrors this control through psychological dominance.

The Dominator

Core Torment & Lie: Aggressive Control

"My way or nothing."

Gifts Under Attack:

- **Mutual Respect** – The Dominator crushes partnership, insisting on control instead of collaboration*("Submit to one another out of reverence for Christ." – Ephesians 5:21)*.
- **Servant Leadership** – It replaces Christlike humility with a hunger for power and position *("Jesus called them together and said, 'You know that those who are regarded as rulers of the Gentiles lord it over them... Not so with you. Instead, whoever wants to become great among you must be your servant.'" – Mark 10:42–45)*.

- **Relational Equality** – It enforces hierarchy where God intended unity, silencing the voices of others *("There is neither Jew nor Gentile, neither slave nor free, nor is there male and female, for you are all one in Christ Jesus." – Galatians 3:28)*.
- **Compassion** – It numbs the heart to the needs of others, seeing kindness as weakness *("Therefore, as God's chosen people, holy and dearly loved, clothe yourselves with compassion, kindness, humility, gentleness and patience." – Colossians 3:12)*.
- **Teachability** – It resists correction and refuses to yield, even to God's Spirit *("Whoever loves discipline loves knowledge, but whoever hates correction is stupid." – Proverbs 12:1)*.

The Dominator manifests through unchecked aggression, authoritarianism, and control at all costs. It demands obedience. It silences dissent, crushes collaboration, and insists its way is the only way. The Dominator shows up in homes, pulpits, boardrooms, and relationships—anywhere it can install a one-way power structure with itself at the top.

Unlike The Intimidator, which rules by emotional tension and fear, The Dominator uses force: verbal, physical, spiritual, or institutional. It is unyielding, training people to stop speaking up. Over time, it creates entire environments where fear is normalized, abuse is rebranded as discipline, and submission is confused with silence.

Scripture Reference:

> *"Woe to the shepherds who destroy and scatter the sheep of my pasture!" (Jeremiah 23:1)*

> *"But among you it will be different. Whoever wants to be a leader among you must be your servant." (Matthew 20:26)*

> *"Do not lord it over those in your care but be examples to the flock." (1 Peter 5:3)*

Common Symptoms:

- Authoritarian or dictatorial leadership style
- Expects obedience without question

- Equates disagreement with disloyalty
- Uses force, shaming, or punishment to keep control
- Creates emotionally or spiritually oppressive environments

Real-Life Example:

Robert is a renowned chef with a string of awards and Michelin stars to his name. He paid his dues under tyrannical culinary legends and now he carries on the tradition with pride. His kitchen operates like a war zone. He screams, throws plates, humiliates staff, and makes even tough line cooks cry. New hires often walk out by day two. Front-of-house managers have resorted to soundproofing the kitchen doors, so diners don't hear the chaos erupting behind them.

The staff is constantly on edge, with some hiding in walk-ins or coatrooms just to mentally break down in peace. Though the food is exquisite and the dining room gorgeous, the atmosphere is oppressive. Guests can sense the weight on the team, especially since no one smiles, and the servers' eyes look red from crying.

The saddest part? Many of the staff come from similarly abusive backgrounds and wear their ability to "survive Chef Robert" as a badge of honor. They mistake resilience for strength, not realizing they're just enduring another form of domination.

Solutions & Declarations:

1. **True strength is shown in mercy, not control.**
   (Micah 6:8 – "He has shown you, O man, what is good; and what does the Lord require of you but to do justly, to love mercy, and to walk humbly with your God?")

2. **I will not lord over others but serve in humility and love.**
   (1 Peter 5:2–3 – "Be shepherds of God's flock... not lording it over those entrusted to you but being examples to the flock.")

3. **Jesus is my model for leadership—serving, not suppressing.**
   (Philippians 2:5-7 – "Let this mind be in you which was also in Christ Jesus... He made Himself of no reputation, taking the form of a servant.")

Turn to Chapter 9 Prayer Index and go to:
Prayer 9: General Prayer for Pride of Life
Prayer 11: Deliverance from Control & Manipulation
Supplemental Prayer: 19

Cross-References:

- **The Intimidator** – The Dominator is the full-grown version of The Intimidator—where fear becomes force and warnings turn into suppression.
- **Jezebel** – While Jezebel cloaks domination in emotional or spiritual manipulation, The Dominator uses direct control to silence and subdue.
- **The Narcissist** – Both crave power, but The Dominator demands loyalty and submission as proof of worth, believing they alone should be obeyed.
- **The Chainkeeper** – Dominators rarely forget a slight. Grudges are held like weapons, and power is used to settle old scores.
- **The Terrifying Father** –Establishes fear as the foundation of authority; The Dominator mirrors this control through physical dominance.
- **The Broken Mirror** – Many Dominators were once deeply wounded. Their need for total control is often an overcorrection to avoid ever feeling powerless again.
- **The Bully** – Uses intimidation and cruelty to assert dominance, especially over the vulnerable. The Dominator and The Bully often partner to control through fear.

The Narcissist

Narcissism is a spiritual distortion of identity rooted in pride, entitlement, and deep insecurity. It builds a false self-image that demands admiration, refuses correction, and devalues others to maintain superiority. It thrives on flattery, control, and emotional detachment while masking deep wounds of rejection and inadequacy.

Core Torment & Lie: Self Exaltation & Lack of Humility

"I am the center of everything."

Gifts Under Attack:

- **Humility** – The Narcissist resists lowliness of heart, rejecting Christ's model of servant leadership *("Do nothing out of selfish ambition or vain conceit. Rather, in humility value others above yourselves. In your relationships with one another, have the same mindset as Christ Jesus." – Philippians 2:3–5).*

- **Empathy** – It numbs compassion, viewing people as tools rather than souls *("Rejoice with those who rejoice; mourn with those who mourn." – Romans 12:15).*

- **Christlike Love** – It replaces unconditional love with performance-based approval and manipulation *("Love is patient, love is kind. It does not envy, it does not boast, it is not proud. It does not dishonor others; it is not self-seeking." – 1 Corinthians 13:4–5).*

- **Accountability** – It avoids repentance or self-examination, resisting the conviction of the Holy Spirit *("The way of fools seems right to them, but the wise listen to advice." – Proverbs 12:15).*

- **True Identity in Christ** – It builds a false identity on praise, power, or performance instead of resting in God's love *("I have been crucified with Christ, and I no longer live, but Christ lives in me." – Galatians 2:20).*

The Narcissist is one of the clearest examples of demon psychology in action, a parasitic spirit that builds an entire false identity in place of the real self. At its core, this demon hollows out its host, leaving a black hole that must be filled by others. The Narcissist survives off "supply"—attention, admiration, control, and energy—and has no sense of self apart from what others reflect back. Their entire personality is a patchwork of traits borrowed from those they manipulate.

They wear masks constantly. Underneath, there is nothing but emptiness and need. These spirits are spiritual vampires who target the kind, the gifted, and the anointed. The brighter the light inside someone, the more determined The Narcissist is to drain it dry. They mimic the talents, speech patterns, and even personality of their victims, cobbling together a persona that looks impressive but is built entirely on stolen identity.

All narcissists operate the same way because it's the same demon running the script. There are no original thoughts, just a recycling of manipulation, projection, and control.

Once a soul tie is formed, the consequences can linger for years unless broken through deliverance. Victims are often left shattered, questioning their worth, their sanity, and even their faith.

This spirit is a vector, carrying and transmitting multiple others:

- The Monarch, who demands submission.
- The Glazer, who uses flattery as bait.
- Jezebel, who orchestrates control through charm and manipulation. She is the head of an entire order of tenacious demons.
- The Puppeteer, who weaponizes guilt to keep people tethered.

The Narcissist is singular in how fully it rewrites reality. It creates a false self that is always the hero or the victim, and always justified, no matter the destruction left behind. Anyone who threatens this illusion becomes the enemy.

Scripture Reference:
"But mark this: There will be terrible times in the last days. People will be lovers of themselves..." (2 Timothy 3:1–2)

"Do not think of yourself more highly than you ought." (Romans 12:3)

"Pride goes before destruction, a haughty spirit before a fall." (Proverbs 16:18)

Common Symptoms:

- Inability to apologize or admit fault
- Hyper-focused on image, admiration, or validation
- Weaponizes emotions or stories to stay the victim
- Keeps a revolving door of admirers or enablers
- Breaks others down to feel powerful or special

Real-Life Example:

Derek is the most well-known lawyer in his small town—respected, admired, and deeply connected. He's helped countless families with legal matters and always seems to know what's going on behind the scenes. People describe him as generous and charming, a pillar of the community. Those closest to him know another truth entirely.

In reality, Derek uses people like tools. He keeps a secret roster of married women, seducing them with flattery and influence while showing utter disregard for his own wife, who's been reduced to a figurehead in a house that feels more like a prison. His children are distant, either mimicking his coldness or disappearing from his life altogether to escape the emotional vacuum he creates.

At work Derek rules by manipulation. He's berated employees, sabotaged business partners, and exploited confidential information to get what he wants, all while maintaining the upper hand through his polished charisma and legal expertise. His paralegal of ten years finally walked out after one too many incidents of psychological abuse, but Derek wasn't done with her. He launched a quiet campaign to destroy her reputation, calling in favors and whispering just enough to ensure no one would hire her again in town. His image stayed intact. Hers did not.

Derek doesn't see himself as cruel. In his mind, he's burdened by his brilliance, surrounded by incompetents and traitors. He recasts every betrayal as proof of his righteousness and every collapse as someone else's fault. To the world, he's a success story. To those he devours, he's a nightmare.

This is The Narcissist fully operational: parasitic, polished, and powerful—building an empire on the emotional wreckage of others while wearing the mask of a savior.

Solutions & Declarations:

1. **I humble myself before the Lord and resist the spirit of pride.**
   (God resists the proud but gives grace to the humble. Therefore, submit to God. Resist the devil and he will flee from you." James 4:6–7")

2. **My worth is secure in Christ—I do not need to be above others.**
   ("I have been crucified with Christ; it is no longer I who live, but Christ lives in me..." Galatians 2:20)

3. **I break agreement with every lie that makes me the center of the story.**
   ("Do nothing out of selfish ambition or vain conceit. Rather, in humility value others above yourselves." Philippians 2:3)

Turn to Chapter 9 Prayer Index and go to:
Prayer 9: General Prayer for Pride of Life
Prayer 11: Deliverance from Control & Manipulation
Supplemental Prayers: 19, 28

Cross-References:

- **The Monarch** – The Monarch feels owed special treatment; The Narcissist believes they are the standard and expects the world to adjust accordingly.
- **The Glazer** – The Narcissist surrounds themselves with flattering enablers who protect and reinforce their false image.
- **Jezebel** – Both operate through charm, emotional manipulation, and domination, masking control as connection.
- **The Broken Mirror** – Narcissists often form out of deep self-hatred and shame, building a false self to survive what they believe is unlovable.

- **The Puppeteer** – Like The Puppeteer, The Narcissist uses manipulation to orchestrate others' behavior, always positioning themselves at the center of attention and loyalty.

The Pretender
Core Torment & Lie: Masking & Fear-Based Pride
"If they saw the real me, they'd leave."
Gifts Under Attack:

- **Authenticity** – It pressures you to project an image instead of living in truth *("Therefore each of you must put off falsehood and speak truthfully to your neighbor, for we are all members of one body." – Ephesians 4:25)*.
- **Vulnerability** – It makes transparency feel dangerous, keeping you emotionally guarded *("But he said to me, 'My grace is sufficient for you, for my power is made perfect in weakness.' Therefore, I will boast all the more gladly about my weaknesses, so that Christ's power may rest on me." – 2 Corinthians 12:9)*.
- **Self-Worth** – It whispers that your real self is unlovable, promoting shame and performance *("I praise you because I am fearfully and wonderfully made; your works are wonderful, I know that full well." – Psalm 139:14)*.
- **True Transformation** – It hinders deliverance by blocking the honesty required for God to fully heal and restore *("Therefore confess your sins to each other and pray for each other so that you may be healed. The prayer of a righteous person is powerful and effective." – James 5:16)*.
- **Trust in God's Love** – It implies that love is conditional, keeping you from resting in God's acceptance *("For I am convinced that neither death nor life, neither angels nor demons, neither the present nor the future, nor any powers... will be able to separate us from the love of God that is in Christ Jesus our Lord." – Romans 8:38–39)*.

This spirit convinces individuals to hide behind false versions of themselves. It tells them to perform, pretend, or shape-shift to be accepted. At its root is a deep fear of rejection, cloaked in pride that says, "I must manage how I'm seen." The Pretender sabotages healing by preventing honesty before God and others. It thrives in secrecy, shame, and self-protection.

The Pretender convinces people that who they are is unacceptable, unsafe, or insufficient. So, they build an identity that's easier to live with, one that earns approval, avoids rejection, or hides the past. The longer they wear the mask, the harder it becomes to take off. Eventually, even they don't remember who they were beneath it.

This demon partners closely with The Narcissist and The Performer, but while the Narcissist demands admiration and the Performer chases applause, The Pretender just wants to be safe. It's a spirit of self-preservation born from shame. It teaches people to be whoever they need to be in order to survive, but survival isn't the same as healing. A mask can't receive love, only maintain performance.

Scripture Reference:

"Woe to you... you clean the outside of the cup and dish, but inside you are full of greed and self-indulgence." (Matthew 23:25)

"Man looks at the outward appearance, but the Lord looks at the heart." (1 Samuel 16:7)

"You were taught... to put off your old self... and put on the new self, created to be like God." (Ephesians 4:22–24)

Common Symptoms:

- Adapts personality based on who is watching
- Secretly feels like a fraud, even when succeeding
- Avoids deep intimacy or exposure
- Becomes a "chameleon" in relationships
- Struggles to identify authentic desires or beliefs

Real-Life Example:

Beau was born beautiful—so beautiful, in fact, that strangers told his mother he belonged on a magazine cover. By the time he was two, his face was on a diaper box. From there, his childhood was spent in front of the camera, eventually landing a role on a long-running hit TV show that made him a household name. America watched him grow up, but Beau never knew who really saw *him*.

Everywhere he went, he was recognized—not as Beau, but as the character he played. People approached him like old friends, laughing, hugging, snapping pictures... but no one knew the boy behind the mask. From before he could even remember, he learned to smile, perform, and stay polished. The mask never came off.

He cycled through relationships, always waiting for the moment someone would use him, betray him, or lose interest. Even when he finally married the mother of his child, he kept his walls up. When his daughter was born, he was devastated to realize he didn't know how to be real with her—how to show her anything other than the version of himself he had learned to perform.

The show ended years ago, but it still played in syndication, and his fame lingered like a shadow. He feared that if he ever truly took off the mask, he'd find nothing underneath—just a boy who never figured out who he really was. The Pretender found the perfect victim in Beau.

Solutions & Declarations:

1. **God loves me as I am, not as I pretend to be.**
   ("But God demonstrates His own love toward us, in that while we were still sinners, Christ died for us." Romans 5:8)

2. **I renounce false identity and step into the truth of who I am in Christ.**
   ("For He chose us in Him before the creation of the world to be holy and blameless in His sight... In love He predestined us for adoption to sonship through Jesus Christ." Ephesians 1:4–5)

3. **I will not perform—I will live in the freedom of the truth.**
   ("Then you will know the truth, and the truth will set you free."
   John 8:32)

Turn to Chapter 9 Prayer Index and go to:
Prayer 9: General Prayer for Pride of Life
Prayer 11: Deliverance from Control & Manipulation
Supplemental Prayers: 28, 34

Cross-References:

- •**The Performer** – The Performer craves applause to feel worthy; The Pretender wears a mask to avoid rejection.
- •**The Narcissist** – Both create false selves, but The Narcissist seeks worship, while The Pretender seeks safety.
- •**The Broken Mirror** – Deep self-rejection often drives the creation of a false identity.
- •**The Guard** – The Guard prevents risk through fear; The Pretender avoids exposure through pretending.
- •**The Liar** – The Pretender doesn't deceive to control others, but to protect themselves from being truly seen.

The Glacier
Core Torment & Lie: Emotional Numbness & Self-Protection
"Feelings are weakness."
Gifts under attack:
Empathy – It dulls your ability to feel with others, leaving relationships cold and disconnected *("Rejoice with those who rejoice; mourn with those who mourn." – Romans 12:15)*.

Compassion – It suppresses your God-given capacity to care deeply for others *("Therefore, as God's chosen people, holy and dearly loved, clothe yourselves with compassion, kindness, humility, gentleness and patience." – Colossians 3:12)*.

Vulnerability – It creates fear of emotional exposure, reinforcing self-isolation *("We have spoken freely to you, Corinthians, and opened* *wide our hearts to you. We are not withholding our affection from you, but you are withholding yours from us. As a fair exchange—I speak as to my children—open wide your hearts also." - 2 Corinthians 6:11–13).*

Love – It chokes the flow of genuine love, both in giving and receiving *("There is no fear in love. But perfect love drives out fear, because fear has to do with punishment. The one who fears is not made perfect in love. We love because he first loved us." - 1 John 4:18–19).*

Intimacy – It shuts down closeness, even with God, making you feel distant, unreachable, and alone *("The Lord is close to the brokenhearted and saves those who are crushed in spirit." - Psalm 34:18).*

The Glacier is the spirit of emotional coldness and detachment. It causes the heart to harden through trauma, pride, or self-preservation, often creating a protective shell that eventually becomes a prison. This demon convinces people that vulnerability is dangerous, empathy is foolish, and love is optional. Over time, it numbs both the desire to feel and the ability to connect. While it often enters through heartbreak, abuse, or rejection, it partners with cruelty, indifference, and pride to preserve its reign. Its ultimate aim is to separate people from love—both giving and receiving—and make even God feel far away.

The Glacier forms when the heart shuts down to avoid pain. It creates a spiritual freeze, convincing individuals that emotions are dangerous, and vulnerability is a threat. This demon numbs compassion, prevents authentic connection, and fosters emotional paralysis. It often emerges after trauma, betrayal, or chronic neglect, whispering that feeling nothing is safer than being hurt again.

Scripture references:

"Because lawlessness will abound, the love of many will grow cold." (Matthew 24:12)

"I will remove your heart of stone and give you a heart of flesh." (Ezekiel 36:26)

"They are senseless, faithless, heartless, ruthless." (Romans 1:31)

Common symptoms:

- Flat emotional affect or inability to cry
- Feeling awkward around intimacy, empathy, or emotional expression
- Keeping conversations shallow or superficial
- Withdrawing when others are vulnerable
- Feeling numb during worship, prayer, or love-centered teaching

Real-life example:

Ted grew up in a house where feelings were not welcome. His father, a hardened member of the Silent Generation, believed emotions were weakness. His mother was in and out of hospitals for most of his childhood, leaving Ted to raise his younger siblings while still a child himself. There was no time to cry, no room to feel—only survive. The only thing that ever gave him joy was his dog, and when it was killed in a hit-and-run, something in him shut down permanently. The Glacier had taken up residence in his heart and froze it.

Ted went through life with that frozen heart. Relationships came and went, mostly shallow, transactional. When he eventually married, he treated his wife like an appliance: useful but not worthy of affection. When she discovered his affairs and walked out, leaving him with their two small children, Ted didn't argue or react. He simply married the woman he'd been cheating with, so he'd have someone to help with the kids.

The house those children grew up in was emotionally desolate. Their stepmother was cruel, and Ted said nothing. He didn't comfort them, didn't protect them, didn't connect at all. He wasn't abusive, but his absence was its own kind of wound. The moment they were old enough to leave, they did, without a backward glance.

Years later, Ted was diagnosed with pancreatic cancer. He never reached out. He ignored the letters, emails, and voicemails from his children—each one a quiet offering of peace and restoration. His heart stayed iced shut. When he died, alone, there was no service, no obituary.

Just a single line on a cremation registry. His children only found out by chance when one of them googled his name out of curiosity.

Ted didn't rage, didn't explode, didn't harm. He simply froze. And in that deep freeze, love couldn't get in or out.

Solutions and declarations:

1. **"God, melt the glacier in my heart. I want to feel again."**
   "I will give you a new heart and put a new spirit in you; I will remove from you your heart of stone and give you a heart of flesh." (Ezekiel 36:26)

2. **"I renounce every vow I made to never need, never cry, never feel."**
   "Because of the increase of wickedness, the love of most will grow cold." (Matthew 24:12)

3. **"I receive the heart of flesh You promised. I welcome the warmth of love again."**
   "God's love has been poured out into our hearts through the Holy Spirit, who has been given to us." (Romans 5:5)

Turn to Chapter 9 Prayer Index and go to:

Prayer 9: General Prayer for Pride of Life
Prayer 11: Deliverance from Control & Manipulation
Supplemental Prayer: 22, 33, 34

Cross references:

- **The Narcissist** – Reinforces emotional detachment and self-preservation through grandiosity or control.
- **The Profane** – Dulls emotional sensitivity and spiritual reverence through constant exposure to corruption.
- **The Critic** – Promotes heartless judgment and rejection of empathy under the guise of discernment.
- **The Bully** – Replaces vulnerability with dominance, maintaining control by staying emotionally unavailable.

- **The Withholder** – Cuts off emotional nourishment to others, especially in close relationships, reinforcing isolation

King Baby (Ahab Spirit)
Core Torment & Lie: Avoidance & Entitlement
"Someone else will handle it."
Gifts Under Attack:

- **Responsibility** – It weakens your ability to own your role and walk in spiritual maturity *("For each one should carry their own load." – Galatians 6:5).*
- **Leadership** – It abdicates God-given authority, creating a vacuum for manipulation *("Be on your guard; stand firm in the faith; be courageous; be strong." – 1 Corinthians 16:13).*
- **Emotional Maturity** – It keeps you stuck in childish patterns of blame and need *("When I was a child, I talked like a child, I thought like a child, I reasoned like a child. When I became a man, I put the ways of childhood behind me." – 1 Corinthians 13:11).*
- **Accountability** – It deflects correction and avoids consequences
- *("Whoever loves discipline loves knowledge, but whoever hates correction is stupid." – Proverbs 12:1).*
- **Integrity** – It undermines consistency between belief and action, damaging trust *("In everything set them an example by doing what is good. In your teaching show integrity, seriousness and soundness of speech that cannot be condemned, so that those who oppose you may be ashamed because they have nothing bad to say about us." – Titus 2:7–8).*

King Baby is the flipside of Jezebel—not the dominant controller, but the passive enabler. In Scripture, Ahab was evil because he refused to wield his God-given authority, instead partnering with Jezebel to accomplish wickedness while keeping his own hands clean. This spirit rules through emotional fragility, silence, withdrawal, and weaponized helplessness.

It expects to be rescued, mothered, or catered to, yet resents the very people who do it.

This spirit thrives on passivity, blame-shifting, and emotional dependence. It resists accountability, expects others to lead or clean up messes, and manipulates through victimhood or neediness. Often paired with Jezebel, King Baby enables domination by surrendering rightful authority.

At its core, this spirit reflects spiritual immaturity, narcissism, and a deep resentment of adult responsibility—all while demanding the privileges of leadership or love.

Scripture references:

"There was no one like Ahab, who sold himself to do wickedness in the sight of the Lord, because Jezebel his wife stirred him up." (1 Kings 21:25)

"He lay on his bed, sulking and refusing to eat." (1 Kings 21:4 — Ahab pouting when Naboth refused to sell his vineyard)

"When I was a child, I thought like a child... but when I became a man, I put the ways of childhood behind me." (1 Corinthians 13:11)

Common symptoms:

- Abdicates decision-making to others but still blames them for outcomes
- Emotionally fragile, sulking, manipulative silence
- Disguises weakness as "niceness" or "not wanting to fight"
- Seeks comfort, control, or affirmation without accountability
- Often attracts domineering partners or friends who "take care of everything"

Real-life example:

Mason was the youngest heir to a powerful political dynasty, but unlike his father and older brothers, he had no fire for leadership, no real competence, and no interest in public service. His mother, however, invested decades grooming him as a fallback, quietly maneuvering school admissions, internships, and public appearances to keep the family name alive. Mason barely noticed. He coasted through life surrounded by handlers, frat brothers, and social privileges that required nothing from him but a last name.

When his father and brothers were tragically killed in a plane crash, everything changed. With the legacy now resting squarely on Mason's shoulders, his mother scrambled to preserve the empire. She arranged a politically advantageous marriage with a sharp, ambitious woman who had no real affection for Mason, only an interest in what he could give her: a platform.

Eager to avoid disappointing anyone and happy to stay in the background, Mason agreed. Soon he was elected to Congress, but behind closed doors, he was barely present. His wife and mother ran the show: crafting speeches, brokering deals, telling him what to wear, say, and sign. Mason just smiled for the cameras, parroting their scripts.

Over time, The King Baby spirit grew stronger. Mason grew comfortable being a figurehead with no spine. The perks of office—luxury, attention, bribes—became his real focus. He fell prey to honey traps, blackmail schemes, and shady lobbying deals. When a massive corruption scandal finally broke, Mason didn't deny or defend. He simply withdrew. While his wife and mother scrambled to protect the brand, Mason hid in a resort abroad, unreachable and emotionally vacant.

That's the fruit of The King Baby spirit: a man who looks like a leader on the outside but is ruled from behind the scenes. He avoids responsibility, flees from conflict, and leaves a trail of destruction he expects others to clean up.

Solutions and declarations:

1. **"I reject spiritual childhood and step into mature manhood."**
   "When I was a child, I talked like a child, I thought like a child, I reasoned like a child. When I became a man, I put the ways of childhood behind me." (1 Corinthians 13:11)

2. **"I will no longer weaponize helplessness to avoid accountability."**
   "Each of us will give an account of ourselves to God." (Romans 14:12)

3. **"I break agreement with passive control and reclaim godly leadership."**
   "Be watchful, stand firm in the faith, act like men, be strong." (1 Corinthians 16:13)

Turn to Chapter 9 Prayer Index and go to:
Prayer 9: General Prayer for Pride of Life
Prayer 11: Deliverance from Control & Manipulation
Supplemental Prayer: 18, 19, 21

Cross-references:

- **Jezebel** – King Baby is her most common counterpart, enabling her dominance by surrendering spiritual authority.
- **The Weak Father** – Often shaped by passive or absent fatherhood, King Baby either becomes or repeats this pattern.
- **The Guard** – Avoids leadership responsibility out of fear of failure or being exposed.
- **The Glazer** – Seeks validation and admiration above correction or growth.
- **The Puppeteer** – Feigns helplessness or confusion to emotionally control outcomes and avoid confrontation.

The Litigator

Core Torment & Lie: Prideful Argumentation

"I can talk circles around them."

Gifts Under Attack:

- **Peace** – It replaces spiritual stillness with constant tension and conflict *("But the wisdom that comes from heaven is first of all pure; then peace-loving, considerate, submissive, full of mercy and good fruit, impartial and sincere. Peacemakers who sow in peace reap a harvest of righteousness." – James 3:17–18).*
- **Humility** – It exalts knowledge over love, making others feel small
- *("But knowledge puffs up while love builds up." – 1 Corinthians 8:1).*
- **Wisdom** – It blinds you to correction and deeper insight from God or others *("The way of fools seems right to them, but the wise listen to advice." – Proverbs 12:15).*
- **Unity** – It causes division and strife, even among believers
- *("Don't have anything to do with foolish and stupid arguments, because you know they produce quarrels. And the Lord's servant must not be quarrelsome but must be kind to everyone, able to teach, not resentful." – 2 Timothy 2:23–24).*
- **Submission to the Spirit** – It prioritizes intellect over intimacy with God *("Trust in the Lord with all your heart and lean not on your own understanding; in all your ways submit to him, and he will make your paths straight." – Proverbs 3:5–6).*

The Litigator cannot let anything go. This demon drives endless debate, correction, and need to win, even in spiritual matters. It operates under the illusion of logic and truth-seeking, but its true goal is control through verbal domination. It sows division, pride, and distraction, often derailing truth in the name of proving a point. While it may masquerade as discernment or "standing up for truth," it is rooted in pride, insecurity, and fear of being seen as wrong.

This demon thrives in families, churches, and comment sections, and it is often spiritually justified by those it controls. Scripture is clear: foolish arguments are unprofitable.

Scripture references:

"Do not answer a fool according to his folly..." (Proverbs 26:4)

"Avoid foolish and ignorant disputes, knowing they generate strife." (2 Timothy 2:23)

"Knowledge puffs up, but love builds up." (1 Corinthians 8:1)

Common symptoms:

- Must have the last word
- Debates everything—even simple facts
- Can't let go of being misunderstood or corrected
- Turns every disagreement into a war of ideas
- Over-identifies with being "right" instead of being righteous

Real-life example:

Brett sees himself as an intellectual heavyweight. Conversations aren't for connection—they're sparring matches. At work, people duck into offices to avoid being cornered by one of his endless monologues. At home, his wife and kids maintain careful diplomacy, knowing any question or disagreement will ignite a verbal barrage.

He constantly moves the goalposts mid-discussion, refusing to stay on topic if it threatens his stance. Word salad, redirection, and talking past people are his default. He always has a comeback, never a question. His family avoids deep conversations, and his coworkers quietly transfer projects to dodge his relentless need to win.

Despite being bright, Brett is emotionally tone-deaf. He doesn't understand why no one wants to be around him. He chalks it up to others being "too sensitive" or "not sharp enough." The truth is The Litigator has made relationship impossible.

Solutions and declarations:

1. **"Being right is not my righteousness—Christ is."**
   "This righteousness is given through faith in Jesus Christ to all who believe." (Romans 3:22)

2. **"I break agreement with the need to control others through argument."**
   "Don't have anything to do with foolish and stupid arguments, because you know they produce quarrels." (2 Timothy 2:23)

3. **"I release my identity from needing to win."**
   "Do nothing out of selfish ambition or vain conceit. Rather, in humility value others above yourselves." (Philippians 2:3)

Turn to Chapter 9 Prayer Index and go to:
Prayer 9: General Prayer for Pride of Life
Prayer 11: Deliverance from Control & Manipulation
Supplemental Prayer: 16, 21, 23

Cross-references:

- **The Idolator** – The Litigator builds identity on being right and superior, idolizing intellect and control.
- **The Guard** – Defensiveness and fear of vulnerability drive the need to dominate every conversation.
- **The Puppeteer** – Skilled in verbal manipulation, The Litigator uses argument to subtly steer outcomes.
- **The Liar** – Truth is often twisted or selectively framed to protect ego or win battles.
- **The Broken Mirror** – At its root, The Litigator is often covering deep insecurity with polished intellect and sharp rebuttal.

The Gossip

Core Torment & Lie: Division & Verbal Poison

"Talking about them makes me feel better about me."

Gifts Under Attack:

- **Integrity** – It tempts you to speak what should remain private, compromising your character *("Sin is not ended by multiplying words, but the prudent hold their tongues." – Proverbs 10:19).*
- **Discernment** – It distorts truth under the guise of concern, making it hard to recognize real harm *("But solid food is for the mature, who by constant use have trained themselves to distinguish good from evil." – Hebrews 5:14).*
- **Trustworthiness** – It erodes the ability to keep confidences, making others feel unsafe around you *("A gossip betrays a confidence, but a trustworthy person keeps a secret." – Proverbs 11:13).*
- **Peacekeeping** – It stirs division and relational tension, sabotaging unity
- *("Let us therefore make every effort to do what leads to peace and to mutual edification." – Romans 14:19).*
- **Love** – It thrives on judgment and comparison, silencing the compassion of Christ *("Love does not delight in evil but rejoices with the truth." – 1 Corinthians 13:6).*

The Gossip is a demon that trades in twisted facts, hidden motives, and masked malice disguised as concern. This spirit thrives in social circles and religious spaces alike—anywhere information becomes currency. Often hiding behind "prayer requests," venting, or "just saying the truth," it feeds off the downfall of others to mask insecurity. In truth, gossip is spiritual arson: it burns down trust, scorches reputations, and leaves division in its wake. God calls it sin.

Scripture References:

> *A perverse person stirs up conflict, and a gossip separates close friends." (Proverbs 16:28)"*

> *"If anyone thinks he is religious and does not bridle his tongue... his religion is worthless." (James 1:26)*

> *"Do not go about spreading slander among your people." (Leviticus 19:16)*

Common Symptoms:

- Compulsion to share information about others
- Feeling "in the know" brings a false sense of power
- Drama follows conversations like a shadow
- Conviction when replaying what was said
- Broken friendships or cliques forming around negativity

Real-Life Example:

Rebecca was the go-to girl for information. In high school, even upper-classmen came to her to get the scoop: who was dating who, who cheated, who cried in the bathroom. She wasn't loud or flashy; she just *knew things*. People told her more because they assumed she already knew everything. What they didn't realize was that the spirit of gossip had been grooming her since childhood.

Her mother—once the reigning social queen of their small town—spent hours each day on the phone, dissecting the lives of neighbors like it was public service. Rebecca absorbed every detail, learning early that gossip wasn't just talk. It was currency, and it made you untouchable.

As an adult, Rebecca turned that "gift" into a business, launching a celebrity gossip site that quickly became one of the most visited in the industry. Publicists and agents whispered in her ear, offering exclusives or trading favors to protect (or sabotage) clients. She built an empire on whispers, casually influencing careers and reputations with a single headline.

Then one day, the script flipped.

Rebecca became a minor celebrity herself. Suddenly, *she* was the story. She watched strangers dissect her looks, her personal life, her mistakes. For the first time, she felt the sting she had so often delivered to others. The shame was suffocating. She dismantled the site and retreated from the spotlight, but her reputation followed her. The Gossip spirit doesn't let go easily. It clings, humiliates, and isolates, especially once its host tries to break free.

What Rebecca once thought was a social gift was really spiritual rot dressed as influence. It gave her power but poisoned her in the process.

Solutions & Declarations:

1. **"I repent for every careless word and break agreement with the spirit of gossip."**
   "But I tell you that everyone will have to give account on the day of judgment for every empty word they have spoken." (Matthew 12:36)

2. **"I will speak life, not death. My words will build, not destroy."**
   "The tongue has the power of life and death, and those who love it will eat its fruit." (Proverbs 18:21)

3. **"I ask God to bridle my tongue and give me discernment before I speak."**
   "Set a guard over my mouth, Lord; keep watch over the door of my lips." (Psalm 141:3)

4. **"I choose love, truth, and self-control over the need to feel important."**
   "But the fruit of the Spirit is love, joy, peace, forbearance, kindness, goodness, faithfulness, gentleness and self-control. Against such things there is no law." (Galatians 5:22–23)

5. **"I declare my mouth belongs to God, and I will no longer be used to divide."**
   "Do not let any unwholesome talk come out of your mouths, but only what is helpful for building others up according to their needs, that it may benefit those who listen." (Ephesians 4:29)

Turn to Chapter 9 Prayer Index and go to:

Prayer 9: General Prayer for Pride of Life

Prayer 11: Deliverance from Control & Manipulation

Supplemental Prayer: 16, 19

Cross References:

- **The Mouth** – Fuels reckless, impulsive speech that spreads harm without restraint
- **The Sower of Strife** – Works alongside gossip to break trust, pit people against each other, and fracture unity.
- **The Critic** – Adds judgment and moral superiority to gossip, cloaking it as "truth-telling."
- **Leviathan** – Twists words and intentions, distorting conversations and fueling offense.
- **The Litigator** – Justifies gossip through arguments and debate, disguising it as necessary discussion.

The Defier

Core Torment & Lie: Rebellion

"No one tells me what to do."

Gifts under attack:

- **Teachability** – The Defier rejects instruction, making growth and correction feel like threats instead of gifts *("Whoever loves discipline loves knowledge, but whoever hates correction is stupid." – Proverbs 12:1).*
- **Honor** – It mocks authority figures and belittles leadership, breaking the biblical order of respect *("Let everyone be subject to the governing authorities, for there is no authority except that which God has established. The authorities that exist have been established by God. Consequently, whoever rebels against the authority is rebelling against what God has instituted." – Romans 13:1-2).*

- **Obedience** – It resists surrendering to God's will, framing obedience as weakness or control *("For rebellion is like the sin of divination, and arrogance like the evil of idolatry. Because you have rejected the word of the Lord, he has rejected you as king." – 1 Samuel 15:23).*
- **Submission to God** – It fosters pride and independence, making it hard to yield to divine direction *("Submit yourselves, then, to God. Resist the devil, and he will flee from you." – James 4:7).*

The Defier is a spirit of rebellion that resists correction and scoffs at instruction. It rises up especially in childhood and adolescence but often lingers well into adulthood, masked as independence or "just being true to yourself." Biblically, rebellion is as the sin of witchcraft (1 Samuel 15:23) because it places self-will above God's will. The Defier despises parents, teachers, bosses, pastors—any structure of accountability. It thrives in cultures that exalt autonomy and self-rule over humility and reverence. The fruit is always bitter: broken relationships, missed wisdom, and eventual destruction. This demon may appear bold, but it always leads people into isolation, deception, and spiritual danger.

Scripture References:

"The eye that mocks a father and scorns to obey a mother will be pecked out by ravens..." (Proverbs 30:17)

"For people will be lovers of self... disobedient to their parents..." (2 Timothy 3:2)

"For rebellion is as the sin of witchcraft..." (1 Samuel 15:23)

Common Symptoms:

- Chronic resistance to authority, even healthy leadership
- Anger or mockery toward parents, pastors, or bosses
- Instinct to disobey simply because a rule exists
- Self-sabotage tied to "no one tells me what to do" mentality
- Pride disguised as independence

Real Life Example:

Dennis was a defiant force since the moment he could speak. His parents, kind and soft-spoken, were baffled by the rage that erupted from such a small child. No punishment worked. No kindness reached him. By age seven, he was diagnosed with oppositional defiant disorder, but even clinical language couldn't explain the spiritual war waging inside their home.

Dennis disobeyed every authority figure placed over him: teachers, coaches, relatives, even kind strangers. His parents often had to leave family events and restaurants before the meal arrived, humiliated by yet another public tantrum. They weren't abusive or harsh. They were just no match for what was riding their son.

The Defier entered the family line long before Dennis was born. His grandfather had been the same way: angry, wild, impossible to restrain. He died young in a bar fight. No one ever made the connection. No one ever tried to break it.

Now an adult, Dennis was taller but not wiser. He couldn't hold a job since he refused to follow instructions or submit to any kind of structure. He floated between shelters, couches, and the beds of those who offered him help, always wearing out his welcome. When things got hard, he lashed out, picked a fight, and vanished.

He occasionally showed up at his parents' door, shouting, accusing, manipulating—just long enough to get something and leave them in tears. Then he disappeared again, fueled by the same spirit that ruled his grandfather: The Defier. The one who cannot kneel. The one who would rather burn bridges than bend the knee.

The last anyone heard, Dennis had been in another fight—this one fatal. The Defier took him the same way it took his grandfather. The family never identified it or learned how to evict it, only how to endure it.

Solutions & Declarations:

1. **"I break agreement with rebellion and choose humility."**
   "God opposes the proud but gives grace to the humble. Humble yourselves, therefore, under God's mighty hand, that he may lift you up in due time." (1 Peter 5:5–6)

2. **"Honor brings blessing—I will not curse what God calls sacred."**

   "Honor your father and your mother, so that your days may be prolonged in the land which the Lord your God gives you." (Exodus 20:12)

3. **"I submit to God's authority and receive His correction with peace."**

   "Moreover, we have all had human fathers who disciplined us, and we respected them for it. How much more should we submit to the Father of spirits and live! ... No discipline seems pleasant at the time, but painful. Later on, however, it produces a harvest of righteousness and peace for those who have been trained by it." (Hebrews 12:9–11)

Turn to Chapter 9 Prayer Index and go to:

Prayer 9: General Prayer for Pride of Life
Prayer 11: Deliverance from Control & Manipulation
Supplemental Prayer: 16, 19

Cross References:

- **The Rude One** – Both operate in prideful disregard for others; The Defier expresses rebellion through disrespect and scorn for correction.
- **Jezebel** – Embodies rebellious control and spiritual defiance; The Defier often serves as a gateway to Jezebel's deeper stronghold.
- **The Coward** – While The Defier appears bold, it ultimately avoids surrender and submission to God out of fear of losing control.
- **The Apostate** – Grows from rebellion into full rejection of truth; The Defier cracks the door that the Apostate slams shut.
- **The Monitor** – Resists correction while harshly correcting others; The Defier hates being told what to do but lives to tell others.
- **The Idolator** – Exalts self-will over God's will; The Defier makes a god out of personal autonomy and rejects divine authority.

- **The Arcane One** – Many who defy spiritual authority fall into false teachings or occult paths as an act of rebellion against biblical truth.
- **The Black Sheep** – Often forms a rebellious identity in contrast to family or authority figures, reinforcing rejection through defiance.

The Glazer

Core Torment & Lie: Manipulation Through Flattery

"You're perfect just the way you are."

Gifts under attack:

- **Accountability** – The Glazer flatters to avoid hard truths, keeping others stuck by shielding them from necessary correction *("Wounds from a friend can be trusted, but an enemy multiplies kisses." – Proverbs 27:6)*.
- **Discernment** – It blurs the line between genuine encouragement and manipulation, making it hard to recognize ulterior motives *("Those who flatter their neighbors are spreading nets for their feet." – Proverbs 29:5)*.
- **Integrity** – It tempts people to compromise honesty for charm, using false praise to gain favor or influence *("Therefore each of you must put off falsehood and speak truthfully to your neighbor, for we are all members of one body." – Ephesians 4:25)*.
- **Humility** – It inflates egos with insincere compliments, feeding pride and resisting refinement *("Pride goes before destruction, a haughty spirit before a fall." – Proverbs 16:18)*.

The Glazer feeds egos until they rot. It disguises itself as kindness but carries no real love. This demon specializes in flattery, enabling, and false encouragement—the kind that tells people what they want to hear, not what they need. It spreads a net for their feet *(Proverbs 29:5)* by removing all friction, truth, or correction, allowing pride and delusion to take root. The Glazer helps people build alternate realities. It convinces them they're misunderstood geniuses, flawless victims, or beyond correction. It inflates humans into idols, then watches as the pedestal becomes a trap.

Scripture references:

*"A man who flatters his neighbor spreads a
net for his feet." (Proverbs 29:5)*

*"Wounds from a friend can be trusted, but an
enemy multiplies kisses." (Proverbs 27:6)*

*"They speak visions from their own minds, not from
the mouth of the Lord." (Jeremiah 23:16)*

Common Symptoms:

- Surrounding oneself with enablers or "yes men"
- Hypersensitivity to correction or feedback
- Resistance to accountability due to constant praise
- Fragile self-image propped up by flattery
- Confusing support with truth avoidance

Real Life Example:

Veronica became a household name through a powerful message: radical self-acceptance. She built her platform on body positivity, trying on clothes from popular brands and showing her unfiltered body to millions. Her audience felt seen. She made space for those who had never been represented and gave them confidence by loving herself publicly. Her authenticity made her a star.

As her following exploded, industry professionals began circling. They told her she could go all the way: mainstream celebrity, endorsement deals, book tours, legacy status. But there was a catch: "You're too good to stay the face of plus-size," they said. "You'd be unstoppable if you just made a few changes."

At first, Veronica resisted. She posted gym content to quiet the murmurs. But soon came the weight loss drugs, then the surgery. When she reappeared weeks later, she was nearly unrecognizable: sleek, sculpted, and suddenly distancing herself from everything that made her famous. She no longer spoke to the community that built her. She dismissed the concerns of her once-loyal followers and brushed off criticism with glossy soundbites about "growth."

What no one knew was that Veronica had made peace with her old self. The "happy fat girl" was her brand, but not her truth. Her new handlers—agents, stylists, publicists—were all Glazers. They praised her constantly, flattered her ego, and shut out every voice of caution. Even as her audience felt betrayed, no one close to Veronica told her the truth. The Glazer filled her world with affirmation not wisdom.

Now, Veronica is followed by a new crowd but haunted by the quiet fury of those she left behind. Her original fans feel deceived, discarded, and disillusioned. Veronica, once a symbol of vulnerability, is trapped behind a mask of polished perfection—shaped by surgery, yes, but also by a spirit that only ever told her what she wanted to hear.

Solutions & Declarations:

1. **"I receive correction as a gift, not an attack."**
   "Whoever loves discipline loves knowledge, but whoever hates correction is stupid." (Proverbs 12:1)

2. **"Better are the wounds of a friend than the kisses of an enemy."**
   "Wounds from a friend can be trusted, but an enemy multiplies kisses." (Proverbs 27:6)

3. **"I value truth over comfort, and growth over ego."**
   "Instead, speaking the truth in love, we will grow to become in every respect the mature body of him who is the head, that is, Christ." (Ephesians 4:15)

Turn to Chapter 9 Prayer Index and go to:
Prayer 9: General Prayer for Pride of Life
Prayer 11: Deliverance from Control & Manipulation

Supplemental Prayer: 16, 17, 19, 21, 23

Cross References:

- **The Liar** – The Glazer flatters through distortion, often exaggerating or twisting the truth to win favor and control.
- **The Doubter** – Feeds confusion and insecurity by praising people into inaction or delusion, while never offering real clarity or challenge.
- **The Monarch** – Both thrive on admiration and control; the Glazer enables the Monarch's self-exaltation with a steady supply of flattery.
- **The Idolator** – The Glazer helps inflate people into idols—either themselves or others—reinforcing image-worship and performance-based value.
- **The Narcissist** – Works hand-in-hand by supplying the validation that fuels narcissistic delusion, often blinding both parties to reality.
- **King Baby** – The Glazer spoils and appeases immaturity, helping King Baby remain stunted and self-centered under the guise of affirmation.
- **The Puppetmaster** – Flattery is one of its strings; the Glazer keeps people manageable by flattering them into dependence.
- **The Guru** – Both use elevated language and false affirmation to establish spiritual or intellectual superiority, often without accountability.

Some demons rot you from the inside out. These spirits take root in the places you've been hurt, dishonored, or overlooked. They feed on offense, resentment, and pride. Over time, they corrupt your character, erode your ability to love, forgive, and relate. What starts as a valid wound becomes a spiritual infection.

These demons are often the most tolerated, because they wear the mask of self-protection: "They hurt me," "I deserve better," "It's not fair." Left unchecked, they poison your relationships, your joy, and your soul. When people find themselves stuck, they think it's because of lack of passion, overlooking these slow, silent strongholds. In this chapter, you'll meet the demons that fester beneath the surface.

Rage & Corruption

67. **The Inferno** – Rage. "Burn it all down."

68. **The Avenger** – Revenge. "I'll make you pay."

69. **The Chainkeeper** – Grudge Holding. "I'll never get over it."

70. **The Withholder** – Ingratitude. "Nothing is ever enough."

71. **The Monarch** – Entitlement. "I deserve it, no matter what."

72. **The Exploiter** – Exploitation & Predatory Selfishness. "People are tools. Use them before they use you."

73. **The Selfish One** – Self-Centeredness. "I come first, everyone else is secondary."

74. **The Rude One** – Pride & Disregard for Others "I just say it like it is. If they can't handle it, that's their problem."

75. **The Unforgiving One** – Unforgiveness. "I'll never forgive them."

76. **The Betrayer** – Treachery. "I'll do what's best for me—even if it destroys you."

77. **The Murderer** – Hatred & Death. "They deserve to be erased."

78. **The Hater** – Malice. "I want bad things to happen to them."

79. **The Cruel One** – Sadistic Domination. "Hurting others makes me powerful."

80. **The Bully** - Tyrannical Intimidation. "If I dominate them, I'll never be dominated."

81. **The Racist** – Prejudice & Dehumanization. "They are beneath you."

The Inferno
Core Torment & Lie: Rage
"Burn it all down."
Gifts Under Attack:

- **Peace** – The Inferno floods the soul with turmoil, replacing calm with volatility and keeping the heart in unrest *("Because human anger does not produce the righteousness that God desires." – James 1:20).*
- **Forgiveness** – It fuels grudges and bitterness, making mercy feel like weakness and vengeance feel justified *("Get rid of all bitterness, rage and anger, brawling and slander, along with every form of malice. Be kind and compassionate to one another, forgiving each other, just as in Christ God forgave you." – Ephesians 4:31–32).*
- **Self-Control** – It overrides restraint, encouraging explosive reactions and emotional recklessness *("Fools give full vent to their rage, but the wise bring calm in the end." – Proverbs 29:11).*
- **Mercy** – It hardens the heart toward others' pain, creating a mindset of retaliation instead of compassion *("Blessed are the merciful, for they will be shown mercy." – Matthew 5:7).*
- **Intimacy with God** – Rage grieves the Holy Spirit and creates distance from God's presence *("Refrain from anger and turn from wrath; do not fret—it leads only to evil." – Psalm 37:8–9).*

The Inferno is a fire. It starts as hurt, then turns to offense, then rage. This demon thrives on keeping old wounds fresh and unhealed, fueling outbursts, bitterness, and inner volcanoes that never fully cool. It makes you feel justified, even noble, for your hatred, but underneath it all, it's corroding your heart. The Inferno will burn through everything unless it's extinguished at the root.

It ultimately becomes about destruction. Rage like this doesn't stay contained or resolve itself. In many situations involving The Inferno, someone ends up dead, particularly in domestic violence cases since women are more likely to be killed by their partner than anyone else.

While the world debates mental health, the spiritual root is rotting beneath the surface. This is demonic.

Scripture Reference:

> *"Human anger does not produce the righteousness that God desires." (James 1:20)*

> *"In your anger do not sin... and do not give the devil a foothold." (Ephesians 4:26–27)*

> *"Anyone who hates a brother or sister is a murderer." (1 John 3:15)*

Common Symptoms:

- Explosive temper or simmering resentment
- Replaying offenses and injustices over and over
- Hatred or disgust toward individuals or groups
- Feeling energized or "alive" when angry
- Difficulty praying, worshipping, or forgiving

Real Life Example:

Rodney can't stop thinking about her.

Crystal was his everything—or so he thought. She stuck with him through some rough seasons, and he always assumed she would keep doing so. He told himself he was just under pressure, that the shouting, the smashed drywall, and the silent treatments were all byproducts of the grind. He was building something. He'd make it all up to her when he "made it."

She didn't wait.

Now Crystal is with Kevin, a clean-cut, well-paid executive with a house in the suburbs and no emotional landmines. Rodney sees the vacation pictures of them on social media. Something deep and cold clenches in his chest. He doesn't just feel abandoned. He feels replaced.

What Crystal saw as survival, Rodney sees as betrayal. She was scared of his temper—scared enough to file a restraining order after he showed up outside her job. He didn't hurt her. He never laid a hand on her. He didn't need to. The tension was its own form of violence, and Crystal's sisters warned her from the start: "He's like your father. You know how that ends."

Rodney replays everything in his mind on a loop. What he should have said. What he could still say. What he'd do to Kevin if given the chance. Humiliate him. Beat him. End him. He wouldn't call it a plan, but it's no longer just a thought.

The Avenger has made its home in him. The spirit says that justice is his to carry out. That rage is righteous. The truth is, it's not about Crystal anymore. It's about the stronghold now festering inside of him turning pain into poison.

Solutions & Declarations:

1. **"I do not repay evil for evil but overcome evil with good."**
   "Do not repay anyone evil for evil. Be careful to do what is right in the eyes of everyone... Do not be overcome by evil but overcome evil with good." (Romans 12:17–21)

2. **"The anger of man does not produce God's righteousness."**
   "Human anger does not produce the righteousness that God desires." (James 1:20)

3. **"I put away bitterness, wrath, and anger, and walk in love."**
   "Let all bitterness and wrath and anger and clamor and slander be put away from you, along with all malice. Be kind to one another, tenderhearted, forgiving one another, as God in Christ forgave you." (Ephesians 4:31–32)

Turn to Chapter 9 Prayer Index and go to:

Prayer 9: General Prayer for Pride of Life
Prayer 12: Deliverance from Rage & Corruption

Cross-References:

- **The Avenger** – Partners with The Inferno by channeling rage into calculated retaliation.

- **The Guard** – Uses anger as a shield to hide fear of failure, rejection, or vulnerability.
- **The Chainkeeper** – Refuses to release offense, allowing bitterness to stoke the flames of rage.
- **The Liar** – Twists perception, convincing you that your anger is justified, righteous, or empowering.
- **The Abyss** – When rage has nowhere to go, it collapses inward into numbness, hopelessness, or depression.

The Avenger
Core Torment & Lie: Revenge
"I'll make you pay."
Gifts Under Attack:

- **Mercy** – The Avenger hardens the heart, making compassion feel foolish and blocking the flow of grace *("Blessed are the merciful, for they will be shown mercy." – Matthew 5:7)*.
- **Trust in God's Justice** – It convinces you that God won't act unless you do, undermining His role as Judge *("Do not take revenge, my dear friends, but leave room for God's wrath, for it is written: 'It is mine to avenge; I will repay,' says the Lord." – Romans 12:19)*.
- **Forgiveness** – It fuels a need for retribution, keeping old wounds fresh and blocking healing *("Bear with each other and forgive one another if any of you has a grievance against someone. Forgive as the Lord forgave you." – Colossians 3:13)*.
- **Emotional Freedom** – It ties your peace to someone else's punishment, trapping you in cycles of bitterness *("See to it that no one falls short of the grace of God and that no bitter root grows up to cause trouble and defile many." – Hebrews 12:15)*.

The Avenger rises when justice feels denied. It tells you someone must pay and if God won't do it, you will. This demon thrives on betrayal, injustice, and unresolved trauma. It turns hurt into fuel and pain into purpose. The Avenger wants punishment. It is crucial to understand the moment you take vengeance into your own hands, God steps back. When you become the judge, jury, and executioner, you step out from under God's protection and straight into demonic influence. The Avenger never delivers justice, only destruction. It tricks you into thinking that vengeance is power, but it always circles back to consume the one holding the sword.

Scripture Reference:

"Vengeance is Mine; I will repay, says the Lord." (Romans 12:19)

*"Do not be overcome by evil but overcome
evil with good." (Romans 12:21)*

*"You have heard it said, 'Eye for eye...' But I tell you, do
not resist an evil person." (Matthew 5:38–39)*

Common Symptoms:

- Fantasizing about revenge or imagining others suffering
- Obsession with making someone "feel what they did to you"
- Bitterness disguised as justice
- Difficulty praying for enemies or wishing them well
- Inner rage when others seem to "get away with it"

Real-Life Example:

A woman was betrayed by her husband personally and professionally. Not only did he cheat on her, but he also used the family business they built together to finance his double life with the other woman. Her devastation turned into obsession. She was determined to ruin him publicly. She went on a scorched-earth campaign: posting receipts, calling clients, dragging his name through the mud. But in her wrath, she didn't realize what she was doing: she torched the very house they built.

In her effort to destroy him, she also destroyed the business. Clients left. Partnerships collapsed. Investors pulled out. And in the end, both their reputations were wrecked, but hers fared worse. People began to see her not as the victim, but as vindictive, unstable, and obsessed. Her husband quietly rebranded the business under a new name and started a family with his affair partner. The wife ended up alone, bitter, and swearing she'd never love again. The Avenger's work was done.

Solutions & Declarations:

1. **"I release judgment and trust God to repay what was done."**
   "Beloved, never avenge yourselves, but leave it to the wrath of God, for it is written, 'Vengeance is mine, I will repay, says the Lord.'" *(Romans 12:19)*

2. **"I choose to bless and not curse those who have hurt me."**
   "But I say to you, Love your enemies and pray for those who persecute you." (Matthew 5:44)

3. **"God is my defender. I will not seek vengeance."**
   "The Lord will fight for you; you need only to be still." (Exodus 14:14)

Turn to Chapter 9 Prayer Index and go to:
Prayer 9: General Prayer for Pride of Life
Prayer 12: Deliverance from Rage & Corruption
Supplemental Prayer: 16, 19

Cross-References:

- **The Doubter** – Undermines trust in God's justice, opening the door for The Avenger to take justice into their own hands.
- **The Inferno** – Fuels the emotional fire that The Avenger channels into retaliation and vengeance.
- **The Chainkeeper** – Refuses to release offense, feeding the grudge that The Avenger seeks to settle.
- **The Liar** – Says that revenge will heal what was broken, masking bondage as empowerment.
- **The Abyss** – When vengeance fails to bring peace, despair and emptiness move in to take its place.

The Chainkeeper
Core Torment & Lie: Grudge Holding
"I'll never get over it."
Gifts under attack:

- **Mercy** – The Chainkeeper refuses to extend grace, believing others should suffer as long as you did *("Blessed are the merciful, for they will be shown mercy." – Matthew 5:7).*
- **Trust in God's Justice** – It resists release because it doesn't trust God to deal with the offense rightly *("Do not take revenge, my dear friends, but leave room for God's wrath, for it is written: 'It is mine to avenge; I will repay,' says the Lord." – Romans 12:19).*
- **Forgiveness** – It delays or denies forgiveness, convincing you that letting go means losing power *("For if you forgive other people when they sin against you, your heavenly Father will also forgive you. But if you do not forgive others their sins, your Father will not forgive your sins." – Matthew 6:14–15).*
- **Emotional Freedom** – It keeps your soul chained to the offender, forcing you to relive the pain and poison *("See to it that no one falls short of the grace of God and that no bitter root grows up to cause trouble and defile many." – Hebrews 12:15).*

The Chainkeeper holds the door open to bitterness, prolonged offense, and relational estrangement. It doesn't demand justice immediately—it wants a grudge. This demon convinces you that holding onto pain protects you from more, that silence is safer than resolution, and that unforgiveness is a shield when it's really a shackle. Unlike The Unforgiving One, which keeps you in a state of visible torment, The Chainkeeper prefers cold silence, passive bitterness, and internal walls. It thrives on long-standing grievances and robs families, marriages, and friendships of decades that could have been whole.

Scripture References:

> *"If you do not forgive others their sins, your Father*
> *will not forgive your sins." (Matthew 6:15)*

> *"Bear with each other and forgive one another... Forgive*
> *as the Lord forgave you." (Colossians 3:13)*

> *"Love keeps no record of wrongs." (1 Corinthians 13:5)*

Common Symptoms:

- Reliving past offenses, especially when emotionally triggered
- Ongoing refusal to reconcile or engage in healing dialogue
- Passive-aggressive behavior or coldness toward offenders
- Emotional shutdown in the presence of unresolved relationships
- Feeling "justified" in cutting off others permanently

Real Life Example:

In Nara, Japan, Otou and Yumi Katayama lived under the same roof for decades, raising three children and maintaining a quiet, traditional household. Behind the calm exterior was a marriage frozen in silence, because Otou hadn't spoken a single word to his wife in over twenty years.

The silence began as a simmering bitterness. Otou felt neglected, quietly resenting how much attention Yumi gave the children. Instead of expressing his feelings, he withdrew. One quiet day blurred into the next, and the longer he remained silent, the harder it became to break the spell. Yumi continued serving him—meals, laundry, companionship—but the man she once laughed with became an unmovable shadow in her own home.

The heartbreaking silence might have gone on forever if not for their grown son, desperate to see healing between his parents. He wrote to a popular television show, asking for help. The hosts staged an emotional reunion in a public park. With cameras rolling and their son watching, Otou finally broke the silence—his voice quiet, uncertain. "Somehow... it's been so long. I was jealous. I felt left out."

By then, twenty years of shared joy, vulnerability, and affection had already been forfeited to pride and passivity. What Otou thought was strength became emotional paralysis—and what he believed was punishment had actually punished the entire family.

The Chainkeeper didn't need to scream or lash out. It just sat quietly, feeding on the unspoken wound until love eroded into silence. The children learned: this is how we suffer in our home—alone, unheard, and unable to reach the ones we love most.

Solutions & Declarations:

1. **"I forgive because I have been forgiven."**
   "Be kind to one another, tenderhearted, forgiving one another, as God in Christ forgave you." (Ephesians 4:32)

2. **"I release every debt, every wrong, and every word spoken against me."**
   "Then Peter came up and said to him, 'Lord, how often will my brother sin against me, and I forgive him? As many as seven times?' Jesus said to him, 'I do not say to you seven times, but seventy-seven times.'" (Matthew 18:21–22)

3. **"I will not let bitterness take root in my heart."**
   "See to it that no one fails to obtain the grace of God; that no 'root of bitterness' springs up and causes trouble, and by it many become defiled." (Hebrews 12:15)

Turn to Chapter 9 Prayer Index and go to:

Prayer 9: General Prayer for Pride of Life
Prayer 12: Deliverance from Rage & Corruption
Supplemental Prayers: 19, 20, 34

Cross References:

- **The Doubter** – Undermines trust in God's justice, making it feel necessary to keep emotional and moral score.

- **The Inferno** – Fuels the smoldering anger that The Chainkeeper refuses to release.
- **The Avenger** – The Chainkeeper stores the offense; The Avenger plots how to make them pay.
- **The Liar** – Twists the truth to say that forgiveness means losing or excusing evil.
- **The Abyss** – Over time, unresolved wounds drag the soul into bitterness, isolation, and despair.

The Withholder
Core Torment & Lie: Ingratitude
"Nothing is ever enough."
Gifts Under Attack:

- **Gratitude** – The Withholder blinds you to your blessings, making you feel entitled rather than thankful. *(1 Thessalonians 5:18 – "Give thanks in all circumstances; for this is God's will for you in Christ Jesus.")*
- **Contentment** – It breeds chronic dissatisfaction, convincing you that joy comes only from what's next. *(Philippians 4:11–12 – "I have learned the secret of being content in any and every situation.")*
- **Emotional Intimacy** – It blocks connection by refusing to express appreciation, leaving others feeling unseen or unloved. *(Proverbs 25:11 – "A word fitly spoken is like apples of gold in settings of silver.")*
- **Appreciation** – It downplays or ignores the good in others, starving relationships of affirmation. *(Romans 12:10 – "Outdo one another in showing honor.")*

The Withholder poisons the atmosphere of blessing. It convinces people that what they have isn't enough, and what others do and give isn't good enough or worthy of thanks. This demon robs the person it inhabits and punishes those around them. The Withholder often shows up in relationships where one person constantly takes but rarely gives back. Affection is withheld. Encouragement is rare. It's an insidious spirit who works with many other demons.

The Withholder starves and leaves people emotionally malnourished in relationships where love should be safe and sustaining. Ingratitude isn't just rude—it's demonic. It slowly trains everyone around it to feel like they're never enough, safe, or worthy of joy. Eventually, it breaks people who were never meant to live like that.

Scripture Reference:

"Although they knew God, they neither glorified Him as God nor gave thanks to Him, but their thinking became futile..." (Romans 1:21)

"Give thanks in all circumstances; for this is God's will for you in Christ Jesus." (1 Thessalonians 5:18)

"The one who offers thanksgiving as his sacrifice glorifies me." (Psalm 50:23)

Symptoms:

- Chronic dissatisfaction, no matter how much is done or given
- Refusal to express appreciation or affection
- Constant criticism or nitpicking
- Emotional coldness or entitlement
- "Walking on eggshells" atmosphere in close relationships

Real-Life Example:

Scott is a self-made man who never believed success gave him an excuse to slack at home. Even while building his company from the ground up, he made sure his half of the household duties never suffered. After long days at work, he'd come home, cook dinner, do the dishes, and help with whatever else needed to be done without being asked.

His wife, Kim, barely looked up when he walked through the door. Her first words were usually corrections: "You forgot the salad." "The towels are folded wrong." "Did you even wipe the counters?" Scott tried not to take it personally. But the silence, criticism, and coldness wore him down.

She had a walk-in closet filled with designer clothes, shelves of handbags, and the freedom to stay home or shop whenever she pleased. Anything she even hinted at wanting, Scott already ordered by the end of the day, but her gratitude never arrived. He felt like he was working for a queen who never crowned him.

Affection was withheld. Appreciation was withheld. The kids had started to notice too—whispering and sidestepping their mother's moods. The home was beautiful, but cold. Scott began to realize he was lonelier in marriage than he ever was alone.

Solutions & Declarations:

1. **I will bless the Lord at all times; His praise will continually be in my mouth.**
   "I will bless the Lord at all times; His praise shall continually be in my mouth." (Psalm 34:1)

2. **I give thanks in all things, for this is God's will for me**
   "Give thanks in all circumstances; for this is the will of God in Christ Jesus for you." (1 Thessalonians 5:18)

3. **I choose to speak life and express gratitude for what I've been given.**
   "Death and life are in the power of the tongue, and those who love it will eat its fruit." (Proverbs 18:21)

Turn to Chapter 9 Prayer Index and go to:

Prayer 9: General Prayer for Pride of Life
Prayer 12: Deliverance from Rage & Corruption
Supplemental Prayer: 16, 24, 19

Cross-References:

- **The Selfish One** – Focuses inward and rarely recognizes the effort, sacrifice, or needs of others.

- **The Narcissist** – Expects admiration but rarely gives honor or thanks in return.
- **The Monarch** – Sees others as servants or pawns, often withholding praise or validation as a form of control.
- **The Curator** – Fixates on appearances and perfection, making it hard to appreciate what's genuine or heartfelt.
- **The Critic** – Picks apart what others offer instead of receiving it with gratitude.
- **The Complainer** – Sees what's lacking in every situation, robbing others of joy and gratitude.
- **The Jealous One** – Can't give thanks because they're too busy resenting what someone else has.
- **The Chainkeeper** – Holds grudges and withholds forgiveness or affirmation, often out of pride or pain.

The Monarch
Core Torment & Lie: Entitlement
"I deserve it, no matter what."
Gifts Under Attack:

- **Humility** – The Monarch elevates self over others, rejecting the servant posture of Christ. *(Philippians 2:3 – "Do nothing out of selfish ambition or vain conceit. Rather, in humility value others above yourselves.")*
- **Gratitude** – It convinces you that blessings are owed, not given— blocking sincere appreciation. *(James 1:17 – "Every good and perfect gift is from above, coming down from the Father of the heavenly lights.")*
- **Responsibility** – It resists accountability, believing others should carry the burden. *(Galatians 6:5 – "For each one should carry their own load.")*

- **Teachability** – The Monarch refuses correction, mistaking rebuke for insult. *(Proverbs 12:1 – "Whoever loves discipline loves knowledge, but whoever hates correction is stupid.")*

The Monarch sits on a throne they didn't build, demanding rewards they never earned. This demon distorts a person's sense of justice, maturity, and self-awareness. It says that effort is optional, that rules are for other people, and that love, success, and recognition should come automatically. The Monarch expects to be served, admired, and exempt from the processes that shape character. When those expectations aren't met, it throws a tantrum or a lawsuit.

Entitlement is spiritual rot. It devours growth and leaves a person emotionally and spiritually stunted. The Monarch often emerges in those raised without discipline, correction, or accountability—especially when provision was mistaken for parenting. This demon isn't confined to the rich. It can be found in anyone who believes they're owed something from life, from God, or from others simply because they want it.

Scripture Reference:

"Pride goes before destruction, and a haughty spirit before a fall." (Proverbs 16:18)

"By your own sword you did not win the land, nor did your own arm bring you victory—it was Your right hand, Your arm, and the light of Your face." (Psalm 44:3)

"The greatest among you must be a servant." (Matthew 23:11)

Symptoms:

- Expecting rewards or positions without effort
- Resenting correction, feedback, or being told "no"
- Seeing oneself as the exception to rules or consequences
- Taking blessings for granted and always wanting more
- Treating others as tools for advancement or convenience

Real-Life Example:

Evan grew up with every advantage: private schools, private tutors, and a mother who built her empire from the ground up. He didn't inherit her drive, though, only her bank account. He paid people to do his homework in school. He got into college as a legacy. When he graduated, he didn't apply anywhere—he simply *expected* to be handed a six-figure role in his mother's company without ever learning the business.

Before that could happen, Evan got caught up in a crypto scheme with his rich friends. He didn't even understand what was happening and when the feds came knocking, the ones who *did* understand let him take the fall. He wasn't smart enough to see it coming and not grounded enough to fight back. Evan went to prison for crimes he barely understood, convinced until the end that his family name would save him.

That's The Monarch: too proud to learn, too entitled to listen, and too blind to see the trap being set. This demon creates people who can't grow, only fall.

Solutions & Declarations:

1. **I humble myself under God's mighty hand, and He will lift me up in due time.**
   "Humble yourselves, therefore, under God's mighty hand, that he may lift you up in due time." (1 Peter 5:6)

2. **I do nothing out of selfish ambition, but in humility, I value others above myself.**
   "Do nothing out of selfish ambition or vain conceit. Rather, in humility value others above yourselves." (Philippians 2:3)

3. **I live to serve, not to be served.**
   "For even the Son of Man did not come to be served, but to serve, and to give his life as a ransom for many." (Mark 10:45)

Turn to Chapter 9 Prayer Index and go to:
Prayer 9: General Prayer for Pride of Life
Prayer 12: Deliverance from Rage & Corruption

Cross-References:

- **The Withholder** – The Monarch sees sacrifice as beneath them and withholds gratitude in return.
- **The Guard** – Entitlement often hides deep fear—of trying, failing, or being exposed as inadequate.
- **The Glazer** – Surrounds the Monarch with constant praise and false affirmation, reinforcing their inflated sense of worth.
- **The Liar** – Feeds the fantasy that the Monarch is inherently more deserving than others.
- **The Doubter** – Refuses to trust God's timing or testing, insisting on elevation without the process.

The Exploiter

Core Torment & Lie: Exploitation & Predatory Selfishness

"People are tools. Use them before they use you."

Gifts Under Attack:

- **Love** – The Exploiter views people transactionally, stripping love of its sacrificial, God-given nature. *(1 Corinthians 13:5 – "Love... is not self-seeking.")*
- **Integrity** – It teaches manipulation over honesty and gain over righteousness. *(Proverbs 10:9 – "Whoever walks in integrity walks securely, but whoever takes crooked paths will be found out.")*
- **Compassion** – It hardens the heart, seeing others' needs as opportunities to exploit rather than serve. *(Colossians 3:12 – "Clothe yourselves with compassion, kindness, humility, gentleness and patience.")*
- **Stewardship of Others** – It rejects responsibility for how you treat others, denying the call to protect and uplift them. *(Philippians 2:4 – "Let each of you look not only to his own interests, but also to the interests of others.")*
- **Covenant Honor** – It treats relationships as expendable, refusing to honor the sacred trust God places between people. *(Romans*

12:10 – "Be devoted to one another in love. Honor one another above yourselves.")

The Exploiter is a cold, calculating spirit that sees people as commodities and extracts their value. Whether through emotional grooming, financial manipulation, sexual coercion, or subtle flattery, The Exploiter thrives on selfish gain. It twists charm into bait and favors into debt. On the surface, it can seem helpful, even generous, but underneath is a heart unmoved by anything but personal advantage. It operates in business, families, churches, and romantic entanglements alike, feeding off power, influence, and control. It is a modern-day slave master, and it has many forms.

Scripture References:

"Woe to the shepherds... who only take care of themselves!... You have ruled them harshly and brutally." (Ezekiel 34:2–4)

"They covet fields and seize them... They defraud people of their homes." (Micah 2:1–2)

"...and human souls" (Revelation 18:13 speaking of Babylon's commerce in human lives)

"Whoever oppresses the poor shows contempt for their Maker." (Proverbs 14:31)

"...brutal, not lovers of good... lovers of pleasure rather than lovers of God." (2 Timothy 3:2–4)

Common Symptoms:

- Using people for favors, sex, status, or influence
- Charismatic manipulation
- Lack of guilt after using someone or betraying trust
- Relationships that revolve around what others can do, not who they are
- Associating love with control, debt, or performance

Real-Life Example:

Jeffrey started as an entertainer: charismatic, stylish, and connected. When the spotlight faded, he reinvented himself as a "Dr." and launched a church in Los Angeles, using his entertainment ties to raise millions for a glamorous new building. His charm worked just as well behind a pulpit. Celebrities showed up, cameras flashed, and crowds lined up early just to claim a seat.

The services were electric—more like concerts than worship. He went on international tours, flaunted designer clothes and luxury vehicles, and told his congregation not to give to the poor, but to him, promising they'd "reap the same favor" if they sowed into his life. Scripture was twisted to support his lifestyle. Behind the scenes, staff members worked around the clock hoping to be "elevated," yet their loyalty was rewarded only with exhaustion and emotional debt.

Jeffrey used social media to harvest personal details, calling out congregants during services under the guise of prophetic insight. Many believed he carried a special anointing, but it wasn't the Holy Spirit; it was witchcraft, manipulation, and spiritual seduction. The Exploiter was strong in him.

Eventually, multiple women came forward—some pregnant, others emotionally destroyed—revealing affairs, coercion, and secret abortions. Nonbelievers, remembering his past, were shocked the Church had ever embraced him. But those inside the system were under a spell. His relationships were never about service or shepherding. They were transactional. Every person was a resource. Every connection had a price.

When the facade finally cracked, the church unraveled. What had once looked like favor was nothing more than spiritual fraud, built on exploitation and ego.

Solutions & Declarations:

1. **I break agreement with every spirit that taught me to use people.**
   "Let love be genuine. Abhor what is evil; hold fast to what is good."
   (Romans 12:9)

2. **I am called to love, not to leverage. People are not resources— they are sacred.**

   "So in everything, do to others what you would have them do to you, for this sums up the Law and the Prophets." (Matthew 7:12)

3. **I repent for the ways I have taken without giving, and I ask God to restore what I corrupted.**

   "Anyone who has been stealing must steal no longer, but must work, doing something useful with their own hands, that they may have something to share with those in need." (Ephesians 4:28)

Turn to Chapter 9 Prayer Index and go to:
Prayer 9: General Prayer for Pride of Life
Prayer 12: Deliverance from Rage & Corruption

Cross References:

- **The Glacier** – The Exploiter shows no emotional connection, using others without empathy or remorse.
- **Jezebel** – Both seek control, but the Exploiter does it through calculated leverage rather than overt domination.
- **The Narcissist** – Sees people as mirrors and tools, valuing them only for what they can provide.
- **Mammon** – The Exploiter turns relationships into transactions, often masking greed as ambition.
- **The Profane** – Treats people, intimacy, and trust as disposable— nothing is off-limits if it serves their gain.

The Selfish One

Core Torment & Lie: Self-Centeredness

"I come first, everyone else is secondary."

Gifts Under Attack:

- **Generosity** – The Selfish One convinces you to hoard instead of share, fearing lack instead of trusting provision. *(2 Corinthians 9:6 – "Whoever sows sparingly will also reap sparingly, and whoever sows generously will also reap generously.")*
- **Empathy** – It dulls compassion, making the pain and needs of others feel irrelevant to your priorities. *(Romans 12:15 – "Rejoice with those who rejoice; mourn with those who mourn.")*
- **Sacrificial Love** – It replaces Christlike giving with self-preservation and entitlement. *(John 15:13 – "Greater love has no one than this: to lay down one's life for one's friends.")*
- **Christlike Humility** – It keeps you focused on your own wants and importance rather than considering others first. *(Philippians 2:3–4 – "Do nothing out of selfish ambition or vain conceit. Rather, in humility value others above yourselves, not looking to your own interests but each of you to the interests of the others.")*
- **Community** – It isolates you in a cycle of taking without giving, eroding the unity and health of the Body of Christ. *(1 Corinthians 12:25 – "So that there should be no division in the body, but that its parts should have equal concern for each other.")*

The Selfish One exalts self above all else. It makes every relationship transactional: "What can I get?" instead of "How can I serve?" This demon distorts love into convenience and turns people into tools. It thrives on entitlement and quietly kills empathy. It shows up in passive forms, like resentment when others don't serve your needs. The Selfish One says that your plans, feelings, and comfort matter most. Underneath is a rejection of surrender, a refusal to see others as sacred, and a deep-rooted pride that mirrors Lucifer's fall. The Selfish One is a signature of the last days.

Scripture References:

"People will be lovers of themselves... proud, abusive..." (2 Timothy 3:2)

"Do nothing from selfish ambition... but in humility count others more significant." (Philippians 2:3–4)

"Where selfish ambition exists, there is disorder and every vile practice." (James 3:16)

"For those who are self-seeking... there will be wrath." (Romans 2:8)

"Let him deny himself and take up his cross daily." (Luke 9:23)

Common Symptoms:

- Constant focus on personal gain, comfort, or convenience
- Resentment when others don't cater to your needs
- Difficulty celebrating others without comparison
- Overusing others' kindness, time, or attention
- Seeing relationships as one-sided or always on your terms

Real-Life Example:

Nicole abandoned her daughter, Amara, as a baby, leaving her with the child's great-grandmother because Nicole "wasn't ready to be tied down." While Amara grew up without birthday calls, holiday visits, or emotional support, Nicole chased men, fun, and freedom. The little girl learned early not to expect anything from her mother.

As Amara got older, she earned a college scholarship and juggled a job to survive. That's when Nicole reappeared, this time needing a place to stay. She moved into Amara's tiny apartment, partied all night, and disrupted her sleep, showing no regard for her daughter's intense schedule. When Nicole found a new boyfriend, she disappeared again without warning.

Amara eventually graduated and landed a high-paying job. As soon as word spread, Nicole came calling, this time demanding to be supported "because I'm your mother." She showed no awareness of the damage she caused, or the sacrifices Amara made. Nicole's sense of entitlement was reinforced her entire life starting with her own mother, who refused to take responsibility for Amara and let the burden fall on an aging great-grandmother.

Amara dreamed of finally building a peaceful, stable life and caring for the woman who raised her, but The Selfish One doesn't honor sacrifice. It demands what it never gave. Every paycheck and bonus Amara earned became Nicole's expectation, reminding Amara she was simply a resource.

Solutions & Declarations:

1. **"I am not the center. God is."**
   "He must increase, but I must decrease." (John 3:30)

2. **"I repent for every time I made others serve my ego instead of my heart."**
   "Do nothing from selfish ambition or conceit, but in humility count others more significant than yourselves." (Philippians 2:3)

3. **"I choose to live a life poured out, not preserved for my own benefit."**
   "Even the Son of Man came not to be served but to serve, and to give his life as a ransom for many." (Mark 10:45)

Turn to Chapter 9 Prayer Index and go to:

Prayer 9: General Prayer for Pride of Life
Prayer 12: Deliverance from Rage & Corruption

Cross References:

- **The Withholder** – Refuses to give love, time, or attention unless there's something to gain.
- **The Greedy One** – Takes more than needed, driven by excess rather than need.
- **The Pauper** – Believes in scarcity and hoards instead of sharing, even in abundance.

- **The Narcissist** – Sees others only in terms of what they can provide or admire.
- **The Abandoner** – Leaves when others require too much or offer too little in return.
- **The Player** – Exploits others emotionally or physically for personal gratification.
- **The Coward** – Chooses self-preservation over sacrifice, even when others are harmed.
- **The Idolator** – Puts self, image, or desire above others—and above God.

The Rude One

Core Torment & Lie: Pride & Disregard for Others

"I just say it like it is. If they can't
handle it, that's their problem."

Gifts under attack:

- **Honor** – The Rude One disregards the value of others, undermining the biblical call to treat every person with respect. *(Romans 12:10 – "Be devoted to one another in love. Honor one another above yourselves.")*
- **Gentleness** – It replaces tenderness with abrasiveness, making harshness seem like strength. *(Philippians 4:5 – "Let your gentleness be evident to all. The Lord is near.")*
- **Discernment in Speech** – It promotes speaking without wisdom or restraint, harming when you're called to heal. *(Proverbs 15:1 – "A gentle answer turns away wrath, but a harsh word stirs up anger.")*
- **Grace** – It disables the ability to speak with kindness, compassion, or understanding—even when truth is needed. *(Colossians 4:6 – "Let your speech always be gracious, seasoned with salt, so that you may know how you ought to answer each person.")*

- **Love** – It twists love into bluntness and writes off empathy as weakness, violating the command to speak the truth in love.
- *(Ephesians 4:15 – "Instead, speaking the truth in love, we will grow to become in every respect the mature body of him who is the head, that is, Christ.")*

The Rude One disguises arrogance as honesty and cruelty as "realness." It convinces people that kindness is weakness and that to be bold means to abandon courtesy. This demon feeds on applause from those who confuse rudeness with strength, but in God's eyes, it is immaturity and a violation of love. Rudeness breaks down connection, causes confusion, and hardens the heart. Whether through sarcasm, bluntness, or disrespect, The Rude One always exalts self over others. It speaks in pride.

Scripture References:

"Love is not rude; it is not self-seeking..." (1 Corinthians 13:5)

"A fool's lips walk into a fight..." (Proverbs 18:6)

"A gentle answer turns away wrath, but a harsh word stirs up anger." (Proverbs 15:1)

"Let your speech always be gracious, seasoned with salt..." (Colossians 4:6)

"Speak evil of no one... show perfect courtesy toward all people." (Titus 3:2)

Common Symptoms:

- Interrupting, dismissing, or talking over others
- Using "truth" as an excuse to insult or offend
- Belittling others under the guise of being "honest"
- Chronic sarcasm, passive aggression, or eye-rolling
- Being known for "saying too much" and apologizing only after damage is done

Real Life Example:

Marjorie poured everything into opening her dream ice cream parlor. Every detail mattered: handmade sprinkles, fresh-baked cookies, slow-cooked sauces. It was a labor of love, the culmination of years of planning, saving, and sacrifice. When opening day arrived, the community buzzed with anticipation.

Because she was handling so much in the kitchen, Marjorie hired a young woman named Isabella to manage the front counter. Isabella came across as no-nonsense and direct, qualities Marjorie initially appreciated. She thought she was leaving the customer service in capable hands.

At first, business boomed. Then it dipped—fast. Despite it being the height of summer, foot traffic slowed to a trickle. Marjorie was baffled. The product didn't change. If anything, it only got better.

Then she read the online reviews.

One after another, customers raved about the quality of the ice cream: "Best I've ever had," "Flavors are unbelievable," "Toppings are insane." But nearly every review ended the same way: "Too bad the girl at the counter is so rude." Some called Isabella "hostile," others "cold," and one customer wrote, "She acted like I was bothering her by being there. I wanted to love this place, but I won't be back until she's gone."

The Rude One had taken root in Isabella, and it cost Marjorie dearly. What should have been the start of something beautiful was slowly being sabotaged by one spirit working through one person. Rudeness isn't just a personality trait. When unchecked, it becomes a tool of destruction, pushing people away, poisoning reputations, and stealing what others have worked hard to build.

Solutions & Declarations:

1. **"My words are meant to bring life, not destruction."**
   "Death and life are in the power of the tongue, and those who love it will eat its fruits." (Proverbs 18:21)

2. **"I break agreement with the lie that cruelty is clarity."**
"Let no corrupting talk come out of your mouths, but only such as is good for building up, as fits the occasion, that it may give grace to those who hear." (Ephesians 4:29)

3. **"I ask for the Spirit to season my speech with grace, humility, and self-control."**
"Let your speech always be gracious, seasoned with salt, so that you may know how you ought to answer each person." (Colossians 4:6)

Turn to Chapter 9 Prayer Index and go to:

Prayer 9: General Prayer for Pride of Life

Prayer 12: Deliverance from Rage & Corruption

Supplemental Prayer: 16, 19

Cross references:

- The Mouth – Empowers unchecked speech that wounds and divides.
- The Critic – Expresses judgment and superiority masked as truth.
- The Glacier – Supports coldness that rejects emotional sensitivity.
- The Litigator – Thrives on arguing rather than understanding.
- The Desperate – Uses rudeness for attention or to dominate conversations.

The Unforgiving One

Core Torment & Lie: Unforgiveness

"I'll never forgive them."

Gifts under attack:

- **Compassion** – The Unforgiving One hardens the heart, blocking empathy and the ability to see others through God's eyes. *(Ephesians 4:32 – "Be kind and compassionate to one another, forgiving each other, just as in Christ God forgave you.")*

- **Peace** – Unforgiveness keeps you in a spiritual prison, tormented by past pain and unresolved anger. *(Colossians 3:13–15 – "Forgive as the Lord forgave you... and let the peace of Christ rule in your hearts.")*
- **Spiritual Authority** – Jesus clearly taught that refusing to forgive cuts off divine authority and releases torment. *(Matthew 18:34–35 – "This is how my heavenly Father will treat each of you unless you forgive your brother or sister from your heart.")*
- **Intimacy with God** – A heart that withholds forgiveness creates spiritual distance, blocking prayer and fellowship with God. *(Mark 11:25 – "And when you stand praying, if you hold anything against anyone, forgive them, so that your Father in heaven may forgive you your sins.")*

The Unforgiving One thrives on wounds that never heal. It keeps pain fresh by replaying offenses on a loop and convincing you that forgiveness is weakness and that justice must come by your own hand. In truth, it chains you to the very people and events you want to escape. Jesus warned plainly: if you do not forgive, you will not be forgiven *(Matthew 6:15)*. The Unforgiving One poisons prayer, warps perception, and blocks spiritual growth. It hardens your heart toward both God and others, cutting off blessing and perpetuating cycles of bitterness, self-pity, and separation from grace.

Scripture References:

> "But if you do not forgive others, your Father will not forgive your sins." (Matthew 6:15)

> "See to it... that no root of bitterness springs up and causes trouble." (Hebrews 12:15)

> "...handed over to the tormentors until he should repay all..." (Matthew 18:34–35)

Common Symptoms:

- Replaying offenses in your mind regularly
- Chronic resentment toward specific individuals

- Inability or refusal to pray for enemies
- Coldness in worship or intimacy with God
- Labeling bitterness as "discernment" or "boundaries"

Real Life Example:

Kayleigh dreamed of a fairytale wedding her entire life, and when the time finally came, she planned an extravagant destination ceremony overseas, complete with a full week of bachelorette events, yacht outings, and luxury spa days. She sent her ten bridesmaids a detailed spreadsheet breaking down the costs, expecting each one to cover not only their share, but to split hers as well.

Three of her bridesmaids—close friends since childhood—called her in tears. They simply couldn't afford the thousands of dollars required. Rather than feel compassion, Kaleigh felt insulted. When her maid of honor gently suggested scaling things back for the group, Kaleigh snapped.

In her eyes, they didn't just decline an invite, they ruined her big day. Fueled by offense and pride, Kaleigh revoked their invitations, disbanded her entire bridal party, and never spoke to those friends again. Years later, she still refers to them as "jealous" and "unsupportive," never acknowledging how unforgiveness hardened her heart and isolated her from the people who once loved her most.

This is The Unforgiving One in action: not just wounded, but unwilling. Offense becomes identity, and pride makes healing feel like losing.

Solutions & Declarations:

1. **"I choose to forgive, even if they never apologize. I release them to God."**
   "And whenever you stand praying, forgive, if you have anything against anyone, so that your Father also who is in heaven may forgive you your trespasses." (Mark 11:25)

2. **"Forgiveness is freedom, not permission. It's how I get my life back."**

   "Judge not, and you will not be judged; condemn not, and you will not be condemned; forgive, and you will be forgiven." (Luke 6:37)

3. **"I will not let bitterness block my blessing."**

   "See to it that no one fails to obtain the grace of God; that no 'root of bitterness' springs up and causes trouble, and by it many become defiled." (Hebrews 12:15)

Turn to Chapter 9 Prayer Index and go to:

Prayer 9: General Prayer for Pride of Life

Prayer 12: Deliverance from Rage & Corruption

Cross references:

- **The Avenger** – Seeks punishment instead of mercy, often driven by the same unresolved pain.
- **The Mouth** – Rehearses old wounds through gossip, venting, or verbal curses instead of seeking healing.
- **The Critic** – Builds harsh judgments and fixed narratives out of offense that was never released.
- **The Chainkeeper** – Refuses to let go, keeping both self and others bound to the past.
- **Leviathan** – Twists perception through pride, convincing people they're justified in not forgiving, even unto hell.

The Betrayer

Core Torment & Lie: Treachery

"I'll do what's best for me—even if it destroys you."

Gifts under attack:

- **Loyalty** – The Betrayer severs bonds of trust, prioritizing personal gain over faithfulness to others. *(Proverbs 17:17 – "A friend loves at all times, and a brother is born for adversity.")*
- **Integrity** – It leads individuals to break promises, act deceitfully, and justify harmful behavior. *(Proverbs 11:3 – "The integrity of the upright guides them, but the unfaithful are destroyed by their duplicity.")*
- **Covenant-Keeping** – The Betrayer mocks sacred commitments, making light of vows in marriage, friendship, or spiritual brotherhood. *(Psalm 15:4 – "...who keeps an oath even when it hurts and does not change their mind.")*
- **Emotional Intimacy** – It destroys safe emotional connection by violating trust, leaving others fearful of vulnerability. *(Proverbs 25:9–10 – "...do not betray another's confidence, or the one who hears it may shame you and the charge against you will stand.")*

The Betrayer walks beside you... until you become a threat. Inspired by the same spirit that entered Judas, this demon values gain over covenant. It says that self-preservation justifies the violation of trust. Whether it manifests as cheating, sabotage, or betrayal of confidence, The Betrayer always leaves devastation in its wake, especially because it comes from someone once close. It often cloaks itself in self-care, strategy, or "what's best for everyone," but its fruit is treachery. It dismantles loyalty and poisons intimacy, always placing personal benefit above relational integrity.

Scripture References:

"Then Satan entered Judas... and he consented and sought an opportunity to betray him." (Luke 22:3–6)

> *"It was not an enemy... but it was you, a man like myself,*
> *my companion, my close friend." (Psalm 55:12–14)*

> *"Do not betray another's confidence." (Proverbs 25:9–10)*

Common Symptoms:

- Willingness to turn on others under pressure
- Justifying betrayal as "protecting yourself" or "just being wise"
- Deep fear of being controlled or "played" by others
- Playing both sides of a conflict
- Cold detachment from people once trusted

Real Life Example:

The world mourned when news broke that four brilliant oncologists died in a tragic boating accident off the coast of Italy. They were celebrating the completion of a groundbreaking medical discovery: a universal cancer cure that showed 100% remission in pre-clinical trials, across all cancer types. To make the milestone, the team chose a private, luxury yacht —an "unsinkable" vessel anchored in calm waters. By morning, the ship was sunk with no survivors. The official story was equipment failure. A fluke.

The tragedy sent shockwaves through the medical community. Behind the headlines, a darker truth began to surface.

Just 48 hours after the sinking, the patent for the cure—previously held jointly by the four researchers—was quietly acquired by the world's largest pharmaceutical conglomerate, Fizzer. A few weeks later, Fizzer released a vague statement: "After internal review, this treatment will not move forward due to regulatory and safety concerns." No further explanation. The cure was shelved. Permanently.

The boat itself? Owned by a shell company that traced back to Blackguard, the most powerful holding corporation on earth, an entity with deep ties to global finance, government, and pharmaceuticals.

The cure wasn't lost. It was buried. Not by natural disaster, but by The Betrayer, the spirit that prioritizes profit over people and kills what should be sacred for the sake of control. This was more than a betrayal of four scientists. It was a betrayal of humanity.

Solutions & Declarations:

1. **"I walk in loyalty and truth, even when it costs me."**
   "Let not steadfast love and faithfulness forsake you; bind them around your neck, write them on the tablet of your heart. So, you will find favor and good success in the sight of God and man." (Proverbs 3:3–4)

2. **"I break every agreement I made with betrayal."**
   "Ah, you destroyer, who yourself have not been destroyed, you traitor, whom none has betrayed! When you have ceased to destroy, you will be destroyed; and when you have finished betraying, they will betray you." (Isaiah 33:1)

3. **"I will not be used to tear others down for gain."**
   "But if you bite and devour one another, watch out that you are not consumed by one another." (Galatians 5:15)

Turn to Chapter 9 Prayer Index and go to:
Prayer 9: General Prayer for Pride of Life
Prayer 12: Deliverance from Rage & Corruption

Cross References:

- **The Liar** – All betrayal is born in deception and cloaked in false intentions.
- **The Achiever** – Will sacrifice others if it means climbing higher.
- **The Narcissist** – Uses people as tools, then discards them when they no longer serve a purpose.
- **The Exploiter** – Betrayal often brings a material reward; the gain is always the goal.
- **Mammon** – At the root of many betrayals lies the love of money, which sells out truth for profit.

The Murderer
Core Torment & Lie: Hatred & Death
"They deserve to be erased."
Gifts under attack:

- **Love** – The Murderer snuffs out the God-given capacity to see others through the lens of grace and worth. *(1 John 3:15 – "Anyone who hates a brother or sister is a murderer, and you know that no murderer has eternal life residing in him.")*
- **Mercy** – It fosters a hardened heart, removing compassion and feeding the desire to judge or destroy. *(Matthew 5:7 – "Blessed are the merciful, for they will be shown mercy.")*
- **Reverence for Life** – The Murderer blinds people to the sacredness of life, whether through violence, abortion, or indifference to suffering.
- *(Genesis 9:6 – "Whoever sheds human blood, by humans shall their blood be shed; for in the image of God has God made mankind.")*
- **Self-Control** – It provokes impulsive rage, premeditated vengeance, or cold indifference—driving people to act without restraint. *(Proverbs 29:11 – "Fools give full vent to their rage, but the wise bring calm in the end.")*

The Murderer begins in the heart. Jesus said anyone who hates their brother is a murderer. This spirit fuels rage, abuse, revenge fantasies, and even verbal assassination. It convinces the host that certain people are so toxic, destructive, or threatening that they must be emotionally or physically eliminated. It is the same spirit that drove Cain to kill Abel, Herod to kill infants, and Pharaoh to enslave and slaughter. The Murderer is hatred fully matured, and it leaves destruction behind in every form.

Scripture References:

"Anyone who hates his brother is a murderer." (1 John 3:15)

"Cain rose up against his brother Abel and killed him." (Genesis 4:8)

*"Anyone who is angry with a brother... is subject
to judgment." (Matthew 5:21–22)*

Common Symptoms:

- Fantasizing about harming someone (emotionally or physically)
- Intense hatred or dehumanization of a person or group
- Abuse (verbal, emotional, physical)
- Using speech to destroy reputations
- Repetitive patterns of outbursts, threats, or intimidation

Real Life Example:

Stephen never had a chance at a normal childhood. His earliest memory was of his father shouting, and then the gunshot that ended his mother's life. She spoke "with an attitude," his father said. That was all it took.

Stephen and his brothers were separated in the system, passed between homes like baggage. Some placements were worse than the home they left. By 16, Stephen was off the grid and into the arms of the streets. A local gang took him in, and before long, the boy who once cowered in corners was the one people feared.

His first murder was senseless. A look. A dare. A trigger pulled to prove something. After that, something in him shifted. The spirit of The Murderer had found a permanent home.

Stephen was the angriest one in the crew. Cold. Empty. Respected. His violence was calculated. He rose quickly in the criminal world and was soon running operations for a cartel by the time most of his peers were trying to get clean or get out.

The spirit of The Murderer is more than just bloodshed. It's a force that celebrates death, desensitizes the soul, and sears the conscience until nothing is sacred. Stephen's humanity was eaten away bite by bite since childhood. By the time he turned 27, he didn't blink while ending lives.

He died the way he lived: shot outside a club on a random Thursday night. No family, no prayer, no chance to repent. No one knows if he ever truly heard the Gospel. The boy who once watched his mother die became the same weapon that stole her. His name was added to The Murderer's growing list of lives stolen too young, too violently, and too far from truth.

Solutions & Declarations:

1. **"I choose life and love over rage and revenge."**
   "This day I call the heavens and the earth as witnesses against you that I have set before you life and death, blessings and curses. Now choose life, so that you and your children may live." (Deuteronomy 30:19)

2. **"The blood of Jesus speaks a better word than murder and hatred."**
   "And to Jesus, the mediator of a new covenant, and to the sprinkled blood that speaks a better word than the blood of Abel." (Hebrews 12:24)

3. **"I repent for every time I partnered with destruction."**
   "If we confess our sins, He is faithful and just to forgive us our sins and to cleanse us from all unrighteousness." (1 John 1:9)

Turn to Chapter 9 Prayer Index and go to:
Prayer 9: General Prayer for Pride of Life
Prayer 12: Deliverance from Rage & Corruption

Cross-references:

- **The Avenger** – Justifies violence as justice.
- **The Unforgiving One** – Feeds the hatred that grows into murder.
- **The Bully** – Dominates through force or fear.
- **The Mouth** – Destroys reputations as a form of emotional murder.
- **The Inferno** – Volatile rage that burns everything in its path.

The Hater

Core Torment & Lie: Malice

"I want bad things to happen to them."

Gifts under attack:

- **Love** – The Hater hardens the heart and shuts off the flow of God's love, replacing it with contempt and cruelty *(1 John 4:20 – "Whoever claims to love God yet hates a brother or sister is a liar.")*.
- **Mercy** – It fuels a desire for others to suffer rather than be forgiven, rejecting the very mercy God extended to us *(James 2:13 – "Judgment without mercy will be shown to anyone who has not been merciful.")*.
- **Empathy** – It numbs the capacity to see others as human or redeemable, feeding dehumanization and cold indifference *(Colossians 3:12 – "Clothe yourselves with compassion, kindness, humility, gentleness and patience.")*.
- **Community** – It isolates and divides, turning connection into hostility and unity into suspicion *(1 John 3:15 – "Anyone who hates a brother or sister is a murderer, and you know that no murderer has eternal life residing in him.")*.

The Hater is a festering spirit. It simmers, seethes, and quietly poisons the soul. It rejoices when others fail, gossips when they succeed, and silently hopes for their downfall. This demon is often born through rejection, jealousy, or comparison. It disguises itself as "realness" or "just being honest," but underneath is an alignment with the Accuser. When left unchallenged, The Hater can evolve into verbal abuse, division, or spiritual contempt and pave the way for The Murderer to move in.

Scripture References:

"Hatred stirs up strife." (Proverbs 10:12)

"Whoever hates his brother is a murderer." (1 John 3:15)

"...living in malice and envy, being hated and hating one another." (Titus 3:3)

Common Symptoms:

- Secret satisfaction when others fail
- Gossip, slander, or public shaming
- Competitive spirit rooted in envy
- Criticism masked as "discernment"
- Withdrawing from community out of bitterness

Real Life Example:

Camila lives in a picture-perfect suburb filled with luxury SUVs, renovated kitchens, and curated Instagram feeds. She's part of a tight circle of moms who brunch together, vacation together, and pose for pictures like they're best friends, but underneath the polished smiles is a cold war of comparison and quiet cruelty.

Their group chat is where the real game is played: screenshots, gossip, and passive-aggressive critiques masked as concern. Camila's days are spent tracking who wore what, who gained weight, who's husband got a promotion, and who's falling behind. The truth is, she's measuring everything and everyone—including herself—with the ruler of The Hater.

Her "best friend" is the one person she feels comfortable enough to hate with out loud. They bond by tearing down the rest. It's the only honest relationship in Camila's life, even though it's entirely built on bitterness.

She calls it "venting." She tells herself it's harmless, but her heart is rotting from being fed daily with envy, comparison, and the secret hope that someone else's perfect life will crack just enough to make her feel better about her own. The Hater has fully taken up residence inside her.

Solutions & Declarations:

1. **"I choose to bless, not curse. I reject the spirit of hatred."**
   "Bless those who persecute you; bless and do not curse." (Romans 12:14)

2. **"Their success does not threaten mine. I release them to God."**
   "For where jealousy and selfish ambition exist, there will be disorder and every vile practice. But the wisdom from above is first pure, then peaceable, gentle, open to reason, full of mercy and good fruits, impartial and sincere." (James 3:16–17)

3. **"My value is not based on comparison—I am complete in Christ."**
   "And you are complete in Him, who is the head of all principality and power." (Colossians 2:10)

Turn to Chapter 9 Prayer Index and go to:
Prayer 9: General Prayer for Pride of Life
Prayer 12: Deliverance from Rage & Corruption
Supplemental Prayer: 16, 19, 21

Cross-references:

- **The Jealous One** – Fuels the root of hatred through comparison.
- **The Mouth** – Turns hatred into verbal destruction.
- **The Critic** – Justifies hostility through constant judgment.
- **The Gossip** – Spreads relational poison to others.
- **The Murderer** – Hatred becomes violence if left unchecked.
- **Leviathan** – Pride twists communication and fuels offense, keeping hatred alive.

The Cruel One

Core Torment & Lie: Sadistic Domination

"Hurting others makes me powerful."

Gifts under attack:

- **Mercy** – The Cruel One severs the heart's ability to extend grace or restraint, choosing vengeance and harm over compassion *(Matthew 5:7 – "Blessed are the merciful, for they shall obtain mercy.")*.

- **Empathy** – It desensitizes the soul to the suffering of others, causing a hardened heart that mocks or enjoys the pain of the weak *(Romans 12:15 – "Rejoice with those who rejoice; mourn with those who mourn.").*
- **Compassion** – This spirit suppresses the emotional reflex to help, replacing it with coldness or indifference *(Colossians 3:12 – "Clothe yourselves with compassion, kindness, humility, gentleness, and patience.").*
- **Reverence for Life** – It distorts the God-given value of others, turning people into targets or tools rather than souls made in His image *(Genesis 9:6 – "Whoever sheds human blood, by humans shall their blood be shed; for in the image of God has God made mankind.").*

The Cruel One is the spirit of sadistic domination. It takes pleasure in pain, especially when inflicted on the weak, voiceless, or defenseless. This demon craves suffering. It whispers to the child who pulls wings off butterflies... to the teen who abuses animals behind closed doors... to the adult who mocks the homeless or torments the vulnerable. Cruelty is its currency.

This spirit is a dark signature of hell: when a person begins to take pleasure in causing pain, they are hosting something demonic. The Bible repeatedly warns against harming the vulnerable for good reason: cruelty is a gateway to evil without limit. Studies have shown that many serial killers began with acts of cruelty toward animals or other children, revealing that this spirit often appears early, especially when left unchecked. The Cruel One erodes the conscience and hollows out the soul, until the screams of others become entertainment. When cruelty is allowed to grow, especially in the young, it becomes a preview of hell on earth.

Scripture References:

"The Lord examines the righteous, but the wicked, those who love violence, he hates with a passion." (Psalm 11:5)

"The righteous care for the needs of their animals, but the kindest acts of the wicked are cruel." (Proverbs 12:10)

"Woe to those who call evil good and good evil..." (Isaiah 5:20)

Common Symptoms:

- Enjoying or justifying the suffering of others
- Cruelty toward animals, children, or the disabled
- Sadistic humor, verbal abuse, or emotional torture
- Viewing mercy as weakness
- Coldness when others are in pain

Real Life Example:

In a quiet suburban neighborhood, residents began noticing a disturbing pattern: family pets were going missing: first a few cats, then several dogs. Flyers went up, search parties were formed, and fear slowly crept in. Eventually, the heartbreaking truth emerged. A recently moved-in neighbor had been abducting and killing the animals. When the story broke, the entire neighborhood gathered in front of his house, some holding photos of their pets, others in tears. The scene was filmed and shared widely online, drawing outrage from across the country.

People sobbed openly as they realized their beloved companions had suffered at this man's hands. Even local politicians showed up, demanding answers and calling for justice. As crowds chanted and mourned, the man stood silently behind his fence unmoved, even smiling. The coldness of his demeanor only added to the horror. When finally brought up on charges of animal cruelty, he pled not guilty, showing no remorse for the lives he took or the grief he caused. The Cruel One had fully taken root, and the entire neighborhood bore witness to what happens when evil begins to delight in the suffering of the innocent.

Solutions & Declarations:

1. **I repent for every act of cruelty and hardness of heart.**
   "I will give you a new heart and put a new spirit in you; I will remove from you your heart of stone and give you a heart of flesh." (Ezekiel 36:26)

2. **I receive the heart of flesh God promised, and I choose compassion over domination.**
   "Therefore, as God's chosen people, holy and dearly loved, clothe yourselves with compassion, kindness, humility, gentleness and patience." (Colossians 3:12)

3. **I will honor and protect the vulnerable as God commands.**
   "Speak up for those who cannot speak for themselves, for the rights of all who are destitute. Speak up and judge fairly; defend the rights of the poor and needy."

   (Proverbs 31:8–9)

Turn to Chapter 9 Prayer Index and go to:
Prayer 9: General Prayer for Pride of Life
Prayer 12: Deliverance from Rage & Corruption

Cross-references:

- **The Bully** – Thrives on power over the weak; often works hand-in-hand with The Cruel One to normalize torment, especially in childhood and adolescence.
- **The Glacier** – Emotional coldness enables cruelty without conscience; The Cruel One strikes, and The Glacier feels nothing.
- **The Mouth** – Turns words into weapons; cruelty often begins with mocking, cursing, or psychological warfare.
- **The Narcissist** – Lacks empathy and sees others as expendable; cruelty becomes a method of self-exaltation and control.
- **The Murderer** – The final destination of unchecked cruelty; when empathy dies, destruction follows—first of spirit, then of life itself.

The Bully

Core Torment & Lie: Tyrannical Intimidation

"If I dominate them, I'll never be dominated."

Gifts under attack:

- **Kindness** – The Bully replaces gentleness with aggression, mocking kindness as weakness and silencing those who extend it *(Ephesians 4:32 – "Be kind and compassionate to one another, forgiving each other, just as in Christ God forgave you.")*.
- **Humility** – This spirit fosters arrogance and superiority, teaching that control and pride are safer than vulnerability *(Philippians 2:3 – "Do nothing out of selfish ambition or vain conceit. Rather, in humility value others above yourselves.")*.
- **Empathy** – It shuts down the ability to see from another's perspective, fueling cruelty and emotional detachment *(1 Peter 3:8 – "Be like-minded, be sympathetic, love one another, be compassionate and humble.")*.
- **Leadership Through Love** – The Bully twists leadership into domination, ignoring the servant-hearted example Christ set
- *(Mark 10:42–45 – "Whoever wants to become great among you must be your servant... For even the Son of Man did not come to be served, but to serve.")*.

The Bully is a spirit of cruel control that seeks to dominate, humiliate, and terrorize others into submission. It operates most often in children and teens, but its roots are deeply generational. This spirit is often passed down through households where emotional abuse is normalized and power is modeled through fear. The Bully thrives when parents excuse bad behavior, teachers look the other way, and communities silently tolerate cruelty. It's not "kids being kids"—it's a demon driving children to suicide.

The Bully doesn't act alone. It recruits others to join its cruelty, forming mobs. It manipulates authority, turns classrooms into war zones, and leaves parents helpless while their child is torn apart socially, emotionally, and spiritually. This is one of the most devastating spirits in this book because it destroys lives young and often, and because most people still don't take it seriously.

Scripture References:

> *"Fools give full vent to their rage, but the wise bring calm in the end." (Proverbs 29:11)*

> *"Blessed are the peacemakers, for they shall be called children of God." (Matthew 5:9)*

> *"Do not repay evil for evil or insult for insult." (1 Peter 3:9)*

Common Symptoms:

- Intimidating others through strength, popularity, or verbal cruelty
- Manipulating authority to stay unpunished
- Targeting peers for social exclusion or public humiliation
- Lack of remorse for harming others
- Patterns of dominance even in adulthood (workplace, family, online)

Real Life Example:

Tori was the latest installment in a long generational line of bullies. Her teachers endured her aunts, uncles, and older siblings in their classrooms and not one of them had been easy. Tori was worse. She carried a sharper cruelty, a more deliberate meanness. She ruled a pack of girls like a young cartel boss, and none of the adults in her life seemed willing or able to stop her.

The worst offender, however, wasn't Tori. It was her mother, Rochelle.

Rochelle built her reputation as a terror in the district, showing up to parent-teacher conferences like a prosecuting attorney with a personal vendetta. She would march into the principal's office with fire in her eyes and a phone camera rolling, demanding to know why her daughter was being "targeted" for "normal childhood behavior." When teachers tried to raise real concerns, she bulldozed them with accusations of bias and threats of lawsuits. If any child or parent dared to speak up about Tori's bullying, Rochelle insisted on confronting them directly, berating administrators until they quietly backed down. In time, staff began giving her a wide berth and by extension, giving Tori quiet permission to continue her reign of terror.

The pack of girls followed Tori's lead like wolves—mocking, isolating, and tormenting anyone who didn't fit into their hierarchy. Things took a horrifying turn when one of their favorite targets, a quiet seventh-grade girl with kind eyes and a soft voice, was driven to attempt suicide. She'd tried to speak up once, but after Rochelle stormed into the classroom and turned her wrath on her, the girl retreated completely.

After her attempt, she was placed in the ICU. What happened next should have been impossible.

Tori and a few members of her clique found a way past hospital staff and entered the girl's room. Once inside, they delivered another round of verbal abuse: quiet enough not to be heard, cruel enough to finish what they started. The girl succumbed to her injuries shortly after.

Tori and the others returned to school as though nothing happened: smiling, laughing, and sitting in class while devastated parents grieved beside an empty locker. No charges were filed. No disciplinary action held. Teachers and staff, terrified of Rochelle's wrath, said little. Parents watched in helpless rage, wondering how such evil could walk through the halls untouched.

Some even began to feel their own hearts darken, dreaming of revenge, feeling the pull of hate, tempted to hurt the very children who had hurt theirs.

That's how The Bully spirit works. It multiplies. It infects a generation and feeds on the weak, the passive, and the silenced.

When justice is withheld, it tries to turn even the righteous into monsters.

Solutions & Declarations:

1. **I renounce every agreement with the spirit of domination and cruelty.**

   "Let all bitterness and wrath and anger and clamor and slander be put away from you, along with all malice. Be kind to one another, tenderhearted, forgiving one another, as God in Christ forgave you."(Ephesians 4:31–32)

2. **I choose humility, compassion, and self-control.**

   "Put on then, as God's chosen ones, holy and beloved, compassionate hearts, kindness, humility, meekness, and patience."(Colossians 3:12)

3. **I was not given power to destroy but to serve.**

   "But whoever would be great among you must be your servant."(Matthew 20:26)

Turn to Chapter 9 Prayer Index and go to:

Prayer 9: General Prayer for Pride of Life

Prayer 12: Deliverance from Rage & Corruption

Supplemental Prayers: 16, 19, 22, 32, 34

Cross References:

- **The Cruel One** – The Bully expresses cruelty through dominance and targeting the weak; The Cruel One takes pleasure in the suffering itself.
- **The Narcissist** – Both seek power through control, but The Bully builds identity through intimidation, not admiration.
- **The Glacier** – Emotional coldness empowers The Bully to dismiss the pain they cause as insignificant or deserved.
- **The Mouth** – Verbal attacks become the Bully's primary weapon— cutting, shaming, and publicly dismantling others.
- **The Suicide Spirit** – The Bully often opens the door for this spirit by isolating and breaking victims until they lose all will to live.

The Racist

Core Torment & Lie: Prejudice & Dehumanization

"They are beneath you."

Gifts Under Attack:

- **Unity among People** – The Racist divides humanity along lines God never drew, fueling hostility and alienation among those made in His image *("From one man he made all the nations, that they should inhabit the whole earth..." – Acts 17:26)*
- **Compassion** – It hardens the heart against others' pain, removing empathy and replacing it with superiority *("Love your neighbor as yourself." – Luke 10:27)*
- **Justice** – It blinds people to fairness and equality, leading them to justify cruelty and ignore wrongdoing *("He has shown you, O man, what is good. And what does the Lord require of you? To act justly and to love mercy..." – Micah 6:8)*
- **Identity in Christ** – It distorts God's design by exalting race over righteousness, denying that all people are equal before Him *("There is neither Jew nor Gentile... for you are all one in Christ Jesus." – Galatians 3:28)*
- **Humility** – It cultivates arrogance by inflating one group above another, forgetting that all fall short and need grace *("For all have sinned and fall short of the glory of God." – Romans 3:23)*

The Racist is a spirit of pride, hatred, and division rooted in the ancient sin of partiality. It whispers that some people are superior, more civilized, more intelligent, or more worthy based solely on race, heritage, or skin tone. It flourishes not only in overt violence but in subtle cultural bias, social hierarchy, and silent agreement. This demon passes through families, institutions, and entire nations, infecting hearts with disdain and distancing communities under the guise of "difference."

The Racist is a direct contradiction to the Gospel, which declares that all people are made in the image of God and united under the blood of

Christ. Where this spirit is present, the image of God in others is denied and the heart grows cold to truth, justice, and empathy.

Scripture References:

"If you show partiality, you commit sin." (James 2:9)

"From one blood God made all nations of men." (Acts 17:26)

"There is neither Jew nor Greek... for you are all one in Christ." (Galatians 3:28)

Common Symptoms:

- Judging a person's value, intelligence, or worthiness based on race or nationality
- Feeling justified in exclusion, cruelty, or suspicion
- Echoing inherited racist language or beliefs "as a joke"
- Dismissing others' experiences with racism as "sensitive" or "exaggerated"
- Believing your group is chosen, exceptional, or inherently better

Real-Life Example:

Essie and John were both mature, kindhearted believers who had waited a long time for love. When they met, it was instant connection: shared values, mutual respect, and a sense of deep peace they both recognized as from God. Their engagement was celebrated by friends and coworkers, but both quietly avoided telling their families one key detail: Essie was Black, and John was white. Both families had deep southern roots where racism was still passed down like family heirlooms.

John's family had known ties to the Klan and even prided themselves on a long lineage of "pure" bloodlines that traced back to slave owners. When he finally brought Essie home, the tension was thick, and the smiles were tight. His parents made it clear: if he married her, he'd be disowned. John didn't argue; he simply walked away, but the loss still stung.

Essie's side was no easier. To them, John represented generational trauma. Her cousins said she was betraying her ancestors. Her aunt told her she'd picked the worst kind of white man, the one with blood on his family's hands. Even those who smiled at the wedding wouldn't look John in the eye.

In public, it didn't get better. In their northern city—liberal on paper but divided in spirit—Essie was often asked why she didn't want a strong Black man. John got side-eyed and accused of having a fetish. Strangers stared. Couples whispered. Waiters ignored them. They never stopped loving each other, but the unseen weight they carried in every room was the same old spirit, just dressed in modern clothes.

The Racist doesn't always wear a hood. Sometimes it hides behind polite silence, generational prejudice, or "just my preference." Its fruit is always the same: division, judgment, and hatred passed down and protected like legacy.

Solutions & Declarations:

1. **I repent of every agreement with pride, hatred, and partiality.**
   "But if you show favoritism, you sin and are convicted by the law as lawbreakers." (James 2:9)

2. **I declare that all people are made in the image of God.**
   "So God created mankind in his own image, in the image of God he created them; male and female he created them. (Genesis 1:27)

3. **I will love as Christ commands—not based on culture, but on covenant.**
   "There is neither Jew nor Gentile, neither slave nor free, nor is there male and female, for you are all one in Christ Jesus." (Galatians 3:28)

Turn to Chapter 9 Prayer Index and go to:
Prayer 9: General Prayer for Pride of Life
Prayer 12: Deliverance from Rage & Corruption

Cross References:

- **The Mouth** – Reinforces racism through slurs, dehumanizing language, or silent complicity that allows hate to fester.
- **The Bitter One** – Cultural and generational wounds twisted into hatred and projected onto others.
- **The Monarch** – Thrives on entitlement and superiority, believing certain groups are inherently better or more deserving.
- **The Sower of Strife** – Sows disunity, tribalism, and suspicion between people groups, often under the guise of "preserving culture".
- **The Hater** – Masks deep-seated contempt as tradition, loyalty, or even humor.

Some demons come to diminish you. These spirits work subtly and cruelly, keeping you from ever becoming who God called you to be. They say that you're not ready, worthy, or chosen. They stoke shame, silence your voice, and convince you it's safer to stay small. Whether through fear, failure, or comparison, these spirits build invisible cages around your calling and convince you to settle inside them.

It's not that they try to destroy you, they only need to stop you.

Shame, Fear & Limitation

82. **The Saboteur** – Self Sabotage & Fear of Success. "You'll ruin it anyway."

83. **The Mute** – Shame-Based Silencing. "No one wants to hear from you."

84. **The Rejector** – Alienation & Rejection. "You'll never belong."

85. **The False Mirror** – Identity Distortion. "You'll never measure up."

86. **The Critic** – Self-Righteous Judgement & Condemnation. "Find their every flaw."

87. **The Despiser** – Misogyny. "Women are weak, manipulative, or inferior."

88. **The Complainer** – Chronic Dissatisfaction & Ingratitude. "Nothing is ever good enough."

89. **The Impatient One** – Restlessness & Distrust in God's Timing. "If it doesn't happen now, it never will."

90. **The Ghoster** – Inconstancy & Broken Loyalty. "If it gets uncomfortable, just disappear."

91. **The Desperate** – Idolatry of Approval. "You're only valuable if someone chooses you."

92. **The Stunted One** – Emotional Immaturity & Stunted Growth. "I shouldn't have to grow up."

93. **The Coward** – Avoidance & Fear of Exposure. "If I hide, nothing can hurt me."

94. **The Appeaser** – Compromise & Fear of Man. "Don't upset anyone."

95. **The Faithless One** – Chronic Distrust in God Despite Proximity to Truth. "God might do it for them, but He won't."

96. **The Suicide Spirit** – Death, Despair & Isolation. "It will never get better. Just end it."

97. **The Cutter** – Self Hatred, Shame & Torment. "You deserve this pain."

98. **The Shrinker** – Fear of Man & False Humility. "If I'm fully seen, I'll be judged, rejected, or attacked."

99. **The Promise Breaker** – Unfaithfulness. "You don't owe anyone."

The Saboteur

Core Torment & Lie: Self Sabotage & Fear of Success

"You'll ruin it anyway."

Gifts Under Attack:

- **Stability** – The Saboteur creates chaos at the edge of breakthrough, making consistency feel dangerous or doomed *("A double minded man is unstable in all his ways." James 1:8)*
- **Fulfillment** – It whispers that you're unworthy of joy, sabotaging blessings before they take root *("The thief comes only to steal and kill and destroy. I came that they may have life and have it abundantly." John 10:10)*
- **Generational Legacy** – It disrupts the ability to build for the future, repeating cycles of dysfunction and missed potential *("A good man leaves an inheritance to his children's children." Proverbs 13:22)*
- Faithfulness – It fosters inconsistency and fear of commitment, convincing you that long-term fruitfulness is for others, not you
- *("Let us not grow weary in doing good, for at the proper time we will reap a harvest if we do not give up." Galatians 6:9)*

The Saboteur attacks your progress. Just as you begin to rise, it whispers doom. It brings up past wounds, childhood programming, or demonic strongholds to convince you that success is dangerous, people will leave, or that it's only a matter of time before everything falls apart. So, you sabotage it first.

This demon partners with trauma, unworthiness, and spiritual instability. It convinces you that blessings are traps, success is unsafe, and chaos is inevitable. It convinces you to burn down your future.

Scripture References:

"The thief comes only to steal, kill, and destroy. I came that they may have life and have it abundantly." (John 10:10)

*"Let us not grow weary in doing good, for in due season
we will reap, if we do not give up." (Galatians 6:9)*

"A double-minded man is unstable in all his ways." (James 1:8)

Common Symptoms:

- Quitting right before big moments or breakthroughs
- Undermining your own success out of guilt, fear, or discomfort
- Self-destructive behaviors (financial, relational, spiritual)
- Expecting collapse or chaos after good news
- Rejecting stability or consistency as "too boring" or "too good to be true"

Real-Life Example:

Angela bounced from relative to relative as a child, always feeling like a burden. Her mother was in and out of rehab, her father nowhere to be found. She grew up learning not to expect consistency and that love came with conditions. By high school, Angela was living with a friend's family and working full time just to survive. Her grades slipped, but she managed to graduate, clawing her way into adulthood without a safety net.

After years of instability, Angela finally landed a job at a company that valued her work ethic. She began to thrive. She met a kind, emotionally steady man who adored her. For the first time in her life, everything was going right. Her bills were paid. Her home was clean and quiet. Her boyfriend showed no signs of leaving. It felt unreal—*too* unreal.

That's when it began.

Angela started picking fights with him over imagined slights. She stopped responding to emails at work and began overspending on credit cards as if it had no consequence. She told herself it was "just stress," but deep down, she didn't believe she was allowed to keep what was good. The Saboteur whispered, *"Ruin it before it ruins you."*

Angela self-destructed because things were going too well. She learned to expect pain, not peace. The Saboteur didn't need to ruin her life. It only had to convince her to do it herself.

Solutions & Declarations:

1. **I was made for abundance, not destruction.**
   "The thief comes only to steal and kill and destroy; I have come that they may have life and have it to the full." (John 10:10)

2. **I will not grow weary. In due season I will reap.**
   "Let us not become weary in doing good, for at the proper time we will reap a harvest if we do not give up." (Galatians 6:9)

3. **I reject instability and receive the mind of Christ.**
   "For, 'Who has known the mind of the Lord so as to instruct him?' But we have the mind of Christ." (1 Corinthians 2:16)

Turn to Chapter 9 Prayer Index and go to:

Prayer 9: General Prayer for Pride of Life
Prayer 13: Deliverance from Shame, Fear & Limitation
Supplemental Prayer: 16

Cross-References:

- **The Abyss** – Once the damage is done, despair floods in, deepening the collapse.
- **The Broken Mirror** – Sabotage often flows from a core belief that you don't deserve good things.
- **The Guard** – Fear of being seen, tested, or vulnerable drives impulsive destruction.
- **The Staller** – Sabotage is sometimes framed as "caution," when it's actually fear in disguise.
- **The Withholder** – Blessings are devalued and discarded when the heart refuses to receive them with thanks.

The Mute

Core Torment & Lie: Shame-Based Silencing

"No one wants to hear from you."

Gifts Under Attack:

- **Communication** – The Mute stifles expression and locks up the voice, especially when it's needed most *("Open your mouth for the mute, for the rights of all who are destitute." – Proverbs 31:8)*
- **Testimony** – It chokes your story before it can bring freedom to others *("They overcame him by the blood of the Lamb and by the word of their testimony." – Revelation 12:11)*
- **Preaching** – It feeds fear of public rejection, undermining confidence in the call to speak God's Word *("Preach the word; be ready in season and out of season." – 2 Timothy 4:2)*
- **Prophetic Expression** – It silences spiritual gifts, especially the ability to speak truth with boldness *("Do not quench the Spirit. Do not despise prophecies." – 1 Thessalonians 5:19–20)*

The Mute is a silencing spirit. It attacks your voice, your story, and your calling, especially if you are called to speak truth, prophesy, teach, or preach. This demon works through shame, fear of rejection, or traumatic experiences where your voice was mocked, dismissed, or punished.

The Kingdom of God advances through spoken truth. The Mute seals mouths through fear, ridicule, insecurity, and spiritual timidity. It doesn't want your healing heard, your victory known, or your praise released.

Scripture References:

"They triumphed over him by the blood of the Lamb and by the word of their testimony." (Revelation 12:11)

"Open your mouth for the mute, for the rights of all who are destitute." (Proverbs 31:8)

"Woe to me if I do not preach the gospel!" (1 Corinthians 9:16)

Common Symptoms:

- Fear of speaking up, even when prompted by God
- Avoiding vulnerable or confrontational conversations
- Feeling resistance when trying to share your testimony
- Holding back in worship, prayer, or spiritual leadership
- Choking or freezing up when it's time to speak truth

Real-Life Example:

Darius had a story that could set people free from addiction to deliverance, from darkness into light. He was surrounded by people who needed to know what he overcame so they could believe they could overcome too. The enemy knew the power of that testimony and assigned The Mute to silence him. Every time the Holy Spirit nudged him to speak, a tightness gripped his throat. He couldn't find the words. He second-guessed the timing. He doubted the impact.

The Mute distorted his perception. It caused him to misread cues from others, convincing him they wouldn't understand, wouldn't care, or might even reject him. The tragedy was that Darius *knew* how powerful testimony could be because it was someone else's story that led him to Christ in the first place. Yet when it came to his own, he hesitated, deferred, and declined.

He canceled events, avoided platforms, and defaulted to silence even while others silently cried out for a sign that transformation was possible. The Mute convinced him his voice was dangerous, and as long as he stayed quiet, others stayed bound.

Solutions & Declarations:

1. **My testimony is a weapon. I will not be silenced.**
   "They triumphed over him by the blood of the Lamb and by the word of their testimony; they did not love their lives so much as to shrink from death." (Revelation 12:11)

2. **God has put His words in my mouth.**

   "Then the Lord reached out His hand and touched my mouth and said to me, 'I have put My words in your mouth.'" (Jeremiah 1:9)

3. **I will open my mouth boldly to declare the gospel.**

   "Pray also for me, that whenever I speak, words may be given me so that I will fearlessly make known the mystery of the gospel." (Ephesians 6:19)

Turn to Chapter 9 Prayer Index and go to:

Prayer 9: General Prayer for Pride of Life

Prayer 13: Deliverance from Shame, Fear & Limitation

Supplemental Prayer: 22

Cross-References:

- **The Guard** – Where the Mute hides in silence, the Guard protects through overreaction; both are rooted in fear of vulnerability.
- **The Rejecter** – The Mute silences the self to avoid rejection, while the Rejecter distances from others before they can get too close.
- **The Liar** – The Liar distorts truth with words; the Mute distorts it with silence. Both manipulate communication to maintain control.
- **The Phantom** – Both vanish emotionally—The Phantom out of anxiety, the Mute out of shame or fear of being misunderstood.
- **The Shrinker** – The Shrinker plays small; the Mute disappears entirely. Both fear that their voice or presence has no worth.

The Rejector

Core Torment & Lie: The External Defense of Rejection

"You'll never belong."

Gifts Under Attack:

- **Belonging** – The Rejector isolates and convinces you that you don't fit anywhere, robbing you of connection and purpose *(Psalm 68:6 – "God sets the lonely in families...")*.
- **Sonship** – It blocks your ability to receive the identity and love of the Father, making you feel like a spiritual orphan *(Romans 8:15 – "The Spirit you received brought about your adoption to sonship. And by him we cry, 'Abba, Father.'")*.
- **Connection** – It erodes trust and community, keeping you from authentic relationship *(Ecclesiastes 4:9–10 – "Two are better than one... If either of them falls, one can help the other up.")*.
- **Self-worth** – It feeds shame and self-rejection, making you feel unwanted or inferior *(Isaiah 43:4 – "You are precious and honored in my sight... and I love you.")*.

The Rejector is one of the most damaging and deeply rooted spirits in the demonic arsenal and one of the most misunderstood. Rejection often begins before a child even takes their first breath. A mother who doesn't want her pregnancy, a father who walks away, or a family burdened by shame can all create an atmosphere of rejection in the womb. And the curse that follows, according to scripture, is *wandering and poverty* (Deuteronomy 28:65–66, Proverbs 13:18).

Rejection is often painfully subtle. A parent can meet every physical need of their child and still withhold affection, emotional connection, or approval—wounds that go unseen but shape a child's entire sense of worth. Children are especially sensitive to rejection and carry that spiritual curse into adulthood if not healed or delivered.

The spirit of The Rejector is not merely about *feeling* rejected, it is the external defense mechanism that *inflicts* rejection. It is the shield a wounded soul raises to protect itself: "Reject them before they reject you." But this is distinct from profiles like The Orphan (fatherlessness and abandonment), The Shrinker (fear of being seen), and The Broken Mirror (self-hatred), which represent the *internalization* of rejection. The Rejector pushes others away in a misguided attempt to preserve the self, but it only deepens the wound.

This spirit thrives in relationships. It appears in marriages when spouses ignore each other's needs, shut down emotionally, or withdraw from intimacy. It disrupts churches, friendships, and workplaces, convincing people that they are unloved, overlooked, or in the way. It makes you scan every interaction for signs you're being left out or discarded. It feeds bitterness, loneliness, and shame.

Ultimately, The Rejector reshapes identity. It leads to isolation, sabotaged relationships, and compensation through perfectionism or people-pleasing. It keeps people in exile when God has already called them home.

The truth remains: In Christ, you are fully accepted, fully loved, and fully known *(Ephesians 1:6, Romans 8:38–39, Psalm 139:1–18)*.

Scripture References:

> *"Even if my father and mother abandon me, the Lord will hold me close." (Psalm 27:10)*

> *"He was despised and rejected by men... yet we esteemed Him not." (Isaiah 53:3)*

> *"To all who believed Him... He gave the right to become children of God." (John 1:12)*

Common Symptoms:

- Fear of rejection or abandonment
- Preemptively withdrawing from groups
- Feeling "too much" or "never enough"
- Shame after conflict or criticism
- Chronic loneliness, even when surrounded by people

Real-Life Example:

Samuel was one of seven children born to six different women, all fathered by the same man. He looked almost exactly like his absent father, a fact his mother used to shame him. With no consistent love or support from either parent, Samuel grew up internalizing the belief that he didn't belong anywhere. His only safe space was the art studio at school, where a kind teacher nurtured his talent. That stability vanished the day he came home to find his family packing up and moving out. His mother told him they'd been evicted and that he needed to figure out where to go—then drove away with her other children, leaving him behind at just 15.

Samuel survived by shutting the world out. Though gifted, attractive, and eventually successful as an artist, he kept everyone at arm's length. He refused romantic relationships, afraid he might carry the same abandonment gene as his father. He trusted no one, expected nothing, and lived his life in a posture of constant bracing: never celebrating or relaxing, always expecting the next rejection to come. The Rejecter convinced him that belonging was for other people.

Solutions & Declarations:

1. **I am not forsaken. I am a child of God.**
   "Yet to all who did receive Him, to those who believed in His name, He gave the right to become children of God." (John 1:12)

2. **Even if others reject me, God never will.**
   "Though my father and mother forsake me, the Lord will receive me." (Psalm 27:10)

3. **I reject the lie of shame. I am accepted in the Beloved.**
   "To the praise of the glory of His grace, wherein He hath made us accepted in the Beloved." (Ephesians 1:6, KJV)

Turn to Chapter 9 Prayer Index and go to:
Prayer 9: General Prayer for Pride of Life
Prayer 13: Deliverance from Shame, Fear & Limitation
Supplemental Prayers: 23, 33, 34

Cross-References:

- **The Broken Mirror** - Distorted self-perception often begins with rejection, convincing the person they are fundamentally unworthy and unlovable.
- **The Guard** - Fear of vulnerability causes the rejected to build walls that block healing and isolate them further.
- **The Shrinker** - Rather than risk more pain, the rejected soul plays small, hides their gifts, and avoids being fully seen.
- **The Abyss** - Long-term emotional isolation and internalized rejection often spiral into depression, hopelessness, and despair.
- **The Chainkeeper** - When past wounds aren't healed, rejection becomes a prison-preventing connection and forgiveness.
- **The Waffler** - Doublemindedness develops in those who long for connection but fear it at the same time, leading to unstable, inconsistent relationships.
- **The Wanderer** - Spirit of rootlessness, detachment, and never settling. Rejection births a life of drifting, unable to trust or stay anywhere long (Genesis 4:12 - the curse of Cain).
- **The Pauper** - Poverty of soul and spirit. Rejection often partners with financial lack, a sense of "never enough," and shame around provision or receiving love.

The False Mirror

Core Torment & Lie: Identity Distortion

"You'll never measure up."

Gifts Under Attack:

- **Contentment** – The False Mirror fuels comparison and jealousy, making it nearly impossible to feel peace with your current portion *(Philippians 4:11–12: "I have learned in whatever state I am, to be content.")*

- **Confidence** – It distorts your perception of self-worth, convincing you that you'll never measure up *(Psalm 139:14: "I praise you because I am fearfully and wonderfully made.")*
- **Purpose** – It distracts you from your God-given assignment by constantly highlighting someone else's path *(Ephesians 2:10: "For we are his workmanship, created in Christ Jesus for good works.")*
- **Vision** – It clouds your ability to see your own journey clearly by fixating your gaze on others *(Proverbs 4:25–26: "Let your eyes look directly forward, and your gaze be straight before you.")*

The False Mirror warps vision by holding up someone else's life as the standard. It uses envy and comparison to poison self-worth and distract from God-given purpose. A person begins to believe they're behind, failing, or unworthy.

This demon lives and thrives on social media but hides in real life too, whenever success is measured by the world's standards instead of God's. The False Mirror convinces one their story doesn't matter, their timing is off, and they'll never catch up. It is the actual thief of "comparison is the thief of joy." We must remember God never called anyone to run someone else's race.

Scripture References:

"Each one should test their own actions... without comparing themselves to someone else." (Galatians 6:4)

"Where you have envy... you find disorder and every evil practice." (James 3:16)

"They... measure themselves by themselves... they are not wise." (2 Corinthians 10:12)

Common Symptoms:

- Feeling perpetually behind in life
- Bitterness at others' win
- Imposter syndrome triggered by peers
- Emotional spirals after scrolling social media

- Resenting friends who have what you've prayed for

Real-Life Example:

Taylor was the kind of woman people envied. Born into generational wealth, she belonged to the top 1%. She had everything: a trust fund with more money than most people would see in five lifetimes, a wardrobe of luxury labels worn only once, multiple homes on both coasts, and a Rolodex of influential friends. Her life was a highlight reel most people couldn't even dream of.

None of it was enough.

Every time she opened Instagram, someone seemed younger, prettier, richer, or more admired. A friend posted her engagement ring—Taylor spiraled. Another friend announced a third degree—Taylor felt behind. Someone she barely knew bought a home in the south of France—and suddenly her Hamptons place felt small. She couldn't see what she had. She could only see what she lacked.

The False Mirror did its job. It distorted reality and fed Taylor a silent script: *You're not enough. You're falling behind. You should be doing more, achieving more, becoming more.* The torment wasn't rooted in truth, but Taylor didn't know that. She thought it was ambition. She thought it was drive.

The truth was as rich as she was, she was the poorest person she knew. She had the world but couldn't enjoy a single part of it. The False Mirror blinded her to her spiritual bankruptcy, keeping her focused on superficialities so she'd never question the deeper reason why she lived in quiet torment and constant comparison.

Solutions & Declarations:

1. **I will not measure my life by someone else's timeline.**
   "Each one should test their own actions. Then they can take pride in themselves alone, without comparing themselves to someone else." (Galatians 6:4)

2. **I am fearfully and wonderfully made—there is no comparison.**

   "I praise you because I am fearfully and wonderfully made; your works are wonderful; I know that full well." (Psalm 139:14)

3. **I break agreement with envy, and I bless those who are ahead of me.**

   "Rejoice with those who rejoice; mourn with those who mourn." (Romans 12:15)

Turn to Chapter 9 Prayer Index and go to:

Prayer 9: General Prayer for Pride of Life

Prayer 13: Deliverance from Shame, Fear & Limitation

Supplemental Prayers: 21, 23

Cross-References:

- **The Collector** – *The False Mirror* fuels the pursuit of external validation through status symbols, which *The Collector* eagerly gathers to prove worth. Together, they trap a person in a cycle of consuming rather than becoming.
- **The Broken Mirror** – Where *The False Mirror* distorts identity through comparison, *The Broken Mirror* compounds it with envy and self-hatred. One says "you'll never measure up," the other "you're not worth fixing."
- **The Idolator** – *The False Mirror* partners with *The Idolator* by placing others' curated lives on pedestals—turning influencers, relationships, or achievements into false gods while dismissing your own identity and journey.
- **The Shrinker** – Feeling inferior leads to shrinking back from calling, voice, or visibility. *The False Mirror* says you're unworthy to lead, while *The Shrinker* convinces you it's safer to stay small.
- **The Rejector** – The belief that you'll never belong—even among "successful" or confident people—is a signature lie of *The False Mirror*. *The Rejector* reinforces it by making every social or professional setting feel like a room you were never meant to be in.

The Critic

Core Torment & Lie: Self-Righteous Judgment & Condemnation

"Find their every flaw."

Gifts Under Attack:

- **Discernment** – The Critic corrupts true spiritual discernment into accusation, making it harder to see with grace *(Hebrews 5:14 – "But solid food is for the mature, who by constant use have trained themselves to distinguish good from evil.")*.
- **Humility** – It fuels a sense of superiority, making you blind to your own weaknesses *(Romans 12:3 – "Do not think of yourself more highly than you ought, but rather think of yourself with sober judgment.")*.
- **Love** – It chokes out compassion and mercy, replacing them with cold comparison *(1 Corinthians 13:1–2 – "If I... do not have love, I am nothing.")*.
- **Encouragement** – It silences the voice that builds up others, replacing it with constant correction *(1 Thessalonians 5:11 – "Therefore encourage one another and build each other up...")*.

The Critic masquerades as discernment but is fueled by insecurity and pride. This spirit compulsively finds flaws, offering commentary instead of compassion. It often begins in homes marked by perfectionism or ridicule, turning the person into a self-appointed judge to protect their own heart from scrutiny.

Its fruit is constant negativity, ruined relationships, and isolation. The Critic hardens your heart, sharpens your tongue, and keeps love at a distance—because love requires grace.

Scripture References:
"Why do you look at the speck in your brother's eye but fail to notice the beam in your own?" (Matthew 7:3)

"Do not grumble against one another... so that
you may not be judged." (James 5:9)

"They tie up heavy burdens... and lay them on
people's shoulders." (Matthew 23:4)

"Satan is the accuser of our brothers and sisters." (Revelation 12:10)

Common Symptoms:

- Sarcastic, harsh, or passive-aggressive language
- Hyper-critical of others' appearance, performance, or beliefs
- Discouraging to be around—always finds what's wrong
- Treats self with same intensity—perfectionist or self-loathing
- Labels criticism as "being honest" or "just trying to help"

Real-Life Example:

Barry prided himself on living a "disciplined" life. He wore his self-control like a badge of honor: same weight since high school, wrinkle-free button-downs, perfect credit score. He believed his perfectionist habits earned him the right to critique everyone else—loudly.

If he saw someone overweight, he'd scoff and say they had no self-respect. Never mind that his wife and daughter were quietly suffering from eating disorders they didn't dare reveal to him. If a friend confided they were struggling financially, Barry would sneer that they should've worked harder, conveniently forgetting that his own debt-free start in life came from wealthy parents who paid his tuition and covered his rent until he was thirty. If he spotted a man wearing a toupee, he'd make a public joke at his expense, believing his own hairline made him superior, as though that were some kind of moral achievement.

Behind the smugness was a secret. Barry knew something was off. Deep down, he felt like a fraud. His surface-level control masked a gnawing sense of failure and shame. He wasn't walking in integrity. He cut corners, lied on deals, compromised in ways no one saw. His perfectionism was a fig leaf, and the constant criticism he hurled at others was really aimed at himself.

The Critic had him trapped. What looked like confidence was self-hatred wearing a mask. Barry couldn't see others clearly because he refused to see himself honestly. The more he judged, the more he decayed.

Solutions & Declarations:

1. **I renounce the need to find flaws in others to feel secure in myself.**
   "Don't grumble against one another, brothers and sisters, or you will be judged. The Judge is standing at the door!" (James 5:9)

2. **I will speak life, not death. My words have the power to build or destroy.**
   "Death and life are in the power of the tongue, and those who love it will eat its fruit." (Proverbs 18:21)

3. **I choose humility over judgment. I lay down the role of the accuser.**
   "You, then, why do you judge your brother or sister? Or why do you treat them with contempt? For we will all stand before God's judgment seat." (Romans 14:10)

Turn to Chapter 9 Prayer Index and go to:
Prayer 9: General Prayer for Pride of Life
Prayer 13: Deliverance from Shame, Fear & Limitation
Supplemental Prayer: 16, 21, 23

Cross-References:

- **The Litigator** – While The Litigator argues to win debates and assert dominance in logic, *The Critic* uses judgment and negativity to gain emotional power and control. One seeks victory through reason; the other through shame.
- **The Broken Mirror** – This spirit fuels internal perfectionism and self-loathing, which often gets projected outward as criticism of others. *The Critic* frequently grows in the soil of unhealed self-judgment.

- **The Idolator** – *The Critic* often evaluates others through a superficial lens, idolizing appearance, success, or performance. This leads to condemnation of those who don't fit the image being worshipped.
- **The Guard** – Criticism becomes a weapon of self-protection. Like *The Guard*, *The Critic* uses harshness to keep people at a distance, masking deeper fears of inadequacy, exposure, or rejection.
- **The Puppeteer** – Manipulation through subtle (or overt) criticism is a hallmark of this pairing. *The Critic* destabilizes others emotionally in order to dominate or steer behavior—often without appearing directly controlling.

The Despiser
Core Torment & Lie: Misogyny
"Women are weak, manipulative, or inferior."
Gifts Under Attack:

- **Honor** – The Despiser mocks the value God placed on women, breaking the command to honor others as image-bearers *(1 Peter 3:7 – "Husbands, in the same way be considerate… and treat them with respect as the weaker partner and as heirs with you of the gracious gift of life.")*.
- **Covenant** – It destroys the sacred unity between man and woman in relationships and marriage, promoting betrayal and domination *(Malachi 2:14 – "The Lord is the witness between you and the wife of your youth. You have been unfaithful… though she is your partner, the wife of your marriage covenant.")*.
- **Identity in Christ** – It suppresses the truth that both male and female were made in God's image and are equal in spiritual inheritance *(Galatians 3:28 – "There is neither… male nor female, for you are all one in Christ Jesus.")*.
- **Intercession** – It dulls the spiritual authority and covering men are meant to carry as protectors, not persecutors, of women

(Ezekiel 22:30 – "I looked for someone among them who would build up the wall and stand before me in the gap...").

- **Nurture** – It mocks or dismisses traits like compassion, tenderness, and maternal strength, which are sacred and often embodied by women *(Isaiah 66:13 – "As a mother comforts her child, so will I comfort you...").*

The Despiser is a demonic distortion of God's design for women, rooted in hatred, fear, or perversion of the feminine. While some forms of misogyny are obvious (abuse, control, violence) others are subtle: devaluing women's voices, mocking their presence, resisting their anointing, or blaming them for all societal or spiritual failure.

This spirit can take hold in both men and women: in men, it drives control, degradation, and resentment of the feminine; in women, it drives internalized hatred of womanhood, rejection of their design, or rivalry with other women.

Biblically, this spirit can be traced back to the serpent's first enmity with Eve. Since then, Satan has sought to undermine, enslave, or destroy women, knowing they carry the ability to birth the next generation of freedom, covenant, and prophecy.

Scripture References:

> *"I will put enmity between you and the woman, and between your seed and her Seed..." (Genesis 3:15)*

> *"She is clothed with strength and dignity; she can laugh at the days to come." (Proverbs 31:25)*

> *"Husbands, love your wives, just as Christ loved the church..." (Ephesians 5:25)*

> *"...this woman, a daughter of Abraham, whom Satan has bound..." (Luke 13:16)*

Common Symptoms:

- Belief that women are inherently manipulative, overly emotional, or untrustworthy

- Contempt for female leadership, even when anointed
- Degrading humor, slurs, or dismissive tones about women
- Women who hate other women, reject their own design, or feel unsafe in their femininity
- Deep relational wounds tied to mother, partner, or female rejection

Real-Life Example:

Andre and Jasmine work for the same Fortune 500 company, but they are on opposite ends of the same spectrum of misogyny.

Andre is a department head who insists his team be staffed with men only. He even has a male assistant, a role typically held by women at the company. "Male energy is the key to business success," he likes to say behind closed doors, justifying his bias as strategy. There are women in the company with stellar track records, sharp minds, and innovative ideas, but Andre would rather hire an average man than give a woman that seat at the table. To him, women are distractions, liabilities, or manipulative climbers. He refuses to acknowledge the real source of his disdain: a childhood shaped by a domineering mother and an absent, passive father. Instead of confronting his wounds, he blames all women.

Then there's Jasmine, the executive assistant to Andre's boss. She knows Andre is problematic but privately agrees with him. She prides herself on being "one of the guys," and uses her proximity to power to protect his all-male team from criticism. When concerns about diversity surface, Jasmine subtly downplays them. She assures her boss that no one cares and that Andre's team is just "high performing." Behind the scenes, she quietly undermines other women by dismissing their achievements, gatekeeping opportunities, and cozying up to the men she sees as worth aligning with.

Jasmine sees herself as superior to other women. She bristles at female leadership and finds camaraderie only with Andre's assistant, the one man among the sea of female admin staff. She takes pride when men tell her she's "not like other women," and uses it as a badge of honor.

Both Andre and Jasmine are under the influence of The Despiser, a spirit that fuels disdain for women and distorts the God-given value of femininity. It poisons organizations from the inside, using both male and female vessels to reinforce a culture of suppression, competition, and spiritual imbalance.

Solutions & Declarations:

1. **I break agreement with hatred of women and rejection of femininity.**

   "Anyone who claims to be in the light but hates a brother or sister is still in the darkness." (1 John 2:9)

2. **I honor God's design—both masculine and feminine—as sacred.**

   "So God created mankind in his own image, in the image of God he created them; male and female he created them." (Genesis 1:27)

3. **I reject every lie that women are weak, evil, or unwanted.**

   "There is neither Jew nor Greek, slave nor free, male nor female, for you are all one in Christ Jesus." (Galatians 3:28)

Turn to Chapter 9 Prayer Index and go to:

Prayer 9: General Prayer for Pride of Life

Prayer 13: Deliverance from Shame, Fear & Limitation

Cross References:

- **The Overbearing Matriarch** – Plants early seeds of resentment in sons and confusion in daughters, creating the root system for The Despiser.
- **The Weak Father** – When male leadership is absent or passive, bitterness often turns toward the women who had to take charge.
- **Jezebel** – Fear of being controlled or manipulated by women often breeds hatred under the guise of "discernment" or male headship.
- **The Broken Mirror** – Women under this spirit may internalize misogyny and perpetuate it against their own gender.
- **The Idolator** – Warps womanhood into an object or performance, reducing feminine identity to appearance, pleasure, or usefulness.

- **The Inverter** – Skews gender design and fuels confusion, often leading to hatred of the feminine and erasure of God's created order.

The Complainer

Core Torment & Lie: Chronic dissatisfaction & Ingratitude

"Nothing is ever good enough."

Gifts Under Attack:

- **Gratitude** – The Complainer keeps your eyes on lack, not blessing, making thankfulness feel impossible. *("Give thanks in all circumstances; for this is God's will for you in Christ Jesus." – 1 Thessalonians 5:18)*
- **Contentment** – It convinces you that nothing will ever be enough, robbing you of peace with your portion. *("I have learned the secret of being content in any and every situation... I can do all this through him who gives me strength." – Philippians 4:12–13)*
- **Faith** – It magnifies problems over promises, making God's goodness seem distant or insufficient. *("Now faith is the substance of things hoped for, the evidence of things not seen." – Hebrews 11:1)*
- **Spiritual Maturity** – Chronic dissatisfaction stunts growth by keeping you focused on offense instead of obedience. *("Do everything without grumbling or arguing, so that you may become blameless and pure." – Philippians 2:14–15)*
- **Leadership** – It undermines influence by modeling ungratefulness and negativity to others. *("Set an example for the believers in speech, in conduct, in love, in faith and in purity." – 1 Timothy 4:12)*

The Complainer is the spirit of chronic grumbling and dissatisfaction. This demon partners with unbelief and rebellion. Israel didn't fall in the wilderness because of giants; they fell because they wouldn't stop grumbling. Complaining invites judgment, blocks blessings, and poisons atmosphere. It accuses God of being insufficient and fosters rebellion against leadership, community, and calling. It is the language of demons.

It often hides behind "high standards," "venting," or "just being real," but in truth, it is spiritual sabotage. The Complainer stirs discontent in marriages, churches, workplaces, and even private prayer lives, making it impossible to see or enjoy what God has already provided.

Scripture References:

"How long will this wicked community grumble against me?" (Numbers 14:27)

"Do all things without complaining or arguing." (Philippians 2:14)

"Do not grumble, as some of them did—and were killed by the destroying angel." (1 Corinthians 10:10)

Common Symptoms:

- Constant dissatisfaction with circumstances or people
- Fixating on flaws instead of blessings
- Discouraging atmosphere—others feel drained around you
- Bitterness masked as honesty
- Entitlement or resistance to spiritual leadership

Real-Life Example:

Francine's adult children were already bracing themselves for Thanksgiving. It was Shelly's turn to host, and the siblings created a group chat to emotionally prepare her. They'd done this for years, predicting and even betting on what Francine would complain about first: the drive, the seasoning, the thermostat, the grandkids' clothes or someone's haircut. It didn't matter that they were a healthy, loving, and successful family. To Francine, everything was always slightly wrong.

Growing up, they noticed how their mother seemed to wake up with complaints already in her mouth. The weather. Her knees. The mail. The news. Their dad. If she wasn't articulating a complaint, she was heavily sighing or exclaiming a curse word, putting everyone on immediate edge as they waited to hear what the problem was.

It wore the children down emotionally to the point their nervous systems were out of whack and their moods uncontrollable. They learned how to compartmentalize and eventually, turned it into a coping game: tallying how many complaints she could make before saying anything positive. Her record was three full days, broken only when she said, "At least it's not ugly outside today."

They laughed to keep from crying, but every one of them left home the moment they were able, desperate to escape the oppressive atmosphere. Their father, who rarely said a word, was dubbed "Chair" because as soon as he walked in the door from work, he'd retreat to his recliner and go completely silent. He learned, like the rest of them, that even neutral conversation could set off the next tirade.

What Francine never realized was that her words created a climate of heaviness. The Complainer ruled that house for decades, and its favorite offering was everyone's peace.

Solutions & Declarations:

1. **I will bless the Lord at all times; His praise shall continually be in my mouth.**
   "I will bless the Lord at all times; his praise shall continually be in my mouth." (Psalm 34:1)

2. **I break agreement with the spirit of grumbling and declare I will walk in gratitude and trust.**
   "Do all things without grumbling or disputing." (Philippians 2:14)

3. **Even when I don't understand, I choose to praise instead of complain.**
   "Give thanks in all circumstances; for this is the will of God in Christ Jesus for you." (1 Thessalonians 5:18)

Turn to Chapter 9 Prayer Index and go to:

Prayer 9: General Prayer for Pride of Life
Prayer 13: Deliverance from Shame, Fear & Limitation
Supplemental Prayers: 15, 21, 23

Cross-References:

- **The Withholder** – Both spirits are fueled by ingratitude, cutting off the flow of gratitude and emotional generosity, which poisons relationships and stifles spiritual growth.
- **The Critic** – The Complainer focuses on what's lacking; the Critic sharpens that dissatisfaction into targeted judgment. Together, they destroy peace through relentless negativity.
- **The Chainkeeper** – When complaints stem from unresolved hurt, they become a cycle of bitterness disguised as commentary, keeping the soul tethered to offense.
- **The Pauper** – Trains the heart to see through a lens of scarcity and lack, so nothing is ever enough. The Complainer vocalizes this internal deficit, reinforcing it with every word.
- **The Liar** – Twists perception to justify dissatisfaction, whispering that grumbling is simply "being real" or "saying what no one else will." It rewrites the narrative to excuse chronic discontent.

The Impatient One

Core Torment & Lie: Restlessness & Distrust in God's Timing

"If it doesn't happen now, it never will."

Gifts Under Attack:

- **Endurance** – The Impatient One weakens your ability to persevere, making every delay feel like a defeat. *("But the one who endures to the end will be saved." – Matthew 24:13)*
- **Maturity** – It sabotages growth by rejecting the process, keeping you spiritually stunted and impulsive. *("Let perseverance finish its work so that you may be mature and complete, not lacking anything." – James 1:4)*
- **Faith** – It distorts trust in God's timeline, convincing you that if it hasn't happened yet, it never will. *("The Lord is not slow in keeping his promise... He is patient with you." – 2 Peter 3:9)*

- **Timing** – It drives rash decisions and premature actions, causing you to move outside of God's appointed season. *("To everything there is a season, a time for every purpose under heaven." – Ecclesiastes 3:1)*
- **Discernment** – It clouds judgment with urgency, making it hard to tell the difference between divine delay and closed doors. *("Test everything; hold fast what is good." – 1 Thessalonians 5:21)*

The Impatient One is a spirit that rushes destiny and derails process. It convinces you that waiting is wasting, and that delays mean God has forgotten you. This demon often enters during seasons of prolonged uncertainty or unfulfilled desire. It makes anxiety feel like ambition. It says, "Take the shortcut. Make it happen yourself. God is too slow." In truth, impatience is unbelief with a motor. It leads people into premature relationships, failed ventures, spiritual burnout, and even demonic detours that look like blessings but are really traps.

Scripture References:

"Desire without knowledge is not good—how much more will hasty feet miss the way!" (Proverbs 19:2)

"Wait for the Lord; be strong and take heart and wait for the Lord." (Psalm 27:14)

"He has made everything beautiful in its time." (Ecclesiastes 3:11)

Common Symptoms:

- Frustration when things don't move quickly
- Settling for "good enough" to avoid waiting
- Constant fear of missing out or being too late
- Jumping into decisions without discernment
- Difficulty trusting God's timing or silence

Real-Life Example:

Chuck waited years for a break, and when a surprise legal settlement finally landed in his bank account, he was convinced it was his moment.

The money felt like freedom, and by the end of the day he received it, Chuck already decided he would start his own business. He didn't wait on counsel, prayer, or planning. By the next morning, he was touring office spaces. That evening, he signed a lease.

Chuck rushed to furnish the space, buying computers, desks, and even branded signage. When the clerk at Office Depot asked what kind of business he was starting, Chuck fumbled to explain. "Something with... charity auctions," he said vaguely. "To help people and make the world better." When she asked where he'd get the items or who would be bidding, Chuck realized he hadn't really thought it through.

Within weeks, the money was bleeding out: rent, furniture, marketing materials, all for a business he couldn't define. By the end of the month, he pivoted to a new vision entirely, one he was sure would work better.

The windfall was mostly gone, and what remained of his confidence was sinking fast. What Chuck didn't realize was that The Impatient One had hijacked his breakthrough. It made him intolerant to waiting, convinced him urgency was the same as purpose, and rushed him right into failure.

Solutions & Declarations:

1. **God's delay is not God's denial. I trust His time, not my timeline.**
   "But if we hope for what we do not see, we wait for it with patience." *(Romans 8:25)*

2. **I break agreement with haste, and I embrace endurance and wisdom.**
   "Whoever believes will not be in haste." (Isaiah 28:16)

3. **I will not forfeit destiny by forcing results. I choose the narrow path.**
   "Enter by the narrow gate. For the gate is wide and the way is easy that leads to destruction... But the gate is narrow, and the way is hard that leads to life." (Matthew 7:13–14)

Turn to Chapter 9 Prayer Index and go to:

Prayer 9: General Prayer for Pride of Life

Prayer 13: Deliverance from Shame, Fear & Limitation

Cross References:

- **The Saboteur** – Impatience often leads to rushed decisions that sabotage long-term success.
- **The Achiever** – Feeds the drive to perform instead of wait, mistaking movement for progress.
- **The Escapist** – Avoids stillness and reflection, constantly jumping into the next distraction.
- **The Doubter** – Doesn't trust God's timing, so it takes control out of fear that nothing will happen.
- **The Loop** – Keeps the mind racing and anxious, unable to rest or discern the right moment to act.
- **The Wanderer** – Moves from one idea or opportunity to the next, never rooted, always chasing what's next.

The Ghoster

Core Torment & Lie: Inconstancy & Broken Loyalty

"If it gets uncomfortable, just disappear."

Gifts Under Attack:

- **Faithfulness** – The Ghoster severs loyalty at the first sign of discomfort, weakening your ability to commit and stay true. *("A faithful person will be richly blessed, but one eager to get rich will not go unpunished." – Proverbs 28:20)*
- **Endurance** – It trains you to flee rather than face, making perseverance in relationships and trials feel impossible. *("Let us not grow weary in doing good, for at the proper time we will reap a harvest if we do not give up." – Galatians 6:9)*

- **Covenant Integrity** – It undermines your word and your presence, attacking the honor of showing up when it counts. *("Let your 'Yes' be 'Yes,' and your 'No,' 'No.'" – Matthew 5:37)*
- **Emotional Maturity** – It avoids discomfort and confrontation, stunting your ability to process feelings and build resilience. *("Be completely humble and gentle; be patient, bearing with one another in love." – Ephesians 4:2)*

The Ghoster is the spirit of inconstancy, an invisible saboteur of relationships, responsibilities, and trust. It convinces people to vanish when things get hard, uncomfortable, or emotionally vulnerable. While the modern term "ghosting" often refers to dating, this demon runs far deeper. It attacks covenant loyalty and causes people to abandon missions, ministries, friendships, and even faith. It partners with fear, shame, rejection, and selfishness, creating a cycle of avoidance and abandonment that prevents true connection. The Ghoster promises freedom but leaves people lonely, immature, and spiritually underdeveloped.

Scripture References:

"A double-minded man is unstable in all his ways." (James 1:8)

"Like a broken tooth or a lame foot is reliance on the unfaithful in a time of trouble." (Proverbs 25:19)

"Let your 'Yes' be 'Yes,' and your 'No,' 'No'; anything beyond this comes from the evil one." (Matthew 5:37)

Common Symptoms:

- Ghosting people after emotional closeness or conflict
- Starting projects or commitments, then vanishing
- Feeling allergic to follow-through
- Difficulty maintaining long-term relationships or accountability
- Regret over repeated patterns of bailing, but unable to stop

Real-Life Example:

Matt thought of himself as a free spirit, someone who didn't let anyone tie him down, but freedom wasn't what he was living. It was avoidance dressed in minimalism. When his ex told him she was pregnant, he never followed up; he just blocked her number and left her to deal with it alone. To this day, he doesn't even know if the child was born. He told himself it was better that way.

His little cousins adored him. Every time he promised to take them to the movies or out for ice cream, they'd light up. But he rarely followed through. He'd forget, flake, or make an excuse, not realizing they'd started to assume disappointment was just part of being loved.

At work, he was talented but undependable. If a meeting felt inconvenient or someone said the wrong thing, he'd disappear for a few days without explanation. The same was true in dating. He gravitated toward women who either shared his emotional avoidance or were so wounded they tolerated his vanishing acts. He'd drop off for weeks, then slide back in with a joke or a compliment, and they'd let him.

Matt thought he was "traveling light"—unattached, untethered, and drama-free. But the truth was, he wasn't free at all. He was running. The Ghoster convinced him that disappearing was safer than staying, that silence was strength, and that detachment was maturity. The wreckage he left behind told a different story: unacknowledged children, broken trust, disappointed families, and a trail of empty relationships. He wasn't traveling light. He was carrying a spirit that made him allergic to roots, connection, and accountability. The Ghoster trained him to flee rather than grow. Behind every ghosted opportunity was a graveyard of potential.

Solutions & Declarations:

1. **I renounce the lie that escape is safer than endurance.**
   "Count it all joy, my brothers, when you meet trials of various kinds, for you know that the testing of your faith produces steadfastness." (James 1:2–3)

2. **I was created for covenant. I will be constant, faithful, and present.**

   "Let love and faithfulness never leave you; bind them around your neck, write them on the tablet of your heart." (Proverbs 3:3)

3. **I break the pattern of inconstancy and receive the Spirit of steadfastness.**

   "May the Lord direct your hearts to the love of God and to the steadfastness of Christ." (2 Thessalonians 3:5)

Turn to Chapter 9 Prayer Index and go to:
Prayer 9: General Prayer for Pride of Life
Prayer 13: Deliverance from Shame, Fear & Limitation
Supplemental Prayer: 22,23, 34

Cross References:

- **The Rejector** – Abandons others before they can be rejected themselves, using withdrawal as self-defense.
- **The Orphan** – Deep wounds of abandonment feed the impulse to disappear rather than connect.
- **The Saboteur** – Destroys meaningful relationships just as they begin to take root.
- **The Escapist** – Runs from discomfort, responsibility, and emotional vulnerability.
- **The Impatient One** – Struggles with the slow pace of relational growth and gives up too soon.
- **The Pauper** – Believes they have nothing to offer, so they leave rather than risk being exposed.
- **The Wanderer** – Drifts from place to place and person to person, avoiding lasting connection or commitment.

The Desperate

Core Torment & Lie: Idolatry of Approval

"You're only valuable if someone chooses you."

Gifts Under Attack:

- **Self-Worth** – The Desperate convinces you that your value is determined by external validation, not by God's design. *("I praise you because I am fearfully and wonderfully made." – Psalm 139:14)*
- **Discernment** – It clouds your judgment with longing, making it hard to recognize red flags or counterfeit connections. *("Above all else, guard your heart, for everything you do flows from it." – Proverbs 4:23)*
- **Confidence** – It erodes boldness by making you dependent on others for identity and affirmation. *("The Lord is my helper; I will not be afraid. What can mere mortals do to me?" – Hebrews 13:6)*
- **Inner Peace** – It keeps your soul restless and anxious, always chasing after love or attention to feel secure. *("You will keep in perfect peace those whose minds are steadfast, because they trust in you." – Isaiah 26:3)*
- **Wholeness** – It fragments your identity, making you believe you're incomplete without someone else's validation. *("You are complete in Him, who is the head of all rule and authority." – Colossians 2:10)*

The Desperate is the spirit behind modern "Pickme" culture, a posture of self-abandonment rooted in rejection and unworthiness. While it often shows up as women competing to be "chosen," the stronghold runs far deeper. It's a spiritual wound that convinces a person to suppress their needs, values, and dignity in order to feel loved or accepted. Whether in relationships, social circles, or ministry, The Desperate leads people to trade identity for attention. It operates like an idol maker, sacrificing wholeness on the altar of validation.

Scripture References:

Proverbs 29:25 – "The fear of man lays a snare, but whoever trusts in the Lord is safe."

Galatians 1:10 – "If I were still trying to please people, I would not be a servant of Christ."

Isaiah 51:12–13 – "Who are you that you fear mere mortals... and forget the Lord your Maker?"

Genesis 29:31–35 – Leah's journey from desperation to praise

Luke 10:41–42 – Martha's striving vs. Mary's contentment

Common Symptoms:

- Over-giving, over-apologizing, or over-performing to be "chosen"
- Silent competition or resentment toward others who are loved
- Settling for emotionally unavailable or toxic relationships
- Avoiding boundaries or needs to avoid rejection
- Emotional crashes when ignored or overlooked

Real-Life Example:

Chanel had everything going for her: beauty, intelligence, a thriving career, and a warm, magnetic personality. To everyone around her, she was the full package. But behind closed doors, Chanel didn't believe any of that mattered unless a man validated it. She hadn't been single since she was thirteen. The idea of being alone—even for a short time—felt unbearable.

She downplayed her needs, morphed into whatever her current boyfriend wanted, and called it "being easygoing." In reality, it was a deep fear of abandonment. When a man lost interest, forgot a date, or ghosted her, Chanel felt worthless. The men she chose left her friends and family baffled. Unambitious, emotionally unavailable, sometimes even manipulative—yet Chanel stayed, convinced she was lucky to be chosen at all.

Then there was George. A competent, kind-hearted man who was burning himself out trying to earn the approval of a boss who belittled him, overworked him, and took all the credit. George's wife and children begged him to walk away, to see how little this man actually cared about him, but he couldn't. For reasons even he didn't fully understand, he needed that man's validation. He ignored the family who adored him, all for the praise of a boss who would forget his name the minute he resigned.

Both Chanel and George were captives of The Desperate, a spirit that hijacks self-worth and attaches it to the most elusive or toxic sources. It says that being chosen by someone—anyone—is what makes you valuable. It drives people to overstay in dead-end relationships, chase conditional approval, and abandon what's healthy for what's familiar. The Desperate doesn't care if you're chosen for the wrong reasons, it only wants you to believe you're nothing if you're not chosen at all.

Solutions & Declarations:

1. **I renounce the lie that I must earn love through submission or performance.**
   "For it is by grace you have been saved, through faith—and this is not from yourselves, it is the gift of God—not by works, so that no one can boast." (Ephesians 2:8–9)

2. **God has already chosen me. I am seen, known, and valued.**
   "You did not choose me, but I chose you and appointed you so that you might go and bear fruit—fruit that will last." (John 15:16)

3. **I break covenant with the spirit of rejection and receive the peace of God.**
   "And the peace of God, which transcends all understanding, will guard your hearts and your minds in Christ Jesus." (Philippians 4:7)

Turn to Chapter 9 Prayer Index and go to:
Prayer 9: General Prayer for Pride of Life
Prayer 13: Deliverance from Shame, Fear & Limitation
Supplemental Prayers: 18, 19, 20, 21, 23, 33, 34

Cross References:

- **he Orphan** – A root of fatherlessness and rejection drives the hunger to be chosen by *someone, anyone.*
- **The Performer** – Compensates through people-pleasing, trying to earn affection instead of resting in worth.
- **The Idolator** – Twists love into worship, placing human approval above God's affirmation.
- **The Harlot** – Settles for connection without covenant, mistaking attention for love.
- **The Critic** – Secretly resents those who are loved or chosen, revealing deep feelings of unworthiness.
- **The Narcissist** – Preys on the needy and approval-seeking, exploiting their desperation for love as a source of narcissistic supply.

The Stunted One

Core Torment & Lie: Emotional Immaturity & Stunted Growth

"I shouldn't have to grow up."

Gifts Under Attack:

- **Maturity** – The Stunted One resists responsibility and spiritual growth, keeping you trapped in childish reactions. *("When I was a child, I spoke like a child... but when I became a man, I put away childish things." – 1 Corinthians 13:11)*
- **Self-Control** – It indulges impulsiveness and excuses undisciplined behavior, sabotaging long-term fruitfulness. *("Like a city whose walls are broken through is a person who lacks self-control." – Proverbs 25:28)*
- **Teachability** – It rejects correction and deflects accountability, making growth and learning feel like personal attacks. *("Whoever loves discipline loves knowledge, but whoever hates correction is stupid." – Proverbs 12:1)*

- **Wisdom** – It chooses comfort over growth, blocking the insight and discernment that come through experience. *("The fear of the Lord is the beginning of wisdom, and knowledge of the Holy One is understanding." – Proverbs 9:10)*
- **Emotional Intelligence** – It stunts awareness of self and others, making relational maturity and empathy feel foreign or burdensome. *("Fools find no pleasure in understanding but delight in airing their own opinions." – Proverbs 18:2)*

The Stunted One arrests emotional and spiritual growth, keeping people trapped in childish reactions long after they've reached adulthood. It shows up as defensiveness, blame-shifting, and emotional outbursts that sabotage relationships. This demon feeds off unhealed wounds and excuses them as personality. But scripture is clear: growth is required, and self-control is a fruit of the Spirit. The Stunted One rewards fragility and makes accountability feel like attack.

Scripture References:

> *"A man without self-control is like a city broken into and left without walls." (Proverbs 25:28)*

> *"You need milk, not solid food... Solid food is for the mature." (Hebrews 5:12–14)*

> *"I gave you milk, not solid food... Are you not acting like mere humans?" (1 Corinthians 3:1–3)*

> *"Whoever hates correction is stupid." (Proverbs 12:1)*

> *"Anger lodges in the bosom of fools." (Ecclesiastes 7:9)*

Common Symptoms:

- Explosive outbursts or shutdowns during emotional conflict
- Chronic defensiveness or inability to receive feedback
- Blaming others for personal immaturity
- Entitlement to comfort without responsibility
- Resisting correction while demanding acceptance

Real-Life Example:

Courtney is a grown woman and a mother of three, but emotionally, she's still a child. Her household excessively accommodates her moods, especially when she's sick, which turns the family into her personal staff more than usual. Meanwhile, if one of the kids is bleeding or feverish, she barely glances up unless it's visibly serious. Her birthday isn't just a day, it's a month-long campaign, complete with a public gift list and her CashApp in her bio.

Her emotional immaturity shows up everywhere: if someone tries to express a hurt feeling, she erupts into self-pity: "I guess I'm the worst mother/friend/wife in the world" — weaponizing guilt to end the conversation. She can say vicious, cutting things to others but crumbles immediately if anyone mirrors it back. She expects lots of applause and encouragement for doing anything, but only comments negatively on anyone else's accomplishments or projects. She is shockingly rude to servers and others, embarrassing whoever she's with.

She has no concept of boundaries. She'll walk into her daughter's room, start rearranging furniture, or claim her things without asking. What's yours is hers, but what's hers is *hers alone*.

Her children are exhausted, emotionally neglected, and confused. They need a mother, but they're stuck with someone who never grew up.

Courtney's body aged, but her soul didn't. The Stunted One kept her locked in a state of emotional immaturity, excused or enabled by others, and unchallenged to grow.

Solutions & Declarations:

1. **I break agreement with the lie that I cannot grow.**
   "I can do all things through Christ who strengthens me." (Philippians 4:13)

2. **The Holy Spirit gives me power, love, and a sound mind.**
   "For God has not given us a spirit of fear, but of power and of love and of a sound mind." (2 Timothy 1:7)

3. **I welcome correction and discipline as the path to freedom.**
   "For the Lord disciplines the one he loves and chastises every son whom he receives." (Hebrews 12:6)

Turn to Chapter 9 Prayer Index and go to:
Prayer 9: General Prayer for Pride of Life
Prayer 13: Deliverance from Shame, Fear & Limitation
Supplemental Prayers: 16, 21, 23, 34

Cross References:

- **The Orphan** – A root of childhood rejection leaves emotional needs unhealed, creating immaturity that persists into adulthood.
- **The Performer** – Craves validation through compliance or charm, masking emotional underdevelopment.
- **The Desperate** – Needs constant attention and reassurance, confusing love with appeasement.
- **The Critic** – Deflects growth by turning every correction into an attack, avoiding accountability.
- **The Narcissist** – Demands special treatment, weaponizes fragility, and cannot handle shared space or boundaries.
- **The Withholder** – Gives selectively, using love and support as leverage while demanding full access to others.
- **The Rude One** – Masks immaturity with arrogance, using defiance and disrespect to avoid growth and correction.

The Coward

Core Torment & Lie: Avoidance and Fear of Exposure
"If I hide, nothing can hurt me."

Gifts Under Attack:

- **Boldness** – The Coward suppresses your voice and presence, convincing you that invisibility is safer than impact. *("The wicked*

flee though no one pursues, but the righteous are as bold as a lion."
– Proverbs 28:1)

- **Faith in Action** – It paralyzes you with fear, keeping you from stepping into what God has called you to do. *("Faith by itself, if it is not accompanied by action, is dead." – James 2:17)*
- **Obedience** – It whispers that the cost of obedience is too high, tempting you to choose safety over surrender. *("If you love me, keep my commandments." – John 14:15)*
- **Courage to Stand for Truth** – It hides from confrontation and waters down conviction to avoid rejection or persecution. *("Be strong and courageous... for the Lord your God goes with you; he will never leave you nor forsake you." – Deuteronomy 31:6)*

The Coward hides in silence. It convinces people that it's safer not to speak, try, or lead. Better to sit back, stay small, and hope trouble passes. This demon often enters after trauma, ridicule, or failure and builds walls around the soul. While others run toward their calling, the one gripped by The Coward flinches from theirs, waiting until it "feels safe." Over time, it stunts purpose, leaves callings unfulfilled, and writes a legacy of regret.

Scripture References:

"But the cowardly... their place will be in the lake of fire." (Revelation 21:8)

"God has not given us a spirit of fear, but of power, love, and a sound mind." (2 Timothy 1:7)

"Fear of man will prove to be a snare." (Proverbs 29:25)

Common Symptoms:

- Chronic indecision or avoidance
- Refusing to stand up for what's right
- Hiding talents, callings, or voice
- Withdrawing in times of pressure
- Letting others lead to avoid responsibility

Real-Life Example:

Tom came from a long line of passive men. His father avoided confrontation at all costs, and his mother constantly made excuses for his father's inaction. Growing up, Tom watched every opportunity shrink under the weight of his own hesitation. Tom had natural talent and could've made the team, landed the lead role, even started his own business, but he never tried. The Coward trained him to stay on the sidelines where it felt "safe."

As an adult, Tom still carried that legacy of fear. He never asked out the girl he truly loved, the one who would've been a faithful partner and loving mother. That one missed step set off a lifetime of detours. He married someone else, settled into a job far below his potential, and kept convincing himself things were "good enough."

Every time a raise or promotion came available, Tom told himself it wasn't the right time. Even when better jobs came knocking, he never answered. He lived quietly and politely, but beneath the surface was a man haunted by what might've been. If you asked him what exactly he was afraid of, he couldn't tell you. The Coward had done its job so well that fear became his baseline. He didn't even recognize it anymore.

Solutions and Declarations:

1. **"I will not fear what man can do to me."**
   "The Lord is on my side; I will not fear. What can man do to me?"
   (Psalm 118:6)

2. **"God has given me boldness, not timidity."**
   "For God gave us a spirit not of fear but of power and love and self-control." (2 Timothy 1:7)

3. **"I step forward in faith—even when I feel afraid."**
   "Be strong and courageous. Do not be afraid; do not be discouraged, for the Lord your God will be with you wherever you go." (Joshua 1:9)

Turn to Chapter 9 Prayer Index and go to:

Prayer 9: General Prayer for Pride of Life

Prayer 13: Deliverance from Shame, Fear & Limitation

Supplemental Prayer: 22

Cross References:

- **The Guard** – Instills paralyzing fear of failure or success, leading to overthinking and inaction instead of bold obedience.
- **The Phantom** – Feeds anxiety about visibility, criticism, or rejection, creating dread at the very idea of stepping into the light.
- **The Critic** – Often represents the internalized voice that first silenced you, making you believe you'll never be enough to risk being seen.
- **The Loop** – Keeps you trapped in obsessive hesitation and fear-based analysis, convincing you to delay until it's "perfect."
- **The Appeaser** – Shares the same root of fear, but copes by pleasing others instead of disappearing.
- **Leviathan** – Twists communication, pride, and identity, convincing you that your voice doesn't matter or that it's safer to hide than to risk being misunderstood. It often masks cowardice in false humility or "wisdom," making retreat feel like discernment.

The Appeaser

Core Torment & Lie: Compromise & Fear of Man

"Don't upset anyone."

Gifts Under Attack:

- **Conviction** – The Appeaser dulls your spiritual backbone, training you to bend truth for the sake of comfort. (*"Woe to those who call evil good and good evil… who put darkness for light and light for darkness." – Isaiah 5:20*)
- **Integrity** – It pushes you to say what others want to hear rather than what is right, fracturing your moral clarity. (*"The integrity of*

the upright guides them, but the unfaithful are destroyed by their duplicity." – Proverbs 11:3)

- **Righteous Leadership** – It weakens your ability to lead with boldness and justice, trading authority for approval. *("Am I now trying to win the approval of human beings, or of God? ... If I were still trying to please people, I would not be a servant of Christ."* – Galatians 1:10)
- **Fear of God over Fear of Man** – It elevates the opinions of others above God's commands, making you a servant to public opinion. *("The fear of man brings a snare, but whoever trusts in the Lord shall be safe."* – Proverbs 29:25)

The Appeaser accommodates evil. It convinces believers that silence is love and that affirming sin is compassion. This spirit fears man's disapproval more than God's judgment. It silences prophets, weakens leaders, and lets corruption grow unchecked in homes, churches, and nations. Often disguised as diplomacy or kindness, this demon is deadly: it keeps the door open to evil while persecuting those who dare close it. The Appeaser is subtle, but in the last days, it is everywhere.

Scripture References:

"Am I now trying to win the approval of human beings, or of God?" (Galatians 1:10)

"They loved the praise of men more than the praise of God." (John 12:43)

"If you do not speak to warn the wicked... I will hold you accountable." (Ezekiel 3:18)

Common Symptoms:

- Avoiding confrontation about sin in friends or family
- Using "grace" as an excuse for moral compromise
- Staying silent to protect relationships or social standing
- Affirming worldly ideologies to be accepted
- Resenting those who speak boldly for truth

Real-Life Example:

Rick recently gave his life to Christ and was all in: baptized, studying the Word, praying daily, and sharing his faith with close friends and family. He knew God saved him for a purpose, and he was eager to walk it out. Then his workplace announced their Pride Month initiative, and something shifted inside him.

Rick worked in a corporate culture where politics and personal beliefs were rarely discussed, but everyone understood that certain views were off-limits. The diversity committee sent out an email instructing employees to add pronouns to their signatures and choose one of two rainbow-themed profile frames: one marked "Ally," the other "LGBTQ+ Community." The email was worded carefully, but the pressure was clear: *participation was expected*. There would also be a mandatory "celebration day" with food, games, and presentations affirming the movement.

Rick hesitated. He knew exactly what Scripture said. He felt the Holy Spirit nudge him. In the back of his mind, another voice spoke louder: *"Don't cause trouble. Don't be the one to make it awkward. You just got here. You'll look like a bigot. It's not a big deal."*

Even though some employees discreetly opted out or never updated their profiles, Rick found himself complying. He added the pronouns. He picked the "Ally" frame. He showed up at the event. All day, he smiled, nodded, and played along, but inside, he was grieving.

He went home feeling sick from the gut-deep knowledge he betrayed what God clearly showed him. He wasn't trying to rebel; he just didn't want to be the odd one out. The Appeaser convinced him that peace with people was worth more than obedience to God.

Solutions & Declarations:

1. **"I fear God more than man."**
   "The fear of man lays a snare, but whoever trusts in the Lord is safe." (Proverbs 29:25)

2. **"I will not be ashamed of the gospel."**

   "For I am not ashamed of the gospel, for it is the power of God for salvation to everyone who believes." (Romans 1:16)

3. **"I choose conviction over comfort."**

   "Am I now seeking the approval of man, or of God? Or am I trying to please man? If I were still trying to please man, I would not be a servant of Christ." (Galatians 1:10)

Turn to Chapter 9 Prayer Index and go to:

Prayer 9: General Prayer for Pride of Life

Prayer 13: Deliverance from Shame, Fear & Limitation

Cross References:

- **The Coward** – Fears the consequences of standing firm, so it chooses silence over conviction.
- **The Critic** – Shames those who take a bold stand, making compromise look like wisdom.
- **The Inverter** – Redefines love as acceptance of sin, twisting truth into hate.
- **Jezebel** – Exerts pressure and manipulation, especially over those who hesitate to resist.
- **The Doubter** – Undermines the urgency of speaking truth, whispering that boldness isn't required.

The Faithless One

Core Torment & Lie: Chronic Distrust in God Despite Proximity to Truth

"God might do it for them, but He won't do it for me."

Gifts Under Attack:

- **Faith** – The Faithless One convinces you that God's promises apply to others but not to you, weakening your ability to trust

Him personally. *("But without faith it is impossible to please Him... He is a rewarder of those who diligently seek Him." – Hebrews 11:6)*

- **Hope** – It steals your sense of future good, making anticipation feel naïve or dangerous. *("May the God of hope fill you with all joy and peace as you trust in him..." – Romans 15:13)*
- **Expectancy** – It conditions you to brace for disappointment rather than believe for breakthrough. *("According to your faith let it be done to you." – Matthew 9:29)*
- **Spiritual Intimacy** – It creates emotional distance from God, replacing connection with doubt and apathy. *("Draw near to God and He will draw near to you." – James 4:8)*
- **Effective Prayer** – It blocks powerful prayer by planting unbelief, making you speak to God without expecting an answer. *("But let him ask in faith, with no doubting..." – James 1:6)*

The Faithless One is a subtle and dangerous spirit because it simply *settles*. This demon keeps people in the pews, in the choir, even in leadership but devoid of expectancy. It wears the mask of maturity, when in reality it's burnout, cynicism, and resignation. It looks like "wisdom," but lives like unbelief. Faith isn't just knowing scripture—it's expecting God to move. The Faithless One rejects that expectation and replaces it with cold survival.

Scripture References:

"When you ask, you must believe and not doubt..." (James 1:6–8)

"He could not do many miracles there because of their unbelief." (Mark 6:5–6)

"See to it that none of you has a sinful, unbelieving heart that turns away..." (Hebrews 3:12)

Common Symptoms:

- Saying the right things but expecting little
- Feeling resentful toward others who get breakthroughs
- Seeing God as distant, selective, or unfair

- Treating prayer like a formality, not a weapon
- Living in self-protection mode to avoid disappointment

Real-Life Example:

Ekon runs one of the most well-known Christian testimony channels online. Every week, he uploads stories from people who've survived the impossible: stage 4 cancer healed, children raised from the brink of death, atheists who encountered Jesus in near-death experiences. He's heard of visions of heaven, warnings of hell, angelic visitations, and supernatural provision. He believes them all. He's never doubted their truth for a moment.

When it comes to his own life, the stories might as well be fiction.

Ekon no longer prays. He used to, but after years of feeling unheard, the silence convinced him he was different, that somehow God loved others more. He still curates stories of faith, but his heart no longer burns with it. He posts about miracles he no longer expects. Shares scriptures he no longer stands on. Even though he champions the testimonies of others, deep down he doesn't believe he'll ever have one of his own.

The Faithless One didn't attack scripture or theology; instead, it just whispered, *"But not for you,"* and Ekon believed it.

Solutions & Declarations:

1. **"I renounce the lie that God has abandoned me."**
   "Be strong and courageous. Do not be afraid or terrified because of them, for the Lord your God goes with you; he will never leave you nor forsake you." (Deuteronomy 31:6)

2. **"My faith is not in what I see, but in who God is."**
   "For we walk by faith, not by sight." (2 Corinthians 5:7)

3. **"I believe again. I trust again. I receive again."**
   "Let us hold unswervingly to the hope we profess, for he who promised is faithful." (Hebrews 10:23)

Turn to Chapter 9 Prayer Index and go to:
Prayer 9: General Prayer for Pride of Life
Prayer 13: Deliverance from Shame, Fear & Limitation
Supplemental Prayers: 15, 24

Cross References:

- **The Doubter** – Struggles with questions and uncertainty, but remains open; The Faithless One has already resigned and withdrawn.
- **The Apostate** – Fully walks away from the faith; The Faithless One stays near but no longer believes God will act personally.
- **The Withholder** – Projects the absence of love onto God, assuming that unanswered prayers mean rejection.
- **The Loop** – Stuck in cyclical thinking, always analyzing but never advancing in trust or surrender.
- **The Critic** – Masks unbelief in sarcasm or cynicism, often mocking what others hope for or believe in.
- **The Mute** – Suppresses testimony and prayer, especially when faith feels fruitless or performative.
- **The Shrinker** – Keeps expectations low to avoid disappointment, settling for spiritual survival instead of victory.

The Suicide Spirit

Core Torment & Lie: Death, Despair, and Isolation

"It will never get better. Just end it."

Gifts Under Attack:

- **Hope** – The Suicide Spirit crushes the expectation of healing or change, making the future feel like a prison instead of a promise. *("For I know the plans I have for you… plans to give you a future and a hope." – Jeremiah 29:11)*

- **Endurance** – It tells you that you've reached your limit, cutting off the strength to persevere one more day. *("Let us run with endurance the race that is set before us." – Hebrews 12:1)*
- **Destiny** – It attacks your divine purpose, trying to abort what God has planned for your life. *("You shall not die but live and declare the works of the Lord." – Psalm 118:17)*
- **Peace** – It floods your mind with torment, drowning out the still voice of comfort and truth. *("The peace of God, which surpasses all understanding, will guard your hearts and your minds." – Philippians 4:7)*
- **Faith** – It makes God's love feel far away or conditional, twisting your trials into proof that He has forgotten you. *("The Lord is close to the brokenhearted and saves those who are crushed in spirit." – Psalm 34:18)*

The Suicide Spirit is a spirit of death that disguises itself as mercy. It says that ending your life is the only way to escape pain. It partners with trauma, grief, isolation, shame, depression, and demonic torment, amplifying every lie and silencing every reason to live. It convinces people that their existence is a burden and that others would be better off without them. The truth is this: God still has plans for your life, and no lie of death can cancel the call of God.

Scripture References:

"The thief comes to steal, kill, and destroy..." (John 10:10)

"The Lord is close to the brokenhearted." (Psalm 34:18)

"Why are you downcast, O my soul? Put your hope in God." (Psalm 42:11)

"I will not die but live and declare the works of the Lord." (Psalm 118:17)

Common Symptoms:

- Persistent thoughts of ending one's life
- Belief that death is the only relief

- Feeling like a burden or irreparably broken
- Obsessive focus on methods, letters, or "exit strategies"
- Isolation from those who care

Real-Life Example From the Author:

I struggled with deep depressive episodes from childhood into adulthood, but never once had a suicidal thought. Not until *the night I was saved*. That's how I know the Suicide Spirit was making a last-minute play for my soul.

At that time, I hit absolute rock bottom. I was jobless, couldn't get hired anywhere despite a stellar resume, had just $5 to my name, and was facing eviction because my building had been sold. There was no safety net. On top of that, my beloved grandmother just died. I spent my last bit of money flying to her bedside, just in time to watch her spirit leave her body. That moment cracked something open in me. I knew there was *something more* to life. Something spiritual. But I had been raised without religion and had no framework to interpret it.

When I got back to my apartment, I found myself standing in the middle of my kitchen, completely stunned at the circumstances I found myself in and without a clue what I was going to do. I was about to be out on the street in New York City, of all places. Could anything be more terrifying? I couldn't even think a thought; I was so overwhelmed.

Then a cardinal landed on my window ledge—a bird I had *never* seen in the city before. My grandmother once told me she'd send one as a sign after she passed. We stared at each other for five solid minutes. Then, out of nowhere, a soft voice said: *"You've seen enough. There's nothing else you want to do or places you want to go. Why don't you just end it now?"*

It wasn't my voice. It certainly didn't come from me.

It *shocked* me awake.

Just a few hours later, I stumbled across a series of personal testimonies online and by the grace of God, I gave my life to Jesus. The *very next morning*, everything started to turn around. He completely delivered me from depression, supplied the funds in an unexpected check which allowed me to move into a new apartment around the corner a couple of days later (a miracle in itself if you're familiar with NYC real estate), and brought me into my first church which gave me the foundation to be the believer I am today.

Now, twenty years later, I know with full conviction: that voice was the Suicide Spirit.

It knew I was about to be rescued. That Jesus was coming for me. That my life was going to get better than I could possibly imagine.

That demon wanted to end me before the light could reach me.

When the enemy knows your rescue is coming, he tries to take you out. This spirit attacks at the edge of deliverance, hoping to end your story before God can rewrite it.

Solutions & Declarations:

1. **"I renounce every agreement with death and despair."**
   "Do not be overcome by evil but overcome evil with good." (Romans 12:21) "The thief comes only to steal and kill and destroy; I have come that they may have life and have it to the full." (John 10:10)

2. **"God's plans for me are good, and I will live to see them."**
   "'For I know the plans I have for you,' declares the Lord, 'plans to prosper you and not to harm you, plans to give you hope and a future.'" (Jeremiah 29:11)

3. **"I will not die but live and declare the works of the Lord."**
   "I shall not die, but I shall live and recount the deeds of the Lord." (Psalm 118:17)

Turn to Chapter 9 Prayer Index and go to:

Prayer 9: General Prayer for Pride of Life
Prayer 13: Deliverance from Shame, Fear & Limitation
Supplemental Prayers: 19, 21, 23, 24, 26, 32, 33, 34

Cross References:

- **The Abyss** – Long-term emotional despair often opens the door for suicidal ideation to take root.

- **The Broken Mirror** – When a person sees themselves as worthless, the Suicide Spirit offers death as the only escape.
- **The Liar** – Twists reality to make pain feel permanent and convince the soul there is no way out.
- **The Doubter** – Undermines faith in God's goodness or deliverance, leading to spiritual surrender.
- **The Cutter** – Prepares the body and mind to accept pain and normalize acts of self-destruction.
- **The Orphan** – Feeds the lie that no one cares and the person is truly alone, increasing the risk of despair.
- **The Phantom** – Creates overwhelming fear about the future, making death feel like a relief from pressure.

The Cutter

Core Torment & Lie: Self-Hatred, Shame, and Torment

"You deserve this pain."

Gifts Under Attack:

- **Identity** – The Cutter convinces you that you are broken beyond repair, unworthy of love or belonging. *("I will give you a new name... no longer called Forsaken." – Isaiah 62:2–4)*
- **Worth** – It trains you to punish yourself for existing, distorting how you see your value in God's eyes. *("Are not five sparrows sold for two pennies? Yet not one of them is forgotten by God... you are worth more than many sparrows." – Luke 12:6–7)*
- **Healing** – It blocks the restoration God offers, keeping you locked in cycles of pain and secrecy. *("He heals the brokenhearted and binds up their wounds." – Psalm 147:3)*
- **Emotional Regulation** – It hijacks your coping mechanisms, making pain feel like the only release from inner turmoil. *("Cast all your anxiety on him because he cares for you." – 1 Peter 5:7)*
- **Purpose** – It convinces you that your life has no meaning, distracting you from the calling and impact God has designed for

you. *("Before I formed you in the womb I knew you; before you were born, I set you apart." – Jeremiah 1:5)*

The Cutter is a spirit of self-harm and torment. It compels people to injure themselves in a twisted attempt to feel control, punishment, or relief. It thrives on secrecy, shame, and cycles of numbness and emotional overload. This demon often partners with depression, rejection, and self-hatred, using pain to counterfeit healing. The blood that heals has already been shed by Jesus.

Scripture References:

"He would cry out and cut himself with stones." (Mark 5:5)

"Your body is a temple... honor God with it." (1 Corinthians 6:19–20)

"They cut themselves... until the blood gushed out." (1 Kings 18:28)

"By His wounds, we are healed." (Isaiah 53:5)

Common Symptoms:

- Cutting, burning, or harming oneself
- Emotional pain "relieved" by physical pain
- Obsessive thoughts about blood, injury, or punishment
- Hiding scars or living in deep shame
- Compulsions that feel too strong to resist

Real-Life Example:

Brianna never meant to become someone who self-harmed. Her home life was tempestuous: loud arguments and emotional instability were the norm. She found some sense of control through disordered eating, but even that wasn't bringing the relief it once had.

One day at school, she noticed a girl accidentally reveal a neat row of small white lines across the top of her thigh. Brianna was fascinated. Not long after, she began noticing the same faint scars on other girls' arms and legs—some not even bothering to hide them. Curious, she looked it up online and discovered an entire subculture around cutting. They didn't call it demonic, but it was.

That night, Brianna tried it. Just once.

The moment the blood beaded on her skin, she felt a strange and fleeting sense of relief. What she didn't know was that she had just participated in a ritual that was a sacrifice to a demon who would begin to demand more and more. Every millimeter of sliced skin, every drop of blood, was an offering.

What began as curiosity became compulsion. She hid it well but carried deep shame.

What she thought was control was actually torment.

Her freedom began the day she realized that Jesus already took the punishment she was inflicting on herself. There was no more debt to pay. No more blood to spill.

Solutions & Declarations:

1. **"I renounce every lie that says pain will heal me."**
   "The Lord is near to the brokenhearted and saves the crushed in spirit."

   (Psalm 34:18) "He heals the brokenhearted and binds up their wounds." (Psalm 147:3)

2. **"I declare my body is God's temple, not mine to destroy."**
   "Do you not know that your bodies are temples of the Holy Spirit, who is in you, whom you have received from God? You are not your own; you were bought at a price. Therefore, honor God with your bodies." (1 Corinthians 6:19–20)

3. **"I release my pain to Jesus, who was wounded so I could be healed."**
   "But he was pierced for our transgressions, he was crushed for our iniquities; the punishment that brought us peace was on him, and by his wounds we are healed." (Isaiah 53:5)

Turn to Chapter 9 Prayer Index and go to:
Prayer 9: General Prayer for Pride of Life
Prayer 13: Deliverance from Shame, Fear & Limitation
Supplemental Prayers: 21, 23, 34

Cross References:

- **The Abyss** – Emotional heaviness and despair often fuel the urge to harm oneself as an outlet.
- **The Broken Mirror** – Self-hatred distorts how one sees their worth, making self-injury feel deserved.
- **The Suicide Spirit** – Cutting can become a gateway or stepping stone to suicidal ideation.
- **The Liar** – Feeds the belief that pain brings control or that suffering proves value.
- **The Critic** – Reinforces internal condemnation, driving a need for punishment and shame.
- **The Withholder** – Withholds compassion and comfort from the self, encouraging pain instead of healing.
- **The Loop** – Keeps individuals stuck in cycles of harm, shame, and regret without resolution or escape.

The Shrinker

Core Torment & Lie: Fear of Man & False Humility

"If I'm fully seen, I'll be judged, rejected, or attacked."

Gifts under attack:

- **Visibility** – The Shrinker convinces you to stay hidden, making you fear exposure instead of embracing your God-given presence. *("No one lights a lamp and hides it... instead, they put it on a stand so that those who come in may see the light." – Luke 11:33)*
- **Influence** – It stifles your voice and impact, keeping you from stepping into the platform God has assigned. *("You are the light of the world. A city set on a hill cannot be hidden." – Matthew 5:14)*

- **Leadership** – It makes you doubt your authority and question your qualifications, shrinking back when you're called to step up. *("Do not let anyone look down on you... set an example for the believers..." – 1 Timothy 4:12)*
- **Creative Expression** – It silences the gifts within you, making self-expression feel dangerous or self-indulgent. *("Having gifts that differ... let us use them..." – Romans 12:6)*
- **Prophetic Voice** – It makes bold truth feel like a liability, suppressing your calling to speak what God says with clarity and courage. *("Cry aloud, do not hold back; lift up your voice like a trumpet..." – Isaiah 58:1)*

This spirit causes individuals to hide their gifts, voices, and callings out of fear. It masquerades as humility but is rooted in pride, shame, and a survival instinct shaped by early criticism or betrayal. The Shrinker convinces you that staying invisible is safer—that obedience should be quiet, cautious, and palatable.

God did not give us a spirit of fear. The Shrinker uses past trauma or failure as a muzzle. It feeds on insecurity and the fear of man, trapping people in smallness when they were called to lead. It thrives among creatives, prophets, and visionaries who feel the spiritual pressure of being "too much."

Scripture references:

"The fear of man lays a snare, but whoever trusts in the Lord is safe." (Proverbs 29:25)

"No one lights a lamp and puts it under a bowl... Let your light shine before others." (Matthew 5:15–16)

"His master replied, 'You wicked, lazy servant!... You should have put my money on deposit...'" (Matthew 25:26–27)

"God has not given us a spirit of fear, but of power, love, and a sound mind." (2 Timothy 1:7)

Common symptoms:

- Chronic self-doubt or downplaying accomplishments
- Avoiding leadership roles, attention, or platforms
- Deep fear of being seen, exposed, or criticized
- False humility that masks fear or shame
- Creativity or ministry ideas that never get shared

Real-life example:

Alina was the most gifted singer in her church, but no one knew it. She only sang in private, where it felt safe. Anytime she was asked to lead worship, she'd panic or politely decline, saying, *"I'm just not that kind of person."*

The truth ran deeper.

In high school, Alina once tried to sing publicly, only to be mocked by classmates. The wound stuck. She vowed in her heart never to put herself in that position again and be that vulnerable. Over the years, she began to spiritualize her avoidance, convincing herself that "staying low" was humble. That maybe she wasn't called to the platform. That maybe God was pleased with her quiet obedience behind the scenes.

Her mother saw the truth and spoke it with love: she reminded Alina that *we were all created to worship*, and that those with anointed voices carried a sacred responsibility. Worship is more than singing, it is ministry. *To sing with anointing is to stand in the gap*, expressing praise on behalf of those who don't have the words or the strength. Alina's voice didn't just fill a room; it invited the presence of God. It helped others enter into deeper worship.

The excuses couldn't hide the truth anymore: Alina wasn't staying low. She was staying afraid. The Shrinker was behind it, silencing her gift, distorting her humility, and keeping her disobedient while the very calling God placed on her life sat untouched.

Solutions and declarations:

1. **"I will not bury what God has given me out of fear."**
   "So I was afraid and went out and hid your gold in the ground. See, here is what belongs to you. His master replied, 'You wicked, lazy servant!'" (Matthew 25:25–26)

2. **"God has not given me a spirit of fear, but of power, love, and a sound mind."**
   "For God has not given us a spirit of fear, but of power and of love and of a sound mind." (2 Timothy 1:7)

3. **"I will let my light shine so others may see and glorify my Father."**
   "Let your light shine before others, that they may see your good deeds and glorify your Father in heaven." (Matthew 5:16)

Turn to Chapter 9 Prayer Index and go to:

Prayer 9: General Prayer for Pride of Life
Prayer 13: Deliverance from Shame, Fear & Limitation
Supplemental Prayers: 21, 23, 34

Cross-references:

- **The Mute** – Silences your voice entirely, preventing you from using your gifts to speak, sing, or declare.
- **The Coward** – Hides out of the fear of rejection, choosing invisibility over the risk of obedience and visibility.
- **The Guard** – Protects through emotional suppression, reinforcing the lie that safety is found in invisibility.
- **The Doubter** – Convinces you you're not ready, not worthy, or not "called" enough to step forward.
- **The Idolator** – Elevates the opinions of others above God's command, making human approval the true god.
- **Leviathan** – Twists humility into prideful self-protection, cloaking fear in a false holiness to avoid vulnerability.

- **The Puffer** – Damages the physical instrument to the point of non-use. Numbs conviction and calling through substances, providing false comfort instead of surrender.

The Promise Breaker
Core Torment & Lie: Unfaithfulness
"You don't owe anyone anything."
Gifts Under Attack:

- **Integrity** – The Promise Breaker undermines your word, making your commitments shallow and easily discarded. *("Let your 'Yes' be 'Yes,' and your 'No,' 'No'; anything more comes from the evil one." – Matthew 5:37)*
- **Trustworthiness** – It erodes your reliability, causing others to question your dependability and intentions. *("A righteous man walks in integrity; blessed are his children after him." – Proverbs 20:7)*
- **Faithfulness** – It sabotages consistency in relationships, assignments, and responsibilities, making follow-through feel optional. *("Whoever can be trusted with very little can also be trusted with much..." – Luke 16:10)*
- **Relational Stability** – It fosters broken agreements and abandoned responsibilities, damaging bonds over time. *("Love always protects, always trusts, always hopes, always perseveres." – 1 Corinthians 13:7)*
- **Witness to Others** – It tarnishes your credibility, making it harder for others to see Christ in your life. *("In everything set them an example by doing what is good. In your teaching show integrity, seriousness..." – Titus 2:7)*

The Promise Breaker demon distorts the sacredness of a vow. It says that promises are optional, especially when they get uncomfortable. Whether in marriages, parenting, business deals, or spiritual commitments, this spirit normalizes betrayal under the guise of "freedom." Over time, it leads to fractured relationships, hardened hearts, and a reputation marked by unreliability. This demon reflects the opposite of God's nature, for God is a covenant-keeping God *(Deuteronomy 7:9)*, and calls His people to reflect that same faithfulness.

Even when the person has good intentions, The Promise Breaker whispers that they won't follow through, feeding a pattern of shame and retreat.

It causes:

- Fear of commitment
- Procrastination and paralysis
- Avoidance of confrontation
- Chronic guilt
- Damaged relationships and credibility

Scripture Reference:

"When you make a vow to God, do not delay to fulfill it. He has no pleasure in fools; fulfill your vow." (Ecclesiastes 5:4)

"Let your yes be yes and your no be no, or you will be condemned." (James 5:12)

"It is better not to vow than to make a vow and not fulfill it." (Ecclesiastes 5:5)

Common Symptoms:

- Serial quitting or ghosting
- Broken relationships or custody arrangements
- Abandoning spiritual callings or ministry
- Betrayal masked as "changing my mind"
- Avoidance of accountability or long-term follow-through

Real-Life Example:

Vlad never set out to be unreliable, but somewhere between failed jobs, broken plans, and promises he couldn't keep, it became his pattern. He meant well in the beginning, but his follow-through never matched his intentions.

He promised his kids he'd pick them up last weekend. Again. He never showed. At first, they used to cry. Now they don't even ask. The disappointment hardened into disillusionment. That's what enrages his ex the most: not just the broken promises, but the fact that their children have stopped expecting anything.

She sees it clearly: the tears have dried, but something far worse has set in. Their innocence was stolen. The one person they should've been able to rely on—their father—is now a figure of inconsistency.

The damage didn't stop there. Now, a quiet lie has taken root in their hearts: *"Fathers don't show up. "*That belief, planted by The Promise Breaker, won't just distort their view of Vlad. It will follow them for life, shaping relationships, weakening trust, and complicating the most important relationship of all: the one with God the Father.

Because how can you trust *Him*...when the word *"father"* is already associated with absence?

Declarations:

1. **"I repent for every vow I broke—spoken or unspoken. I will be known by integrity."**
   "Better is it that you should not vow than that you should vow and not pay." (Ecclesiastes 5:5)

2. **"I break every generational curse of broken promises, abandonment, and betrayal."**
   "Know therefore that the Lord your God is God; He is the faithful God, keeping His covenant of love." (Deuteronomy 7:9)

3. **"By God's grace, my word will be trustworthy. I reflect the faithfulness of Christ."**
   "Let your 'yes' be yes and your 'no' be no." (James 5:12)

Turn to Chapter 9 Prayer Index and go to:
Prayer 9: General Prayer for Pride of Life
Prayer 13: Deliverance from Shame, Fear & Limitation

Cross-References:

- **The Betrayer** – Violates sacred trust and loyalty, compounding the pain of broken promises.
- **The Ghoster** – Abandons without closure, leaving others confused and emotionally stranded.
- **The Liar** – Breaks promises by twisting truth, avoiding confrontation, or omitting key details.
- **The Defier** – Rejects godly authority and refuses accountability, making vows with no intention of honoring them.
- **The Orphan** – Often the wounded recipient of broken promises, leading to generational patterns of distrust and abandonment.
- **The Weak Father** – Fails to lead or protect, leaving children spiritually vulnerable and modeling unreliability as the norm.

Before we identify the spirits embedded in family systems, we must first understand the demons that target individuals within them. These spirits often attach early—sometimes even before birth—using rejection, abandonment, fear, and performance to distort identity and sever healthy bonds. Their goal is to isolate, mislabel, and reroute destiny before it can take root. These are demons of distortion, and their primary mission is to separate us from love, truth, and our divine assignment.

Not all demonic influence enters through trauma alone; some comes through inheritance. These are the *familiar spirits*—named not just because they feel familiar, but because they come through family. They often hide in plain sight: passed down in parenting styles, cultural expectations, or what's dismissed as *"just how we were raised."* These spirits embed themselves in generational patterns and relational roles, especially within dysfunctional or narcissistic systems. Children become characters in a script they never agreed to, cast as The Performer, The

Black Sheep, or The Golden Child, each role designed to meet the emotional needs of broken adults rather than reflect God's design.

Some of the most insidious spirits assign the roles. Unless confronted, they repeat. What you don't cast out, your children may inherit.

Generational & Familiar Spirits

100. **The Severer** – Estrangement. "You don't need them. Be alone."

101. **The Orphan** – Internal Wound of Rejection. "You are unwanted."

102. **The Performer** – Approval Addiction & Identity Through Performance. "Be who they want."

103. **The Golden Child** – Pride, Idolatry & Control. "You can do no wrong."

104. **The Black Sheep** – Rejection, Condemnation & Isolation. "You're the problem."

105. **The Truth Teller** – Isolation, Rejection & Spiritual Backlash. "Telling the truth ruins everything."

106. **The Overbearing Matriarch** – Control, Emasculation & Pride Disguised as Protection. "Only I know best."

107. **The Meddling Mother-in-Law** – Manipulation, Control & Boundary Violation. "They still belong to me."

108. **The Withholding Father** – Absence, Conditional Love & Emotional Starvation. "Earn my approval."

109. **The Weak Father** – Passivity, Abdication of Responsibility & Fear of Failure. "I won't lead."

110. **The Terrifying Father** – Domination, Intimidation & Punishment Based Authority. "Obey or suffer."

111. **The Neglectful Parent** – Emotional Abandonment, Apathy & Misprioritized Affection. "You're on your own."

112. **Sibling Rivalry** – Competition, Envy, Comparison & Favoritism. "There's only room for one."

113. **The Burnt-Out Child** – Parentification, Chronic Responsibility & Emotional Exhaustion. "You're not allowed to be a child."

114. **The Wanderer** – Aimlessness from Rejection. "I don't belong anywhere."

115. **The Jealous Mother** – Insecurity, Control, Competition & Emotional Manipulation. "You can't outshine me."

116. **The Enmeshed Mother** – Emotional Incest, Identity Theft & Soul-Tie Bondage. "You belong to me."

The Severer

Core Torment & Lie: Estrangement

"You don't need them. Be alone."

Gifts Under Attack:

- **Connection** – The Severer breaks the natural bonds of human relationship, convincing you that isolation is safer than vulnerability. *("Two are better than one... If either of them falls, one can help the other up." – Ecclesiastes 4:9–10)*

- **Intimacy** – It drives emotional distance and relational sabotage, making closeness feel threatening or unnecessary. *("Carry each other's burdens, and in this way, you will fulfill the law of Christ." – Galatians 6:2)*

- **Covenant** – It attacks long-term loyalty, replacing enduring love with detachment and bitterness. *("What God has joined together, let no one separate." – Mark 10:9)*

- **Reconciliation** – It hardens the heart against forgiveness and healing, making division seem justified and permanent. *("All this is from God, who reconciled us to himself through Christ and gave us the ministry of reconciliation." – 2 Corinthians 5:18)*

- **Spiritual Family** – It isolates you from the Body of Christ, making independence seem holy and community seem optional. *("Now* *you are the body of Christ, and each one of you is a part of it." – 1 Corinthians 12:27)*

The Severer is a generational demon assigned to destroy natural bonds between men and women, parents and children, brothers and sisters. Its mission is far greater than individual heartbreak. It is a direct assault on God's design for the family, which is the foundational unit of society. When families fracture, homes no longer raise children in truth and love, and those children grow up to reproduce the same cycles until the very fabric of culture begins to unravel. We're seeing the consequences now: rising loneliness, mental illness, fatherlessness, and widespread relational dysfunction.

The Severer thrives in this chaos. It cloaks division in the language of empowerment: self-protection disguised as independence, and estrangement disguised as boundaries. It thrives in a world of ghosting, divorce, and cutoff culture, where love is seen as a liability and trust is viewed as weakness. It often enters through generational trauma, early abandonment, or spiritual betrayal. Once it takes root, it says the same lie over and over: "You're better off alone."

Scripture References:

> *"For the Lord... hates divorce... So, guard your heart; do not be unfaithful." (Malachi 2:16)*

> *"God places the lonely in families; he sets the prisoners free..." (Psalm 68:6)*

> *"Many will turn away from the faith... betray and hate each other... the love of most will grow cold." (Matthew 24:10–12)*

Common Symptoms:

- Estrangement from family without closure
- Feeling "safer" without emotional bonds
- Relationship sabotage when intimacy deepens
- Fierce independence masking fear of abandonment
- Cynicism about love, covenant, or reconciliation

Real-Life Example:

Danielle has cut off both her parents, her siblings, and even her former best friend. She says she's setting boundaries, but in truth, she's setting fires. Anyone who gets too close, who pokes at the pain she's tried to forget, is quickly removed. No confrontation. No conversation. Just silence.

Danielle is carrying on the tradition she saw modeled for generations.

Her earliest memory of this spiritual inheritance was at her great-grandmother's house. She found an old black-and-white photo tucked in a drawer. On the back, it read "Violet, 1920." Curious, Danielle asked who the woman was. Her great-grandmother snatched the photo away and said flatly, *"That's my sister. She got up from the breakfast table one day and walked out of this house. Never came back. That's all you need to know."* The conversation ended and Violet was never mentioned again.

Danielle didn't need an explanation. Even as a child, she noticed something missing. There were no aunts or uncles at holidays. No cousins in the family photo albums. She had grown up surrounded by silence and severance.

So, when she got older and started cutting people off herself, it didn't feel unnatural. It felt *familiar*. It was the way her family handled pain: amputate the limb and move on.

Tamika's story is different, but the outcome is the same.

Her father was abusive, and she's proud she survived without him. She doesn't speak his name or think of him—except maybe once a year when Father's Day ads show up in her inbox. In her mind, his absence justifies her silence. *If he wanted a relationship, he'd reach out.* Since he hasn't, she tells herself it's settled, but the wound is still there.

Tamika avoids dating, downplays her desire for marriage, and scoffs at emotional dependency. Her independence is worn like a badge of honor, but beneath it is grief, mistrust, and fear. The only man who was supposed to protect her didn't, and now no man gets the chance. In her world, men don't even exist anymore.

Both Danielle and Tamika believe they've taken control of their lives when the truth is The Severer has taken control of their legacy.

This spirit thrives on generational division, snapping bonds before they can form, rewriting trust into trauma, and teaching hearts to expect abandonment before they ever learn how to belong. It destroys families, reprograms them, and convinces people families are not worth forming or maintaining.

Solutions and Declarations:

1. **"I was made for covenant. I break agreement with the lie that I must be alone."**

   "The Lord God said, 'It is not good for the man to be alone. I will make a helper suitable for him.'" (Genesis 2:18)

2. **"I forgive those who wounded me and reject the spirit of estrangement."**

   "Bear with each other and forgive one another if any of you has a grievance against someone. Forgive as the Lord forgave you." (Colossians 3:13)

3. **"God restores what was lost. I invite healing into my family line."**

   "I will repay you for the years the locusts have eaten... you will have plenty to eat, until you are full, and you will praise the name of the Lord your God." (Joel 2:25–26)

Turn to Chapter 9 Prayer Index and go to:
Prayer 9: General Prayer for Pride of Life
Prayer 14: Deliverance from Generational & Family Spirits
Supplemental Prayers: 25, 26, 27, 28, 33, 34

Cross References:

- **The Orphan** – Deepens the wound of fatherlessness or rejection, reinforcing the belief that attachment always leads to abandonment.
- **The Rejector** – Feeds the lie that you're too broken for connection, making disconnection feel safer than risking rejection.

- **The Broken Mirror** – Uses a distorted self-image to justify isolation and sabotage close relationships.
- **The Guard** – Encourages emotional walls and mistrust, warning that vulnerability will only lead to pain.
- **The Black Sheep** – Reinforces estrangement by convincing the individual they're the problem in a dysfunctional family.
- **The Wanderer** – Adds rootlessness and instability, promoting a pattern of drifting rather than bonding.
- **The Pauper** – Introduces scarcity in relationships as well as resources, convincing the person they're unworthy of belonging or investment.

The Orphan

Core Torment & Lie: Internal Wound of Rejection
"You are unwanted."
Gifts Under Attack:

- **Belonging** – The Orphan convinces you that you'll always be on the outside, rejected and alone. *("God sets the lonely in families..." – Psalm 68:6)*
- **Identity** – It distorts your understanding of who you are in Christ, making you feel like a spiritual outsider instead of a beloved child. *("The Spirit you received brought about your adoption to sonship. And by him we cry, 'Abba, Father.'" – Romans 8:15)*
- **Trust** – It makes you suspicious of love and care, expecting abandonment or betrayal at every turn. *("Trust in the Lord with all your heart and lean not on your own understanding." – Proverbs 3:5)*
- **Security** – It creates instability in your emotional and spiritual life, making it hard to rest in God's promises. *("I have made you and I will carry you; I will sustain you and I will rescue you." – Isaiah 46:4)*
- **Connection to the Father** – It blocks intimacy with God by projecting earthly rejection onto Him. *("Though my father and mother forsake me, the Lord will receive me." – Psalm 27:10)*

The Orphan is a spirit of abandonment that attacks the core of human identity: the need to be chosen, covered, and loved. It often enters through the physical or emotional absence of a father or primary caregiver, but can also take root after trauma, neglect, or spiritual disappointment. Even if a person grows up in a full household, The Orphan convinces them they are fundamentally alone and must fend for themselves. It sabotages intimacy with both God and others, whispering that vulnerability is weakness and that no one is coming to stay.

Scripture References:

"I will not leave you as orphans; I will come to you." (John 14:18)

"The Spirit you received brought about your adoption to sonship. And by him we cry, 'Abba, Father.'" (Romans 8:15)

"A father to the fatherless... God sets the lonely in families." (Psalm 68:5–6)

Common Symptoms:

- Hyper-independence disguised as self-sufficiency
- Fear of needing or relying on anyone
- Belief that love must be earned, not received
- Feeling spiritually "outside" even in the church
- Deep longing for affirmation, protection, or covering

Real-Life Example:

Jake's mother died when he was just a baby. His father was physically present but emotionally vacant. From as early as Jake could remember, their relationship functioned more like distant roommates than family. His father never asked to see a report card, never offered advice or help with schoolwork, and never really checked in on him at all. If Jake needed something—clothes, food, money—he'd ask. His father would give him a few bills, and Jake would figure the rest out on his own.

He learned quickly that dependence was a liability.

By the time he was a teenager, Jake was driving himself to school illegally, but his father didn't care. Jake taught himself how to drive and was good at it, so that was enough. He got a job bussing tables at a casino using a fake ID and worked nights while going to school during the day. He stacked cash in his room, proud of the fact that he didn't need anyone. When college came, he paid tuition in cash but dropped out once a business he started from his dorm room began to take off.

On paper, Jake was impressive: resourceful, street smart, wildly independent. But if you looked closer—or asked the people in his life—they'd all say the same thing: No one ever got close to him.

Jake was his own source of comfort, protection, and provision. He had never learned to rely on anyone else, and in adulthood, that hasn't changed. He only maintains relationships that place no expectations on him. Even with people he truly likes, who make him feel something he can't explain, he just can't open the door all the way. There's a wall he doesn't know how to lower.

To Jake, this is normal. To everyone else, it's heartbreaking.

Because the truth is, The Orphan still lives inside Jake, telling him that closeness is dangerous, that vulnerability is weakness, and that the only person he can count on is himself.

Solutions and Declarations:

1. **"I am not abandoned — I have been adopted by God and am fully loved."**
   "The Spirit you received does not make you slaves, so that you live in fear again; rather, the Spirit you received brought about your adoption to sonship. And by him we cry, 'Abba, Father.'" (Romans 8:15)

2. **"I renounce the lie that I must survive alone. I belong in the Father's house."**
   "Even the sparrow has found a home, and the swallow a nest for herself, where she may have her young—a place near your altar, Lord Almighty, my King and my God." (Psalm 84:3)

3. **"Where others failed me, God Himself will cover and restore me."**

   "Though my father and mother forsake me, the Lord will receive me." (Psalm 27:10)

Turn to Chapter 9 Prayer Index and go to:
Prayer 9: General Prayer for Pride of Life
Prayer 14: Deliverance from Generational & Family Spirits
Supplemental Prayers: 15, 27, 32, 33, 34

Cross References:

- **The Severer** – Normalizes detachment and reinforces the belief that needing others leads to pain.
- **The Rejector** – Feeds self-rejection by convincing the person they were left because they weren't worthy of love.
- **The Broken Mirror** – Distorts identity by turning abandonment into a reflection of personal failure.
- **The Performer** – Pushes the person to overcompensate, striving to be chosen by becoming who others want.
- **The Phantom** – Keeps them in emotional hypervigilance, always expecting the next wound or departure.
- **The Wanderer** – Reinforces the feeling of being spiritually and relationally homeless, driving instability and rootlessness.

The Performer

Core Torment & Lie: Approval Addiction
& Identity Through Performance

"Be who they want."

Gifts Under Attack:

- **Authenticity** – The Performer pressures you to curate a version of yourself that's acceptable to others, not aligned with who God created you to be. *("Am I now trying to win the approval of human beings, or of God?" – Galatians 1:10)*

- **Identity** – It distorts your sense of self by tying your worth to applause, productivity, or validation. *("You are my Son, whom I love; with you I am well pleased." – Mark 1:11)*
- **Rest** – It refuses to let you slow down, equating stillness with failure or invisibility. *("In repentance and rest is your salvation, in quietness and trust is your strength..." – Isaiah 30:15)*
- **Freedom in Christ** – It keeps you in a cycle of striving instead of standing firm in grace. *("It is for freedom that Christ has set us free..." – Galatians 5:1)*
- **Emotional Honesty** – It suppresses your true needs and feelings, teaching you to perform rather than connect. *("Therefore, each of you must put off falsehood and speak truthfully to your neighbor..." – Ephesians 4:25)*

The Performer is a spirit that trades identity for acceptance. It tells you that love must be earned through excellence, likability, or usefulness and that your worth is directly tied to how well you meet other people's expectations. Often rooted in childhood environments where love was conditional or where approval had to be maintained, The Performer breeds anxiety, burnout, and spiritual shallowness. Instead of being known and loved for who they are, those bound by this spirit become experts in wearing masks, adjusting to every room, and performing their value into existence.

Scripture References:

"Am I now trying to win the approval of human beings, or of God?" (Galatians 1:10)

"Come to me... and you will find rest for your souls." (Matthew 11:28–30)

"We are not trying to please people but God, who tests our hearts." (1 Thessalonians 2:4)

Common Symptoms:

- Chronic people-pleasing or approval addiction
- Deep fear of disappointing others or being exposed as "not enough"
- Identity confusion from constantly adapting to others
- Exhaustion from over-performing at work, church, or home
- Spiritual shallowness from being too "on" to ever be real

Real-Life Example:

Talley is the one everyone calls when they need something: advice, help, money, a last-minute rescue. She's poised, polished, reliable. At work, she's admired for her sharp instincts and emotional intelligence. People say she's a natural people person. But the truth is, she's neither extroverted nor relaxed—she's just highly trained.

Talley's childhood home was a minefield.

The emotional weather could change without warning, and no one ever knew which version of her parents they'd get. Disownment was a regular threat. So, from an early age, Talley developed a skill set: anticipate moods, meet unspoken needs, perform the right version of herself to stay safe. The attention she gives others may feel flattering, but it's not born of connection. It's survival.

Those instincts served her well in adulthood. She excelled professionally, spotting opportunities and reading rooms better than most. She earned enough to support herself and her relatives, who weren't doing as well. That dynamic came with a hidden price: she could give, but she couldn't receive. She wouldn't even know how. To need help would lower her score on the invisible scoreboard in her mind—a score she's been keeping since childhood to measure her worth.

As long as she had the lead, she felt safe. It was exhausting.

Her idea of peace? Being alone in a hotel room on a business trip, with zero chance that someone might barge in and ask for something. That's the only time she really relaxes.

No one sees the toll it takes because Talley doesn't let anyone close enough to see her unmasked. She doesn't even know who she is without the performance.

The Performer has robbed her of rest, identity, and true intimacy. Part of her fears that if she stops the act, there might be no one underneath it.

Solutions and Declarations:

1. **"I am not what I do — I am who God says I am."**
   "See what great love the Father has lavished on us, that we should be called children of God! And that is what we are!" (1 John 3:1)

2. **"I renounce the lie that I must earn love. I receive the gift of grace."**
   "For it is by grace you have been saved, through faith—and this is not from yourselves, it is the gift of God—not by works, so that no one can boast." (Ephesians 2:8–9)

3. **"My worth is not found in approval, but in identity."**
   "Am I now trying to win the approval of human beings, or of God? Or am I trying to please people? If I were still trying to please people, I would not be a servant of Christ." (Galatians 1:10)

Turn to Chapter 9 Prayer Index and go to:
Prayer 9: General Prayer for Pride of Life
Prayer 14: Deliverance from Generational & Family Spirits
Supplemental Prayers: 25, 28, 31, 34

Cross References:

- **The Orphan** – Uses performance to secure love and belonging, fearing that without achievement, they are invisible.
- **The Broken Mirror** – Masks deep-rooted unworthiness with constant overachievement and perfectionism.
- **The Rejector** – Convinces the person that their true self isn't acceptable, so they must become whatever others want.

- **The Idolator** – Elevates image, success, or status as a false source of worth, chasing admiration instead of identity.
- **The Guard** – Fuels the fear that failure will lead to rejection, making the stakes of every effort feel life-or-death.

Assigned Roles in Dysfunctional Families

Spiritual Assignments Hiding in Psychological Labels

In many homes, children are assigned roles that serve the emotional or narcissistic needs of the adults in charge. These roles may seem psychological, but they carry spiritual weight. Demons exploit dysfunction by locking individuals into roles that shape how they see themselves, relate to others, and receive love — often for life.

These are not "types" of people. They are assignments, often imposed through trauma, favoritism, silence, or survival. Moreover, the spirits behind them know exactly what they're doing.

These are the generational and cultural demons: spirits that root themselves in families, cultural expectations, and inherited patterns. They operate subtly, often camouflaged as "just the way we are" or "how I was raised."

These spirits hide behind personalities, family values, cultural norms, and even love, but their true fruit is control, division, performance, favoritism, and rejection. Left unchallenged, they reproduce across generations, assigning the same roles and strongholds to children and grandchildren, like a script no one remembers agreeing to.

These roles include:

- **The Golden Child** – Idolized to uphold the family's image, pressured to be perfect. The Golden Child appears favored but is trapped in pressure. They're not seen — they're *used*. Their "goodness" becomes a mask, and their fall is often private and devastating.
- **Biblical Parallel:** Joseph *(Genesis 37)* — His father's favoritism incited division and hatred.

- **The Black Sheep** – Blamed, punished, or cast out to preserve the illusion of harmony. The Black Sheep may actually be the most spiritually gifted — that's why they're targeted. This role distorts identity, drives rebellion or despair, and creates spiritual exhaustion from fighting to be seen.
- **Biblical Parallel:** David *(1 Samuel 16)* — Left out by his own family when greatness was at the door.
- **The Truth Teller** – Punished for exposing hidden dysfunction, often isolated for seeing too clearly. The Truth Teller often becomes the outcast or martyr. They're seen as "the problem" when in fact, they are often the beginning of healing. The enemy tries to silence them early, before they can lead others out.
- **Biblical Parallel:** Jeremiah, Stephen, and Jesus Himself — each rejected for exposing uncomfortable truth.

The Golden Child

Core Torment & Lie: Pride, Idolatry & Control

"You can do no wrong."

Gifts Under Attack:

- **Authenticity** – The Golden Child creates a false self to maintain approval, making it unsafe to be real, flawed, or vulnerable. *("The Lord detests lying lips, but he delights in people who are trustworthy." – Proverbs 12:22)*
- **Humility** – It nurtures superiority or perfectionism, making you believe you're only valuable when you're outperforming others.
- *("God opposes the proud but gives grace to the humble." – James 4:6)*
- **Intimacy** – It keeps relationships shallow or performative, since true closeness requires imperfection. *("Confess your sins to one another and pray for each other so that you may be healed." – James 5:16)*
- **Identity in Christ** – It attaches worth to achievement and image rather than being rooted in sonship and grace. *("See what great*

love the Father has lavished on us, that we should be called children of God!" – 1 John 3:1)

- **Grace** – It blocks the ability to receive unearned love, making self-sufficiency feel safer than surrender. *("By grace you have been saved through faith... not by works, so that no one can boast." – Ephesians 2:8–9)*

The Golden Child appears favored, but they are used, not loved. Chosen as the "perfect one" in a dysfunctional family system, they are placed on a pedestal to uphold the family's image. The praise they receive is conditional, and their identity becomes fused with performance. Over time, this creates a false self rooted in pride, pressure, and unrelenting fear of failure. Their "goodness" becomes a prison. Even as adults, Golden Children often become high achievers, moral authorities, or religious leaders, but struggle deeply with burnout, self-righteousness, and hidden shame.

Beneath their polished surface lies an untended soul crying out to be known without the mask.

Idolatry is elevating anything above God in your heart. The Golden Child exalts perfection, performance, approval, and image above God's grace, truth, and definition of worth.

They begin to worship the identity they've been assigned: *"the good one," "the successful one," "the example,"* instead of the identity given by Christ. *"They exchanged the truth of God for a lie, and worshiped and served created things rather than the Creator..."* (Romans 1:25)

The Golden Child can appear obedient, successful, even religious, but it's fueled by fear and idolatry, not freedom in Christ. Their need to maintain "perfection" becomes their altar. This is the serious danger.

This is why it's not just pride and control, but idolatry that locks them into a spiritual trap.

Scripture References:

Joseph is favored by his father, inciting family division. (Genesis 37)

*"Pride goes before destruction, a haughty
spirit before a fall." (Proverbs 16:18)*

"Everything they do is done for people to see..." (Matthew 23:5)

Common Symptoms:

- Deep identity confusion when performance is no longer praised
- Chronic fear of failure or moral collapse
- Over-identification with status, morality, or perfection
- Disdain for those who threaten the family's image
- Secret inner exhaustion from constantly performing

Real-Life Example:

Max was the oldest of three, and from a young age, he carried the hopes and the image of his entire family. It all began the winter he knocked on his neighbor's door and offered to shovel the walkway for a few bucks. What he didn't know was that the man behind the door was a successful software entrepreneur. Impressed by Max's hustle and maturity, the man offered him a summer internship. That single moment changed everything.

By the time Max finished college, he had a full-time job waiting for him. Within a few years, he was promoted to Vice President of Product Development and was being groomed to take over the company when the founder retired. He had earned it—every bit of it. But back at home, Max's success had become the family's identity.

Every birthday, barbecue, and holiday dinner turned into a celebration of *their* golden boy, but not in a way that honored Max. Instead, his parents used his accomplishments as a mirror to reflect their own greatness—taking subtle credit for every win. When neighbors complimented Max's achievements but raised an eyebrow at how much his parents bragged, Max always defended them: *"If they hadn't given us such a good life, I wouldn't have even lived in this neighborhood. They taught me how to work hard. I owe everything to them."*

It sounded humble, but it wasn't the full truth.

Behind the scenes, his siblings told a different story. His younger brother, the black sheep, had rejected the family script altogether—traveling with an indie band, broke, couch-surfing, and the constant subject of family ridicule. His middle sister cut ties almost completely. She went off to college and rarely came back. When she did visit, she refused to play along. She'd call out the favoritism, the manipulation, the way Max was being used to prop up a family image. Eventually, the invitations stopped coming.

Max stayed. He stayed because his success had become part of the family's emotional economy. Any other dream he might have—starting his own business, moving away, doing something less "impressive"—would feel like betrayal.

He told himself he loved his job, and maybe he did. But the truth is, he never asked what *he* wanted. He was too afraid of what it might cost.

The Golden Child may wear the crown, but it's heavy and it's often welded on with guilt, obligation, and the unspoken warning: *"Don't ruin this for us."*

Solutions & Declarations:

1. **"I am not my performance—I am God's child, loved without conditions."**
   "But God demonstrates His own love for us in this: While we were still sinners, Christ died for us." (Romans 5:8)

2. **"I renounce the idol of perfection and receive the gift of grace."**
   "My grace is sufficient for you, for my power is made perfect in weakness." Therefore, I will boast all the more gladly about my weaknesses, so that Christ's power may rest on me." (2 Corinthians 12:9)

3. **"I don't have to hold everything together. God is the source of my worth."**
   "He is before all things, and in Him all things hold together." (Colossians 1:17)

Turn to Chapter 9 Prayer Index and go to:

Prayer 9: General Prayer for Pride of Life

Prayer 14: Deliverance from Generational & Family Spirits

Supplemental Prayer: 25, 26, 28

Cross-References:

- **The Performer** – Reinforces the need to maintain love and approval through achievement and perfection.
- **The Monarch** – Encourages internalized superiority or control, especially when the child is idealized above others.
- **The Idolator** – Shifts identity toward titles, success, or admiration rather than God's purpose and grace.
- **The Rejector** – Fuels anxiety around failure, suggesting that being anything less than exceptional will lead to abandonment.
- **The Critic** – Uses judgment and comparison to protect the fragile identity built on praise and external validation

The Black Sheep

Core Torment & Lie: Rejection, Condemnation & Isolation

"You're the problem."

Gifts Under Attack:

- **Identity** – The Black Sheep distorts how you see yourself, making you internalize blame and shame as who you are—not what you've experienced. *("Therefore, if anyone is in Christ, the new creation has come..." – 2 Corinthians 5:17)*
- **Belonging** – It convinces you that you're fundamentally different or unlovable, cutting you off from healthy connection. *("You are no longer foreigners and strangers, but fellow citizens with God's people..." – Ephesians 2:19)*
- **Authority** – It keeps you from walking in your spiritual power by constantly second-guessing your worth and right to lead. *("See, I*

have given you authority... to overcome all the power of the enemy."
– Luke 10:19)

- **Voice** – It silences you with shame, making you believe your perspective is unwelcome or unnecessary. *("Open your mouth for the mute, for the rights of all who are destitute." – Proverbs 31:8)*
- **Prophetic Calling** – It twists your set-apartness into alienation, making you doubt that your difference was God-ordained. *("Before I formed you in the womb, I knew you... I appointed you as a prophet to the nations." – Jeremiah 1:5)*

The Black Sheep is the family scapegoat, blamed for everything that goes wrong, excluded from praise, and punished for disrupting the illusion of harmony. While their siblings are praised for compliance, the Black Sheep is cast out for authenticity, emotion, or truth. This is a spiritual assignment. The enemy marks them because of what they carry. Often the most sensitive, intuitive, or spiritually gifted child, the Black Sheep is spiritually targeted through the family system.

This role breeds rebellion, bitterness, despair, or over-compensation. Some fight for visibility. Others disappear. The torment is the same: being unloved for who they truly are.

Scripture References:

David is left out by his family when the prophet comes. *(1 Samuel 16)*

"He was despised and rejected by men..." (Isaiah 53:3)

"Though my father and mother forsake me, the Lord will receive me." (Psalm 27:10)

Common Symptoms:

- Feeling emotionally unsafe in family systems
- Repeatedly accused or misunderstood, even without cause
- Rebellion or withdrawal after prolonged rejection
- Shame over emotional expression or confrontation
- Unshakeable sense of "I don't belong"

Real-Life Example:

Joey always felt like the only sane one in the house, which made him feel insane. His siblings went along with their parents' bizarre, oppressive rules without protest. No using the bathroom after dark. Showers limited to 120 seconds. No doors on any bedroom, ever. They called it "order," but Joey saw it for what it was: control. He could stomach being the family's unpaid labor force—mowing lawns, fixing appliances, raising the younger kids—but it was the emotional climate that broke him down. There was no warmth, only venom. His parents barked commands and handed out punishments that came without warning and made no sense.

What hurt most was the isolation. Whenever he tried to speak up, to name what was happening, his parents called him rebellious, ungrateful, dramatic. His siblings didn't defend him. Some even joined in—distancing themselves so they wouldn't get punished too. Joey was blamed for "disrupting the peace," for "making everything harder," simply because he wouldn't lie about how bad it really was. Family gatherings became landmines. He was ignored, accused of holding grudges, or guilt-tripped for not "forgiving and forgetting" like everyone else claimed to have done.

Eventually, he stopped speaking, but the silence didn't bring peace, only shame. Was he the problem? Was he just too sensitive? Too angry? Too much?

No. Deep down, he knew the truth. He wasn't broken. He was awake. That's why they tried to break him.

Solutions & Declarations:

1. **"I am not rejected—I am chosen by God."**
   "You did not choose Me, but I chose you and appointed you so that you might go and bear fruit—fruit that will last." (John 15:16)

2. **"I break the assignment of scapegoating and receive my true identity."**
   "To all who did receive Him, to those who believed in His name, He gave the right to become children of God." (John 1:12)

3. **"The voice that called me 'too much' was never God's."**

   "The Lord your God is with you, the Mighty Warrior who saves. He will take great delight in you; in His love He will no longer rebuke you but will rejoice over you with singing." (Zephaniah 3:17)

Turn to Chapter 9 Prayer Index and go to:

Prayer 9: General Prayer for Pride of Life

Prayer 14: Deliverance from Generational & Family Spirits

Supplemental Prayer: 25, 26, 28, 32, 33, 34

Cross-References:

- **The Orphan** – Feeds the sense of being unloved and uncared for, even within one's own home.
- **The Rejector** – Reinforces the belief that you'll never be accepted, no matter what you do.
- **The Abyss** – Opens when the weight of exclusion and emotional neglect turns inward.
- **The Critic** – Often speaks through family members, twisting everything into blame and shame.
- **The Chainkeeper** – Makes it nearly impossible to forgive those who should have protected you.

The Truth Teller

Core Torment & Lie: Isolation, Rejection & Spiritual Backlash

"Telling the truth ruins everything."

Gifts Under Attack:

- **Prophetic Vision** – The Truth Teller sees what others miss, but this gift is attacked with fear of backlash or being labeled divisive. *("Son of man, I have made you a watchman... so hear the word I speak and give them warning from me." – Ezekiel 3:17)*

- **Discernment** – It causes you to question your insight, making you doubt what the Holy Spirit has revealed to you. *("But solid food is for the mature, who by constant use have trained themselves to distinguish good from evil." – Hebrews 5:14)*
- **Boldness** – It makes you timid about speaking up, especially when truth threatens comfort or status quo. *("Pray... that whenever I speak, words may be given me so that I will fearlessly make known the mystery of the gospel." – Ephesians 6:19)*
- **Justice** – It silences your call to confront wrongdoing, replacing righteous indignation with fear of conflict. *("Speak up and judge fairly; defend the rights of the poor and needy." – Proverbs 31:9)*

The Truth Teller sees what others pretend not to. Assigned this role in dysfunctional families, they are often the first to name abuse, hypocrisy, or lies and are punished for it. Rather than being protected, they are labeled "troublemakers," "too sensitive," or "rebellious." This is spiritual retaliation. The enemy uses the family's dysfunction to isolate the one who could expose it.

Truth Tellers are often the first to leave toxic systems and the first to be blamed for their collapse. Make no mistake: their presence threatens the demonic strongholds that others have made peace with. That's why they're silenced early.

Scripture References:

"The word of the Lord has brought me insult and reproach all day long." (Jeremiah 20:8)

Stephen speaks truth and is stoned for it. (Acts 7:54–59)

"A prophet is not without honor except in his own hometown..." (Matthew 13:57)

Common Symptoms:

- Being labeled the "difficult" one for exposing dysfunction
- Frequent relational fallout after telling the truth
- Internalized guilt for the discomfort of others

- Feeling spiritually attacked or alone after confrontation
- Suppressing gifts to keep peace

Real-Life Example:

Nichola always had an eye for what was really going on, and the courage to say it out loud. In school, the other kids admired the way she spoke up respectfully but directly when something wasn't right. She wasn't trying to rebel or get attention. She simply couldn't stand seeing everyone punished because a few kids couldn't behave. *Why were the rest of them being held hostage?* she'd ask. Even the troublemakers would quiet down when Nichola spoke. She had that rare authority that truth gives: calm, clear, undeniable.

At home, it was the same. She would ask her parents why they were still married if all they did was fight and ignore each other. Why live this way and make everyone else miserable, too? She wasn't trying to be disrespectful; she genuinely wanted answers. But the truth made people squirm. It was easier to label her difficult than to face what she was exposing.

At church, she was told to be quiet. At home, she was told she was stirring up drama. In friendships, people praised her honesty until it touched their own blind spots. Slowly, Nichola learned that most people don't really want the truth. They want comfort, even if it's a lie. So, she began to silence herself.

The silence didn't bring peace, it brought dissonance. She could still feel the tension when something was off and the unease when someone was pretending. Her "discomfort" was discernment. Her boldness was a holy gift that made her a target in the spiritual realm.

The Truth Teller will be actively silenced by the enemy as long as possible.

Solutions & Declarations:

1. **"I am not the problem—God gave me eyes to see."**
   "The spiritual person judges all things but is himself to be judged by no one. For who has understood the mind of the Lord so as

to instruct him? But we have the mind of Christ." (1 Corinthians 2:15–16)

2. **"I will speak truth in love, no matter the cost."**
"Instead, speaking the truth in love, we will grow to become in every respect the mature body of Him who is the head, that is, Christ." (Ephesians 4:15)

3. **"My calling is not to please man, but to honor God."**
"For am I now seeking the approval of man, or of God? Or am I trying to please man? If I were still trying to please man, I would not be a servant of Christ." (Galatians 1:10)

Turn to Chapter 9 Prayer Index and go to:
Prayer 9: General Prayer for Pride of Life
Prayer 14: Deliverance from Generational & Family Spirits
Supplemental Prayers: 26, 28, 31, 34

Cross-References:

- **The Guard** – Instills fear of backlash, making honesty feel dangerous instead of brave.
- **The Coward** – Tempts the Truth Teller to stay silent rather than risk confrontation.
- **The Critic** – Distorts discernment, accusing the truth-teller of being judgmental or harsh.
- **The Doubter** – Creeps in when repeated rejection makes them question if they're just imagining things.
- **The Ghoster** – Pushes the Truth Teller to withdraw completely, avoiding conflict by disappearing.

The Overbearing Matriarch

Core Torment & Lie: Control, Emasculation & Pride Disguised as Protection

"Only I know best."

Gifts Under Attack:

- **Divine Order** – The Overbearing Matriarch disrupts God's design for family and leadership, placing herself at the center instead of Christ. *("But I want you to understand that the head of every man is Christ, the head of a wife is her husband..." – 1 Corinthians 11:3)*
- **Trust** – It refuses to release control, assuming that others—especially men—will fail or disappoint. *("Trust in the Lord with all your heart and lean not on your own understanding." – Proverbs 3:5)*
- **Godly Partnership** – It undermines unity in marriage or family by overpowering rather than co-laboring. *("Two are better than one... if either of them falls, one can help the other up." – Ecclesiastes 4:9–10)*
- **Generational Blessing** – It reproduces dysfunction by modeling dominance instead of discipleship, creating cycles of fear and resentment. *("The righteous who walks in his integrity—blessed are his children after him!" – Proverbs 20:7)*

This spirit rules through fear, guilt, and emotional dominance. Under the appearance of nurturing or "holding the family together," The Overbearing Matriarch becomes the spiritual head of the home even when men are present. She may be the grandmother, the mother, or the elder daughter, but her authority is out of alignment. What looks like strength is often spiritual pride: control masked as care. This demon emasculates sons, overrides fathers, and teaches daughters that dominance is love. Its influence breaks homes, undermines godly authority, and replaces biblical order with matriarchal rule.

This stronghold often enters through trauma, widowhood, fatherlessness, or generational patterns where men have historically been passive, absent, or dishonored.

Scripture References:

"You tolerate that woman Jezebel..."(Revelation 2:20)

"She is loud and defiant..."(Proverbs 7:11)

"Wives, submit to your husbands as to the Lord..."(Ephesians 5:22–24)

Common Symptoms:

- Sons who are indecisive, passive, or fearful of leading
- Daughters who dominate relationships but long for safety
- No strong male figures in the family line
- Family members who fear upsetting "Mama" more than disobeying God
- Generational legacy of resentment, silent rebellion, and male withdrawal

Real-Life Example:

In Keisha's family, the women ruled everything. Her grandmother was called "the queen," her mother "the boss," and it was understood that Keisha would one day take her place in that matriarchal throne. The men were voiceless, powerless and infantilized.

Every son in the family handed over his paycheck to the grandmother, who controlled the budget like a warden, allocating what the men could spend and when. None of them owned anything—not even the home they lived in. The deed was in the grandmother's name. The will would pass everything to Keisha's mother. The men were allowed to live there, but only if they followed orders. Any resistance meant exile. Even the adult sons had their rooms searched for "contraband" like cigarettes, as though they were teenagers sneaking out after curfew.

Keisha never met her father. He was spoken of like a ghost story, a cautionary tale about how no man could be trusted. The women kept the family polished and presentable, showing up to church dressed in perfect order. Her grandmother and mother led the procession proudly to the front pew. The men trailed behind, mute and diminished.

When Keisha began dating, she didn't know how to be in partnership, only power struggle. Every man she chose became either a project to fix or a pawn to control. She wanted love but panicked at the thought of submission. Authority had only ever looked like domination. Control was what had been modeled. Softness, safety, and mutuality were foreign concepts.

She came from a line of strong women, but it wasn't just strength. It was spiritual distortion. The Overbearing Matriarch isn't just a personality type. It's an ancient principality—one that silences godly men and crowns wounded women in their place.

Solutions & Declarations:

1. **"God's order is not oppression. I release control and receive His covering."**
   "Wives, submit yourselves to your own husbands as you do to the Lord. For the husband is the head of the wife as Christ is the head of the church." (Ephesians 5:22–23)

2. **"I break agreement with the lie that no man can be trusted or lead."**
   "Trust in the Lord with all your heart and lean not on your own understanding; in all your ways submit to Him, and He will make your paths straight." (Proverbs 3:5–6)

3. **"I forgive the women who taught control as love. I choose truth."**
   "Then you will know the truth, and the truth will set you free." (John 8:32)

Turn to Chapter 9 Prayer Index and go to:
Prayer 9: General Prayer for Pride of Life
Prayer 14: Deliverance from Generational & Family Spirits
Supplemental Prayers: 19, 28, 30

Cross-References:

- **Jezebel** – Operates through domination and control, presenting a counterfeit version of godly leadership.
- **The Puppeteer** – Uses emotional manipulation to orchestrate outcomes and keep others dependent.
- **The Idolator** – Elevates the matriarch to an untouchable pedestal, making family loyalty a form of worship.
- **The Guard** – Instills fear of vulnerability, teaching that surrender is weakness rather than trust.
- **The Weak Father** – Enables the imbalance through silence, absence, or passive complicity.

The Meddling Mother-in-Law

Core Torment & Lie: Manipulation, Control & Boundary Violation

"They still belong to me."

Gifts Under Attack:

- **Marital Unity** – The Meddling Mother-in-Law drives wedges between spouses by inserting herself into decisions, affections, and loyalties. *("Therefore, a man shall leave his father and his mother and hold fast to his wife..." – Genesis 2:24)*
- **Autonomy** – It undermines a couple's ability to form their own household by keeping emotional or financial control tethered to the parent. *("You were bought at a price; do not become slaves of human beings." – 1 Corinthians 7:23)*
- **Honor Without Idolatry** – It confuses biblical honor with submission to manipulation, turning respect into bondage. *("Honor your father and your mother..." – Exodus 20:12; not "obey them forever")*
- **Emotional Boundaries** – It erodes healthy separation by using guilt, obligation, or passive aggression to maintain influence. *("Let*

what you say be simply 'Yes' or 'No'; anything more comes from evil." – Matthew 5:37)

- **Spiritual Priorities** – It subtly positions family above God's order, distorting allegiance and spiritual headship. *("Whoever loves father or mother more than me is not worthy of me..." – Matthew 10:37)*

This demon disrupts the sacred bond of marriage by refusing to let go. Operating through well-meaning but controlling mothers (often of sons), it uses guilt, favoritism, and passive aggression to maintain emotional power long after children have left home. The Meddling Mother-in-Law inserts herself into decisions, undermines spouses, and creates division, then claims innocence.

Though disguised as care or concern, this is a breach of biblical order. It fosters unholy allegiance, fractures generational trust, and delays spiritual maturity in the adult child.

Scripture References:

"A man shall leave his father and mother and be joined to his wife..." (Genesis 2:24)

"A house divided against itself cannot stand." (Mark 3:25)

"Honor your father and mother" (but not above God's order) (Exodus 20:12)

Common Symptoms:

- Spouse feels like a third wheel in their own marriage
- Adult child afraid to set boundaries or say "no"
- Frequent loyalty conflicts between partner and parent
- Constant guilt or shame tied to perceived disloyalty
- Family secrets, triangulation, or "you've changed" accusations

Real-Life Example:

Laci felt like she'd married into a triangle. From the start, Aaron's mother Susan made herself a fixture in their lives. She showed up uninvited, let herself into their home while they were at work, rearranged furniture, and threw away food from their fridge without asking. She called relentlessly until Aaron picked up, and if he didn't, she'd appear on their doorstep—no warning, no boundaries.

When Laci went into labor with their first child, Susan demanded to be in the delivery room, even though only Laci's mother was invited. When she was told no, she caused a scene in the hallway, accusing Laci of "reigniting old trauma" about Aaron's premature birth, as if the birth of Laci's child was somehow about Susan. Aaron didn't see the issue. He brushed it off, leaving Laci feeling alone in what should've been one of the most sacred moments of her life.

That was the turning point. The quiet resentment Laci had been swallowing began to harden. When Susan began giving Laci advice on how to "treat her son better," something inside her snapped. It was clear: there were three people in this marriage, and Susan had no intention of letting go. Laci finally drew the line and told Aaron he had to choose, but deep down, she already knew he'd made his choice a long time ago.

Aaron thought Laci was trying to divide the family. but it wasn't Laci who fractured the bond. It was the spirit of The Meddling Mother-in-Law in Susan, who did its work well and Aaron let it happen.

Solutions & Declarations:

1. **"I honor my parents, but I cleave to my spouse. God's order is clear."**
   "Therefore a man shall leave his father and his mother and hold fast to his wife, and they shall become one flesh." (Genesis 2:24)

2. **"I break every ungodly soul tie, guilt bond, and emotional leash."**
   "Am I now trying to win the approval of human beings, or of God? Or am I trying to please people? If I were still trying to please people, I would not be a servant of Christ." (Galatians 1:10)

3. **"My marriage is protected. My loyalty is first to God, then to my covenant."**

   "So they are no longer two, but one flesh. Therefore, what God has joined together, let no one separate." (Matthew 19:6)

Turn to Chapter 9 Prayer Index and go to:

Prayer 9: General Prayer for Pride of Life

Prayer 14: Deliverance from Generational & Family Spirits

Supplemental Prayers: 19, 28, 30

Cross-References:

- **The Severer** – Works to dismantle godly connection between spouses by inserting division at the root.
- **Jezebel** – Uses veiled manipulation disguised as concern to maintain control and influence.
- **The Guard** – Causes fear of confrontation, making the spouse passive and conflict-avoidant.
- **The Idolator** – Elevates family ties above God's design for marriage, disguising it as loyalty.
- **The Withholding Father** – His emotional or spiritual absence enables the mother to dominate unchecked.

The Withholding Father

Core Torment & Lie: Absence, Conditional Love & Emotional Starvation

"Earn my approval."

Gifts Under Attack:

- **Identity** – The Withholding Father creates a performance-based self-image, making you earn value instead of receiving it as a child of God. (*"This is my Son, whom I love; with him I am well pleased."* – *Matthew 3:17)*

- **Security** – It destabilizes your inner world by making love feel unpredictable, fragile, or dependent on success. *("The Lord is my rock, my fortress and my deliverer... in him I take refuge." – Psalm 18:2)*
- **Confidence** – It instills a deep fear of failure and rejection, breeding anxiety in relationships and assignments. *("For the Spirit God gave us does not make us timid, but gives us power, love and self-discipline." – 2 Timothy 1:7)*
- **Sonship** – It blocks the ability to receive freely from the Father, keeping you in a slave mindset of striving and shame. *("You are no longer a slave, but God's child; and since you are his child, God has made you also an heir." – Galatians 4:7)*
- **Capacity for Intimacy** – It limits emotional depth by teaching you that vulnerability is unsafe or never enough. *("We love because he first loved us." – 1 John 4:19)*

The Withholding Father is often silent, as opposed to being violent or overt. This spirit operates through fathers who are physically present but emotionally unavailable, distant, or spiritually disengaged. Whether through perfectionism, pride, or their own unhealed wounds, these men fail to offer what children need most: affirmation, tenderness, and safe identity.

Instead of being nurtured, children of The Withholding Father are left striving for approval that never comes. Sons grow up unsure of their manhood, driven by success but never satisfied. Daughters swing between craving male validation or rejecting men entirely. This is a defining wound. It distorts how we see God, how we love others, and how we value ourselves. The vacuum left behind becomes a landing pad for demons like The Orphan, The Performer, and The Idolator.

Scripture References:

"This is my beloved Son, in whom I am well pleased." (Matthew 3:17)

"Fathers, do not exasperate your children..." (Ephesians 6:4)

"A good man leaves an inheritance to his
children's children..." (Proverbs 13:22)

Common Symptoms:

- Inability to recall specific moments of emotional warmth from their father
- High-achieving adults who fall apart when affirmation is withdrawn
- Fear of failure linked to fear of abandonment
- Deep discomfort in receiving love, especially from God
- Pattern of relationships where love must be earned or proven

Real-Life Example:

Gina could count on one hand the moments her father acknowledged her—*really* acknowledged her. After winning the national debate championship, he gave a curt "Good job." On prom night, when she descended the stairs in her dress, he smirked—not warmly, but in a way she desperately hoped was approval. Then he turned away.

That was the pattern. Distant. Dry. Unimpressed.

One day, she tried to name it. "It feels like my emotional bank account starts at zero with you every day," she said flatly. "Like I have to earn your interest from scratch."

He didn't argue. He just nodded. "That's exactly right."

Gina carried that mindset into every relationship. Was this person worth the effort? Did she want to spend her emotional energy on someone who'd likely never deposit anything back? Usually, the answer was no. But when someone who carried the spirit of The Withholding Father crossed her path—same aloofness, same cold charm—she became obsessed. Professors, mentors, bosses. Men who held their praise like a trophy. She would break herself to win their approval, only to realize, far too late, that she was being used.

They were just like her father: emotionally unavailable, withholding, and quietly narcissistic because they were all animated by the same spirit.

Gina didn't struggle to love others. She struggled to believe she was worth loving in return. The Withholding Father taught her that love was earned through performance. It haunted her into adulthood until she realized that God is nothing like her earthly father. His love is not distant. It's not earned. It's given freely.

Solutions & Declarations:

1. **"I renounce the lie that I must earn love."**
   "But God shows his love for us in that while we were still sinners, Christ died for us." (Romans 5:8)

2. **"God is not like my earthly father—He affirms me freely and completely."**
   "This is my beloved Son, in whom I am well pleased." (Matthew 3:17)

3. **"I forgive my father for the words he never said and the love he didn't give."**
   "Be kind to one another, tenderhearted, forgiving one another, as God in Christ forgave you." (Ephesians 4:32)

Turn to Chapter 9 Prayer Index and go to:
Prayer 9: General Prayer for Pride of Life
Prayer 14: Deliverance from Generational & Family Spirits
Supplemental Prayers: 20, 21, 23, 26, 28, 29, 32, 33, 34

Cross-References:

- **The Orphan** – Fuels the deep ache of emotional abandonment and fatherlessness, even when the father is physically present.
- **The Guard** – Builds protective walls to avoid further rejection, making vulnerability feel unsafe.

- **The Broken Mirror** – Forms a distorted self-image in the silence of withheld affirmation.
- **The Performer** – Teaches that love must be earned through achievement and excellence.
- **The Idolator** – Projects father wounds onto God or other authority figures, seeking approval in all the wrong places.
- **The Narcissist** – Echoes the cold detachment and self-centeredness of the father, drawing the wounded child into toxic cycles.
- **The Critic** – Reinforces the internalized voice of the father, replaying judgment even in moments of success.

The Weak Father

Core Torment & Lie: Passivity, Abdication of Responsibility & Fear of Failure

"I won't lead."

Gifts Under Attack:

- **Authority** – The Weak Father surrenders his God-given role, creating a vacuum where spiritual leadership should stand. *("Be watchful, stand firm in the faith, act like men, be strong." – 1 Corinthians 16:13)*
- **Courage** – It paralyzes action through fear of getting it wrong, silencing boldness and moral conviction. *("Have I not commanded you? Be strong and courageous... For the Lord your God will be with you wherever you go." – Joshua 1:9)*
- **Spiritual Headship** – It disrupts the divine order of the home by placing emotional or spiritual leadership on the mother or children. *("For the husband is the head of the wife as Christ is the head of the church..." – Ephesians 5:23)*
- **Protection** – It leaves the family vulnerable to spiritual and emotional attack due to lack of covering. *("The prudent see danger*

and take refuge, but the simple keep going and pay the penalty." – Proverbs 27:12)

- **Legacy** – It stunts generational strength, modeling avoidance rather than courage, leaving children unsure of what godly leadership looks like. *("A good man leaves an inheritance to his children..." – Proverbs 13:22)*

The Weak Father is a spirit that works through men who abandon spiritual leadership out of fear, shame, trauma, or confusion. They avoid hard conversations, defer to their wives, and retreat into comfort zones. While they may appear gentle or non-threatening, their passivity leaves the family uncovered, unanchored, and unguarded.

Instead of cultivating safety and direction, they leave their wives overburdened and their children spiritually orphaned—even if everyone still lives under the same roof. This demon thrives in men who were never taught to lead and who believe falsely that peacekeeping is the same as leadership. However, a passive man is not a harmless man. In the absence of his voice, protection, and covering, other spirits rise up, especially Jezebel, The Overbearing Matriarch, and The Severer.

Scripture References:

"Act like men; be strong." (1 Corinthians 16:13)

"The husband is the head of the wife, as Christ is the head of the church." (Ephesians 5:23)

"He who does not provide for his own household has denied the faith..." (1 Timothy 5:8)

Common Symptoms:

- Men who avoid confrontation or decisions at all costs
- Wives who lead not by design, but because there's no choice
- Children who lack boundaries, guidance, or a sense of safety
- Emotionally disconnected fathers who default to hobbies or work
- Generational patterns of men shrinking back when leadership is required

Real-Life Example:

Nate grew up barely knowing his father. Richard left their family when Nate was still young, pulled away by his wife's best friend, a woman with two daughters of her own. He remarried quickly and never looked back. His new wife ran the show, loud and domineering, and her daughters followed suit. Richard faded into the background and stayed there.

Richard gave them everything—money, time, obedience—but never once stood up for himself. He raised those girls like they were his own, let them talk down to him, boss him around, and spend his money freely. Meanwhile, Nate and his mother were left behind, barely a memory.

Years passed. Richard's second wife eventually landed in a nursing home, and the stepdaughters moved away, only calling when they needed money. One of them had maxed out his credit card behind his back, leaving him over $100,000 in debt. When their mother died, they came back—not to mourn, but to take. They pillaged the house for valuables, not caring whether the items belonged to their mother, to Richard, or to the family he abandoned.

Neighbors noticed Richard was deteriorating and needed help. Word reached Nate's mother, who hadn't heard from Richard in decades. She and Nate showed up. They got him the care he needed, placed him in a respectful facility, organized his finances, and gave him a second chance at dignity.

But the pattern repeated.

The stepdaughters returned, asking for more money—the same money Richard now needed to survive. And he gave it. He even let them take the house.

Nate called his father, begging him to stop. "She's gone! You're free! Why are you still letting them ruin your life?" Richard would murmur "I know, I know," and then do nothing. The housekeeper he hired was using his car and debit card to buy groceries for herself. Everyone saw what was happening. Richard did nothing.

His niceness turned into surrender. His passivity became a prison, and the people he once abandoned were now the only ones willing to stand by him.

The Weak Father can look kind, polite, and agreeable. Under the surface, though, he refuses to lead, protect, and stand. In his silence, the people who need him most are left unshielded, and the wrong ones rise to power.

Solutions & Declarations:

1. **"I step into the role God gave me without fear or shame."**
   "For God gave us a spirit not of fear but of power and love and self-control." (2 Timothy 1:7)

2. **"I break agreement with passive masculinity and silence."**
   "Be watchful, stand firm in the faith, act like men, be strong." (1 Corinthians 16:13)

3. **"I will not confuse peacekeeping with godly leadership."**
   "If anyone does not know how to manage his own household, how will he care for God's church?" (1 Timothy 3:5)

Turn to Chapter 9 Prayer Index and go to:

Prayer 9: General Prayer for Pride of Life
Prayer 14: Deliverance from Generational & Family Spirits
Supplemental Prayers: 26, 29, 34

Cross-References:

- **The Overbearing Matriarch** – Fills the power vacuum when fathers refuse to lead, dominating the family structure in his absence.
- **The Guard** – Encourages avoidance and passivity, rooted in fear of failure or confrontation.
- **The Severer** – Leads children to emotionally disconnect from fathers who are physically present but spiritually and emotionally absent.
- **The Performer** – Emerges in children who strive to earn approval or create stability that the father never provided.

- **The Idolator** – Causes the wife to turn to children, career, or church leadership to fulfill the protective and spiritual role the father neglected.
- **Lazybones** – Promotes apathy and comfort-seeking, whispering that retreat is easier than the burden of responsibility.

The Terrifying Father

Core Torment & Lie: Domination, Intimidation & Punishment-Based Authority

"Obey or suffer."

Gifts Under Attack:

- **Gentleness** – The Terrifying Father teaches that strength equals harshness, suppressing the fruit of tenderness and patience. *("Let your gentleness be evident to all. The Lord is near." – Philippians 4:5)*
- **Mercy** – It replaces compassion with control, making forgiveness seem weak and correction feel like vengeance. *("Be merciful, just as your Father is merciful." – Luke 6:36)*
- **Trust** – It conditions others to obey out of fear, not love, creating fractured relationships built on compliance, not connection. *("There is no fear in love. But perfect love drives out fear..." – 1 John 4:18)*
- **Emotional Safety** – It creates an atmosphere of tension and anxiety, where honesty and vulnerability feel dangerous. *("Fathers, do not provoke your children to anger, but bring them up in the discipline and instruction of the Lord." – Ephesians 6:4)*
- **Right View of God** – It distorts the image of the heavenly Father, making Him seem angry, distant, or impossible to please. *("The Lord is compassionate and gracious, slow to anger, abounding in love." – Psalm 103:8)*

This spirit distorts fatherhood into fear-based control. It masquerades as "discipline" but rules through dread, perfectionism, and emotional volatility. Whether it's raised voices, cold silence, harsh punishments, or rigid expectations, The Terrifying Father convinces children that love must be earned and that failure equals wrath.

Many who grow up under this spirit develop deep father wounds, associating God with punishment instead of mercy. It's common in cultures that praise "strictness" as strength, but the fruit is spiritual distortion, emotional shutdown, and generational trauma. This demon may not always be violent, but it's always oppressive. Often, the children who survive it either become it... or marry it.

Scripture References:

"Fathers, do not provoke your children to wrath..." (Ephesians 6:4)

"There is no fear in love. But perfect love drives out fear..." (1 John 4:18)

*"The Lord is compassionate and gracious,
slow to anger..." (Psalm 103:8)*

Common Symptoms:

- Walking on eggshells in the household
- Children who hide, lie, or people-please to avoid punishment
- Adults who fear vulnerability, failure, or divine judgment
- Cold, emotionally unavailable fathers who call it "tough love"
- Sons who grow up and replicate the same intimidation

Real-Life Example:

Ben grew up in a house where noise of any kind was a liability. His father, Jason, stood 6 foot 7 and was built like a wall of muscle. He carried an atmosphere of constant threat. The house was dead quiet most of the time, not out of peace, but fear. If someone dropped a dish or laughed too loud, the whole house would freeze. Seconds later, they'd hear the stomp of heavy footsteps, the door slam open, and the belt come flying.

Ben's nervous system never settled. He lived in a constant state of high alert, waiting for the next explosion. Sometimes Jason would leap out from nowhere just to start swinging. The beatings were routine, not discipline—just raw, senseless rage.

As the kids got older and less physically vulnerable, the punishments evolved. Jason would strip their rooms bare, leaving only a mattress and clothes. Or he'd force them to walk miles to school in brutal weather, trailing them silently in his car like a predator watching prey. His cruelty was calculated, and his dominance complete. No amount of obedience could calm him. The children had excellent grades. His wife was kind, submissive, and never talked back. Jason always found a reason to erupt anyway.

When the children finally left home, they didn't look back. They pleaded with their mother to leave him. Years later, Jason dropped dead in the kitchen from an aneurysm. No one grieved. His name was never spoken again because even his memory carried fear.

Jason wasn't just a harsh parent; he was a terrorizing force. A bully in the body of a father. The trauma he left behind didn't die with him. It echoed in his children's bodies, long after his footsteps stopped.

Solutions & Declarations:

1. **"God is not like the man who raised me."**
   "The Lord is compassionate and gracious, slow to anger, abounding in love." (Psalm 103:8)

2. **"I break agreement with fear as leadership."**
   "Fathers, do not provoke your children to anger, but bring them up in the discipline and instruction of the Lord." (Ephesians 6:4)

3. **"I choose compassion, humility, and grace in my authority."**
   "Clothe yourselves, all of you, with humility toward one another, for 'God opposes the proud but gives grace to the humble.'" (1 Peter 5:5)

Turn to Chapter 9 Prayer Index and go to:
Prayer 9: General Prayer for Pride of Life
Prayer 14: Deliverance from Generational & Family Spirits
Supplemental Prayers: 26, 29, 34

Cross-References:

- **The Guard** – Builds internal walls to survive judgment, criticism, and emotional landmines.
- **The Abyss** – Opens beneath children forced to suppress all feeling in an atmosphere of fear.
- **The Broken Mirror** – Forms when a child believes their worth is tied to avoiding punishment or earning impossible approval.
- **The Puppeteer** – Uses fear and guilt to manipulate and maintain dominance over others.
- **The Weak Father** – Often the adult child of a tyrant, swinging between passivity and paralysis in the name of "peace."
- **The Bully** – Shares the same spirit of intimidation and dominance, often appearing in both homes and schoolyards.
- **The Inferno** – Burns with unchecked rage, punishing not to correct but to release fury.
- **The Glacier** – Sometimes follows the Terrifying Father's reign, creating emotional freeze in children who learn that feeling anything is dangerous.

The Neglectful Parent
Core Torment & Lie: Emotional Abandonment, Apathy & Misprioritized Affection
"You're on your own."

Gifts Under Attack:

- **Security** – The Neglectful Parent creates instability in the heart, leaving children to self-soothe and fend for themselves emotionally. *("The eternal God is your refuge, and underneath are the everlasting arms." – Deuteronomy 33:27)*
- **Worth** – It sends the message that you are not worthy of time, attention, or care, distorting your sense of value. *("Are not five*

sparrows sold for two pennies? Yet not one of them is forgotten by God... you are worth more than many sparrows." – Luke 12:6–7)

- **Trust** – It damages the foundation of safe attachment, making it difficult to rely on others or God. *("Trust in the Lord with all your heart and lean not on your own understanding." – Proverbs 3:5)*
- **Emotional Engagement** – It numbs connection, teaching you that your emotions are burdens or invisible. *("Rejoice with those who rejoice; mourn with those who mourn." – Romans 12:15)*
- **Capacity for Intimacy** – It hinders closeness by normalizing distance, causing you to withhold vulnerability and expect rejection. *("We have spoken freely to you... open wide your hearts also." – 2 Corinthians 6:11–13)*

The Neglectful Parent is absent in quiet, insidious ways. This demon works through parents who are physically present but emotionally disengaged, distracted by addictions, busyness, or selfish pursuits. It tells the child, *"You don't matter unless I feel like engaging."* Over time, that silence becomes identity. Children of neglect don't always rebel— they often become invisible, hyper-independent, or hyper-responsible, parenting themselves while slowly starving for affirmation.

This spirit sows confusion and bitterness masked as self-reliance. As adults, these children struggle to receive love or ask for help because their foundational experiences taught them no one would come.

Misprioritized affection means that love is present but wrongly directed.

It's not always a lack of love, but a distortion in where and how that love is invested.

The parent may only devote energy to their career, hobbies, or social image. They might prioritize other children while ignoring the emotional needs of one. Sometimes they show more attention to a spouse, friends, or even pets than to their child. They could even be more emotionally invested in television, phones, or virtual relationships than the child in front of them

Warmth could be reserved for moments of pride (good grades, performance), but the parent is cold otherwise.

In all these examples, the child witnesses love and focus—but not for them. The wound is compounded by knowing the parent can show care but chooses not to toward them. Misprioritized affection is a counterfeit of love that wounds as deeply as absence.

The result from this kind of affection misplacement is invisible or forgotten children who carry internal messages like: "I'm not interesting enough to love."

"I have to perform or achieve to earn attention." "Others will always come first." "Presence doesn't equal care."

God's love is never misprioritized. He says: *"Can a mother forget the baby at her breast and have no compassion on the child she has borne? Though she may forget,* I will not forget you!" (Isaiah 49:15)

God's attention is deliberate, personal, and perfectly directed.

Scripture References:

"Can a mother forget the baby at her breast and have no compassion?" (Isaiah 49:15)

"Children are a heritage from the Lord." (Psalm 127:3)

"Train up a child in the way he should go..." (Proverbs 22:6)

Common Symptoms:

- Parents who are emotionally unavailable, preoccupied, or dismissive
- Children taking on adult roles prematurely (parentified)
- Adults who suppress needs and fear emotional dependence
- Deep loneliness hidden behind achievement or stoicism
- Distrust in affection, closeness, or sustained attention

Real-Life Example:

Janelle doesn't recall bruises or shouting matches, only a suffocating absence. Her mother was physically present but emotionally tethered to someone else: a tiny designer dog. The dog had a wardrobe, home-cooked meals, spa-like grooming appointments, and more eye contact in a week than Janelle received in years. Her mom spoke to it in a sweet, animated voice Janelle never heard directed at her.

She remembered watching her mother hold the dog and wondering, What did I do wrong? Why don't I matter like that?

Her father was no different: quiet, detached, living like a roommate instead of a parent. Neither of them knew anything about her: not her favorite subject, not her dreams, not when she was hurting. The kitchen was always stocked with their preferences; no one asked what she liked or even if she'd eaten. It was like they had a child without ever stepping into parenthood.

Janelle stopped trying. No point asking for what would never come. No conversations. No hugs. No checking in. Not even a goodbye when she left home for good. She packed in silence, walked out the front door, and no one even looked up. Unless she called, she knew she'd never hear from them again.

Now an adult, Janelle prides herself on being independent, but it's a brittle kind of strength. She flinches when people show care. Deep down, she still wonders why she didn't deserve the love so freely given to a dog.

The Neglectful Parent leaves a void. That emptiness teaches something cruel: that love is optional, presence is a luxury, and closeness is unsafe.

Solutions & Declarations:

1. **"My value is not based on how others treated me."**
   "Are not five sparrows sold for two pennies? And not one of them is forgotten before God. Why, even the hairs of your head are all numbered. Fear not; you are of more value than many sparrows." (Luke 12:6–7)

2. **"God never left me. He sees, hears, and chooses me."**
   "The Lord is near to the brokenhearted and saves the crushed in spirit." (Psalm 34:18)

3. **"I release the burden of raising myself. I receive the Father's healing."**

   "Even if my father and mother abandon me, the Lord will hold me close." (Psalm 27:10, NLT)

Turn to Chapter 9 Prayer Index and go to:

Prayer 9: General Prayer for Pride of Life

Prayer 14: Deliverance from Generational & Family Spirits

Supplemental Prayers: 26, 29, 30, 31, 32, 33, 34

Cross-References:

- **The Orphan** – Cultivates a deep sense of abandonment and emotional exile, even when the parent is physically present.
- **The Broken Mirror** – Forms when a child receives no reflection of their worth, leading to confusion about identity and value.
- **The Performer** – Emerges from the belief that love must be earned through perfection, since attention was never freely given.
- **The Burnt-Out Child** – Develops when the child is forced to self-manage or emotionally parent themselves from an early age.\
- **The Guard** – Builds protective emotional walls to cope with constant invisibility and disappointment.
- **The Selfish One** – Prioritizes their own comfort, desires, and preferences over the basic needs of their child.
- **The Narcissist** – Sees children as accessories or burdens rather than souls to be nurtured, withholding attention unless it serves their image.

Sibling Rivalry / Warfare

Core Torment & Lie: Competition, Envy, Comparison, Favoritism

"There's only room for one."

Gifts Under Attack:

- **Unity** – Sibling rivalry fractures the family bond, turning allies into adversaries and undermining God's design for brotherhood and sisterhood. *("How good and pleasant it is when God's people live together in unity!" – Psalm 133:1)*
- **Identity** – It fosters performance-based worth, making each sibling feel they must outshine the other to be seen. *("We are God's workmanship, created in Christ Jesus to do good works..." – Ephesians 2:10)*
- **Peace** – It breeds ongoing tension, conflict, and resentment, making rest and safety in the home feel impossible. *("Blessed are the peacemakers, for they will be called children of God." – Matthew 5:9)*
- **Mutual Honor** – It discourages celebration of one another's gifts, replacing honor with jealousy and suspicion. *("Be devoted to one another in love. Honor one another above yourselves." – Romans 12:10)*
- **Godly Perspective** – It twists the view of family into a battleground, obscuring God's sovereign choice in gifting, timing, and purpose. *("Now you are the body of Christ, and each one of you is a part of it." – 1 Corinthians 12:27)*

Sibling Rivalry is a demon that embeds itself in families through comparison, favoritism, and emotional neglect. It whispers that love is scarce, and only one child can win. Whether through overt favoritism or subtle differences in treatment, this spirit turns siblings into competitors, fostering lifelong resentment, jealousy, and division.

It thrives across generations, using the same script over and over: one child exalted, another ignored. It builds families where siblings become strangers or enemies. Left unaddressed, this spirit poisons marriages, inheritance, family legacy, and even ministry callings born in the same household.

Scripture References:

"Now Israel loved Joseph more than all his children..." (Genesis 37:3)

"Cain rose up against Abel his brother and killed him." (Genesis 4:8)

"Where jealousy and selfish ambition exist,
there is disorder..." (James 3:16)

Common Symptoms:

- Assigned sibling roles (the favorite, the scapegoat, the forgotten)
- Adults still trying to win approval from parents or compete with each other
- Deep-rooted resentment masked by distance or fake civility
- Generational echo—same patterns passed down to children
- Celebration of one sibling feels like loss to another

Real-Life Example:

Peter and Porter grew up under the same roof but lived in two different stories.

Their parents were high-achieving professionals who expected nothing less from their sons. Porter, the younger of the two, declared at six years old that he wanted to be a lawyer, and everything about him seemed to align with that path. As he grew up, he could absorb complex information, argue persuasively, and keep up in any intellectual setting. Their parents were thrilled. They bragged about his brilliance, sparred with him like he was already a peer, and rewarded him with trust, privileges, and admiration.

Peter, on the other hand, had to work harder just to stay afloat. He needed private tutors and still struggled with standardized tests. He didn't want to be a lawyer. He wanted to write music. Their parents gave him the best gear and paid for an elite music school, but it was always clear they viewed his dreams as a hobby, not a calling.

Porter lived up to the plan. He graduated from law school, landed prestigious clients, and became a regular commentator on national news. Peter dropped out of music school to tour, hoping passion would open doors faster than a degree. Sometimes it did—he'd get a rave review or a packed show—but nothing ever stuck. He spent most of his 30s doing open mics and patching together income from day jobs, while Porter moved toward early retirement.

Deep down, Peter believed that if he could just become *famous*, it would level the playing field. It wasn't just about making it; it was about *beating* Porter. Earning his parents' pride. Finally being the golden child.

But the more time passed, the wider the gap grew. Porter stopped answering Peter's calls. Peter started burning bridges: borrowing money from everyone he knew, then disappearing. Even now, as a grown man, Peter's heart is broken over his failures, fractured by years of comparison, favoritism, and a silent war no one ever tried to stop.

Sibling Rivalry can sound like applause in one direction and silence in the other. If it goes unchecked, it becomes generational, repeating itself in the next set of siblings.

Solutions & Declarations:

1. **"I break agreement with the lie that love is scarce."**
   "Love is patient and kind; love does not envy or boast; it is not arrogant or rude. It does not insist on its own way... Love never ends." (1 Corinthians 13:4–5, 8)

2. **"I release every spirit of comparison, envy, and rivalry."**
   "For where jealousy and selfish ambition exist, there will be disorder and every vile practice." (James 3:16)

3. **"My value is not in performance or position, but in who God says I am."**
   "See what great love the Father has lavished on us, that we should be called children of God! And that is what we are!" (1 John 3:1)

Turn to Chapter 9 Prayer Index and go to:
Prayer 9: General Prayer for Pride of Life
Prayer 14: Deliverance from Generational & Family Spirits
Supplemental Prayer: 25

Cross-References:

- **The Golden Child** – The favored sibling whose pedestal creates resentment and unrealistic pressure on both sides.
- **The Broken Mirror** – Forms in the overlooked sibling who internalizes the belief that they'll never be enough.
- **The Idolator** – Turns family dynamics into a performance arena, where love must be earned and appearances are everything.
- **The Guard** – Builds emotional defenses after years of comparison, favoritism, or betrayal.
- **The Withholder** – Reinforces the divide by offering love, affirmation, or resources selectively, deepening resentment between siblings.
- **The Wanderer** – Reflects the sibling who leaves emotionally or physically, seeking belonging elsewhere after being edged out of the family system.

The Burnt-Out Child

Core Torment & Lie: Parentification,
Chronic Responsibility &
Emotional Exhaustion

"You're not allowed to be a child."

Gifts Under Attack:

- **Rest** – The Burnt-Out Child was trained to carry burdens too big, too soon, making rest feel lazy or unsafe. *("Come to me, all you who are weary and burdened, and I will give you rest." – Matthew 11:28)*

- **Joy** – It stifles playfulness and delight, replacing it with pressure, survival mode, and over-functioning. *("The joy of the Lord is your strength." – Nehemiah 8:10)*
- **Innocence** – It forces maturity prematurely, exposing the child to adult concerns and emotional loads they weren't built to carry. *("Out of the mouth of babes and nursing infants You have perfected praise..." – Matthew 21:16)*
- **Identity** – It roots self-worth in being useful or needed, not in simply being a child of God. *("You are my beloved child; in you I am well pleased." – Luke 3:22, paraphrased)*
- **Godly Order** – It reverses roles in the home, often requiring the child to emotionally or practically parent the adults. *("Children are not obligated to save up for their parents, but parents for their children." – 2 Corinthians 12:14)*

This demon targets children who are forced to grow up too fast, becoming caretakers, mediators, or emotional support for adults. Whether through neglect, addiction, abuse, divorce, or a parent's emotional immaturity, this spirit enters early and convinces the child that their needs are unimportant. They become the "mature one," the "helper," the "rock," while burying their own desires, fears, and pain.

As adults, Burnt Out Children are reliable, competent, and deeply weary. They never learned how to rest or receive love without performing. Their identity is tied to usefulness, and they often feel guilty for having needs. Even in safe environments, they carry an internal tension: If I don't hold everything together, it will all fall apart.

Scripture References:

"It would be better... than to cause one of these little ones to stumble." (Luke 17:2)

"Children are a heritage from the Lord..." (Psalm 127:3)

"Come to me, all who are weary... and I will give you rest." (Matthew 11:28)

Common Symptoms:

- Grew up supporting parents emotionally, financially, or practically
- Childhood labeled as "mature," "responsible," or "old soul"
- Reluctance or inability to ask for help
- Constant exhaustion, even in seasons of peace
- Hidden anger or grief from a stolen childhood

Real-Life Example:

Diego was the second oldest of five, but he may as well have been their father. His own dad was long gone, and his mother floated in and out of the picture like a ghost. When she *was* home, she acted more like another child than a parent: sleeping for hours, crying unpredictably, needing constant reassurance. The real work of keeping the family together fell on Diego.

By twelve, he was collecting bottles and cans for money, washing dishes under the table at a local restaurant, and coming home to bathe his siblings, help them with homework, and cook what little food they had. His mom would call him "the man of the house," and ask him accusingly why there wasn't more food in the fridge, as if he were the parent who had failed.

No one told Diego to grow up overnight, but no one else stepped up either.

Even into adulthood, the pattern didn't stop. When his mother got sick and had no one to care for her, Diego moved her into his home and nursed her until the day she died. By then, he had his own house, his own career, and his own bills, but no childhood to speak of. He had never known what it felt like to be nurtured, protected, or carefree.

People praise him now, calling him dependable, selfless, hardworking. But inside, Diego is exhausted. Not just tired from life but weary in his soul. He has spent his entire existence carrying others, and no one has ever carried him.

The Burnt-Out Child doesn't come from nowhere. It's forged in the fire of abandonment and adultification. Even when the childhood ends, the weight doesn't lift.

Solutions & Declarations:

1. **"I renounce the lie that my worth is tied to responsibility."**
   "Come to me, all who labor and are heavy laden, and I will give you rest." (Matthew 11:28)

2. **"God does not need me to carry what He already bore."**
   "Surely he has borne our griefs and carried our sorrows... and the Lord has laid on him the iniquity of us all." (Isaiah 53:4–6)

3. **"I receive rest, healing, and the freedom to be God's child."**
   "The Spirit you received does not make you slaves, so that you live in fear again; rather, the Spirit you received brought about your adoption to sonship. And by him we cry, 'Abba, Father.'" (Romans 8:15)

Turn to Chapter 9 Prayer Index and go to:

Prayer 9: General Prayer for Pride of Life
Prayer 14: Deliverance from Generational & Family Spirits
Supplemental Prayers: 26, 28, 29, 30, 31,32, 33, 34

Cross-References:

- **The Orphan** – Grows up emotionally or spiritually unfathered, forced to fill adult roles too early.
- **The Broken Mirror** – Blames themselves for being overlooked, interpreting neglect as a personal defect.
- **The Guard** – Hides exhaustion and buried resentment behind strength and self-reliance.
- **The Severer** – Eventually detaches emotionally or physically to escape the crushing weight of responsibility.
- **The Withholding Father** – Models emotional absence and teaches that care must be earned, not given.

- **Lazybones** – May rise later in life as a backlash—manifesting as collapse, fatigue, or refusal to carry more.
- **The Performer** – Finds identity in usefulness, believing love must be earned through constant effort.
- **The Neglectful Parent** – Fails to provide nurturing or structure, forcing the child into a caretaker role far too young.
- **The Stunted One** – Halts emotional development by robbing the child of a true childhood, leaving them overgrown in duty but undergrown in freedom.
- **The Wanderer** – Struggles to find a true sense of home or rest after being displaced by responsibility their soul was never designed to carry.

The Wanderer

Core Torment & Lie: Aimlessness from Rejection

"I don't belong anywhere."

Gifts Under Attack:

- Purpose – The Wanderer erodes confidence in God's plan, making the future feel out of reach *("For I know the plans I have for you..." – Jeremiah 29:11)*.
- Stability – It breaks roots and sabotages commitment, leaving people spiritually and relationally unmoored *("You will be cursed in your coming in and going out." – Deuteronomy 28:19)*.
- Obedience – The spirit of wandering resists discipline, always seeking escape from structure *("A man who strays from the path of understanding will rest in the assembly of the dead." – Proverbs 21:16)*.
- Calling – It blinds you to the places and people you're assigned to help, pulling you into fruitless cycles *("They wandered in the wilderness in a solitary way..." – Psalm 107:4)*.

The Wanderer is a fruit of rejection. When a child is not wanted—even from the womb—a spiritual door is opened to this curse. This demon causes people to drift from job to job, city to city, relationship to relationship, always running from something they can't name. It resists spiritual covering and accountability, often interpreting correction as attack.

This spirit works subtly at first: an itch for "freedom," a desire to detach when things get hard. But behind the restlessness is a spiritual orphan who's been cast out—and who now self-casts. The Wanderer ensures they never feel safe long enough to heal, grow, or be known.

Scripture References:

"A fugitive and a vagabond you shall be on the earth." (Genesis 4:12)

"You will grope about at noon, as the blind grope in the darkness... You will be unsuccessful in everything you do." (Deuteronomy 28:29)

"He who strays from the path of understanding will rest in the assembly of the dead." (Proverbs 21:16)

Common Symptoms:

- Frequent moves or job changes without clear direction
- Avoidance of long-term commitments
- Aversion to spiritual authority or church accountability
- Difficulty settling into a calling or career
- Intense fear of being "trapped" or "stuck"

Real-Life Example:

Brady carried the curse of rejection for as long as he could remember. It started at home with parents who were cold and dismissive, and that rejection followed him into school. Teachers seemed irritated by him. Other kids avoided him. It was like something invisible was repelling people, and he didn't understand why.

Spiritually, something was clinging to him. Spirits of rejection, poverty, and abandonment had been invited in—some through generational sin, some through his parents' neglect—and they began to shape his life from the ground up.

As soon as he was old enough, Brady left. No plan, just escape. He hit the road with nothing but his instincts. He was sharp, resilient, and deeply resourceful. He learned to survive through camping, scavenging, and odd jobs. He never stayed long, never let anyone get close. He lived off the grid, off the map, and as far outside the system as possible.

Once, at a campground, a kind couple noticed how young he was and tried to help. They offered him food and warm clothes, even forced some cash into his hands. He accepted it with gratitude but disappeared by morning, terrified they might report him to the authorities or worse—*try to keep him.*

That was the story everywhere he went. Brady had chances to re-enter society. Outreach programs tried. Churches tried. But the very idea of being brought back into the world he'd escaped from filled him with panic. He didn't want to be found. He didn't want roots. The pain of being rejected had taught him that *attachment was dangerous,* and freedom meant staying detached.

Brady thought he was surviving on his own terms. But really, he was still being driven by wounds, by spirits, and by the lie that he would never belong.

The Wanderer compels its host to run and hide, convincing him the world has decided there's no place for him in it.

Solutions & Declarations:

4. **I have a place in God's plan. I will not wander in vain.**
   "'For I know the plans I have for you,' declares the Lord, 'plans to prosper you and not to harm you, plans to give you a future and a hope.'" (Jeremiah 29:11)

5. **I will not fear commitment; God plants me where I will bear fruit.**
   "They are like trees planted along the riverbank, bearing fruit each season. Their leaves never wither, and they prosper in all they do." (Psalm 1:3)

6. **I submit to God's leadership and timing.**

"Submit yourselves therefore to God. Resist the devil, and he will flee from you." (James 4:7)

Turn to Chapter 9 Prayer Index and go to:

Prayer 9: General Prayer for Pride of Life

Prayer 14: Deliverance from Generational & Family Spirits

Supplemental Prayers: 15, 27, 33, 34

Cross-References:

- **The Orphan** – Roots the pattern of wandering in a deep sense of being unwanted, unclaimed, or spiritually uncovered.
- **The Rejector** – Deflects connection by pushing others away first, projecting the pain of past abandonment.
- **The Guard** – Protects the heart through distance, fleeing from vulnerability and emotional exposure.
- **The Shrinker** – Equates invisibility with safety, retreating into smallness to avoid being seen—and hurt.
- **The Pauper** – Keeps the Wanderer in cycles of lack and instability, convincing them that survival is all they can expect.
- **The Severer** – Encourages the cutting of relational ties before they can deepen, mistaking detachment for freedom.
- **The Burnt-Out Child** – May underlie the desire to flee, shaped by early exhaustion and the need to escape responsibility and pressure.

The Jealous Mother

Core Torment & Lie: Insecurity, Control, Competition & Emotional Manipulation

"You can't outshine me."

Gifts Under Attack:

- **Identity** – The Jealous Mother distorts your sense of self by making your growth feel threatening or unacceptable. *("I praise you because I am fearfully and wonderfully made..." – Psalm 139:14)*
- **Confidence** – It chips away at self-assurance through comparison, criticism, or silent withdrawal when you succeed. *("Do not throw away your confidence; it will be richly rewarded." – Hebrews 10:35)*
- **Voice** – It suppresses expression and opinion, making you feel like your voice brings tension instead of value. *("Open your mouth wide, and I will fill it." – Psalm 81:10)*
- **Femininity** – It fosters shame or rivalry around beauty, grace, or strength, especially from mother to daughter. *("She is clothed with strength and dignity; she can laugh at the days to come." – Proverbs 31:25)*
- **Leadership** – It undermines your influence by treating your strength as rebellion or arrogance. *("Do not let anyone look down on you because you are young, but set an example..." – 1 Timothy 4:12)*

The Jealous Mother is a deeply wounding spirit that turns the sacred role of motherhood into a rivalry. Rather than nurturing, she competes. Rather than covering, she critiques. This demon is most common between mothers and daughters, but it can also affect sons. At its core is an insecure, unhealed woman who sees her child's beauty, gifts, or joy as a threat instead of a blessing.

She may appear charming to others, but behind closed doors, she manipulates through sarcasm, comparison, control, or withholding love. Her child becomes a mirror that reflects what she hates or mourns in herself, and rather than breaking the cycle, she becomes its enforcer.

This demon is often rooted in generational trauma, internalized misogyny, or a life of disappointment and missed potential. If not cast out, it evolves into full-blown Jezebel, where control and manipulation replace true love.

Biblical Basis:
While there's no explicit "jealous mother" named in scripture, the spirit is present in multiple biblical patterns:

- **Jezebel** (1 Kings 19–21) – Not a mother in name, but motherlike in control, manipulation, and fear of being replaced.
- **Michal** (2 Samuel 6:16, 20–23) – Saul's daughter who mocked and despised David's worship, reflecting resentment toward joy and anointing.
- **Hagar & Sarah** (Genesis 16, 21) – Though Sarah was the "legitimate" wife, her jealousy toward Hagar led her to exile a mother and child.

Most relevant:

- **Ezekiel 16:44** – "Like mother, like daughter." This proverb exposes the cycle of sin passed down between generations of women.

Common Symptoms:
- Criticizing a daughter's beauty, body, choices, or voice
- Competing for attention with children, especially around men
- Withholding praise or sabotaging success
- Shaming independence or spiritual growth
- Infantilizing adult children to maintain control

Real-Life Example:
Kayla grew up in the shadow of a woman everyone adored. Her mother, Cynthia, had been a model in her youth and still turned heads well into middle age. Online, Cynthia was bubbly, glamorous, and constantly posting selfies—even in swimsuits—basking in praise from followers

who told her she looked incredible for her age. But behind the scenes, something darker was festering.

As Kayla grew into her own beauty, her mother's warmth began to curdle. Cynthia started sabotaging Kayla subtly at first. She discouraged Kayla from wearing flattering clothes and only bought her outfits that made her look frumpy or childish. If Kayla liked a boy, Cynthia would flirt with him or share embarrassing information about Kayla. If Kayla made a new friend, Cynthia would find a way to insert herself or poison the connection.

It didn't make sense. Cynthia was still beautiful, still admired—why resent her daughter for becoming the same?

Envy doesn't respond to logic. It responds to fear. Cynthia couldn't stand the idea of being outshined, even by her own child. She needed the spotlight and saw Kayla as competition.

People often wondered why someone as lovely and kind as Kayla carried such obvious insecurity. They had no idea the source was her own mother, the one person who should have been her biggest supporter. Cynthia always masked her cruelty with charm. In public, she was funny, fun, and full of laughter. Behind closed doors, she was Kayla's greatest opposition.

It nearly worked. Cynthia almost convinced Kayla to turn down a scholarship that would have changed her life. But something in Kayla snapped awake. She realized this was sabotage and for the first time, she saw her mother clearly.

The Jealous Mother competes with the very child she raised, and unless that cycle is broken, it repeats through generations.

Solutions & Declarations:

1. **"I break agreement with the lie that I must dim my light to be loved."**
   "Let your light shine before others, so that they may see your good works and give glory to your Father who is in heaven." (Matthew 5:16)

2. **"I am not in competition with the one who raised me—I am called to freedom."**

   "It is for freedom that Christ has set us free. Stand firm, then, and do not let yourselves be burdened again by a yoke of slavery." (Galatians 5:1)

3. **"God is not like my mother. He celebrates me without condition."**

   "The Lord your God is with you, the Mighty Warrior who saves. He will take great delight in you; in his love he will no longer rebuke you but will rejoice over you with singing." (Zephaniah 3:17)

Turn to Chapter 9 Prayer Index and go to:

Prayer 9: General Prayer for Pride of Life

Prayer 14: Deliverance from Generational & Family Spirits

Supplemental Prayers: 19, 26, 30, 34

Cross-References:

- **Jezebel** – Operates through manipulation and control, driven by deep insecurity and fear of being replaced.
- **The Broken Mirror** – Leaves daughters with a distorted self-image, shaped by comparison and criticism instead of nurture.
- **The Critic** – Delivers cruelty in disguise—often through sarcasm, backhanded compliments, or public humiliation.
- **The Idolator** – Competes for attention and praise, turning motherhood into a platform for self-worship.
- **The Guard** – Instills fear of closeness with other women, teaching daughters that female relationships are unsafe.
- **The Withholder** – Uses affection, affirmation, and approval as tools of control, never freely given.
- **The Saboteur** – Undermines opportunities and confidence under the guise of "just being honest" or "looking out for you."

The Enmeshed Mother

Core Torment & Lie: Emotional Incest, Identity Theft & Soul-Tie Bondage

"You belong to me."

Gifts Under Attack:

- **Autonomy** – The Enmeshed Mother blurs emotional boundaries, making you feel responsible for her well-being and unable to live freely. *("Each one should carry their own load." – Galatians 6:5)*
- **Identity in Christ** – It hijacks your self-concept, binding your worth and decisions to her approval rather than God's purpose. *("For we are God's masterpiece... created in Christ Jesus to do good works..." – Ephesians 2:10)*
- **Relational Freedom** – It interferes with friendships, dating, and marriage by enforcing loyalty through guilt, control, or emotional dependency. *("For this reason, a man shall leave his father and mother and be joined to his wife..." – Genesis 2:24)*
- **Marriage** – It creates spiritual and emotional conflict between spouses, forcing a partner to choose between honoring their parent or cleaving to their spouse. *("What God has joined together, let no one separate." – Mark 10:9)*
- **Emotional Maturity** – It stunts personal development, keeping you emotionally entangled and infantilized well into adulthood. *("When I became a man, I put the ways of childhood behind me." – 1 Corinthians 13:11)*

The Enmeshed Mother may appear loving, nurturing, even "best friend" material, but behind the closeness is a deep spiritual bondage. This spirit binds children emotionally, spiritually, and sometimes physically, in a way that stunts independence, disrupts marriages, and replaces God's voice with hers.

This demon masks control as closeness, guilt as love, and boundary-breaking as loyalty. It's often a result of her own abandonment, betrayal, or rejection, which she compensates for by clinging too tightly to her children, especially sons.

The Enmeshed Mother doesn't raise her children to leave the nest; she raises them to orbit her forever. The spiritual result is a soul tie that functions like idolatry and produces confusion, stagnation, and delayed destiny.

Scripture References:

"For am I now seeking the approval of man, or of God? Or am
I trying to please man? If I were still trying to please man,
I would not be a servant of Christ." (Galatians 1:10)

"The soul who sins shall die. The son shall not bear the guilt of the
father, nor the father bear the guilt of the son." (Ezekiel 18:20)

"The fear of man lays a snare, but whoever trusts
in the Lord is safe." (Proverbs 29:25)

Common Symptoms:

- Parent and adult child share an inappropriate emotional closeness ("best friends" or codependency)
- Child feels responsible for parent's emotions or decisions
- Inability to make independent choices without fear or guilt
- Parent interferes in romantic/marital relationships
- Spouse of the child feels like an outsider or competition

Real-Life Example:

Amy was the baby of the family, born ten years after her closest sibling. With the house already quiet and settled, her mother poured all her attention into her. They dressed in matching outfits, went everywhere together, and shared every detail of life. Amy felt loved and chosen. But she didn't realize that the closeness came at a price.

As Amy grew older and naturally began to crave a bit of space, her mother saw it as betrayal. A sleepover with friends? Silent treatment. A little independence? Manipulation. From that point on, Amy learned that her autonomy came with consequences, and she stopped testing the boundaries. Her mother remained her best friend, and Amy stopped forming meaningful friendships with girls her own age.

When it came time for college, there was only one option: the university down the street. Of course, Amy would live at home. The idea of moving away was dismissed immediately, and Amy didn't push it. Her world had already shrunk around her, and she told herself it was fine.

Then came the dream offer: a job in fashion in New York City, everything Amy had worked for. But when she shared the news, her mother collapsed into bed, suddenly and mysteriously ill. It was a pattern Amy recognized (her mother had always gotten "sick" when Amy tried to break free) but this time felt more severe. Amy declined the offer. Her mother quickly recovered.

Later, Amy met someone she truly connected with, a man who wanted to build something real with her. Her mother hated him from the moment they met. She belittled him, gave him cold stares, and accused him of "taking Amy away." Amy tried to see him in secret, but eventually, the emotional toll became too great. She broke it off; not because she wanted to, but because she couldn't take the pressure.

Now in her thirties, Amy still lives at home. She cooks, cleans, and cares for her mother like a dutiful daughter. She tells herself this is the life she wants—that it's safe, simple, even ideal. But deep down, a quiet ache lingers. She's never truly been free.

The Enmeshed Mother doesn't need chains to keep her children bound. She uses guilt, neediness, and manufactured crisis to confuse love with ownership, ensuring that her children never really leave. Not emotionally. Not spiritually. Not completely.

Solutions & Declarations:

1. **"I was created for covenant with God—not emotional captivity with man."**
   "For you were bought with a price; do not become slaves of men."
   (1 Corinthians 7:23)

2. **"I break ungodly soul ties with those who claimed me as their own."**
   "Therefore a man shall leave his father and his mother and hold fast to his wife, and they shall become one flesh." (Genesis 2:24)
   (Note: this verse affirms God's design for healthy separation and individual identity within covenant.)

3. **"I honor my mother, but I belong to Christ."**
   "If anyone comes to me and does not hate his own father and mother... he cannot be my disciple." (Luke 14:26)

   (Note: this verse emphasizes allegiance to Christ above all earthly ties.)

Turn to Chapter 9 Prayer Index and go to:
Prayer 9: General Prayer for Pride of Life
Prayer 14: Deliverance from Generational & Family Spirits
Supplemental Prayers: 20, 26, 30, 34

Cross-References:

- **The Idolator** – Turns the parent-child relationship into a sacred bond that replaces God's design for healthy boundaries.
- **The Meddling Mother-in-Law** – Often the evolved form of enmeshment, where the parent continues to dominate even after the child marries.
- **The Severer** – Children who break free may swing to the opposite extreme, cutting ties completely to escape the emotional entanglement.
- **The Performer** – Trains the child to live for approval, shaping their identity around pleasing rather than becoming.
- **The Ghoster** – Avoids direct confrontation by disappearing emotionally or physically, struggling to speak truth to power.
- **The Stunted One** – Prevents emotional and spiritual maturity, keeping the child in a perpetual state of dependence and delayed development.

SOLUTIONS
8

The Full Gospel Message
You were born into a war.

It's not metaphorical. It's the truth, and your life has always been proof of it. The pain, the confusion, the torment you've felt wasn't random. It was targeted. You were born with a calling, and the enemy knew it before you did.

The Bible says the whole world lies under the power of the evil one *(1 John 5:19)*. Jesus came to destroy the works of the devil *(1 John 3:8)* and to redeem you from the grip of sin and death. He wasn't just a teacher or a martyr. He was God in human flesh, prophesied centuries before His birth, crucified for your sin, and raised to life with power.

You don't need to earn salvation; you need to accept it. God is not waiting for you to be perfect; He's waiting for you to surrender. Once you do, the same Spirit that raised Jesus from the dead will live in you *(Romans 8:11)*. You will be sealed, empowered, and given new life.

Why the Bible is True
The Bible proves itself:

- **Prophecy Fulfillment:** Over 900 prophecies have come true in exact detail. The odds of this are incalculable.
- **Manuscript Evidence:** The Bible has more accurate ancient copies than any book in history—far more than Plato, Homer, or Aristotle.

- **Science Before Science:** Leviticus 17:11 declares that "the life of the flesh is in the blood" thousands of years before scientists confirmed that blood carries oxygen, nutrients, immunity, and DNA. Today a single drop of blood can tell a person's entire biological story, just as scripture said all along. In Genesis 6:15, God gave Noah ship dimensions in a 30:5:3 ratio, now recognized by engineers as the ideal proportion for stability and load bearing in large vessels, showing the Bible knew long before blueprints did. Scripture spoke of air-borne illness germ theory and proper sanitation to prevent cross contamination *(Leviticus 13:45, 11:32-36)*, the water cycle *(Ecclesiastes 1:7)*, and atomic theory *(Hebrews 11:3)*. These are only a few examples.

- **Revelation 13 Technology:** Ancient prophecy now makes sense in light of modern tools like RFID chips, digital IDs, and biometric surveillance. The "Mark of the Beast" is no longer a fable. It's a prototype.

- **Earthquakes, Plagues, Wars & Rumors of Wars:** Jesus predicted these as birth pains *(Matthew 24)*. They're here. In the past century, earthquakes have not only increased in number, but also in intensity and diversity of locations, with significant seismic activity now occurring in regions that were once considered geographically stable. In recent decades, plagues have become more diverse, frequent and global, with new diseases emerging at a rate never seen before, often jumping from animals to humans and spreading faster than ever through modern travel. Wars and rumors of wars have intensified across the globe, with rising conflict not only between nations, but also within them, through civil unrest, terrorism, and political upheaval, just as Jesus warned. He said, "nation will rise against nation" *Ethnos* against *ethnos*, in the Greek. Today ethnic and cultural conflicts are escalating worldwide.

- **The Bible is supernaturally consistent.** Written over 1,500 years by 40+ authors across 3 continents... yet it tells one unified story.

The Battle You're In

You were born into enemy territory. The Bible says the whole world is under the control of the evil one *(1 John 5:19)*. That's why life has never felt fair, because it isn't. We live in a fallen world where darkness operates by default unless light pushes back.

This is spiritual law. Whether you believe in demons or not, they believe in you, and they've been studying you your whole life.

You're not defenseless. God has given you spiritual armor *(Ephesians 6:10–18)*. He's given you weapons: His Word, His Spirit, and your voice. And He's given you authority to tread on serpents and scorpions *(Luke 10:19)*. That means demons and unclean spirits and all the powers of the enemy.

One of your most powerful weapons is discernment, the ability to recognize what's really going on underneath the surface. This is what is meant when we hear someone say "I was blind, but now I see" after they've been saved. To hear God's voice clearly and know when the enemy is trying to counterfeit it is another major feature of having sight in God. Think about the alternative: walking through this dark world completely blind to what is around you, targeted by an enemy you cannot see but who has a perfectly clear view into you and your life.

The Bible says to test every spirit *(1 John 4:1)* and to be transformed by the renewing of your mind so you can recognize God's will *(Romans 12:2)*. Discernment sharpens as you spend time in His presence and His Word.

Spiritual Maturity and the Battle for Strength

We are called to grow in grace and in the knowledge of Jesus Christ *(2 Peter 3:18)*. Scripture refers to new believers as babies in the faith still drinking milk, not yet ready for solid food: *"I gave you milk, not solid food, for you were not yet ready for it. Indeed, you are still not ready."* (1 Corinthians 3:2) and *"Though by this time you ought to be teachers, you need someone to teach you the elementary truths of God's word all over again. You need milk, not solid food! ... But solid food is for the mature..."* (Hebrews 5:12–14)

That's not a criticism—it's a starting point. Every believer begins somewhere. Over time, we are meant to mature, to grow strong in the Lord, and to graduate from milk to meat, from passivity to power.

In the spiritual realm, the enemy can see the difference. Just like predators in the natural world go after the young, the sick, or the isolated, demons look for spiritual vulnerability, specifically the believer who doesn't yet know their authority, who doesn't yet use their weapons, who isn't yet walking in the fullness of what Jesus paid for.

"My people are destroyed for lack of knowledge." (Hosea 4:6) This is why discernment and spiritual growth are survival. *"...in order that Satan might not outwit us. For we are not unaware of his schemes." (2 Corinthians 2:11)*

The same way the enemy can see spiritual weakness, he can also recognize when a believer is covered in God's power and has access to authority. The prophet Zechariah describes God's presence as a wall of fire around His people and glory within: *"'For I,' says the Lord, 'will be a wall of fire all around her, and I will be the glory in her midst.'" (Zechariah 2:5)*

In the spirit, that fire is real. Demons can see it. But for many believers, that fire burns low because they've never been taught how to stoke it. The enemy preys on believers who don't know the power they carry.

Another demon repellent is faith, which is more than belief—it is a substance in the spirit: *"Now faith is the substance of things hoped for, the evidence of things not seen." (Hebrews 11:1)*

That's why faith is both a gift and a key piece of the armor of God *"Above all, taking the shield of faith, wherewith ye shall be able to quench all the fiery darts of the wicked." (Ephesians 6:16)*

If we want to grow in faith, we have to be under sound teaching and preaching that feeds our spirit and isn't simply motivational speaking. We cannot wield power in a truth we've never heard. *"How shall they believe in Him of whom they have not heard? And how shall they hear without a preacher?" (Romans 10:14)*

"Faith comes by hearing, and hearing by the Word of God." (Romans 10:17). The last clause of that verse means that true *listening* happens

when God's word is spoken. It has the power to cut through confusion and open our ears like nothing else can. This is why Jesus said, "He who has ears to hear, let him hear." We all have physical ears, but only the Spirit of God can awaken our ability to hear truth in a way that builds faith.

A Word of Warning: Stay Pure

Nothing attracts demonic attention quite like a lukewarm believer, someone who knows the truth but refuses to walk in it. *"I know your works, that you are neither cold nor hot. I wish you were one or the other! So, because you are lukewarm—neither hot nor cold—I will spit you out of My mouth." (Revelation 3:15–16)*

Lukewarm Christianity is dangerous ground. It invites judgment and spiritual attack. There is something about a believer in willful sin that draws more attention than an unbeliever in both the natural and spiritual realms. In the spirit, the enemy sees a mixture of light and darkness—an unstable position of compromise —and demons love to exploit that. In the natural world, unbelievers seem to instinctively know what a Christian should be doing, and when a believer doesn't live up to that standard, the world is quick to call it out. There is something about spiritual compromise that draws scrutiny and invites mockery. The same people who reject God still expect His people to reflect him.

Make no mistake, God is holding everyone accountable: believers who are supposed to reflect God and lead others to repentance, and those mocking who muddle and distort the message. They have proved God's own point where He states: *"For since the creation of the world , God's invisible qualities— his eternal power and divine nature — have been clearly seen, being understood from what has been made, so that people are without excuse." (Romans 1:20)*

So be pure. Be intentional. Grow. *"Do not give the devil a foothold." (Ephesians 4:27)*

> *"Be strong in the Lord and in the power of His might. Put on the full armor of God..." (Ephesians 6:10–11) "Like newborn babies,*

crave pure spiritual milk, so that by it you may grow up in your salvation." (1 Peter 2:2)

The longer you walk with God, the stronger your weapons become.

Here's the main truth the enemy doesn't want you to know: you have authority. You are dangerous to darkness. Once you start walking in that truth, the war changes. So don't back down and retreat. Suit up, speak truth, and push back. You were born for this.

What To Do Next

You've come this far for a reason. Now it's time to take your next step.

1. Say Yes to Jesus

   There's a prayer in the next section to help you do just that. Speak it when you're ready.

2. Get Baptized

   This is a command. Even Jesus was baptized as an example for us *(Matthew 3:13-17)*. Baptism is a public declaration of your new life in Christ. It announces your allegiance to people, the heavenly realms, and the enemy himself. It is a spiritual line in the sand that says, "I belong to Jesus."

   Baptism can be done by any true believer; it doesn't have to be a pastor, and you don't need to be in a church building. It can happen in a bathtub, a river, a pool — any place with water and faith. What matters is your heart and obedience. If you don't belong to a church yet, ask a trusted believer to baptize you, or reach out to a Bible-teaching church and let them know you're ready; many list their baptism services online. Some ministries like Kayla Gabbard's hold services all over the country for thousands of people. Jesus said, "Repent and be baptized, every one of you..." *(Acts 2:38)*. Don't put it off.

3. Read the Word

   Start with the Gospels—Matthew, Mark, Luke, and John—to meet Jesus for yourself.

Each Gospel gives a unique perspective:

- **Matthew** was written primarily for a Jewish audience, showing how Jesus fulfilled Old Testament prophecy as the promised Messiah.
- **Mark** is fast-paced and action-driven—great if you're just getting started.
- **Luke** was written by a physician and historian; it emphasizes Jesus' compassion and includes details no other Gospel mentions.
- **John** focuses on the divinity of Christ and offers deep spiritual insight into who Jesus is.

After the Gospels, read Acts, which records the miracles of the early Church and the boldness of the first believers. It will ignite your faith and show you what the Holy Spirit can do through surrendered people.

Romans is a letter Paul wrote to believers in a culture not unlike our own: full of idolatry, confusion, and moral decay. It clearly explains sin, grace, salvation, and how to live in the Spirit.

Proverbs is a collection of practical wisdom that King Solomon wrote for his son, yet it applies directly to us as sons and daughters of God. Much of what the world celebrates as "life advice" or "personal growth" originated here, it's just stripped of God's name.

As you read, always ask: Who is speaking? Who are they speaking to? What is being said and what does it show me about God? That's a great place to start.

Having a physical Bible you can highlight, underline, and write notes in is incredibly helpful—it becomes a personal record of your journey with God. There are also excellent Bible apps that give you access to nearly every translation, study tools, and audio versions. These are especially helpful if you're reading the King James Version, which can be rich but challenging. Comparing translations can deepen your understanding and help the Word come alive.

4. Pray Every Day

   You don't need fancy words for a conversation with God, just honesty. Prayer invites God into your situation. It opens the door for heaven to move.

5. Invite the Holy Spirit

   Ask Him to fill you, lead you, and convict you. He's your helper, your guide, and your comforter. He is also a gentleman and won't force himself upon you.

6. Fast

   Some strongholds only break through prayer and fasting *(Matthew 17:21)*. Start simple—a meal, a day, sunup to sundown—but seek God as you do it. Replace your normal meal prep, eating, and cleaning up time with reading the Bible and talking to God. Fasting is the best way to humble ourselves, which God honors. *"If the people, which are called by my name, shall humble themselves, and pray, and seek my face, and turn from their wicked ways, then will I hear from heaven, and will forgive their sin, and will heal their land." (2 Chronicles 7:14)*

7. Connect with Other Believers

   No church is perfect, but it is necessary. You weren't meant to fight alone. Most churches stream online if you're unsure where to start. As you visit, churches will be excited to bring you into their fold. Take your time and make sure God approves of where you're thinking of being planted. Tell anyone who may be pressuring you that you're bringing it to God first. Then do so. *"...not forsaking the assembling of yourselves together, as is the manner of some, but exhorting one another, and so much more as you see the Day [of Jesus's return] approaching." (Hebrews 10:35)*

8. Use Declarations Daily

   Speak the truth over your life. Hang declarations where you'll see them: your mirror, your dashboard, your fridge *(Deuteronomy 11:18–20)*. Words are power. *"Death and life are in the power of the tongue" (Proverbs 18:21)*. It's spiritual law. The devil knows it. That's why music, mantras, and media are filled with repetition. Your brain doesn't distinguish between reality and imagination. Spoken words shape your inner world and invite spiritual alignment. That's why the Sword of the Spirit is the Word of God *(Ephesians 6:17)*. You defeat lies with truth, out loud.

9. Sharpen Your Discernment

   Test everything *(1 John 4:1)*. Just because something feels good doesn't mean it's from God. The Holy Spirit will advise you, just listen for his still quiet voice, which often sounds like your own thought — except you know it didn't come from you. People call this intuition or a gut feeling, but it's all the Holy Spirit. Anytime you argue back, that's also a sign it's the Holy Spirit and not you. So do yourself a favor and just listen!

Finding Your Calling

You were born with a purpose.

God says, *"Before I formed you in the womb, I knew you" (Jeremiah 1:5)*. You're not an accident. The incredible odds you beat to even being born are mind-boggling. The very torments you've faced are proof that your life has meaning, because hell doesn't fight what doesn't matter.

Ask God to reveal what He put inside you. James 1:5 says He gives wisdom generously to all who ask. The Holy Spirit will guide you. As you heal, your gifts will become clearer.

This book has already shown you: the area of your greatest attack often reveals the area of your greatest gift. You were never just a victim. You are being equipped to set others free.

Final Word

Deliverance is a journey. Some demons leave fast. Others take time, prayer, and perseverance. Don't be discouraged if you don't feel different overnight.

What matters is that you're no longer in the dark. You've been given language for your struggle, weapons for your freedom, and the truth about your identity.

You are not alone or powerless or beyond repair. You are chosen, called, and loved. Now you are equipped.

PRAYER INDEX

9

What is Prayer?

From the beginning, God delegated rulership to mankind. That dominion means He operates through willing partnership, not force. *"Then God said, 'Let Us make man in Our image, according to Our likeness; let them have dominion... over all the earth...'" (Genesis 1:26-28)*

Earth is under human stewardship. God works through people who invite His will. *"The heavens are the Lord's heavens, but the earth He has given to the children of man." (Psalm 115:16)*

Jesus does not barge in—He waits to be invited into our lives and situations. *"Behold, I stand at the door and knock. If anyone hears My voice and opens the door, I will come in..." (Revelation 3:20).*

Even Jesus taught us to ask for God's will to be done. It's not automatic—we must invite it. *"Your kingdom come, Your will be done, on earth as it is in heaven." (Matthew 6:10 The Lord's Prayer).*

He needs legal access through human agreement. We see in Ezekiel 22:30 God looked for someone to intercede so He could act with mercy but found none. *"So, I sought for a man among them who would make a wall and stand in the gap before Me on behalf of the land, that I should not destroy it; but I found no one."*

God gives us the choice. Our decisions determine access to blessing or destruction. *"I have set before you life and death, blessing and cursing; therefore, choose life..." (Deuteronomy 30:19).*

Submission is a prerequisite. God doesn't force Himself into battles we won't give Him. *"Submit yourselves, then, to God. Resist the devil, and he will flee from you."* (James 4:7)

Why We Need to Pray

Let's look at what the Bible says about the power, necessity and purpose of prayer.

Prayer is a daily, dynamic defense. We should pray about everything: *"And pray in the Spirit on all occasions with all kinds of prayers and requests."* (Ephesians 6:18)

Prayer brings revelation and wisdom only God can give. Who doesn't want that? *"Call to Me and I will answer you and tell you great and unsearchable things you do not know."* (Jeremiah 33:3)

Best of all, prayer replaces every bad feeling with peace by anchoring us in God's presence. God says, *"Do not be anxious about anything, but in every situation, by prayer and petition, with thanksgiving present your requests to God. And the peace of God that surpasses all understanding will guard your hearts and minds in Christ Jesus."* (Philippians 4:6-7)

Do you see the simple instructions and prescription in that verse? 1. Don't be anxious. 2. Present your requests to God with thankfulness.

"Ask and it will be given to you: seek and you will find; knock and the door will be opened to you." (Matthew 7:7). God invites us to keep asking. Sometimes the answers to prayers come quickly and sometimes we have to wait longer than we want to.

The Psalms are the Original Prayer Index.

Long before modern prayer guides, God gave us a collection of raw, honest, Spirit-breathed prayers in the book of Psalms. These ancient words cover every emotion—joy, grief, rage, despair, hope, and praise—and give us a model for how to cry out to God with reverence and truth.

One of the most effective ways to deepen your prayer life is to read the Psalms out loud in the first person, for example turning *"The Lord is my shepherd"* into *"You are my Shepherd, Lord."* Let these living words become your own. When you speak scripture, you're wielding a sword.

Please note prayer was never meant to be formulaic. It was meant to be a fresh conversation anchored in truth, lifted by the Spirit, and directed toward the Father. The psalms will never lose their power, and you should use them when you can't find the words, as an example and training for your own prayer. Just don't forget to have your own conversations with God.

Resistance to Prayer

Even seasoned believers sometimes struggle to pray. For one thing, that uneasy feeling of being watched when you go to pray is not just in your head. You are not praying alone. Besides Jesus, the Holy Spirit, and God, your guardian angels are in the audience as well as whoever wants to attend from the enemy's side – though they will run away when we put up an active defense: *"Resist the devil and he will flee from you." (James 4:7).*

Resisting means to refuse to accept or comply with something; it means the attempt to prevent something by action of argument. You are resisting the enemy, and he is resisting you. Praying is resistance and is like setting off nuclear bombs in the spirit, making the enemy run for cover. No wonder that when you decide to pray, all kinds of distractions start, including ringing phones, notifications, barking dogs, crying children...

"When you pray, go into your room, close the door and pray to your Father, who is unseen..." (Matthew 6:6) That "room" might be a closet, a car, a corner of your yard, or your actual war room. It's a space where you can talk to God freely, without shame or self-consciousness or interruption.

Remember *"The fervent prayer of a righteous person avails much." (James 5:16).* Fervent means heartfelt, honest, and full of fire. Righteous doesn't mean you're perfect — nobody is —but a righteous person gets back up and keeps going: *"For though the righteous fall seven times, they rise again..." (Proverbs 24:16).*

He sees your effort, not just your outcome. He cares about how hard you're trying. God is looking for people who are running their race the best they can, fighting the good fight the best they know how, and keeping the faith, even when it's hard *(2 Timothy 4:7)*

He's looking for a heart that is committed: *"For the eyes of the Lord range throughout the earth to strengthen those whose hearts are fully committed to him." (2 Chronicles 16:19)*

God is pleased by a heart that's striving to make the effort, is humble, and repentant: *"The sacrifices of God are a broken spirit: a broken and contrite heart, O God, You will not despise." (Psalm 51:17)*

How to Use These Prayers

The following prayers are not magic words or formulas. They are examples of how to pray with boldness, truth, and intention. Feel free to use them word-for-word or let them inspire your own conversation with God.

Prayer should be fresh, not stiff. It's about connection. Sometimes we don't even have words, only tears. Those tears are prayers within themselves: *"...the Holy Spirit helps us in our weakness. For example, we don't know what God wants us to pray for. But the Holy Spirit prays for us with groanings that cannot be expressed in words." (Romans 8:26 NLT)* and *"You keep track of all my sorrows. You have collected all my tears in your bottle." (Psalm 56:8 NLT).*

God already knows your thoughts *(Psalm 139)*, but speaking out loud shifts the spiritual atmosphere. Hearing the prayer come from our own mouths helps our brain to wire itself for belief and that we will see the results of our prayer. *"Death and life are in the power of the tongue, and he who loves it shall eat the fruit of it." (Proverbs 18:12).*

Introduction to the Foundational Prayers

While this book could easily include an entire volume of prayers, we've chosen to begin with these three Foundational Prayers. They speak to the spiritual core of every believer: salvation, protection, and purpose. These are the starting points, prayers that every person, no matter where they are in life, can pray with authority and expectation.

Following these, you'll find deliverance prayers that align with the rest of the book, each crafted to confront and break the specific spiritual attacks and demonic strongholds exposed in the demon profiles.

You'll see scripture references included throughout the prayers. These don't need to be spoken out loud, but they're there so you can study them later or use them in prayer like, "Lord, you said in Matthew…" to stand on His word with boldness. God loves when we pray His Word back to Him.

This is a spiritual toolkit. Use it often. Speak these prayers out loud. Write them down. Let them guide your own words when you don't know what to say. The Holy Spirit intercedes for us with groanings too deep for words *(Romans 8:26)*, but He also empowers us to pray with boldness and precision.

Let these words be a starting point for deeper communion with the One who hears every whisper and answers every cry.

FOUNDATIONAL PRAYER:
SALVATION: BECOMING A CHILD OF GOD

Dear Jesus,

I come before You humbly, recognizing that I am a sinner in need of a Savior. I have lived apart from You, going my own way, and I no longer want to live that way. I believe that Jesus Christ is Your Son, that He lived a sinless life, died on the cross for my sins, and rose from the dead so that I could be saved and have eternal life.

Today, I repent. I turn away from my old ways and surrender my life to You, Jesus. I invite You to be my Lord and Savior. I believe in my heart and confess with my mouth that Jesus is Lord *(Romans 10:9)*, and I receive Your gift of salvation by grace through faith *(Ephesians 2:8–9)*.

From this moment on:
- I am a new creation *(2 Corinthians 5:17)*.
- I am washed clean by the blood of Jesus *(1 John 1:9)*.

- I am adopted into Your family *(Romans 8:15)*.
- My name is written in the Lamb's Book of Life *(Luke 10:20)*.
- The Holy Spirit now lives in me *(1 Corinthians 6:19)*.

Help me to follow You all the days of my life. Teach me Your ways. Lead me in truth. Protect me from deception and strengthen me in faith. I give You my whole life, my heart, my mind, and my soul.

In Jesus' mighty name, Amen.

FOUNDATIONAL PRAYER:
PROTECTION OVER SELF, HOME & LOVED ONES

Heavenly Father,

You are my refuge and my fortress, my God in whom I trust *(Psalm 91:2)*. I dwell in the shelter of the Most High and rest in the shadow of the Almighty *(Psalm 91:1)*. I ask now for Your divine protection over every area of my life.

I plead the blood of Jesus over myself, my home, my family, my possessions, and everything under my authority. Surround me with a hedge of protection. Assign angels to guard me in all my ways, whether I'm in the city or the field, coming in or going out *(Psalm 91:11, Deuteronomy 28:6)*.

I declare:

- No weapon formed against me shall prosper *(Isaiah 54:17)*.
- No evil shall befall me, nor shall any plague come near my dwelling *(Psalm 91:10)*.
- The Lord is my shepherd; I shall not lack *(Psalm 23:1)*.
- He will deliver me from every trap and protect me from deadly disease *(Psalm 91:3)*.
- A thousand may fall at my side, ten thousand at my right hand, but it will not come near me *(Psalm 91:7)*.

Holy Spirit, expose every plot of the enemy. Shield my mind from fear, my heart from anxiety, and my path from danger. I declare peace over my household and traveling mercies wherever I go.

Whether I am asleep or awake, at home or abroad, You are with me. Your rod and Your staff comfort me. You go before me and You are my rear guard.

I trust You, Lord, as my Defender, my Fortress, and my Safe Place.

In Jesus' powerful name, Amen.

FOUNDATIONAL PRAYER:
DIRECTION & REVEALING OF CALLING AND PURPOSE

Father God,

You are the Author of my life and the One who knit me together with intention *(Psalm 139:13)*. Before I was formed in the womb, You knew me. Before I was born, You set me apart *(Jeremiah 1:5)*. I come before You asking for clarity, direction, and the full revealing of the purpose for which You created me.

Your Word says that You know the plans You have for me, plans to prosper me and not to harm me, plans to give me a future and a hope *(Jeremiah 29:11)*. I surrender every distraction, delay, and detour that has clouded my path and ask You to light the way.

I declare:

- The steps of the righteous are ordered by the Lord and my righteousness comes from you *(Psalm 37:23, Isaiah 54:7)*.
- I will trust in the Lord with all my heart and lean not on my own understanding; in all my ways I will acknowledge Him, and He will direct my path *(Proverbs 3:5–6)*.
- God has not given me a spirit of fear, but of power, love, and a sound mind *(2 Timothy 1:7)*.

- I am God's workmanship, created in Christ Jesus to do good works, which He prepared in advance for me to do *(Ephesians 2:10)*.

Holy Spirit, reveal the gifts You've placed within me. Show me how to serve, where to go, and what to lay down. Close every wrong door and swing wide the ones You've ordained. Let me not waste one more day in confusion, fear, or stagnation.

I break agreement with every lie that says I have no value or that my time has passed. I speak purpose over my life, clarity over my mind, and courage into my next step.

I am not lost, I am led.
I am not useless, I am chosen.
I am not late, I am right on time in God's perfect plan.

In Jesus' mighty name, Amen.

Deliverance Prayers:
The Lust of the Flesh

Prayer 1: General Prayer for Lust of the Flesh
Heavenly Father,
You have called me to walk in the Spirit and not fulfill the lusts of the flesh *(Galatians 5:16)*. I confess that my flesh has been strong and my resistance weak, but Your power is made perfect in my weakness *(2 Corinthians 12:9)*. I bring every craving, impulse, appetite, and indulgence to the foot of the cross, where the flesh was crucified with Christ *(Romans 6:6)*.

In the name of Jesus, I renounce every spirit that feeds the flesh instead of the spirit *(Romans 8:13)*. I repent for every agreement I've made with sin, secrecy, and spiritual compromise. I reject the lie that I have to obey my cravings, for sin shall no longer be my master, because I am not under law, but under grace *(Romans 6:14)*. I belong to Christ, and I crucify the flesh with its passions and desires *(Galatians 5:24)*.

I declare:

- I am not ruled by impulse or appetite. I am ruled by the Spirit of God *(Romans 8:14)*.
- I am not a slave—I am free *(Romans 6:22)*.
- I am not weak—I am empowered *(Ephesians 6:10)*.
- I am not condemned—I am covered *(Romans 8:1)*.

Create in me a clean heart, O God, and renew a right spirit within me *(Psalm 51:10)*. Set my mind on things above, not on earthly things *(Colossians 3:2)*. Fill me with a hunger for righteousness that drowns out every fleshly desire *(Matthew 5:6)*. Let me walk as a living sacrifice, holy and acceptable to You *(Romans 12:1)*.

In Jesus' name, Amen.

Prayer 2: Deliverance from Addiction & Indulgence

Lord God,

You are the Bread of Life *(John 6:35)*. You are Living Water *(John 4:14)*. I confess I've turned to lesser things to satisfy the ache in my soul. I've fed the flesh instead of the spirit, and I've looked to created things instead of the Creator *(Romans 1:25)*. I've used substances, food, screens, fantasies, and distractions as a form of escape and in doing so, I opened the door to bondage *(Romans 6:16)*.

In the name of Jesus, I renounce the spirits of addiction, indulgence, and sensory escape. I come out of agreement with every lie that tells me, "just one more" will fix the pain *(John 8:44)*. I reject the deceitful cravings of the old nature, which is being corrupted by its deceitful desires *(Ephesians 4:22)*. I command every spirit feeding on my dependence to leave now, in the mighty name of Jesus Christ *(Mark 16:17)*.

Every impulse that controls me, every craving that rules me, every reward system twisted by darkness—I break your hold. You will not have my body. You will not hijack my mind. You will not speak to me like I belong to you.

Holy Spirit, fill the space where those cravings lived. Teach me how to wait in discomfort instead of medicating it. Teach me how to feel again. Show me the root beneath the cycle—and heal it.

I declare:

- I am not mastered by anything *(1 Corinthians 6:12)*.
- My body is the temple of the Holy Spirit *(1 Corinthians 6:19–20)*.
- I offer my body as a living sacrifice, holy and pleasing to God *(Romans 12:1)*.
- I put to death the deeds of the flesh by the Spirit *(Romans 8:13)*.
- Whom the Son sets free is free indeed *(John 8:36)*.

Let every craving be uprooted. Let every chemical grip be shattered. Let every demonic stronghold break under the authority of Jesus' name *(2 Corinthians 10:4)*. Rewire my desires. Retrain my appetite. Fill the emptiness with Your presence and power *(Psalm 107:9)*. I trade addiction for anointing. I walk not in the counsel of the wicked, nor stand in the path of sinners, nor sit in the seat of mockers, but I delight in the law of the Lord *(Psalm 1:1–2)*.

I seal this deliverance in the blood of Jesus. I declare that I am not a slave to my appetite. I am not addicted—I am delivered. I belong to Christ.

In Jesus' name, Amen.

Prayer 3: Deliverance from Perversion & Sexual Sin

My Father in Heaven,

You are holy, and You have called me to be holy in all that I do *(1 Peter 1:16)*. I confess that I have misused the gift of sexuality. I have allowed lust, perversion, and compromise to corrupt what You created to be sacred and good *(Genesis 2:24; Hebrews 13:4)*. I have believed lies about my identity, my worth, and what love truly is.

In the name of Jesus, I break every soul tie formed through sexual sin *(1 Corinthians 6:15–16)*. I renounce every spirit of perversion, lust, adultery, and corruption that has entered through open doors. I come out of agreement with every unholy fantasy, impulse, and temptation that exalts itself against the knowledge of God *(2 Corinthians 10:5)*.

I declare:

- I am a new creation in Christ *(2 Corinthians 5:17)*.
- I am not my past—I am redeemed and washed clean *(1 John 1:9)*.
- I was bought with a price and will honor God with my body *(1 Corinthians 6:20)*.
- I flee from sexual immorality *(1 Corinthians 6:18)*.
- I clothe myself with the Lord Jesus Christ and make no provision for the flesh *(Romans 13:14)*.
- The Spirit helps me put to death the misdeeds of the body *(Romans 8:13)*.

Cleanse my memories. Heal my history. Restore what was stolen or misused *(Joel 2:25)*. Remove every image, imprint, and lie that the enemy planted in my mind and body. Let purity rise in me like a fire that cannot be quenched *(Matthew 5:8)*. Strengthen me to walk in self-control, not in shame. Let my body be an instrument of righteousness, not unrighteousness *(Romans 6:13)*. I yield to Your Spirit and reject the lust of the flesh *(Galatians 5:17)*.

In Jesus' name, Amen.

Prayer 4: Deliverance from Sloth & Apathy

Lord Jesus,

You did not save me to drift through life. You saved me for a purpose and prepared good works in advance for me to do *(Ephesians 2:10)*. Forgive me for every time I said, "I'll do it later" and delayed what You've called me to pursue. Forgive the spirit of laziness, apathy, numbness, and avoidance I've allowed to grow.

In Jesus' name, I renounce every spirit of spiritual sloth, procrastination, passivity, and fatigue. I reject the lie that I am too tired, too broken, too unmotivated, or too late to begin. I break every agreement with stagnation and complacency. I will no longer say, "A little sleep, a little slumber," and let poverty or spiritual decay overtake me *(Proverbs 24:33–34)*.

I declare:

- I can do all things through Christ who strengthens me *(Philippians 4:13)*.
- The Spirit of the Lord gives me power, love, and a sound mind *(2 Timothy 1:7)*.
- The same Spirit that raised Christ from the dead gives life to my mortal body *(Romans 8:11)*.
- Whatever I do, I work at it with all my heart as working for the Lord *(Colossians 3:23)*.
- The diligent will prosper, but the lazy will come to ruin *(Proverbs 10:4; Proverbs 13:4)*.

Wake me up. Stir me up. Light the fire again. Renew my strength like the eagle's *(Isaiah 40:31)*. Make me faithful in little and trusted with much *(Luke 16:10)*. I trade stagnation for steadfastness, apathy for action, and delay for diligence. I break every spiritual paralysis and receive divine energy to move forward in obedience and purpose. In

Jesus' name, Amen.

Deliverance Prayers:
The Lust of the Eyes

Prayer 5: General Prayer for Lust of the Eyes

Heavenly Father,

You said that the eyes are the lamp of the body *(Matthew 6:22)*, and I confess mine have strayed. I have desired what glitters, chased what fades, and compared myself to others instead of seeking Your face. I repent for the lust of the eyes, for pursuing possessions, appearances, and knowledge apart from You.

In Jesus' name, I renounce every spirit that fuels desire through what I see: greed, envy, comparison, vanity, idolatry, and counterfeit light. I reject the illusion that more—more stuff, more beauty, more status—will fulfill what only You can satisfy.

I declare:

- My eyes are fixed on Jesus, the author and finisher of my faith *(Hebrews 12:2)*.
- I will not set any worthless thing before my eyes *(Psalm 101:3)*.
- I turn my eyes away from worthless things and live according to Your Word *(Psalm 119:37)*.

Purify my vision. Let me see with spiritual eyes. Show me the eternal, not the temporary. Take away the darkness and fill me with light.

In Jesus' name, Amen.

Prayer 6: Deliverance from Greed, Materialism & Vanity

Lord God,

You are Jehovah Jireh, my provider. Yet I've looked to money, things, and appearances to define my worth. I confess the sin of greed, the fear of lack, and the pride of life that has driven me to chase status over surrender. I've stored up treasures on earth instead of in heaven *(Matthew 6:19–21)*.

In Jesus' name, I renounce the spirits of Mammon, materialism, vanity, and idolatry. I break agreement with every lie that says my value comes from what I have, how I look, or how others perceive me. I will no longer serve two masters *(Matthew 6:24)*.

I declare:

- God will supply all my needs according to His riches in glory *(Philippians 4:19)*.
- My life does not consist in the abundance of possessions *(Luke 12:15)*.
- I will clothe myself with humility, not pride *(1 Peter 5:5)*.

Teach me to steward, not hoard. To reflect Your image, not culture's idols. Let my heart be rich toward You, not this world.

In Jesus' name, Amen.

Prayer 7: Deliverance from Envy, Comparison & Discord
Heavenly Father,

I repent for comparing myself to others when You created me to be unique. I've looked sideways instead of upward. I've envied what others have instead of celebrating who You made me to be. I confess the sin of jealousy, competition, insecurity, and resentment. I repent for every grudge, secret bitterness, and inward curse I've spoken in my heart.

In Jesus' name, I renounce the spirits of envy, comparison, pride, and strife. I break agreement with every lie that says I am less because someone else is more. I reject the fear of insignificance and the need to compete for value.

I declare:

- I am fearfully and wonderfully made *(Psalm 139:14)*.
- Love does not envy or boast—it rejoices with the truth *(1 Corinthians 13:4–6)*.

- I will live at peace with others, as far as it depends on me *(Romans 12:18)*.

Let my heart be clean. Let my thoughts be generous. Let my mouth speak blessings and not bitterness. I choose to honor, not compete. To bless, not resent. To rejoice with those who rejoice (Romans 12:15).

In Jesus' name, Amen.

Prayer 8: Deliverance from False Illumination & Occult Influence
Almighty God, Maker of Heaven and Earth,
You are the Way, the Truth, and the Life *(John 14:6)*. I confess that I have opened doors—out of curiosity, pain, pride, or ignorance—to spiritual counterfeits. I've sought power, healing, insight, or identity in places You did not author. I repent for every step into the occult, witchcraft, divination, or New Age lies.

In the name of Jesus, I renounce all spirits of false light, deception, occultism, sorcery, astrology, manifestation, goddess worship, familiar spirits, and hidden knowledge. I sever every soul tie to practices, people, or rituals not from You. I tear down every high thing that exalts itself against the knowledge of God *(2 Corinthians 10:5)*.

I declare:

- I will have no other gods before You *(Exodus 20:3)*.
- I will not consult mediums or seek hidden knowledge *(Leviticus 19:31)*.
- I am filled with the Spirit of truth, not deception *(John 16:13)*.

Close every open door. Cleanse every lingering residue. Purge the atmosphere and renew my spirit. I surrender to Your truth and shut every gate to the enemy.

In Jesus' name, Amen.

Deliverance Prayers:
The Pride of Life

Prayer 9: General Prayer for Pride of Life

Heavenly Father,

You oppose the proud but give grace to the humble *(James 4:6)*. I humble myself before You now. I confess that I have sought glory, control, recognition, and security apart from You. I have exalted myself when I should have bowed low. I have trusted in my own strength instead of depending on Yours.

In the name of Jesus, I renounce every spirit rooted in the pride of life: self-exaltation, rebellion, and striving for identity apart from You. I repent for thinking more highly of myself than I ought *(Romans 12:3)*. I cast down every high thing that exalts itself against the knowledge of God and take every thought captive to the obedience of Christ *(2 Corinthians 10:5)*.

I declare:

- I boast in nothing but the cross of Jesus Christ *(Galatians 6:14)*.
- The fear of the Lord is the beginning of wisdom *(Proverbs 9:10)*.
- I must decrease, and Christ must increase *(John 3:30)*.
- I humble myself under Your mighty hand, and in due time You will lift me up *(1 Peter 5:6)*.

Purge me of pride. Break every idol of self. Help me to humble myself like Christ, who humbled Himself unto death—even death on a cross *(Philippians 2:8)*. Let Your Spirit rule over my mind, my will, and my identity.

In Jesus' name, Amen.

Prayer 10: Deliverance from Mind & Identity Distortion

Father God,

You are not the author of confusion but of peace *(1 Corinthians 14:33)*. You formed me in my mother's womb, and all my days were written in Your book before one of them came to be *(Psalm 139:13–16)*. The enemy has tried to hijack my mind and distort my identity. I have believed lies about who I am, what I'm worth, and whether I truly belong.

In the name of Jesus, I renounce every spirit of identity confusion, mental torment, and false self-image. I break agreement with every lie spoken over me—by others or by myself—that contradicts Your Word. I silence the voice of the Liar *(John 8:44)*, Doubt, Fear and Anxiety, the Division of Mind, and the Distorted Self Image.

I declare:

- I have the mind of Christ *(1 Corinthians 2:16)*.
- I am fearfully and wonderfully made *(Psalm 139:14)*.
- I am not conformed to this world, but transformed by the renewing of my mind *(Romans 12:2)*.
- I am God's workmanship, created in Christ Jesus for good works *(Ephesians 2:10)*.
- I am not given a spirit of fear, but of power, love, and a sound mind *(2 Timothy 1:7)*.

Let every fragmented thought be made whole. Let every counterfeit identity be torn down. Let clarity replace confusion and peace replace anxiety. Anchor my mind in truth and renew me daily through Your Word.

In Jesus' name, Amen.

Prayer 11: Deliverance from Control & Manipulation

Heavenly Father,

You alone are sovereign. You alone are worthy to rule. I confess that I've tried to control what was never mine to command. I've manipulated, dominated, or retreated in fear, trying to preserve a false sense of safety. I've been controlled by others, and I've tried to control them in return.

In the name of Jesus, I renounce every spirit of control, manipulation, fear, and domination. I break agreement with the spirit of Jezebel and every partnering force including Intimidation, Narcissism, Flattery, and Gossip. I reject the lie that control equals security.

I declare:

- The Lord is my refuge and fortress; I will trust in Him *(Psalm 91:2).*
- I humble myself under God's mighty hand, and He will lift me up *(1 Peter 5:6).*
- I trust in the Lord with all my heart and lean not on my own understanding *(Proverbs 3:5–6).*
- Where the Spirit of the Lord is, there is freedom *(2 Corinthians 3:17).*
- My life is hidden with Christ in God *(Colossians 3:3).*

Father, break every soul tie formed by control and emotional manipulation. Sever the spiritual influence of those who have claimed authority over me that You never gave them. Heal what made me seek control in the first place. I release every person I've tried to manage. I release every outcome I've tried to force. I surrender all control to You for my future, my relationships, my reputation. I choose trust. I choose freedom.

In Jesus' name, Amen.

Prayer 12: Deliverance from Rage & Corruption

Dear Jesus,

Your Word says, "Be angry and do not sin" *(Ephesians 4:26),* but I confess that I've let my anger take root and corrupt me. I've acted out of vengeance, bitterness, pride, and pain. I've allowed the enemy to stir up wrath, resentment, and destruction where You have called me to peace.

In the name of Jesus, I renounce every spirit of rage, revenge, pride, cruelty, and corruption. I break agreement with every demonic stronghold tied to unhealed offense and unchecked ego.

I declare:

- "The anger of man does not produce the righteousness of God." (James 1:20)
- "Vengeance is Mine, I will repay, says the Lord." (Romans 12:19)
- "Do not be overcome by evil but overcome evil with good." (Romans 12:21)
- "Let all bitterness and wrath and anger… be put away from you." (Ephesians 4:31)
- "Blessed are the peacemakers, for they shall be called sons of God." (Matthew 5:9)

God, heal the wound that gave rage its foothold. Remove the poison of unforgiveness and restore my heart to peace. Let the fire of the Holy Spirit consume every unclean flame of anger in me. Give me a spirit of self-control and compassion. Replace my reflex for wrath with a readiness to forgive. I lay down the sword I was never meant to carry. You are my defender. You are my justice. I choose peace over pride and humility over heat.

In Jesus' name, Amen.

Prayer 13: Deliverance from Shame, Fear & Limitation

Dear God,

You did not give me a spirit of fear, but of power, love, and a sound mind *(2 Timothy 1:7)*. Yet shame has silenced me, fear has bound me, and limitation has made me small. I've believed the lie that I am broken beyond repair or too weak to change.

But You are the lifter of my head *(Psalm 3:3)*, and in You, I am not condemned *(Romans 8:1)*. Today I renounce every spirit of shame, insecurity, fear, hiding, self-hatred, and self-sabotage. I break agreement with every spirit sent to make me doubt my worth and silence my voice.

I declare:

- "I praise You, for I am fearfully and wonderfully made." *(Psalm 139:14)*
- "Those who look to Him are radiant; their faces are never covered with shame." *(Psalm 34:5)*
- "In Christ, I am a new creation; the old has passed away." *(2 Corinthians 5:17)*
- "I can do all things through Christ who strengthens me." *(Philippians 4:13)*
- "The Lord is my light and my salvation—whom shall I fear?" *(Psalm 27:1)*

God, restore the truth of who I am. Silence every accusing voice and shut the mouth of the enemy. Let me walk with boldness, not in arrogance but in the confidence of Your love. I strip off every false label. I release the weight of past failures. I receive the robe of righteousness and the name You gave me before I was born. I am not invisible, You see me. I am not rejected; You call me Your own. I am not disqualified; I am a co-heir with Christ.

In Jesus' name, Amen.

Prayer 14: Deliverance from Generational & Family Spirits

Heavenly Father,

You are the God of Abraham, Isaac, and Jacob—the God of generations. You said that sin can pass down through the bloodline *(Exodus 20:5)*, but You also promised that the curse would be broken in Christ *(Galatians 3:13)*. Today, I come before You to break every generational spirit, pattern, and stronghold that has tried to claim my life and family.

In the name of Jesus, I renounce every familiar spirit and generational curse. I break agreement with every unclean spirit tied to my bloodline, culture, or upbringing.

I declare:

- "Christ redeemed us from the curse of the law by becoming a curse for us." *(Galatians 3:13)*
- "If anyone is in Christ, he is a new creation; the old has gone, the new has come." *(2 Corinthians 5:17)*
- "The sins of the parents will no longer be held against the children." *(Ezekiel 18:20)*
- "He sets the lonely in families." *(Psalm 68:6)*
- "Whom the Son sets free is free indeed." *(John 8:36)*

Father, I choose to forgive my family where they failed me. I release the weight of unhealthy roles and expectations. I step into my identity as a child of God, not a product of dysfunction. I cancel every inherited lie, every generational wound, and every word curse spoken over my name. The line of destruction ends with me, and the line of blessing begins.

In Jesus' name, Amen.

Supplemental Prayers

Prayer 15: Spiritual Growth, Discernment & Being Planted in the Right Church

Heavenly Father,

You are the Gardener, and I am the planting of the Lord *(Isaiah 61:3)*. I ask You to plant me in the right spiritual soil where I will grow in grace and in the knowledge of Jesus Christ *(2 Peter 3:18)*. Lead me to the church, community, teachers, and relationships that will sharpen me, disciple me, and hold me accountable in love.

Remove me from environments that are spiritually dry, deceptive, or misaligned with Your truth. You said in your Word, *"Those who are planted in the house of the Lord shall flourish in the courts of our God."* (Psalm 92:13)

Lord, give me a hunger for Your Word—deeper than I've ever known. Let me crave it like food. You said, *"Man shall not live by bread alone, but by every word that proceeds from the mouth of God."* (Matthew 4:4)

Increase my discernment. Your Word says, *"But solid food is for the mature, who by constant use have trained themselves to distinguish good from evil."* (Hebrews 5:14)

Make me sensitive to truth and bold in conviction. Give me the fear of the Lord, which is the beginning of wisdom *(Proverbs 9:10),* and protect me from false teaching, flattery, and distraction.

Let the words of my mouth and the meditation of my heart be acceptable in Your sight, O Lord, my strength and my redeemer *(Psalm 19:14).* Cleanse my thoughts, purify my motives, and make my life a testimony of holiness.

I ask You for the voice of the Holy Spirit to be clear in my life—through Scripture, through wise counsel, and even through dreams and visions. You said, *"Your young men shall see visions, your old men shall dream dreams."* (Joel 2:28) and *"Whether you turn to the right or the left, you will hear a voice behind you saying, 'This is the way; walk in it.'"* (Isaiah 30:21)

Give me faith that moves mountains. Let me grow in faith and walk by it daily—not just in word, but in demonstration and power *(1 Corinthians 2:4–5).*

I ask You to activate and increase the spiritual gifts, especially the gift of prophecy, that I may build others up and point them back to You *(1 Corinthians 14:1, 12).* Open my ears to hear and enlighten the eyes of my understanding *(Ephesians 1:18),* so I may know the hope of Your calling and walk fully in it.

Make me a vessel of Your light. May others come to know Jesus through the way I live, speak, love, and obey. You said, *"Let your light so shine before men, that they may see your good works and glorify your Father in heaven." (Matthew 5:16)*

I give You permission to direct, prune, strengthen, and send me. Plant me deep and grow me strong—so that I bear fruit that lasts.

In Jesus' name,
Amen.

Prayer 16: Control of the Tongue

Dear Lord,
Your Word says that death and life are in the power of the tongue *(Proverbs 18:21),* and I ask You now to take full control over my words.

"Set a guard, O Lord, over my mouth; keep watch at the door of my lips." (Psalm 141:3)

I repent for every idle, careless, critical, or harmful word I've spoken—over myself, over others, over my family, and even over my pets. Forgive me for gossip, slander, unkindness, rash judgments, and casual negativity that did not reflect Your heart.

You said in your Word, *"But I tell you that everyone will have to give account on the day of judgment for every idle word they have spoken." (Matthew 12:36)* Help me to remember this daily, Lord—not out of fear, but out of love and reverence for You. Let me be quick to repent when I misspeak and sensitive to conviction when my words don't align with Your truth.

"May the words of my mouth and the meditation of my heart be pleasing in Your sight, O Lord, my Rock and my Redeemer." (Psalm 19:14)

Give me self-control, which is a fruit of Your Spirit *(Galatians 5:23)*. Teach me to be slow to speak and quick to listen *(James 1:19)*. Let my words bring healing, not harm—truth, not confusion—blessing, not curses.

Let my mouth become a well of life *(Proverbs 10:11)*, and may the fear of the Lord govern my speech, so that I may never be ashamed when I stand before You and give account for how I used my voice.

I consecrate my tongue to You. Let my mouth be used for praise, intercession, and speaking life—nothing else.

In Jesus' name,
Amen.

Prayer 17: To Be Counted Worthy and Not Deceived in the Last Days
Lord God Almighty,
I ask You now, in humility and awe, to count me worthy to escape what is coming on the earth and to stand before You unashamed *(Luke 21:36)*.

You said in your Word, *"Watch therefore, and pray always that you may be counted worthy to escape all these things that will come to pass, and to stand before the Son of Man." (Luke 21:36)*

Give me supernatural discernment to recognize the times, and to see through every trap, scheme, and deception of the enemy. You said, *"Let no one deceive you by any means." (2 Thessalonians 2:3)* and that *"Even the elect would be deceived—if that were possible."* (Matthew 24:24)

Do not let me fall for the strong delusion, no matter what signs, wonders, or emotional appeals I may witness. Expose every lie with the light of Your Word and the truth of the Holy Spirit.

Give me the strength to endure when the days grow dark and the pressure intensifies. You said, *"The enemy will speak words against the Most*

High and wear out the saints of the Most High." (Daniel 7:25) Sustain me. Shield me. Keep my lamp burning.

Clothe me daily with the full armor of God so that I can stand in the evil day *(Ephesians 6:13)*. Let me be alert, anchored in truth, and protected under the shadow of Your wings *(Psalm 91:1–4)*.

I ask for supernatural provision and divine protection—physically, emotionally, and spiritually. Let my life count for the saving of souls. Direct my time, energy, and resources toward work that lays up treasure in heaven *(Matthew 6:19–20)*.

Give me eyes to see through the illusion of this world. Let me never forget I am a sojourner, a citizen of Heaven. *"This world is not my home—I'm just passing through."* (Hebrews 11:13–16)

Keep my heart awake. Keep my hands clean. Keep my focus on You. And if I must stand alone, let me stand with You.

In the name of Jesus Christ,
Amen.

Prayer 18: Deliverance from Witchcraft

Heavenly Father,
I come before You in the name of Jesus Christ, the One who has all power and authority in heaven and on earth *(Matthew 28:18)*. I renounce and break every agreement—whether from my own actions or those done against me—with witchcraft, divination, sorcery, or the occult. I repent for any personal involvement, bloodline connection, or curiosity I've entertained toward things You call detestable *(Deuteronomy 18:10–12)*.

Whether I am the target or the participant, I reject all involvement with witchcraft and break its power over my life. What was sent against me is returned to the pit of hell in Jesus' name.

I declare: no weapon formed against me shall prosper, and every tongue that rises against me in judgment I condemn *(Isaiah 54:17)*. I reject every hex, spell, curse, incantation, or ritual spoken over me or my bloodline. I cancel every demonic assignment sent through witchcraft, knowingly or unknowingly, and I declare that it shall not stand, and it shall not prosper *(Isaiah 8:10)*. I plead the blood of Jesus as my covering and my shield *(Revelation 12:11)*.

Your Word says that You do not allow a sorceress to live *(Exodus 22:18)*, and that You frustrate the signs of liars and make diviners mad *(Isaiah 44:25)*. You alone are God, and there is no power above Yours.

I rebuke every spirit of fear, manipulation, confusion, control, and counterfeit "light" that has entered through witchcraft or familiar spirits. I declare that I do not receive the spirit of bondage again to fear, but the Spirit of adoption, by which I cry Abba, Father *(Romans 8:15)*. Every monitoring spirit, spiritual parasite, or demonic assignment sent against me is now cast out in the name of Jesus.

I speak the authority of Luke 10:19 over my life: *"I have been given authority to trample on snakes and scorpions and over all the power of the enemy; nothing shall harm me."*

I cancel every dream invasion, astral projection, or spiritual attack sent against me through witchcraft or sorcery. I command every portal opened through rebellion or idolatry to be shut now in the name of Jesus. Your Word says rebellion is as the sin of witchcraft *(1 Samuel 15:23)*, so I renounce all rebellion and submit to You fully, Lord.

You are my refuge and my fortress, my God in whom I trust *(Psalm 91:2)*. You deliver me from the snare of the fowler and from the deadly pestilence *(Psalm 91:3)*. A thousand may fall at my side, ten thousand at my right hand, but it will not come near me (*Psalm 91:7)*.

I bind the spirit of Jezebel, Python, and every unclean spirit associated with witchcraft, false prophecy and counterfeit power. I bind them in the name of Jesus and declare that where the Spirit of the Lord is, there is freedom *(2 Corinthians 3:17)*.

Fill me now with Your Holy Spirit. Seal every space with Your truth and Your presence. I receive the mind of Christ *(1 Corinthians 2:16)* and the peace that surpasses all understanding *(Philippians 4:7)*. I choose to walk in the light, and I sever all ties with darkness.

In the name of Jesus Christ, every curse is broken, every chain destroyed, and every spirit of witchcraft cast out. I am free. Amen.

Prayer 19: Deliverance from The Jezebel Spirit & Cluster – Severing Control, Intimidation & Seduction

Lord God,

You are holy and powerful, and there is no spirit above Yours. Today I come boldly to confront the influence of Jezebel in my life—in my mind, my relationships, and my lineage. I renounce every way I've been controlled, manipulated, or seduced—and every way I've participated in those tactics myself. I ask for complete deliverance by the blood of Jesus Christ.

In the name of Jesus, I renounce the spirits of Jezebel and all in her order. I sever every demonic contract tied to seduction, domination, vanity, fear, guilt, emotional blackmail, or unholy sexuality. I break the chains of every soul tie forged through control, trauma, lust, or false intimacy. I cast down every high thing that exalts itself against the knowledge of God (2 Corinthians 10:5).

I declare:

- I submit to God. I resist the devil, and he must flee. *(James 4:7)*
- I am not a slave to sin, but a servant of righteousness. *(Romans 6:18)*

- I walk by the Spirit and do not gratify the desires of the flesh. *(Galatians 5:16)*
- Greater is He who is in me than he who is in the world. (1 John 4:4)

Holy Spirit, cleanse my mind, my body, and my history.

Restore purity to my thoughts, peace to my heart, and discernment to my soul.
Fill the void where intimidation and seduction once lived.
Fortify me with Your power, Your truth, and Your authority.
Where Jezebel once reigned, let Jesus now rule.

I am no longer under the dominion of this spirit.
I walk in boldness, not fear.
I walk in truth, not control.
I walk in purity, not manipulation.

Every agreement with Jezebel is now null and void.
I belong to Christ—and Christ alone.

In Jesus' mighty name, Amen.

Prayer 20: Deliverance from Limerence & Emotional Bondage
Heavenly Father,
I come to You in the name of Jesus Christ—my Deliverer, my Healer, and my Source of truth. I lift before You the emotional bondage that has entangled my heart and mind. I confess that I have formed unhealthy attachments—whether emotionally, mentally, physically, or spiritually—and I repent for giving anyone a place in my soul that belongs to You alone.

I break every soul tie now in the name of Jesus.
Whether it formed through physical intimacy, emotional obsession, fantasy, repeated thoughts, idolization, or unspoken longing—I renounce it now.

"What God has joined together, let no one separate" (Mark 10:9)—but what God did not join, I have no covenant with.

I surrender every feeling of infatuation, fantasy, and longing that has consumed me.

"[I cast] down imaginations, and every high thing that exalts itself against the knowledge of God..." (2 Corinthians 10:5) I tear down the stronghold of limerence—the obsession, the emotional high, the mental loops, the dependency. I refuse to give power to a person or relationship that is not from You.

I declare: my soul belongs to Jesus. Not to the person I've fixated on, not to my past, and not to the lies of the enemy. I sever the tie in Jesus' name. I break every spiritual, emotional, and chemical bond that has formed between us. I uproot every seed of fantasy, false hope, and torment. *"You restore my soul." (Psalm 23:3)*
"Whom the Son sets free is free indeed [and I am free]." (John 8:36)

I speak Your Word over my mind: *"[I] do not conform to the pattern of this world but [am] transformed by the renewing of [my] mind." (Romans 12:2)*

Renew my thoughts, Lord. Cleanse my imagination. Heal my nervous system where it has been conditioned by craving and emotional highs. Where my body and emotions are addicted to fantasy or connection—break that cycle in Jesus' name.

I ask You to shut every spiritual doorway I've opened through obsession, idolatry, emotional fixation, or longing for someone who is not mine to carry. I repent for trying to fill emotional voids in my own strength.

I tear down the altar I built in my heart to this person. *"[I] shall have no other gods before [You]." (Exodus 20:3)*

Lord, I invite Your holy presence to fill the space where that soul tie used to live.

I ask You for righteous relationships.

Ordain my connections. Remove what's not from You and establish what is.

Bring me into godly alignment with people who will sharpen me, honor You, and lead me toward truth and wholeness. *"Every good and perfect gift is from above..." (James 1:17)*

"Two are better than one... for if one falls, the other can help them up." *(Ecclesiastes 4:9–10)*

I wait on You, Lord—not another person. *"My soul waits for the Lord more than watchmen for the morning." (Psalm 130:6)*

Seal this deliverance by the power of the Holy Spirit. I receive Your peace, clarity, and joy. I am whole. I am Yours. I am free.

In Jesus' name,
Amen.

Prayer 21: Healing From Identity Distortion

Heavenly Father,

You are the One who formed me in my mother's womb. You make no mistakes, but somewhere along the way, I believed I was one. I've carried distorted images of myself formed by trauma, comparison, rejection, and lies that did not come from You.

Right now, I lay down every false identity I've worn and every lie I've believed about who I am. I renounce every label that came from pain, people, or the enemy.

In the name of Jesus, I reverse the curses of the enemy and declare:

- I will no longer see myself through the lens of shame or self-hatred.
- I will not measure my worth through the approval of others.
- I refuse to hide my light or play small out of fear.
- I will no longer destroy what You're trying to build in me.

- I don't have to earn love or prove my value.
- I silence every voice that condemns what You've called good.
- I reject the lie that I'm unworthy or unloved.
- I will not accept twisted definitions of truth, identity, or morality.
- I renounce every fractured view of myself and receive wholeness in Christ.

I declare the truth:

- I am fearfully and wonderfully made *(Psalm 139:14)*.
- I am created in the image of God *(Genesis 1:27)*.
- I am God's workmanship—His masterpiece—created for good works *(Ephesians 2:10)*.
- I am chosen, loved, and set apart *(1 Peter 2:9)*.
- I have been given a spirit of power, love, and a sound mind *(2 Timothy 1:7)*.

Jesus, wash my eyes. Restore my mind. Help me see myself as You do. I receive healing for my identity, and I choose to walk in the truth of who I am in You.

In Your name, Amen.

Prayer 22: Freedom From Fear, Anxiety & Avoidance

Dear Jesus,

You have not given me a spirit of fear, yet I have been living as though fear has the final say. It has ruled my thoughts, guided my decisions, and kept me from fully stepping into what You've called me to do. I confess that I have obeyed fear more than I've obeyed faith. I've avoided, shrunk back, and run—not because You told me to, but because fear did.

In the name of Jesus, I renounce the spirit of fear and every way it has influenced my life. I break agreement with anxiety, avoidance, dread, and panic. I no longer accept the lie that I must stay hidden or that I'm safer in isolation.

I renounce the spirits of: Fear, Anxiety, Cowardliness, Avoidance, Unfaithfulness, Unreliability, Desperation, and People Pleasing.

I declare the truth:

- God has not given me a spirit of fear, but of power, love, and a sound mind *(2 Timothy 1:7)*.
- Perfect love casts out fear *(1 John 4:18)*.
- I will be strong and courageous; I will not be afraid or discouraged, for the Lord my God is with me *(Joshua 1:9)*.
- Even though I walk through the valley of the shadow of death, I will fear no evil *(Psalm 23:4)*.
- In righteousness I will be established, and I will be far from oppression *(Isaiah 54:14)*.

I command every tormenting spirit of fear and anxiety to leave now. Every whisper of doom, every racing thought, every invisible hand holding me back—I cut you off in Jesus' name. I will not be ruled by panic. I will not be dictated by dread. My mind is not your playground.

Holy Spirit, breathe peace into my spirit. Teach me to walk in confidence, not caution. Show me what safety in You really feels like. Let the comfort of Your presence replace the pressure of fear. Teach me stillness, teach me trust.

I seal this deliverance in the name of Jesus and by His blood. My mind is covered. My heart is guarded. My peace is restored.

In Jesus' name,
Amen.

Prayer 23: Deliverance from Shame & Insecurity

Dear Jesus,

You formed me with care and purpose, yet shame has tried to bury my identity. I have carried labels You never gave me—unworthy, unlovable, broken, invisible. I confess that I've believed lies about who I am, and I've let insecurity rule my actions, relationships, and voice.

But today, I come into agreement with Your truth instead.
I break the curse of shame, the cycle of hiding, and the weight of false identity.

I declare the truth of God's Word:
- I am fearfully and wonderfully made *(Psalm 139:14)*.
- I am God's workmanship, created in Christ Jesus for good works *(Ephesians 2:10)*.
- There is no condemnation for those who are in Christ Jesus *(Romans 8:1)*.
- Those who look to Him are radiant; their faces are never covered with shame *(Psalm 34:5)*.
- God chose the weak things of the world to shame the strong *(1 Corinthians 1:27)*.

I command every spirit of shame and insecurity to leave me now in Jesus' name.
You are not my portion. My confidence is not based on performance, appearance, or approval—it is anchored in Christ. I no longer need to perform, prove, or earn worth. I have it because He gave it.

Holy Spirit, wash me in the truth of who I am.
Restore what shame stole. Rebuild what insecurity cracked. Let me walk in boldness—not arrogance, not fear—but holy boldness rooted in You.
I receive the courage to be seen, to speak, to stand.

I seal this deliverance in the name of Jesus and under the authority of His blood. Shame is broken. The mirror is cleared. My identity is secure.

In Jesus' name,
Amen.

Prayer 24: Deliverance From Confusion, Doubt & Faithlessness

Heavenly Father,

You are not the author of confusion but of peace *(1 Corinthians 14:33)*. Yet my thoughts have been scattered, my faith shaken, and my heart weary. I confess that I've let fear and doubt take root where faith once lived. I've questioned Your promises and let circumstances speak louder than Your Word.

But today, I draw a line. I will no longer be tossed by every wind or buried in uncertainty. I anchor myself to Your truth and Your voice.

In the name of Jesus, I renounce the spirits of Doubt, Confusion, and Faithlessness that have clouded my mind and shaken my confidence— but no more. I command you to leave me now in the name of Jesus Christ. You will not distort God's voice, delay His plans, or keep me stuck in fear or overthinking.

I declare the truth of God's Word:

- If any of you lacks wisdom, let him ask of God... and it will be given to him. *(James 1:5)*
- I will trust in the Lord with all my heart and lean not on my own understanding. *(Proverbs 3:5–6)*
- God is not a man, that He should lie... Has He said, and will He not do it? *(Numbers 23:19)*
- Let us hold fast the confession of our hope without wavering, for He who promised is faithful. *(Hebrews 10:23)*
- Your word is a lamp to my feet and a light to my path. *(Psalm 119:105)*

Holy Spirit, sharpen my discernment.

Give me clarity of mind and purity of heart. Remove every whisper of the enemy and replace it with the fire of conviction. Let me no longer entertain the idea that You are silent, distant, or indifferent.

Jesus, restore my faith. You are the author and finisher of it *(Hebrews 12:2)*. Breathe life into every place that has been dulled by disappointment. I repent of faithlessness, and I choose today to believe again.

I seal this deliverance in the name of Jesus and by the authority of His blood.
My faith will not fail. My mind is not a battlefield; it is a dwelling place of truth and wisdom. Confusion has no home here.

In Jesus' name, Amen.

Prayer 25: Deliverance From Family Rivalry, Comparison & Sibling Wounds
Heavenly Father,
I lift to You the pain I've carried from within my own family. You see the wounds of being overlooked, misjudged, compared, or cast aside. You see what favoritism did. You see the shame that settled in my bones.

I break every word curse and unspoken expectation placed upon me by my family. I cancel the lie that I must earn love or be like someone else to be worthy. I release jealousy, bitterness, resentment, and inferiority. I cancel the script of sibling comparison and competition.

I declare:

- Before I was born, You formed me and called me by name. *(Isaiah 49:1)*
- I am fearfully and wonderfully made. *(Psalm 139:14)*
- Each one of us has different gifts, according to the grace given to us. *(Romans 12:6)*
- Where the Spirit of the Lord is, there is freedom. *(2 Corinthians 3:17)*
- You prepare a table before me, even in the presence of those who have hurt me. *(Psalm 23:5)*

Father, restore what was broken. Heal the unspoken wars that lingered in silence.

Give me eyes to see myself the way You do—not through the lens of a role I was assigned in childhood. Teach me how to love my family without being ensnared by the dysfunction. Set me free from comparison, performance, and legacy wounds.

Lord, bring healing to the fractures. Even if reconciliation is not possible, I ask for restoration in my soul. I lay down every offense and every unmet need.

Fill the void with Your perfect love and give me new spiritual family as You promised.

I forgive my parents, my siblings, and myself. I bless those who seemed favored. I bless those who didn't know better. I step into my God-given identity—without shame, without rivalry, and without regret.

In Jesus' name, Amen.

Prayer 26: For Deliverance From Parental Wounds

Father God,

You are the perfect parent—the one who never fails, never forgets, never forsakes. I was not raised by perfection. You see the wounds left by my earthly parents, whether through control, neglect, fear, absence, or misplaced expectations.

In the name of Jesus, break the power of generational dysfunction, unhealthy attachments, favoritism, silence, shame, fear, and manipulation. I cancel the curse of emotional abandonment and overcontrol. I release the burden of parenting my parent. I forgive every wound that shaped me.

I declare:

- Though my father and mother forsake me, the Lord will receive me. *(Psalm 27:10)*

- God sets the lonely in families. *(Psalm 68:6)*
- You are my Father; I am the clay; You are the potter. *(Isaiah 64:8)*
- I have received the Spirit of adoption by whom I cry, 'Abba, Father!' *(Romans 8:15)*
- I am no longer an orphan—I belong to You. *(John 14:18)*

Lord, re-parent me in Your love. Show me who I am apart from how I was raised. Rebuild my sense of safety, identity, and belonging. Tear down the inner vow that says I must never need anyone. Help me to set healthy boundaries without guilt and to offer forgiveness without letting toxicity continue.

Holy Spirit, hold me like I was never held. Protect me like I was never protected.
Speak truth where I was silenced. Establish safety where there was fear. Rebuild my identity from the inside out. Break the template of control, abuse, and rejection. Replace it all with Your perfect love.

I forgive them—not because they were right, but because I refuse to carry this wound one more day.
I release their failure and receive Your fullness.
I release their absence and receive Your presence.
I release their control and receive Your comfort.
I am no longer under the shadow of their choices.
I am under the covering of the Most High.
I walk in freedom, healing, and wholeness.

I forgive my parents, and I release them from the debt of shaping me perfectly.
I bless them with freedom, even as I step into mine. I receive the comfort, healing, and identity of my true Father.

In Jesus' name, Amen.

Prayer 27: Deliverance From Generational Poverty & Rejection

Heavenly Father,

You are the God of abundance and belonging. I have lived under the curses of scarcity and rejection. I have believed I am unwanted, unseen, and always lacking—never enough, never provided for.

In the name of Jesus, I break every generational curse of instability, fatherlessness, financial lack, and emotional exile. I sever agreements with homelessness, rootlessness, and worthlessness. I cancel every lie that says I must strive to earn love or scavenge to survive.

I declare:

- My God will supply all my needs according to His riches in glory by Christ Jesus. *(Philippians 4:19)*
- I am accepted in the Beloved. *(Ephesians 1:6)*
- I am no longer a slave, but a son—and if a son, then an heir through God. *(Galatians 4:7)*
- God gives me the power to produce wealth. *(Deuteronomy 8:18)*
- I am planted, not forsaken; rooted, not drifting. *(Psalm 1:3, Hebrews 13:14)*

Father, plant me in Your provision and truth. Show me that I am not disposable. I am not invisible. I am Yours. Break the poverty mindset off my life. Heal the places in me that wander, starve, and hide.

I receive Your adoption, Your abundance, and Your anchor.

In Jesus' name, Amen.

Prayer 28: Deliverance From Narcissistic Systems & False Identity

Father God,

You are the God of truth and freedom—not confusion, distortion, or control. But I have lived inside a system that twisted love into performance, identity into roles, and connection into competition. I have been labeled, compared, and molded to fit someone else's broken image.

In Jesus' name, I cancel every assignment of manipulation, favoritism, triangulation, and emotional invalidation. I break agreement with the lie that my worth is based on what I do, how I appear, or whether I am chosen by people.

I declare:

- I am fearfully and wonderfully made. *(Psalm 139:14)*
- Where the Spirit of the Lord is, there is freedom. *(2 Corinthians 3:17)*
- The truth will set me free. *(John 8:32)*
- I no longer live to please man, but God who tests my heart. *(1 Thessalonians 2:4)*
- God does not show favoritism. *(Romans 2:11)*

Father, restore my identity. Release me from false roles. Heal what was broken by performance-based love. Remove every mask and mantle that was forced on me in childhood or in dysfunctional families. I receive Your voice above every other—Your truth above every label.

I step out of the system and into sonship.

In Jesus' name, Amen.

Prayer 29: Deliverance From Father Wounds & Fragmented Masculinity

Heavenly Father,

You are the Father to the fatherless *(Psalm 68:5)*, and You are not like the one who hurt me, abandoned me, or left me guessing. I come to You not just as a child needing healing—but as one ready to be re-fathered by You.

In the name of Jesus, I break agreement with fear, neglect, abuse, silence, intimidation, and performance-based love. I uproot the lies that said I had to earn affection, that I was too much, or not enough.

I declare:

- I have been adopted by God, and by His Spirit I cry, "Abba, Father." *(Romans 8:15)*
- The Lord is close to the brokenhearted and saves those who are crushed in spirit. *(Psalm 34:18)*
- My identity is not in the wounds of a man, but in the love of my Heavenly Father. (1 John 3:1)
- I will not project the failure of a man onto my perfect God. *(Numbers 23:19)*

Lord, rewire the way I see You—and myself.
Where there was absence, fill me with Your presence.
Where there was cruelty, show me Your compassion.
Where there was rejection, affirm me with Your truth.

I forgive my father, whether passive or abusive.
I release him and receive You.

In Jesus' name, Amen.

Prayer 30: Healing From Mother Wounds & Enmeshment

Father God,

You are the one who knit me together in my mother's womb *(Psalm 139:13)*, and You alone define who I am. I come before You to release the wounds caused by maternal control, absence, jealousy, or over-attachment and to be restored to wholeness in You.

In the name of Jesus, I reject false loyalty, emotional blackmail, and the lie that I exist to fulfill someone else's needs. I break ungodly soul ties and unhealthy attachments formed through guilt, fear, or manipulation.

I declare:

- I was bought with a price, and I will not become a slave to human expectations. *(1 Corinthians 7:23)*
- For this reason a man shall leave his father and mother and be united to his spouse. *(Genesis 2:24)*
- Those who do the will of God are my true family. *(Mark 3:35)*
- I will honor my parents, but I will not be controlled by them. *(Ephesians 6:1–2)*

Holy Spirit, restore my sense of self. Show me how to set boundaries without fear.

Help me to discern love from control. Unravel every false narrative I've believed about womanhood, worth, and my role in others' lives.

I forgive my mother for what she did and what she failed to do.

I release her to You and reclaim the life You've designed for me.

In Jesus' name, Amen.

Prayer 31: Healing From Parentification & Adultification

Father God,

You are the God who sees me *(Genesis 16:13)*. You saw every moment I was forced to grow up too soon. You saw when I was treated like the adult, the caretaker, the stabilizer—when I needed to be held, not depended on. You did not design children to carry the burdens of parents. So today, I come to You and lay those burdens down.

In the name of Jesus, I reject the lie that I am only loved when I am useful. I break every agreement that says I must be responsible for everyone else in order to have worth. I cancel the curse of reversed roles and the spirit of false maturity that has stolen my rest.

I declare:

- Come to Me, all who are weary and burdened, and I will give you rest. *(Matthew 11:28)*

- I cast all my cares on You, for You care for me. *(1 Peter 5:7)*
- I am a child of God, not a slave to the needs of others. *(Romans 8:15)*
- It is for freedom that Christ has set me free. *(Galatians 5:1)*

God, I invite You into my earliest memories of carrying too much. Rescue the little version of me who felt responsible for everyone's survival. Release me from shame, guilt, and exhaustion. Restore to me the years the locusts have eaten (Joel 2:25).

I receive the gift of rest.
I receive the love of a perfect Father.
I give You permission to reparent me—to teach me how to live free, not just function.
I trust You to carry what was never mine to hold.

In Jesus' name, Amen.

Prayer 32: Restoring Innocence & Safety to the Wounded Child
Father God,
You are my refuge and my healer. You know every moment that wounded my innocence. You saw the things I never should've witnessed, the words that pierced too deep, the touch that should never have happened, the loneliness that became my hiding place. You are not just the God of my adult self—you are the God of my inner child too.

In the name of Jesus, I break every word curse, every trauma imprint, and every lie spoken over me as a child. I sever the influence of demons that entered through abuse, abandonment, exposure to evil, or lack of protection. I command every tormenting spirit tied to those memories to leave now in the name of Jesus.

I declare:

- Let the little children come to Me, for to such belongs the kingdom of heaven. *(Matthew 19:14)*

- The Lord is near to the brokenhearted and saves the crushed in spirit. *(Psalm 34:18)*
- He heals the brokenhearted and binds up their wounds. *(Psalm 147:3)*
- You will be secure, because there is hope; you will look around and rest in safety. *(Job 11:18)*
- I will repay you for the years the locusts have eaten. *(Joel 2:25)*

Holy Spirit, go into the places I've buried. Retrieve the parts of me that shut down in order to survive. Restore the joy that was stolen. Replace the shame with tenderness.

Rebuild the safety that was shattered. Surround the little version of me with Your angels, Your peace, and Your presence.

I will no longer hate the child I was.
I will no longer replay the pain I endured.
I am not damaged—I am deeply loved.
I am not forsaken—I am being made whole.

I receive my healing.
I receive my restoration.
I receive the arms of my true Father.

In Jesus' name, Amen.

Prayer 33: Deliverance From The Orphan Spirit – Restoring Belonging & Divine Adoption

Abba Father,

You are not distant or silent. You are near to the brokenhearted and faithful to adopt the abandoned. I come to You today as one who has felt spiritually orphaned rejected, overlooked, and unloved. But I believe Your Word: that You have not left me as an orphan. You have come to me. *(John 14:18)*

In the name of Jesus, I break every agreement with the lie that I am unwanted, unloved, or unworthy of belonging. I sever every spiritual chain that ties me to fatherlessness, instability, emotional exile, or a poverty mindset. I declare that my inheritance is not rejection, but righteousness.

I speak the truth of scripture over my soul:

- I have been adopted as God's child. *(Ephesians 1:5)*
- I am no longer a slave, but a child and an heir. *(Galatians 4:7)*
- God sets the lonely in families. *(Psalm 68:6)*
- Even if my father and mother forsake me, the Lord will receive me. *(Psalm 27:10)*
- The Spirit I received brought about my adoption as a child of God. *(Romans 8:15)*

Holy Spirit, restore my sense of home. Anchor me in Your love. Speak identity where there has been confusion. Wrap me in Your covering where I've felt exposed.

Surround me with the family of God—spiritual mothers, fathers, and true brothers and sisters. Unplug every orphan voice in my mind and teach me to hear Your voice clearly.

I am not abandoned.
I am not fatherless.
I am not forgotten.
I am seen. I am known. I am wanted. I am Yours.

I receive my adoption, my inheritance, and my place at Your table.

In Jesus' name, Amen.

Prayer 34: Freedom From Rejection & Abandonment

Heavenly Father,

You are the God who sees me, the God who calls me chosen, not forsaken. I come before You with the ache of being overlooked, unloved, or cast aside. I confess that I've carried rejection like a second skin. I've feared abandonment and believed lies that I was unwanted or invisible. But today, I break agreement with every lie and every spirit that fed them.

In the name of Jesus, I renounce every spirit of rejection, abandonment, orphanhood, and emotional exile—known and unknown, personal and generational.

I declare the truth:

- I am accepted in the Beloved *(Ephesians 1:6)*.
- Though my mother and father forsake me, the Lord will receive me *(Psalm 27:10)*.
- I have received the Spirit of adoption *(Romans 8:15)*.
- I am no longer an outsider but part of God's household *(Ephesians 2:19)*.
- God sets the lonely in families *(Psalm 68:6)*.
- I am chosen, holy, and dearly loved *(1 Peter 2:9; Colossians 3:12)*.
- I am fearfully and wonderfully made *(Psalm 139:14)*.

In Jesus' name, I command every spirit of Rejection, Orphanhood, Neglect, Wandering, Inconstancy, Poverty, Fear, Anxiety, Unforgiveness, Grudge-Holding, Exhaustion, Distortion and Abandonment to leave me now. You no longer have legal ground in my life. I sever every soul tie, word curse, and generational wound that opened the door. I cancel the enemy's assignment over my identity and future.

Holy Spirit, come now. Fill every empty and wounded place. Teach me to receive love and correction without fear. Rebuild what was broken by abandonment and neglect. Restore my trust. Plant me firmly in Your love.

Father, heal my heart. Heal the cracks left by abandonment. Repair the damage caused by those who should have stayed but left. Fill the empty places with Your love. Teach me how to receive—love, connection, correction, and care—without fear. Show me that my worth is not defined by human treatment, but by divine truth.

I forgive those who rejected me. I release them to You. I will not live from the wound but from Your Word.

I seal this deliverance in the blood of Jesus. I am no longer alone. I am chosen. I am claimed. I am home.

In Jesus' name,
Amen.

ACKNOWLEDGEMENTS

Thank you to Bill Larkin for sharing your testimony,
which led to my salvation.

I am indebted to the churches who welcomed me as a member
and grew me in grace and the knowledge of Jesus Christ:

Greater St. Stephen United Church of God, Brooklyn, NY
and the entire Marvin Williams Family,
with Special Thanks to Dr. & Mrs. Jerome Williams
Pastor & First Lady Craig Williams

Smith Temple Baptist Church, Raleigh, NC
Pastor and First Lady Oscar Holland, Sr

Door of Hope Christian Church, Marion, SC
Pastor and First Lady Michael A. Blue

God Bless You

INDEX

T